T5-DGS-667

DATE DUE

FEB 0 8 2006			
GAYLORD			PRINTED IN U.S.A.

THE CLARINET
IN THE CLASSICAL PERIOD

The Clarinet
IN THE CLASSICAL PERIOD

ALBERT R. RICE

3 12 08 03641 8590

Mannes College of Music
Harry Scherman Library
150 W. 85th st.
New York, NY 10024

OXFORD
UNIVERSITY PRESS

2003

ML
945
R52
2003
c. 1

OXFORD
UNIVERSITY PRESS

Oxford   New York
Auckland   Bangkok   Buenos Aires   Cape Town   Chennai
Dar es Salaam   Delhi   Hong Kong   Istanbul   Karachi   Kolkata
Kuala Lumpur   Madrid   Melbourne   Mexico City   Mumbai   Nairobi
São Paolo   Shanghai   Taipei   Tokyo   Toronto

Copyright © 2003 by Oxford University Press, Inc.

Published by Oxford University Press, Inc.
198 Madison Avenue, New York, New York 10016

www.oup.com

Oxford is a registered trademark of Oxford University Press

All rights reserved. No part of this publication may be reproduced,
stored in a retrieval system, or transmitted, in any form or by any means,
electronic, mechanical, photocopying, recording, or otherwise,
without the prior permission of Oxford University Press.

Library of Congress Cataloging-in-Publication Data
Rice, Albert R.
The clarinet in the classical period / Albert R. Rice.
   p. cm.
Includes bibliographical references (p.   ) and index.
ISBN-13 978-0-19-514483-3
ISBN 0-19-514483-X
1. Clarinet—History—18th century.   2. Clarinet—History—19th century.
I. Title.
ML945 .R52 2003
788.6'219'09033—dc21   2003014197

9   8   7   6   5   4   3   2
Printed in the United States of America
on acid-free paper

To my mother, Mary Agresta Rice,

a very fine coloratura singer,

and to two dear departed friends

and wonderful musicians,

Rosario Mazzeo and Charlotte Zelka

ACKNOWLEDGMENTS

This book has benefited from the input of many people all over the world. Any errors that remain are only my own. First, I must give my heartfelt thanks to my friends Sir Nicholas Shackleton and Dr. David Ross for advice and much help. Jean Jeltsch has provided many documents from the Paris archives regarding makers and shared much knowledge with me concerning eighteenth-century clarinets. Ingrid Pearson has contributed a number of thought-provoking conversations on many aspects of the clarinet, searched for items at the British Library, and generously shared some of her discoveries from her own doctoral research. Joseph Moir has also been very helpful in sharing his vast knowledge of the early clarinet as well as many instruments from his collection. Luigi Magistrelli has been very kind and helpful in sending many published and manuscript works for the clarinet written in Italy. He has also been generous in sending many of his CD recordings of clarinet works. Robert Eliason has very generously provided the musical examples. Many others have been extraordinarily kind and helpful. These include Stewart Carter, Jane Ellsworth, Michael Finkelman, Otto Himmer, Eric Hoeprich, Gunther Joppig, Marketta Kivimäki, Kathryn Shanks Libin, Andreas Masel, William Maynard, Rosario Mazzeo, Renato Meucci, Charles Mould, Beryl Kenyon de Pascual, Pamela Poulin, Harrison Powley, Keith Puddy, Thomas Reil, John Rice, Xavier Salaberry, Marlowe Sigal, Hans Rudolph Stalder, Johan Van Kalker, Himie Voxman, Denis Watel, William Waterhouse, Howard Weiner, Pamela Weston, Eugene K. Wolf, and Phillip Young.

Many curators of musical instrument collections and museums have been very helpful in allowing me access to instruments, obtaining photographs, and answering questions. I would like to thank Margaret Birley (London, Horniman Museum), Kurt Birsak (Salzburg), James Borders (Ann Arbor), E. Isolde Clerc (Geneva), Martin Elste and Tom Lerch (Berlin), Florence Gétreau (Paris), Veronika Gutmann (Basel), Cynthia Adams Hoover (Washington), Jerry Horne (Little Rock), Günther Joppig (Munich), Ignace de Keyser (Brussels), Peter Kjeldsberg (Trondheim), Dieter Krickeberg (Nuremberg), Darcy Kuronen (Boston), Jeannine Lambrechts-Douillez (Antwerp), André Larson (Vermillion), Michael Latcham (The Hague), Laurence Libin (New York), Jeremy Montagu (Oxford), Arnold Myers (Edinburgh), Robert Sheldon (Washington, Miller Collection), Gerhard Stradner (Vienna), Susan Thompson (New Haven), and Elisabeth Wells (London, Royal College of Music). Many librarians have helped me to obtain books and microfilms. My special thanks go to the Interlibrary Loan staff of the Honnold Library at The Claremont Colleges, and to the staffs of the Music Library of the University of California at Los Angeles, New York Public Library, Huntington Library, Harvard University, Vassar College, British Library, Bodleian Library, Staatsbibliothek in Munich, Oesterrichische Nationalbibliothek in Vienna, and Bibliothèque Nationale in Paris. Research funds for the completion of this book were partially provided by a grant from the National Endowment for the Humanities for 1990–91.

The last person that I must thank for her expert editing, helpful prodding, and enormous patience is my wife, Eleanor Montague. Without her constant support and insight, I would never have been able to complete this book.

CONTENTS

FIGURES

ABBREVIATIONS, CONVENTIONS, NOTES TO READERS, AND MUSICAL NOTATION

Abbreviations: Musical Instruments

Abbreviations are adapted from Dibley, *Historic Musical Instruments*, vol. 2, pt. F, fasc. i: Clarinets. The orientation is from the top of the instrument downward.

S	speaker key
B♭	b♭¹ key
A–B	a¹–b¹ trill key
A	a¹ key
G♯	g♯¹ key
f/c	f¹/c³ key
E♭/B♭	e♭¹/b♭² key
C♯/G♯	c♯¹/g♯² key
B/F♯	b/f♯² key
B♭/F	b♭/f² key
A♭/E♭	a♭/e♭² key
F♯/C♯	f♯/c♯ key
F/C	f/c² key
E/B	e/b¹ key
E♭	e♭ key
D	d key
C♯	c♯ key
C	C key
Lo	left-hand thumb
L1	left-hand index finger
L2	left-hand middle finger
L3	left-hand ring finger
L4	left-hand little finger
Ro	right-hand thumb
R1	right-hand index finger

R2	right-hand middle finger
R3	right-hand ring finger
R4	right-hand little finger

Abbreviations: Journals, Dictionaries, and Reference Sources

AMZ	*Allgemeine Musikalische Zeitung*
BD	*A Biographical Dictionary of Actors, Actresses, Musicians, Dancers, Managers, and Other Stage Personnel in London, 1600–1800*
BTC	*The Breitkopf Thematic Catalogue*
CWB	*The Collected Works of Johann Christian Bach*
EM	*Early Music*
FoMRHIQ	*Fellowship of Makers and Researchers of Historical Instruments Quarterly*
GSJ	*The Galpin Society Journal*
HW	*Joseph Haydn Werke*
JAMIS	*Journal of the American Musical Instrument Society*
LS	*The London Stage, 1660–1800*
DMf	*Die Musikforschung*
MGG	*Die Musik in Geschichte und Gegenwart*
MGG, 2d ed.	*Die Musik in Geschichte und Gegenwart, 2d ed.*
NAMIS	*Newsletter of the American Musical Instrument Society*
New Grove	*The New Grove Dictionary of Music and Musicians*
New Grove, 2d ed.	*The New Grove Dictionary of Music and Musicians, 2d ed.*
NGDAM	*The New Grove Dictionary of American Music*
NGDMI	*The New Grove Dictionary of Musical Instruments*
NGDO	*The New Grove Dictionary of Opera*
NLI	*The New Langwill Index of Musical Wind Instrument Makers*
NMA	*Neue Ausgabe sämtlicher Werke*, Wolfgang Amadeus Mozart
MB	*Musica Britannica*
MW	*Wolfgang Amadeus Mozart's Werke*
PACN	*The Performing Arts in Colonial Newspapers, 1690–1783*
RRMCE	*Recent Researches in the Music of the Classical Era*
Recherches	*"Recherches" sur la Musique Français Classique*

SWG   *Sämtliche Werke*, Christoph Willibald Gluck
TS   *The Symphony, 1720–1840*

Abbreviations: General and Countries

A   Austria
Abb.   Abbildung
B   Belgium
c.   century
ca.   about
CH   Switzerland
cf.   compare with
CR   Czech Republic
d.   died
D   Germany
diss.   dissertation
DK   Denmark
ed.   edition, editor, edited by
F   France
fasc(s).   fascicle(s)
fl.   flourished, was active
GB   United Kingdom
Hz   Herz
I   Italy
ill(s).   illustration(s)
J   Japan
m(m).   measure(s)
MS.   manuscript
NL   Netherlands
no(s).   number(s)
op.   opus
pl(s).   plate(s)
pt(s).   part(s)
Q   quarter
rev.   revised
sec(s).   section(s)
ser.   series
Sign.   Signatur
trans.   translation, translated by
US   United States of America
vol(s).   volume(s)
wg.   Werkgruppe

Abbreviations: Museums and Collections

Abbreviations are taken from Waterhouse, *The New Langwill Index.*

A-Graz-D	Diözesanmuseum
A-Graz-L	Landesmuseum Joanneum
A-Salzburg	Museum Carolino Augusteum
A-Salzburg-C	Cubasch Collection
A-Wien	Sammlung alter Musikinstrumente, Kunsthistorisches Museum
B-Bruxelles	Musée des instruments de musique
B-Liège	Musée d'Art wallon
C-Toronto	Galper Collection
CH-Basel	Historisches Museum
CH-Genève	Musée des Instruments anciens de Musique
CH-Luzern	Triebschen, R. Wagner Museum
CH-Zumikon	Stalder Collection
D-Berlin	Musikinstrumenten-Museum, Staatlisches Institut für Musikforschung
D-Biebrich	Wiesbaden-Biebrich, Musikhistorisches Museum Heckel
D-Bonn	Beethoven-Haus
D-Darmstadt	Hessisches Landesmuseum
D-Eisenach	Bachhaus
D-Göttingen	Städtische Museum
D-Hamburg	Museum für Hamburgische Geschichte/ Museum für Kunst und Gewerbe
D-Ingolstadt-S	Stadtmuseum
D-Leipzig	Musikinstrumenten-Museum der Karl-Marx-Universität
D-Markneukirchen	Musikinstrumenten-Museum
D-München-J	Joppig Collection
D-München-S	Musikinstrumentenmuseum im Stadtmuseum
D-Nürnberg	Germanisches Nationalmuseum
D-Uhingen	Reil Collection
DK-Copenhagen	Musikhistorisk Museum
DK-Copenhagen-H	Himmer Collection
DK-Copenhagen-R	Rosenwald Collection
DK-Tåsinge	Nielsen Collection
F-Arnouville-lés-Gonesse	Watel Collection
F-Bayonne	Sallaberry Collection
F-Le Mans	Jeltsch Collection
F-Nice	Conservatoire municipal de musique
F-Paris	Musée de la Musique
GB-Cambridge	Shackleton Collection

GB-Edinburgh	Edinburgh University Collection of Historical Musical Instruments
GB-Keighley	Cliffe Castle Museum
GB-London-H	Horniman Museum
GB-London-RCM	Royal College of Music
GB-London-W	Waterhouse Collection
GB-Manchester	Royal Northern College of Music
GB-Oxford	Bate Collection of Musical Instruments
I-Milano	Museo Teatrale alla Scala
I-Roma-M	Museo Nazionale degli Strumenti Musicali
I-Roma-S	Santa Cecilia Museum
J-Tokyo	Musashino Academia Musicae
N-Trondheim	Ringve Musikhistorisk Museum
NL-Amsterdam	Hoeprich Collection
NL-Den Haag	Haags Gemeentemuseum
NL-Onnen	Varel Collection
S-Stockholm	Musikmuseet
SF-Helsinki	National Museum
US-AK	Band Museum
US-CA-Claremont	Kenneth G. Fiske Museum, Claremont Colleges
US-CA-Claremont-R	Rice Collection
US-CA-Santa Monica	Moir-Bouquet Collection
US-CT	Yale University Collection of Musical Instruments, New Haven
US-DC	Smithsonian, Washington
US-DC-S	Sheldon Collection
US-MA-Boston	Museum of Fine Arts
US-MA-Boston-C	Casadesus Collection, Boston Symphony
US-MA-Newton Centre	Sigal Collection
US-MI-Ann Arbor	Stearns Collection, University of Michigan
US-MI-Dearborn	Henry Ford Museum
US-MN	Polley Collection
US-NY-Dewitt	D'Mello Collection
US-NY-Massapequa Park	Maynard Collection (now dispersed)
US-NY-New York-C	Caplin Collection (now dispersed)
US-NY-New York-M	Metropolitan Museum
US-SD	Shrine to Music, University of South Dakota, Vermillion
US-UT	Museum of Church History and Art of the Church of Jesus Christ of Latter Day Saints, Salt Lake City

Notes to Readers

The term "America" or "American" is used for the United States of America even when referring to the colonial period. When known, for extant instruments, information is given in parentheses in the following order: date, location, and identification number assigned by that location.

Musical Notation

The following system of musical notation is used throughout.

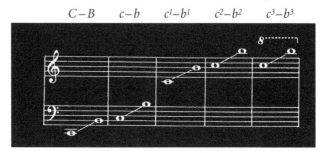

THE CLARINET
IN THE CLASSICAL PERIOD

INTRODUCTION

As the Clarinet, is an Instrument much esteemed in Regimental Bands as well as in Concerts, a short Description of it and it's effects will be necessary before the Method of playing on it is shewn. It is divided into four Parts; the Mouth Piece, (on which a flat Reed is tied) the upper Joint, the middle Piece, and the Bell or bottom Piece. It has thirteen Holes, five of which are stopped by Keys; it is to those Keys that the Instrument is indebted for its chief Use, as before they were contrived, the Clarinet could not be used in Concert, as at present it is. When played by itself, the fullness and sweetness of Tone is very pleasing, but when Joined with French Horns only, or in Concert with other Instruments, it's charming Effect is too obvious to be particularly described.

The Clarinet Instructor (London, ca. 1780)

Made in Germany, Belgium, the Netherlands, Austria, France, and the Czech Republic, the two- or three-key baroque clarinet was played until about 1760 and continued to be used by some military bandsmen and amateur musicians until the beginning of the 1800s. During the late 1750s and early 1760s, owing to the reciprocal efforts of makers, composers, and players, the somewhat limited baroque clarinet evolved into a more flexible classical clarinet, first in France as an instrument with four keys followed shortly thereafter in England and Germany by ones with five and six keys. By the 1770s, classical clarinets were found throughout Europe and had appeared in the Czech Republic, Scandinavia, Spain, Austria, and America. By 1800, the clarinet had spread to parts of Asia and South Africa. From about 1800 to 1830, clarinets were made with larger finger holes and a larger, redesigned mouthpiece that increased the instrument's projection and power. New keys were added and metal pillars were employed to mount them, improving intonation and allowing greater technical fluency. These changes occurred concurrently with the increasing technical and musical demands of early romantic composers.

The clarinet that developed during the years 1760 through 1830 and the music utilizing it are the focus of this volume. It continues the story started in the author's book *The Baroque Clarinet*, which traces the instrument from its origin in Nuremberg in 1700 through its development to 1760. The evolution of the classical clarinet is an intricate, complex story involving numerous people working in a variety of countries during times of stunning societal, musical, and technological changes. To tell the story, new research is integrated with a comprehensive summary and analysis of extant evidence. It is grounded in careful examination of numerous instruments by European and American makers; detailed review of published and manuscript sources and patents; analysis of musical scores and clarinet parts; and study of pictorial references. Several of these sources are reproduced here for the first time. The purpose of the book is to extend our knowledge and understanding of the development and evolution of the classical clarinet by tracing developments in four focus areas: (1) changes in the design, construction, mechanisms, and playability of the physical instrument; (2) playing techniques and performance practices that emerged as players and composers gained experience with the classical clarinet; (3) music utilizing the instrument and the derivation of a clarinet idiom; and (4) the introduction and use of the classical clarinet in performing groups.

A modest amount of technical musical knowledge is assumed, but the text is accessible to the general reader as well as to players, composers, instrument makers, and organologists. The book can be read from start to finish, of course, if one wishes to acquire a comprehensive view of the evolution of the classical clarinet. The reader can also use the volume as a reference, dipping into specific chapters for selected information. Extensive footnotes are supplied so the interested reader can follow the thread of research underpinning the work reported here. The original texts are provided primarily for sources that have not been reprinted.

Beginning in the 1760s and 1770s, in order to achieve a variety of goals, makers in various countries experimented with virtually every design and construction feature of the clarinet. Each change had the potential to modify the clarinet's playability and influence its utilization. The outcomes varied substantially, ranging from significant to incidental to outright dead ends. By the end of the eighteenth century, three national design schools had developed in Germany, France, and England. About 1780, an important Viennese movement established its own distinct fourth school that continues today. From the 1760s, a few makers in Belgium made distinctive clarinets, but a separate school did not emerge later in the century. However, beginning in the 1860s — outside the chronological limits of this book — several makers in Brussels, Paris, and America constructed thousands of the popular Belgian-designed Albert-system clarinets. The instruments from these various schools exhibit tonal differences and respond differently throughout the clarinet's range.

A history of the classical clarinet would be incomplete without attention to the body of performance practices that evolved. Topics discussed include range, registers, and fingerings; embouchure and mouthpiece positions; articulation; selection of a clarinet; transposition; notation of parts and clefs; and the use of a mute.

The third focus area explores the utilization of the classical clarinet by selected composers in various genres. During the second half of the eighteenth century, the exceptionally rapid acceptance of the clarinet as a significant woodwind instrument coincided with the development of preclassical music as exemplified by the works of Jean-Phillipe Rameau and Johann Stamitz, who wrote parts that required the baroque three-key clarinet pitched in A and the classical four-key clarinet in B♭. The classical clarinet had a distinctive timbre that projected well out of doors and blended with other woodwinds and brasses, thus making it a valuable addition to any orchestra and essential to military and civic bands and to Harmoniemusik ensembles—wind bands consisting of pairs of oboes, horns, bassoons, and clarinets. The enormous popularity of opera in the main European musical centers also exposed the public to the classical clarinet during the late eighteenth century. A large amount of chamber music from solos for clarinet alone to nonets for nine players contributed to the clarinet's popularity and use among amateurs and professionals. In addition, music arranged from opera and theater productions for wind bands became quite popular among aristocrats and amateurs. In several instances, analysis of the music or knowledge of the instrument played supports associating a type of clarinet (e.g., four-key French, five-key German, six-key English, thirteen-key French) with specific music.

As an added dimension, the book explores the relationships among composers, makers, and players and how their associations affected the development of the clarinet and its music. For example, composers influenced the evolution of key mechanisms on clarinets by writing music that could not be played on simpler instruments. The best-known early-romantic examples are the first and second concertos and the Concertino (1811) by Carl Maria von Weber, and the first (1809) and second (1810) concertos by Ludwig Spohr, which literally required ten- and eleven-key clarinets.

The development of the classical clarinet ultimately affected the modern instrument. Early-nineteenth-century instrument makers contributed original design aspects that later became incorporated into the modern clarinet, as is revealed by an examination of patents and instruments by James Wood and Teobaldo Monzani and the designs and instruments by the maker Jean-François Simiot and the player-inventors Iwan Müller and César Janssen.

The fourth focus area concerns the development of performing groups that made use of the clarinet, often in a prominent leading position, such as wind and military bands, and as a distinctive member of the woodwind choir in opera and orchestral works. All of these organizations contributed greatly to the public's acceptance and enjoyment of the classical clarinet.

A future monograph will provide an historical account of the lower-pitched clarinets: the clarinet d'amour, basset horn, alto clarinet, bass clarinet, contralto clarinet, and contrabass clarinet.

Organization

The first chapter lays the foundation for the rest of the book with a detailed survey of the physical instrument. It is a basic chapter probably of most value to the general reader. The second chapter surveys the historical development of the instrument to about 1830 via published and written descriptions, extant instruments, and patents. A separate section is devoted to the basset clarinet and the type of instruments used by Anton Stadler, an Austrian player and friend of Mozart.

The techniques and practices used by performers are the focus of chapter 3. In chapter 4 I analyze selected music written from about 1755 to 1830 and the establishment of a clarinet idiom during the eighteenth century. The discussion includes a number of clarinet parts in eighteenth-century operas, choral works, concertos, orchestral, and chamber music, such as Mozart's *Don Giovanni*, Haydn's *Creation*, Beethoven's Eighth Symphony, Mozart's and Weber's concertos, and Mozart's quintet. In chapter 5 I trace the dissemination and use of the classical clarinet in wind bands and orchestras, and the development of conservatories and music schools.

The history of the clarinet will probably never be completely revealed. Its many facets and byways will continue to be explored and our understanding will evolve. New music will be unearthed; there will be fresh interpretations of performance; and a fuller appreciation of the potential of eighteenth- and nineteenth-century instruments will enhance our knowledge of this music and its performers. Such is the lure of the clarinet. One thing is worth emphasizing, though. The early clarinet should not be considered an inferior forerunner of the modern instrument, but rather a different instrument that can produce beautiful and enlightening musical results.

The acoustic nature of the clarinet is not investigated in this book; however, the reader may benefit from a number of recent books and articles devoted to this subject. Detailed measurements of tone holes and bore graphs are not included, although some specific measurements are given for selected instruments. The interested reader or instrument maker is directed to the list of instrument plans presented by Van Acht, Bosma, and Hoekman (1992). Clarinets discussed in the text are identified by the location and a specific identification number, if available.

Sources

Sources of inspiration for this book are many. Recordings abound of music written during the eighteenth and nineteenth centuries played on the modern clarinet. Clarinetists who have enriched us include Jacques Lancelot, Jack Brymer (whose book includes a wealth of information), Gervase de Peyer, Hans Rudolf Stalder, Karl Leister, Thea King, Georgina Dobrée, Thomas Friedli, Luigi Magistrelli, and especially Dieter Klöcker, who recorded numerous concertos and chamber works of diverse combinations of instruments. In the past few years, the early-nineteenth-century clarinet has been featured in recordings of the works of Beethoven, Schubert, Berlioz, and Schumann, played by Hans Rudolf Stadler, Alan Hacker, Keith Puddy, Colin Lawson, Kurt Birsak, Eric Hoeprich, Antony Pay, Jean-Claude Veilhan, Gilles Thomé, Luigi Magistrelli, Jiři Krejči, and Joost Hekel, to mention only a few.

Countless editions of early clarinet music have been published since the 1950s. Himie Voxman, formerly professor at the University of Iowa, edited many concertos and chamber works and advised dozens of students in writing dissertations concerning specific clarinet works. György Ballása issued several important articles and numerous editions from early manuscript works preserved in European libraries. Others who have also contributed editions include Jost Michaels, Stanley Drucker, Dieter Klöcker, Jack Brymer, Pamela Weston, Georgina Dobrée, Colin Lawson, and Mitchell Lurie.

The literature concerning the history of the clarinet is abundant, including two classic studies. They were written by Oskar Kroll (1965; rev. Eng. ed., 1968) and F. Geoffrey Rendall (rev. ed., 1971) and published posthumously. The former deals mainly with the historical and musical development of the clarinet, particularly in Germany. The latter is divided equally between practical and historical considerations, concentrating on the development of the instrument in England. Pamela Weston's books on clarinet virtuosi (1971 and 1977) provide a broad base of information. Other significant studies include David Ross's D.M.A. dissertation on the construction of the eighteenth-century clarinet (1985); David Charlton's article on classical clarinet technique (1988); and the article by Nicholas Shackleton ("Clarinet") for the *New Grove Dictionary of Musical Instruments* (1984) and the *New Grove Dictionary of Music and Musicians* (2001), which include valuable data on instrument construction, playing techniques, and music.

Recent books by Michael Jacob (1991), William Waterhouse (1993), Phillip T. Young (1993), Kurt Birsak (1992; English trans., 1994), Colin Lawson (1995, 1996, 2000), Johan van Kalker (1997), Jean Jeltsch (1997), Fabrizio Meloni (2000), and Günther Dullat (2001) provide a wealth of information. Jacob provides a thorough investigation of the concertos by Carl Stamitz and his contemporaries and a short history of the eighteenth-century clarinet. Waterhouse contributes much new information in his invaluable index of instrument makers and Young gives information on several hundred clarinets in his survey of 4,900 woodwinds. Birsak's book is a general history of the clarinet with an emphasis on the eighteenth and nineteenth centuries, primarily in Austria. Lawson's *Cambridge Companion to the Clarinet* includes several essays by English clarinetists examining the history, construction, and repertory of the instrument. His 1996 book is a thorough investigation of Mozart's clarinet concerto and Anton Stadler's instrument and provides an historical sketch of the clarinet's development; and his newest offering is a practical guide to the early clarinet that addresses many important issues of playing and interpreting music playing early instruments. Van Kalker reviews the past literature on the clarinet and provides detailed listings of treatises and method books, and a large bibliography. Jeltsch's book is a thorough investigation of a set of six-key clarinets made by Jean-Jacques Baumann that includes biographical information on Baumann culled from French archival documents. Meloni provides a general book with a long initial chapter on history and many photographs of early clarinets (written by Luigi Magistrelli), followed by chapters on important Italian players and teachers; physics; pedagogy; jazz; and photographs of the construction of modern clarinets. Dullat presents an organological history of eighteenth-, nineteenth-, and twentieth-century clarinets with many reproductions of instrument photographs and patent drawings, as well as some archival documents.

1

GENERAL DESIGN
AND CONSTRUCTION
CHARACTERISTICS

Around the late 1750s and early 1760s, changes were made to the some-what limited two- and three-key baroque clarinets that led to more-flexible four- or five-key classical models. Makers experimented with virtu-ally every design and construction element of the clarinet to achieve various outcomes, and from 1810 to 1830, a radical redesign of the keys, tone holes, and bore resulted in a thirteen-key clarinet ready for the technical and mu-sical demands of early romantic music. The process of evolution of the clar-inet is a fascinating story, played out by numerous characters working in various geographic areas against the backdrop of steady changes in technol-ogy, society, and music. A key element of the history is the changing nature of the instrument itself. It is appropriate, therefore, to begin our study of the classical clarinet with a careful look at its physical developments.

General Characteristics

The classical clarinet, like the modern one, is a closed tube with a bore of cylindrical cross-section throughout most of its length, played with a single reed, made in sections, utilizing keys, and designed from the begin-ning as a transposing instrument. From about 1760 to 1830, boxwood (*Buxus sempervirens*), occasionally ebony (*Drospyros ebeninus*), or ivory was used. By the early nineteenth century there were some brass clarinets, but these were generally not accepted until the twentieth century. Dark-colored woods such as African blackwood (*Dalbergia melanoxylon*, also called grenadilla) and cocus (*Brya ebenus*) were used only occasionally from the mid-1830s but became the most popular woods after about 1860.[1] Apart from the maker's desire to experiment with a specific material, often the choice was a matter of economics and/or availability. However, some believe that material does affect tone quality. For example, the writer and clarinetist Geoffrey Rendall expresses the opinion that boxwood instruments provide the sweetest and most expressive tone, while those made of cocus and African blackwood sound the fullest and most brilliant. In addition, body wall thickness has an audible effect on tone quality; a thick wall results in a dull flat tone, a thin one in a shrill tone.[2]

At its upper and lower ends, the largely cylindrical bore turns very slightly into a conical section or cone in order to control tuning. The quality of the bore's surface affects tone quality and response. A smooth finish produces a clear, resonant tone; a rough finish results in an uneven, dull tone. Holes are drilled into the bore to be covered by a finger, thumb, or key head. Generally, the earliest classical clarinets feature round finger holes with a smaller right-hand first finger (R1) hole. After about 1815 many have oval-shaped finger holes, with a large R1[3] for more precise intonation and a louder sound. Eighteenth-century German clarinets (such as those by A. Grenser and Grundmann) sometimes feature doubled tone holes for the third (L3) and/or seventh (R4) finger holes, placed in a cove or depression in the wood surface. A few early-nineteenth-century makers include a doubled finger hole for L3, but it is not common.

The clarinet's compass or range consists of four registers: chalumeau, intermediate or throat, clarinet, and extreme.[4] The first register corresponds roughly to the range of the eighteenth-century chalumeau and includes the notes from e to f^1. The clarinet register comprises the overblown twelfths above the chalumeau register, that is, from b^1 to c^3. Separating the chalumeau and clarinet registers is the intermediate register ($f\sharp^1$ to $b\flat^1$), with notes above g^1 (played with all fingers removed and left thumb removed) produced with the aid of keys. The extreme register, from $c\sharp^3$ to g^3, can be seen as fifth harmonics, or the result of twice overblowing the corresponding fingerings from a to $d\sharp^1$ in the chalumeau register.[5] Beyond g^3, many fingerings are possible, and the pressure exerted by the lips becomes quite important in playing a note.

The greatest difficulty in clarinet manufacture during the eighteenth and nineteenth centuries was adjusting precise twelfths between the chalumeau and clarinet registers. Makers adjusted the width of these twelfths mainly by modifying, by a very small amount, the cross-section at the top and bottom of the bore. In most eighteenth-century instruments the transition from the lower end of the cylindrical bore to the flared cone of the bell is rather sharp and is situated below the lowest tone hole. By the first quarter of the nineteenth century, many makers controlled intonation by making a conical section as far up as the fourth finger hole above the bell.[6] At the upper end, intonation is influenced by a combination of variations in the bore shape; the bore of the barrel; and the inner construction of the mouthpiece. Intonation within each register is refined by subtly altering finger hole size and by enlarging or undercutting the under side of the tone holes. When makers developed the four-key classical clarinet during the 1760s, the placement of the key touches determined hand position, with left hand above and the right hand below. All eighteenth-century clarinets have one thumbhole, three finger holes for the left hand, and four finger holes for the right.

The earliest classical clarinet, one with four keys, emerged during the 1750s and early 1760s. These were made and played as late as the early nineteenth century, along with clarinets of earlier and later design, and are essentially transition instruments between the three-key baroque clarinet and the popular classical five-key clarinet. Like that of some of its two- and three-key predecessors, the body of four-key instruments is divided into four sections or joints, including a mouthpiece joined to a long socket.

The sections join by means of tenons and sockets. A tenon is formed by thinning the end of one section by about one half and taking away a corresponding amount from the inside of the section receiving the tenon to form a socket. To give the socket greater strength, the wood around it is left thicker, and the end is often protected against strain and splitting by adding a ring or ferrule of ivory, horn, bone, wood (often the same kind as the body), or metal around the socket. Each tenon is wrapped with waxed thread to make the connection airtight.

Over time, various makers changed the number and configuration of individual sections. For example, several eighteenth-century mouthpieces have a very long tenon constituting a section called a mouthpiece-barrel. During the last third of the eighteenth century, the lower section of the mouthpiece was divided to create a separate barrel with two sockets, one to fit the mouthpiece tenon and one to fit the left-hand finger-hole-section tenon. The bell was also divided during the late eighteenth century. Several eighteenth-century instruments have a bell with a long wood section with mounted keys and R4, called a stock-bell. During the late eighteenth century, makers created a separate stock section with tenons at both ends to fit the sockets of the right-hand finger hole joint and a smaller bell. As a result, many late-eighteenth- and early-nineteenth-century clarinets have six sections: mouthpiece, barrel, left-hand joint, right-hand joint, stock, and bell. By the 1820s, some instruments were made with the stock section joined to the right-hand finger hole section providing a platform for mounting additional keys. Often, the maker's motivation to divide a section was economic since larger pieces of wood are more expensive.

Keys may be forged; hammered, punched, and filed from a flat sheet of brass; or cast by pouring molten metal (silver for more-expensive instruments) into a mold. Each has three parts: a key head or flap to cover the tone hole; a shank to attach the key head to the body; and a touch or touch piece, usually at the end of the shank, to open or close the key head when pressed. A pad of leather is affixed with shellac or sealing wax onto the underside of each key head in order to make an airtight seal with the tone hole.

On eighteenth- and early-nineteenth-century instruments, key heads are rectangular or trapezoidal and occasionally feature decoration on the top surface, such as diagonal lines pointing to each corner of the key head, part of a maker's stamp, or even an owner's name. A flat leather pad is glued underneath the key head, which commonly closes on a flat area created in the surface of the section called a key seat.[7] By the 1810s, makers also made key heads in a flat, circular shape.

For the speaker key, a metal liner or tube extends the tone hole into the bore of the section, or a raised flat chimney projects above the section to assist in the production of the overblown or clarinet register. The player produces the clarinet register when the speaker key is open and the player increases the air pressure and tension of the lips. A thin piece of brass or a pin acts as an axle on which the key shank pivots. All the keys are attached to the body in a similar manner. For example, the speaker key is laid in a channel or slot cut in a raised ring or mounted in a wood block that is left standing when the section is turned on the lathe. The pin is inserted in a hole drilled in the ring or block, then either through a hole placed horizontally in the middle of the key shank or through a hole in a rocker or metal lug bent down from the shank. The pin is often made with a hook on one end to facilitate removal so the pad on the key head can easily be changed as it becomes worn.

Keys are positioned to facilitate playing. Those mounted lengthwise are called side-keys (e.g., the S or A key); keys placed perpendicular to the bore axis are cross-keys (e.g., the C♯/G♯ or B♭/F key). Clarinets with more than six keys often have one or more cross-keys. The touch of the speaker is angled upward on the dorsal side to enable the thumb simultaneously to cover its finger hole and to depress the touch. The raised rings for mounting the A key on the frontal side and the speaker on the dorsal side of eighteenth-century instruments often include a line in the center for decoration and as a guide for boring the hole for the axle pin on which the keys pivot. On many late-eighteenth- and early-nineteenth-century instruments these rings are reinforced with an iron, brass, or steel pin inserted horizontally through the wood above or below the ring. Some makers place the pin in the center of the upper rings adjacent to the axle pins. If the clarinet includes blocks, this pin is often situated horizontally through the blocks below the axle pins, particularly on the better quality instruments. More-expensive, high-quality instruments are pinned above and below the blocks.

The keys for both L4 and R4 and the R4 finger hole are set in a swelling or boss of the stock section. On most continental instruments, the swelling is fusiform or tapered; most instruments made in England or America exhibit a bell shape. The E/B key is positioned for L4 with a long shank set in a slot in the swelling of the stock section. It is mounted a little more than halfway down the length of the shank with an axle pin inserted into a hole drilled through the swelling, and through a metal rocker attached to the underside of the shank. The E/B key has a two-part construction: the shank and a separate key head mounted to a small wood block. When the E/B touch is pressed, it closes the key head by pressing on a pilot or tongue that fits through a loop attached to the end of the key head. Each key and the E/B shank have a flat metal spring that rests against the bottom of the shank to provide sufficient tension to open or close the key head. The other end of the spring is inserted partway into the wood, and on later instruments, the other end is soldered to the bottom of the shank.

Several surviving four-key examples reveal a short fourth key for A♭/E♭ positioned for the right-hand little finger and mounted in the stock-bell socket swelling. R4 covers a finger hole for F/c² that is bored at an angle on the swelling, just above the tone hole for the A♭/E♭ key. Theoretically, the A♭/E♭ key tone hole should be placed above the F/c² hole, but because of the extra width at the socket swelling, it must be placed lower to achieve the correct tuning. Considerable documentation from France and a few extant French instruments show that some makers prefer the long F♯/C♯ (rather than the A♭/E♭) key mounted in the same swelling as the E/B key, with its touch positioned for L4. Both types of four-key clarinets were played during the second half of the eighteenth century, but it is not known which type was constructed first.

The most popular clarinet during the eighteenth and nineteenth centuries was the five-key instrument with A♭/E♭ and F♯/C♯ keys, which allowed greater flexibility in fingering. The F♯/C♯ key tone hole is higher on the right-hand section than that for the E/B key, and the touch pieces are close together for easy reach by L4. This is the typical classical clarinet although many instruments, particularly by English makers, include a sixth A–B trill key. A slot is provided for the long touch of the A–B key in one or two rings or blocks adjacent to the thumbhole on the right side of the left-hand section (from the player's viewpoint), operated by R1. The five-key clarinet was the standard model during the late eighteenth century for players around the world and continued to be made in Germany as an inexpensive instrument as late as the early twentieth century.[8] Figure 1.1 illustrates the sectional divisions of classical clarinets, and figure 1.2 illustrates keys and their associated terms.

Some eighteenth- and early-nineteenth-century clarinets were made with *corps de réchange*—two additional finger hole sections that, when inserted, change the pitch by one-half step, usually from B♭ to A. However, surviving corps de réchange are scarce, which suggests that their use was not always satisfactory in intonation. A few makers supplied additional mouthpieces and longer barrels in addition to the corps' finger hole sections, thus providing better intonation.

Beginning in the 1820s, a thumb rest was sometimes fashioned as part of the wood body on the dorsal side of the right-hand joint, usually between the fourth and fifth finger holes. These integral thumb rests varied in shape but were often cut as short, curved protrusions. In 1824, Backofen was the first to illustrate integral thumb rests in his fingering charts for five- and eleven-key clarinets.[9] Some makers preferred to attach separate thumb rests of horn, ivory, or metal to the dorsal side by means of small screws.[10]

During the first decade of the nineteenth century, makers slowly added

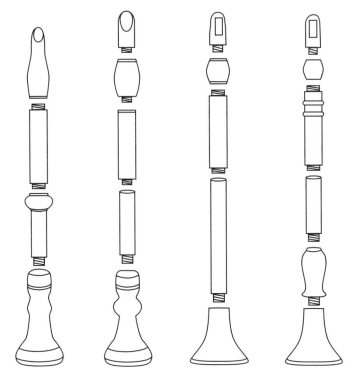

FIGURE 1.1   Sectional divisions of the classical clarinet.

keys to the common five- or six-key instrument to facilitate playing trills, improve the tuning and quality of sound, and provide a smoother transition in slurring from one note to another. An eight-key clarinet with cross-keys for E♭/B♭ positioned for L3 and B/F♯ for R3 was successfully introduced in London about 1800 by John Hale.[11] The keys provide additional fingerings and help to produce a fuller and more accurate tone than was possible with the older cross-fingerings. The clarinetist and inventor Iwan Müller is responsible for a clarinet that would play in all tonalities, thus eliminating the need for corps de réchange. His thirteen-key clarinet of 1811 has keys mounted on the sections with saddle-shaped brass pieces now called saddles. By 1821, his pillars were soldered onto a metal base-plate screwed to the body; later pillars were threaded and individually screwed into the body. Screws attach the key shanks to the top of the pillars.[12] Müller developed a new type of soft pad, called an elastic plug, to fit into round or domed key heads called salt-spoon keys and countersunk tone holes to leave a raised rim of wood for the round key pad to rest on; the latter characteristic is utilized on modern instruments. Shortly after the appearance of salt-spoon keys, pads became thinner and flatter, so the key head design changed to become shallow cups.[13]

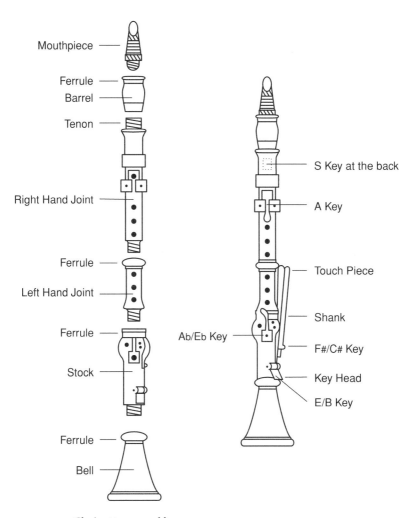

FIGURE 1.2   Clarinet terms and keys.

Mouthpieces, Barrels, and Tuning

The earliest classical clarinets are constructed with a mouthpiece made of the same material as the body, usually boxwood. Whether separate or part of a mouthpiece-barrel combination, the mouthpiece has a beak-shaped profile with thin side and top rails; a rectangular, trapezoidal, or (in the earliest classical instruments) V-shaped window or opening; a flat surface or table below the window; and a slight curving away of the side and top rails, called the lay. Eighteenth- and early-nineteenth-century mouthpieces have grooves below and around the window to guide the twine wound around the mouthpiece, which secures the reed against the flat table and rails.[14] The flat side of the reed is placed on the table with the butt end resting against a ledge to prevent it from slipping off the table and moving sideways when being tied on.[15] The thin upper section of the reed vibrates against the side and top rails. Two engravings from Robinet's 1777 *Suite de recueil de planches* illustrate a frontal view of a mouthpiece-barrel with its reed unattached and a side view of both (see figure 1.3). Castillon's description of this mouthpiece from a four-key clarinet provides a clear picture.

> The head is made of boxwood like the rest; it terminates in a beak somewhat resembling that of a recorder but instead of the mouthpiece, this beak has on its upper flat part a triangular hole. The beak is pierced obliquely so that the interior profile exactly corresponds to the outline shown. The triangular orifice is covered by a tongue of cane, suitably shaped and adapted, and tied on with thread; so that the mouthpiece of the clarinet is something like the tongue of brass that one finds on a child's wooden trumpet.[16]

During the 1770s on the continent, makers separated the upper section of the mouthpiece-barrel from its lower end, resulting in a mouthpiece

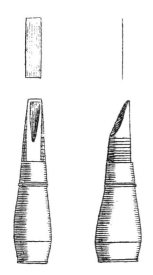

with a tenon about one-quarter the length of the barrel. The barrel is pear-shaped, with sockets on both ends. With this change, the barrel is used as a tuning slide on the tenon of the right-hand joint, leaving the mouthpiece flat against the upper end of the barrel when playing. Documentation of separate mouthpieces made of blackwood or ebony is found during the 1780s.[17] Brass mouthpieces on military clarinets are included in a description of the clarinet in Köster's 1781 *Deutsche Encyclopädie*. However, metal mouthpieces did not enjoy wider use until the 1820s, initially in Germany. Nineteenth-century mouthpieces are also made of African blackwood (grenadilla) or cocus and sometimes have a thin ring turned just below the window to help bind the cord around the reed.

FIGURE 1.3   Mouthpiece-barrel of a four-key clarinet, Robinet, *Suite de recueil de planches* (Paris, 1777).

After about 1785, English makers also separated the mouthpiece-barrel into two sections, but with different results. English mouthpieces are shorter and narrower than continental mouthpieces, with a very long tenon about three-quarters the length of the English waisted-shape or incurved barrel. The barrel does not have sockets, but at its thick end the bore is narrowed up to a point to form a thin ledge. Thus, the mouthpiece tenon fits snugly against the ledge in the bore of the barrel, forming an efficient seal. Fully engaged, the mouthpiece and barrel sections are shorter than the earlier combined mouthpiece-barrel section. With this change, the long tenon mouthpiece rather than the barrel could be used for tuning and provided a longer slide than was available on continental instruments. On the basis of a few early examples, Shackleton suggests that the London maker John Hale was the inventor of the long-tenon mouthpiece.[18] The fingering chart in the earliest English tutor, *The Clarinet Instructor* (ca. 1780), includes an engraving of a clarinet with its mouthpiece pulled out so that the long tenon is visible.[19]

Regardless of design, separate mouthpiece and barrel sections enable the maker to utilize smaller pieces of wood—an economic advantage. Shackleton notes two other benefits from this change. Material more resistant to warping, such as cocus or blackwood, could be used for the mouthpiece rather than boxwood, and the bore of the mouthpiece and upper part of the barrel could be more easily modified by the maker to control intonation. On earlier instruments with mouthpiece-barrel combinations, the bore is cylindrical up to the mouthpiece chamber.[20] By the beginning of the nineteenth century, different methods had developed to control intonation. For example, makers in Dresden such as Heinrich Grenser made a rather short barrel with a bore over a millimeter wider than that of the body, with a sharp gradation in the top tenon of the right-hand joint. The longer barrels of French instruments have a smaller gradation in the bore, while in England the bore remained essentially cylindrical, as in baroque clarinets. Unfortunately, the evidence from extant clarinets is incomplete since mouthpieces and barrels are often missing or damaged.

Mouthpieces made by August Grenser and his nephew Heinrich are unusual in that they are scored on the outside in three different places rather than symmetrically grooved, in order to hold the twine or string ligature. This may be unique to the Grensers, or it may represent a local characteristic of Dresden makers.[21]

An 1812 British patent (No. 3586) by the Monzani firm illustrates two small wooden knobs glued or attached to either side of the base of the mouthpiece "to assist in taking out the mouth piece from socket"[22] without disturbing the twine holding the reed. However, this design feature was not adopted by other British makers and possibly by only one French maker.[23]

The mouthpieces of the earliest clarinets are often stamped with the maker's mark on the table below the reed, which, when aligned with marks on the other joints, suggests the practice of placing the reed against the upper lip while blowing. By the 1840s, the Lyonais maker Louis Muller offered mouthpieces stamped on either the table or dorsal side because some players changed their technique to play with the reed below.[24]

Iwan Müller was the first to illustrate a metal ligature (*anneau*) with two screws (still in present use) in his *Gamme* or fingering chart for his thirteen-key *nouvelle clarinette*, published about 1812. In his subsequent tutor, Müller advocated using a metal ligature with two screws to secure the reed onto the

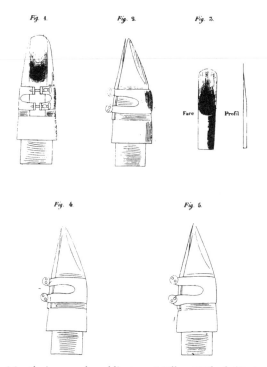

FIGURE 1.4   Mouthpiece, reed, and ligature, Müller, *Méthode* (Paris, ca. 1821).

mouthpiece. He reasoned that it was much easier to remove the reed from the mouthpiece using a ligature than to unwrap twine; in addition, it was more elegant looking (see figure 1.4).[25] Mouthpieces were constructed without twine grooves after the widespread adoption of ligatures about 1850, except for those made in Germany and Austria, where the older tradition persists to the present.

During the nineteenth century, makers sought a substance for mouthpieces that would not warp from the moisture generated during playing. Mouthpieces were made of ivory, pewter (with a brass tenon), metal, or hard crystal glass.[26] For example, in 1828 the maker Streitwolf advertised a thirteen-key ebony clarinet with gilded silver keys, a metal mouthpiece, and a case.[27] Later, Streitwolf made adjustable metal mouthpieces, one of which was played by Johann Hermstedt at an 1832 concert in Leipzig. For tuning purposes, it has a movable tenon adjustable up or down from its base by means of a screw.[28] During the 1830s, pewter mouthpieces appeared, with a brass tenon used as a tuning slide and a barrel with a brass lining.[29] Although several examples of these mouthpieces survive on American-made clarinets, it is by no means certain that American makers developed pewter mouthpieces.[30]

Mouthpiece caps made of wood (usually not boxwood) stained brown are commonly found on English eighteenth- and nineteenth-century clarinets. They protected the thin tip of the mouthpiece and the fragile reed tip. English makers provided these caps by the 1770s, as shown in an engraving of a left-handed five-key clarinet in volume 1 of Corri's *Select Collection of the Most Admired Songs,* published in 1779.[31]

A few makers experimented with an extendable metal-lined barrel for use as a tuning slide. In Vanderhagen's 1819 tutor, the fingering chart for a twelve-key clarinet includes a metal-lined barrel that separates in the center. The metal tube is marked with six lines, enabling the player to calibrate the extent of the slide, and the slick surface of the metal accumulates less water than a wooden surface. Vanderhagen mentions that it is very easy to use a barrel with a metal slide on a twelve-key or older clarinet, but the slide must be made very long. He suggests that the maker consider the length of the upper joint when constructing a metal-lined barrel with a slide.[32] Other French makers during the 1820s constructed mouthpieces with metal tenons or metal-lined barrels that fit on metal tenons of the left-hand joint, for use as a tuning slide.[33]

Reeds

The reed is essential, since its tip vibrates to produce the tone as the player blows into the mouthpiece. Ivory, bone, whalebone, lancewood (*Calophyllum brasiliense*), boxwood, ebony, and silver are among the materials that were tried over time to create these vibrations, but cane (*Arundo donax*) has been the material of choice for clarinet reeds since the eighteenth century. Invariably players prefer the musical results of cane because of its resilience and responsiveness to embouchure pressure changes and its ability to tolerate moisture without adverse effects.[34] A beautiful tone is produced only if a reed of the finest cane is matched to a well-made mouthpiece.

Reed size varies with the mouthpiece design. For example, eighteenth-century English mouthpieces are generally shorter and narrower at the tip than contemporary continental mouthpieces; English reeds of the time are correspondingly smaller. Eighteenth- and early- nineteenth-century Austrian mouthpieces are also narrower than German and French mouthpieces and require a narrower reed. During the 1820s and 1830s, English makers began to make mouthpieces with a socket and barrels that fit on a tenon on the right-hand section, for use as a tuning slide. These mouthpieces require longer and wider reeds, as measurements from a few English, French, and Austrian mouthpieces indicate (see table 1.1).[35] Reeds are easily broken and separated from their instruments, so precise dating is problematic.

Premade clarinet reeds have been available from makers and musical instrument dealers at least since the 1760s. One of the earliest firms to offer them was John Longman and Company (London), as noted in a 1769 cata-

TABLE 1.1
English, French, and Viennese mouthpieces

Maker[1]	Clarinet	Total length (cm.)	Reed length (cm.)	Table length (cm.)	Width at tip (cm.)	Date	Stamp
G. Miller	B♭ 5-key	62	43	13	11	ca. 1775	Miller London
Anon. English	B♭ 6-key	60	41	11	10	ca. 1785	Unstamped
Astor	C 5-key	65	47	11	10	ca. 1790	Unstamped
Astor & Co.	C 6-key	61	42	12	11	ca. 1810	Unstamped
Goulding & Co.	C 5-key	60	43	16	11	ca. 1820	I. Wood-Fecit
F. M. Amelingue	C 5-key	69	47	34	14	ca. 1820	Unstamped
K. Hammig	B♭ 5-key	66	61	31	11	ca. 1820	Unstamped
D'Almaine & Co.	B♭ 10-key	65	57	30	12	ca. 1835	Unstamped with socket
J. Printemps	B♭ 13-key	68	51	21	13	1837	Printemps Lille

1. Miller, Anonymous English and Printemps (US-CA-Santa Monica) Astor & Co., Goulding & Co., Amelingue, and Hammig (US-CA-Claremont-R), Astor (US-CA-Claremont, W119), D'Almaine & Co. (US-CA-Claremont, W155).

log.[36] Regardless of the availability of premade reeds, there have always been players who cut and shape their own reeds to produce a fine tone quality and the desired response.[37] Players can purchase cane and prepare it following written instructions or instructions from a teacher.

Information detailing the preparation of cane reeds initially appeared in 1803 in Backofen's *Anweisung*. He recommends starting with a hard cane reed that approximates the proportions of the mouthpiece. After soaking it in water to soften it, cut the cane with a sharp knife. If the back of the reed is not flat, use a wide file to flatten it. Use thin pieces of glass, Dutch rush, or a tubular piece of green cane as an abrasive. Players who want elasticity thin the reed at the tip while others thin it more in the middle and leave the tip thicker. Others make the reed convex on both surfaces or flat on top and concave underneath.[38] Equally spaced grooves are cut on the bark side of the reed in order for the cord ligature to secure it to the mouthpiece.[39]

Dates, Hallmarks, and Serial Numbers

Eighteenth- and early- nineteenth-century clarinets were occasionally stamped with a date of manufacture on the bell or barrel. Of surviving eighteenth-century instruments the largest number were dated by three Dresden makers: Grundmann (1775, 1789, and 1795), A. Grenser (1777, 1785, and 1796), and Floth (1806). One Swiss maker is M. Sutter (1788); Czech makers are Doleisch (1793 and 1794) and Bauer (1789); Italian makers were Magazari (1798) and Fornari (1806), and one Austrian is Friedrich Hammig (1798). The only English maker who dated his instruments was Thomas Collier (1770 and 1774).[40] Beginning in the 1820s, a few French makers, including Lefèvre and Printemps, dated their instruments, as did Charles Sax (Brussels).

The undersides of the long forged brass keys for F♯/C♯ and E/B on some eighteenth-century English clarinets were stamped in an oval or rectangular die with the initials of the key makers, such as "I H" for John Hale; "I W" for James Wood; and "W M" for William Milhouse. Hale's mark is on key touches on instruments by Collier, Miller, Astor, Cahusac, and Kusder. The Monzani and Key firms sometimes have hallmarks stamped on top of the silver key touches of the S, A–B trill, F♯/C♯, and E/B. These are useful in dating the keys and by implication the instruments, but caution is in order because keys were replaced and key makers made them in batches and sold them later. The number of marks constituting an English hallmark varied over the years, but there are usually five depictions: a leopard's head, a date letter, a lion passant (or resting), a king's or queen's head, and a key maker's mark.[41]

The use of serial numbers on woodwinds began about 1809 by the Monzani firm in London. On early-nineteenth-century clarinets, the serial number was usually stamped on the frontal side of the barrel below the maker's stamp. The serial number, sometimes with the additional evidence of hallmarked keys, may provide evidence for an approximate date of an instrument.[42] Other firms whose clarinets included stamped numbers that may be serial numbers are Firth, Hall, and Pond (New York), and Hanken (Rotterdam).[43]

Nominal Pitch and Pitch Levels

Makers started marking the nominal pitch on clarinets during the late eighteenth century, a practice increasingly desirable as clarinetists had to play differently pitched clarinets in various tonalities, particularly in eighteenth-century operas. Makers stamped or carved the sounding pitch of the clarinet, when playing c^2, on the finger hole sections and additional corps de rechange, and sometimes on the barrel and bell. For example, pitch letters for clarinets in C are marked "C;" instruments in B♮ are marked "H" (German for B); those in B♭ are marked "B" (German for B♭); and clarinets in A are marked "A." The stock, bell, and mouthpiece do not have to be marked because these sections are used with different corps. During the eighteenth century, William Milhouse and a few continental makers made use of pitch letters, and during the nineteenth century, it became common. Only a few corps survive pitched in B♮, and the letter "E" was found on a corps in B♮ for a C clarinet (F-private collection) by Viennen.[44] The Italian writer Francesco Antolini mentions that "E♯" indicates the pitch of B♮,[45] but this mark is not verified from extant instruments. Other pitch letters on nineteenth-century E♭ clarinets include "Es" (German for E♭) and "E♭." By the 1820s, some French makers, such as Simiot, stamped syllables to indicate nominal pitch, "La" for A and "Si♭" for B♭. Nominal pitch names are not marked on modern clarinets since players predominately use the B♭ and A clarinets, transposing parts when they occur for the C clarinet.

An unofficial standard pitch level for English woodwinds during the early nineteenth century was A = 440 Hz, a fact supported by the practical experience of many players and collectors as well as by playing tests on several instruments. During this time, a few English makers used numerical systems to indicate gradations of this pitch level and stamped a number on sections of the clarinet. This practice was probably adapted from the use of numbers on the graduated wooden tenons of tuning heads by the flute maker Richard Potter. John Cramer's firm was one of the earliest to use numbers on clarinets, with the flattest instruments marked "1" and the sharpest "6."[46] During the early nineteenth century, Cramer's former partner, Thomas Key, stamped 1 through 6 on barrels, finger hole sections, and bells, probably to indicate specific pitch levels.[47] One twelve-key clarinet (GB-Edinburgh, 143) by Key includes two barrels, the shorter stamped with the word "sharp."[48]

The systematic investigation of classical clarinet pitch levels began only during the 1980s. Stradner reports pitch levels between A = 430 and A = 445 for eighteenth- and early-nineteenth-century clarinets by the Viennese makers Rockobaur (a three-key clarinet d'amour), Hammig (or Hammich), Griesbacher (a basset horn), Tauber, and Merklein. He also suggests that Viennese makers utilized these pitch levels for oboes and flutes during the same period.[49] Ross arrives at a similar conclusion after establishing that a clarinet by the Viennese maker Lotz (CH-Genève, 136) plays between A = 435 and A = 437.[50] Baur, Griesbacher, and Doleisch made clarinets between A = 430 and A = 440.[51]

Pitch levels reported to Haynes indicate that most German, English, French, and Italian clarinets from about 1765 to 1800 are pitched A = 415 to A = 430 and that instruments after 1800 are often at A = 440 or higher. Only two French clarinets in C, by Savary Père, are found to be as low as A = 397 to A = 399.[52] The vast majority of English five- and six-key clarinets are pitched at A = 440, verified by the author's testing and that of many other players and collectors. Most of these instruments were probably made for use in military or church bands. It is assumed that the few existing English instruments pitched at about A = 430 were made for orchestral playing, including the only known English eighteenth-century clarinet in A (ca. 1800, GB-Edinburgh, 131), by George Miller.[53] Pitch levels of eighteenth- and nineteenth-century clarinets vary from as low as A = 397 to as high as A = 455 Hz. Since there was no standard for pitch level, each town established its own standard from existing instruments with an immovable pitch source, such as a church organ.

Cases

Surviving eighteenth-century clarinet cases are rare; the few that do survive are wooden boxes.[54] Leather bags were utilized in the late eighteenth century; they were first documented in a 1780 inventory of instruments kept at the library of the king of France at Versailles that includes six pairs of clarinets with corps de réchange and mouthpieces in leather pouches.[55] Leather bags continued to be in use by the London firm of Wood and Ivy, which sent an invoice for five clarinet bags to the Edinburgh firm of J. and R. Glen in 1839.[56]

2

HISTORICAL DEVELOPMENT

M any of the earliest classical clarinet makers were of German origin. They worked in England and France, and their influence is apparent in other countries as well, particularly Denmark and Italy. However, native makers in these countries soon further developed the initial designs. In America, many clarinets were imported from England throughout the first half of the nineteenth century, and the majority of instruments manufactured in America were imitations of English clarinets.

Caution is appropriate in using evidence from extant instruments because many exist in altered form. For various reasons, an instrument may have had one or more alterations over time including, but not limited to, shortening to raise the pitch; modifying tone holes to correct pitch problems; or adding keys for greater flexibility.[1] Others, cracked or damaged over time, have been repeatedly repaired. For example, Shackleton notes that many excellent Viennese clarinets from Mozart and Beethoven's time were altered and repaired to extend their usefulness.[2] Thus, the reader should understand that numerous extant classical clarinets are likely to have been altered or changed at one point during their history, thus unavoidably complicating, and perhaps misleading, historical and playing analysis.

Makers sometimes modified baroque three-key clarinets by adding a key, an operation that made them the earliest four-key classical clarinets. In fact, there is no definitive documentation as to where and when the earliest four- and five-key classical clarinets were developed. However, examination and comparison of extant instruments, treatises, tutors, and music provides an account of the development of the instrument in various countries. The historical record is complicated, and an erroneous overall picture of the development of the clarinet has been painted by many nineteenth- and twentieth-century authors who attributed the addition of keys to certain makers or players simply by copying previous sources rather than by examining the original documents and establishing the validity of their claims.[3] Future research and examination of extant instruments will reveal new information about the classical clarinet and its makers, such as Jeltsch's work (1997) on Jean-Jacques Baumann.

The Classical Clarinet: Developments by Country

France

The clarinet was only occasionally required as a special instrument in Parisian operas during the 1750s. During the 1760s, a number of composers published works for the instrument. Pinpointing the date for the instrument's transformation from a baroque three-key clarinet to a classical four-key instrument is problematic. For example, in 1758, the writer and musician Michel Corrette specified the range of the clarinet as f to c³, identical to the range of the two-key clarinet described by Eisel in his 1738 treatise; Garsault described a two-key high-F clarinet in his 1761 general encyclopedia.[4] These sources suggest that clarinets in Paris were still the two-key variety.

During the 1760s and 1770s, three sources were published regarding a four-key clarinet with an F♯/C♯ key. The first appears in an interesting 1764 description of the clarinet by Du Moutier in the *Dictionnaire portatif des arts et métiers*.

> For some years, clarinets have been popular in Paris, and they make them quite skillfully there. They are instruments with a reed, about as long as the oboe, but with a much wider and even diameter, so that one needs only a single reamer for boring this instrument. The reed of a clarinet is not the same as that of a bassoon or oboe. It is a thin tongue of cane attached with twine to the upper part of the mouthpiece which, when animated by breath, gives this instrument a unique sound. In the low range, it has the sound of the chalumeau; and in the high range, it has the sound of a soft trumpet, and does not produce the octave as in the other wind instruments but the fifth above the octave. Clarinets, played with taste and intelligence, create a beautiful effect in symphonies, and they are also very pleasant to listen to in a quartet with hunting horns. The skill of the craftsman consists in tuning this instrument with much care and exactitude, for the high notes must be perfectly a twelfth above the low notes. The two small keys placed on top of the clarinet must be in their proper position. Two keys have recently been added to the foot or lower part of clarinets that make this instrument complete, because it was lacking one pitch (B natural) in the diatonic scale. At the same time, it has all the semi-tones at least in the hands of good players. Until now, this instrument could only be played in the keys of C and in F, although it has a much greater range than the oboe.[5]

Du Moutier states that clarinets were skillfully produced in France for some years, presumably at least since the early or mid-1750s. The earliest French makers in Paris were Johann Gottfried Geist (from 1750), Gilles Lot (active from 1752), Michel Amlingue (active as a wood turner from 1766, master from 1780), Martin Lot (master from 1769), and Jean Baptiste Prudent (master from 1771), all represented by extant four- and five-key examples.[6] Du Moutier observed that only one reamer or tapered boring bar is needed to produce the clarinet's cylindrical bore. A boring bar with a sharp spoon-shaped tip and a groove along its length to remove waste wood was the most popular.[7] The conical bores of other woodwinds such as flutes, oboes, and bassoons require more than one type of reamer. Du Moutier also acknowledges the difficulty of producing in-tune twelfths between the chalumeau and clarinet registers. He states that two keys were recently added to the two-key clarinet to overcome the lack of a b♮[1]. Du Moutier also notes that for good players, all the other semitones are playable, and although the clarinet is restricted to the tonalities of C and F, it has a much greater range than the oboe.

Valentin Roeser, a German composer and clarinetist, prepared the earliest known instrumentation manual, entitled *Essai d'instruction à l'usage de ceux qui composent pour la clarinette et le cor* (1764),[8] and wrote an important account of the four-key French clarinet. He did not provide a detailed description, but the specific mention of large keys for E/B and F♯/C♯ and his illustration of difficult passages that composers should avoid leave little doubt that his clarinet was a four-key instrument. Roeser states, "These two keys were added not long ago, because earlier, neither the b♭[1] [E/B key] nor the c♯[2] [F♯/C♯] were available. The a[1] [A] and b♭[1] [S] are likewise played with keys, but the latter are much smaller and less awkward than the former."[9] Undoubtedly, awkwardness in playing occurred when slurring between b[1] and c♯[2], since the player had to lift L4 from one touch piece to the other. Given the lag time in publication and dissemination of knowledge typical of the period, Roeser was probably referring to a time not less than ten years prior to his *Essai* for the addition of these keys (that is, about 1754).

Roeser subsequently published the earliest fingering chart in a *Gamme de la clarinette avec six duos* about 1769.[10] The clarinet engraving in this chart has four sections: two finger hole joints, mouthpiece-barrel, and stock-bell (see figure 2.1). The unusual shank of the F♯/C♯ lever has a noticeable upward curve that brings its touch piece closer to the E/B touch. Four subsequent publications copy most of Roeser's fingerings and model their engravings on his four-key clarinet.[11]

The German Johann Gottfried Geist, known as Jean Godeffroy Geist or Geitz, made the earliest extant French-made clarinet. Geist arrived in Paris from Weimar about 1750 to work as a woodwind maker. By 1775, he was suffering a mental illness and was prohibited by the Châtelet de Paris from making instruments.[12] In 1992, a four-key C clarinet (ca. 1760, F-Paris, E.922.2.1) by Geist marked "[dove bearing twig]/I. G. GEIst/A PARIS/[five-petal flower]" was sold at a Paris auction to the Musée de la Musique (see figure 2.2).[13] It is similar to the instrument in Roeser's *Gamme* but features a straight rather than a curved touch piece for the F♯/C♯ key. There are mouthpiece-barrel and stock-bell sections, two squared-off rings with dec-

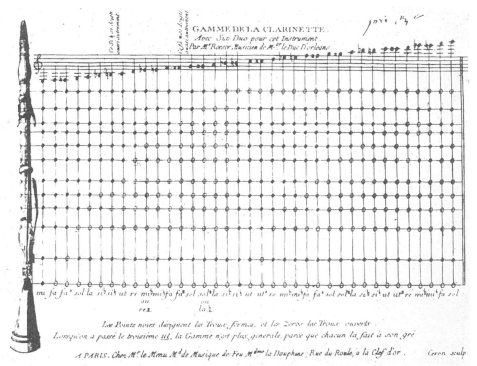

FIGURE 2.1   Four-key clarinet, Roeser, *Gamme* (Paris, ca. 1769).

orative scoring for mounting the S and A keys, one ferrule, and a block for
the E/B key. The Geist clarinet is an appropriate instrument to perform the
duets in Roeser's *Gamme de la clarinette* (ca. 1769) and the C clarinet parts in
Les deux avares (1770) by André-Ernest-Modeste Grétry. Only three more
four-key clarinets with an F♯/C♯ key by French makers, built after Geist completed his instrument, were reported to the author. These include an ebony
C clarinet with ivory ferrules by Michel Amlingue, a clarinet by Martin Lot,
and a clarinet marked "Champlain" made during the 1770s or 1780s.[14]

Seven years after Roeser's *Gamme*, Frédéric Adolphe Maximilian Gustav
de Castillon provides an informative description of the four-key clarinet and
a fingering chart in his article "Clarinette" in the *Supplément à l'Encyclopédie*
(1776). Although Castillon was writing in Berlin, he was associated with the
Prussian court of Frederick the Great and would have been familiar with the
latest Parisian-made instruments.[15] He includes four engravings of a four-
key instrument in the 1777 *Suite du recueil de planches* that differ only slightly
in construction from the Geist clarinet (see figure 2.3).[16]

Castillon and Geist's clarinets have square-turned rings with scribe lines
on the upper section and a rounded but small ferrule of the right-hand finger hole joint socket. Both have a straight shank for the F♯/C♯ key, instead of

Roeser's more rounded rings, and a curved shank. Castillon's socket swelling on the stock-bell is smoother and expands less than Geist's. He also includes one single scribe line and one double line on the swelling of the stock-bell for mounting the F#/C# and E/B keys. Castillon's mouthpiece-barrel has a window that is slightly more V-shaped than Geist's. In general appearance Castillon's clarinet, in particular the shape and appearance of the mouthpiece-barrel, resembles a five-key D clarinet (ca. 1780, F-Paris, 533) stamped "G. A. Rottenburgh."[17] Castillon's description in the *Supplément à l'Encyclopédie* includes significant information on the construction and use of the instrument.

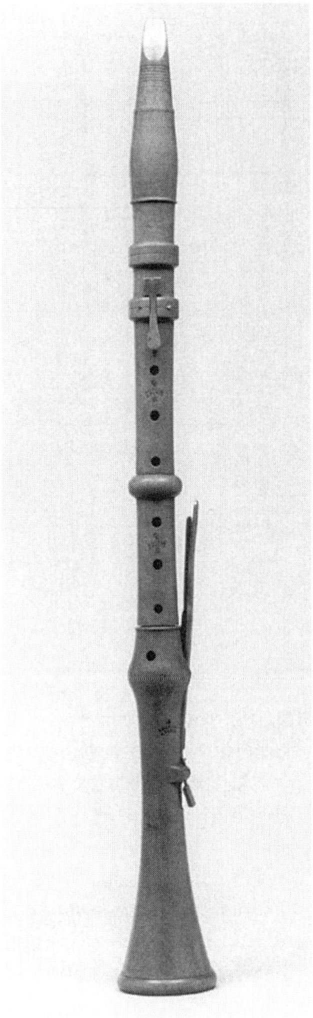

One important observation is that the clarinet is a minor third lower than other instruments; that is, its lowest C is in unison with the lowest A on the violin. By this reckoning, the compass of the clarinet extends from 4 ft. C#, the first C# of the cello [*sic*] to E, the triple octave of the minor third of this C# or the fingered E on the top string of the violin. This is why, when the clarinet plays with other instruments, the part is written a minor third higher than theirs. For example, if the piece is in A major, the part is in C; if in D, it is in F. Owing to fingering difficulties, obbligato passages are written only for the clarinet in C (the A of other instruments) and in F major (the D of other instruments). To remedy this want of variety, the middle joints containing the holes 2, 3, 4, 5, 6, and 7 are now made in duplicate. With these new pieces the clarinet is raised a major semitone, giving two more tonalities, Bb and Eb major. The two things to remember are that the clarinet is usually a minor third below other instruments, but that one should state which middle joints the player must select. At the time of writing, there is in Berlin, a musician who plays a clarinet with six keys on which he obtains all the modes. It has already been remarked how much difficulty four keys cause. It must be much worse with six![18]

FIGURE 2.2   Four-key clarinet in C, Johann Gottfried Geist, Paris (ca. 1765, F-Paris, E.922.2.1).

Castillon emphasizes that the clarinet is pitched in A, with two new middle sections to raise the pitch one-half step to Bb. His preference for the

A clarinet is apparently based on the large number of A clarinet parts in French operas, since the most favored clarinet later in the eighteenth century for concertos, chamber music, and wind ensembles was the B♭ instrument.

Castillon is one of the earliest to mention corps de réchange to change the pitch, a practice that became popular throughout Europe.[19] His mention of the Berlin musician with a six-key clarinet highlights that instruments of a more advanced design were available to a few adventurous players.

Four-key clarinets were utilized in the C clarinet parts of the Parisian operas of the 1770s and were still being used during the early 1780s, as proven by the publication of a fingering chart by Abraham about 1782.[20] The five-key instrument first appeared in Paris after 1780 and was probably played in productions of *Iphigénie auf Tauris* (1781) by Christoph Willibald Gluck and *Panurge dans l'Isle des Lanternes* (1785) by Grétry.

A few French makers constructed four-key clarinets with an A♭/E♭ key, presumably for the Belgian or German market. Three four-key clarinets with an A♭/E♭ key were made by Martin Lot (in B♭), Michel (in D), and Charlier (in C) but were destroyed during World War II.[21] Martin Lot's clarinet was made probably after he attained master status in Paris in 1769. Michel and Charlier were active during the late eighteenth and early nineteenth centuries.[22] Charlier's clarinet has the touch for the A♭/E♭ key on the dorsal side for the thumb. Lot's instrument originally had the touch in the same position as that of Charlier's, but the tone hole was filled and a new one drilled in order to reposition the key on the frontal side. A metal saddle was mounted for the E/B key, probably to repair damage to the original mounting.[23] The dorsal position of the A♭/E♭ key also appears on a few German instruments in the 1770s, prefiguring what came to be its usual place on the front of the instrument.

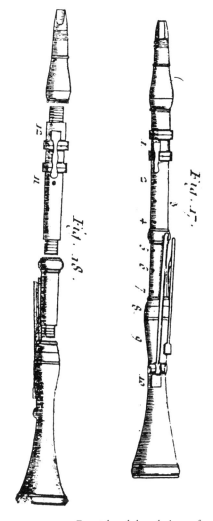

FIGURE 2.3   Frontal and dorsal views of a four-key clarinet, Robinet, *Suite de recueil de planches* (Paris, 1777).

The first published illustration in France of a five-key clarinet appears about 1785 with a fingering chart in the important *Méthode* by Amand Vanderhagen (see figure 2.4).[24] The drawing is somewhat inaccurate—the stock-bell is shortened in order to fit it into the fingering chart, and the Ab/Eb key touch points to the right instead of the left. Nevertheless, Vanderhagen illustrates a four-piece instrument having a mouthpiece, no barrel, two finger hole sections, and an hourglass-shaped stock-bell. His instrument is similar to an unmounted boxwood five-key clarinet (ca. 1780, F, private collection) by Gilles Lot without a barrel and a single ivory ferrule on the top of the left-hand section.[25] Its S and A keys are mounted in square rings without scribe marks; its E/B key is mounted in a block. During the 1780s, French makers made clarinets with a separate barrel for tuning as a better alternative to a mouthpiece with a long tenon used by English makers. All subsequent five-key French clarinets include a separate mouthpiece and barrel. An early boxwood Martin Lot five-key C clarinet (ca. 1785, F-Paris, 1024) has horn ferrules, a stock-bell, and a pear-shaped barrel. The instrument is similar to his cousin's clarinet which has its S and A keys mounted in square rings without scribe marks and its E/B key mounted in a block.[26]

In 1796, Frédéric Blasius wrote a clarinet tutor with a fingering chart illustrating a five-key clarinet in five sections: mouthpiece, barrel, two finger hole sections, and stock-bell.[27] The earliest French illustration with divided stock and bell sections appears in Jean Xavier Lefèvre's 1802 tutor written for clarinet students at the newly formed Conservatory of Music in Paris.[28]

Michel Amlingue was born about 1741 in Trier in the western part of Germany. He arrived in Paris in 1760 and became a wood turner (*tourneur sur bois*) in 1766. Amlingue (who attained master level in 1780) made all types of woodwinds but specialized in clarinets. At least twenty clarinets with three to thirteen keys have been reported.[29] A shop inventory after the death of Amlingue's wife Marie Catherine Ducollet in 1806 indicates more than one hundred clarinets priced from five to nine francs with only three made of ebony at twelve francs each.[30] In 1803, the Swedish virtuoso Bernhard Crusell, studying at the Paris Conservatory, purchased a mouthpiece by Amlingue and clarinet by Baumann at the suggestion of his clarinet teacher, Lefèvre. After Amlingue's death in 1816, his son François-Michel Amlingue continued to make clarinets using his father's stamp and another marked "AMELINGUE."[31]

FIGURE 2.4   Five-key clarinet from fingering chart, Vanderhagen, *Méthode* (Paris, ca. 1785).

Amlingue made a beautiful B♭ five-key clarinet (ca. 1790, US-MA-Boston, 38.1750) with an ebony body and ivory ferrules in six sections: blackwood mouthpiece (plus a second mouthpiece), barrel, two finger hole sections, stock, and bell. In addition, there are corps de réchange in A with two finger-hole sections and a barrel for tuning to A. When the corps is inserted, a lever attached to the end of the F♯/C♯ touch piece for L4 may be extended (see figure 2.5).[32] This is one of the only surviving ebony examples by Michel Amlingue and one of a few eighteenth-century clarinets with corps de réchange. According to Bessaraboff, it belonged to Captain Bryant P. Tilden and arrived at the museum in a wooden case with brass fittings and the following letter, which documents its existence before 1794.

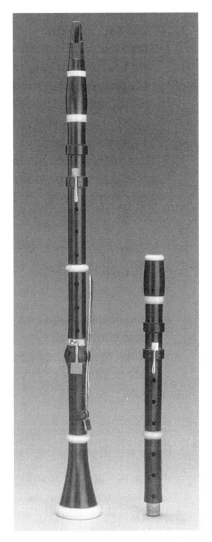

> My Clarionett was bo't for me by my music master D'Anglebert, a German professor at Bordeaux in 1794. It was made, years previously, by Amlingue of Paris. I paid twenty silver crowns (6 livres ca.) on account of its superior excellence. My music lessons were on every day—during one hour: about 18 mo. at three francs per lesson. It has now traveled with me six times, to various parts of Europe and Asia Minor. Twice to Brazils. [A check mark is inserted here.] Four times to China,—besides many trips shorter distances, Java, Manilla, etc. etc. etc. making over 200,000 miles. Near St. Helena. Ship Globe from Canton for Philadelphia. April 8th 1832. Bryant P. Tilden

FIGURE 2.5   Five-key clarinet in B♭ and A, Michel Amlingue, Paris (ca. 1790, US-MA-Boston, 38.1750).

Below this is added a check mark and a postscript: "3 times more. Batavis Manila and Canton. Sept. 1837."[33]

This clarinet was played a great deal as shown by heavy wear on the finger holes of the B♭ joints, but the A joints appear to have been hardly used. One of the mouthpieces is signed "Debost," presumably a Parisian mouthpiece maker. Both sections produce an attractive, full sound. A clarinet like this was probably played in the B♭ and A orchestral parts in the Parisian productions of Giovanni Paisiello's *Il barbier di Siviglia* (1784) and *Il re Teodoro in Venezia* (1786), and of Grétry's *Guillaume Tell* (1791).

According to Bragard and Hen, who do not cite their source, Amlingue advertised six- and seven-key clarinets in 1782.[34] This is possible, although no extant Amlingue clarinets with more than five keys can be dated with certainty to the eighteenth century. Simiot credited Amlingue as the first French maker to construct an A clarinet with a corps de réchange in B♮.[35] It seems likely that Amlingue offered corps with his instruments during the 1780s since they had been available since the 1770s. Furthermore, B♮ clarinets or corps de réchange are required in several operas produced in Paris, such as Grétry's *L'amitie à l'epreuve* (1772), *Colinette à la cour* (1782), and *La caravane du Caire* (1784); and Floquet's *L'union de l'amour et des arts* (1774) and *Le Siegneur Bienfaisant* (1780).

The woodwind maker Prudent Thierriot, also known as Thierriot fils, apprenticed with the Parisian maker Charles Joseph Bizey from 1747 to 1753 and became a master in 1759. Prudent worked with a minimum of eight workers, and his son Jean Baptiste Prudent (who, as the son of a maker, was granted master status in 1771). Extant instruments from their shop are stamped only with the name "Prudent." After Thierriot's death in 1786, the shop closed and the makers Porthaux and Delusse completed an inventory, discussed by Jeltsch and Giannini,[36] showing 142 differently pitched clarinets and supplies. A tally by nominal pitch reveals 93 clarinets in C, 30 in B♭ (14 with corps in A), 9 in D, and 10 in F. The large number of C clarinets and the F clarinets suggest that Thierriot's firm was a major supplier for wind bands and band regiments in Paris and other French cities. Some of the D and B♭ instruments, particularly with corps de réchange in A, were meant for orchestral or chamber music. Considering the large inventory, it is surprising that only 3 instruments marked "Prudent" are extant.[37]

Late-eighteenth-century five-key clarinets (all GB-Cambridge) include Theodore (Paris? 1780–90); Alexis Bernard (Lyon, 1780–90); Cuvillier (St. Omer, ca. 1790, B♭ clarinet with A corps); and Bodin (Paris, ca. 1800, B♭ clarinet with A corps). The instruments by Theodore and Cuvillier have one-piece stock-bells. Other late-eighteenth-century five-key clarinets (both F-Le Mans) with a stock-bell are by Nicolas Viennen (Paris, ca. 1790) and Jean Chréstien Proff (Tours, ca. 1780). The Proff clarinet has scribe marks on the two rings for the S and A keys and a single line on the swelling for the A♭/E♭ key, similar to the four-key clarinet illustrated in the plate for the 1777 *Supplément à l'Encyclopédie*. Proff was born in Strasbourg and was a wind instrument maker in Tours ("faiseur d'instrument à vent à Tour"), according to his "actes de marriage" in the municipal archives of Tours. Five key clarinets were also made during the eighteenth century by Jean Jacques Tortochot (Paris, master from 1779), Dominique Antony Porthaux (Paris, master from 1780), Boisselot aîné (Montpellier, from about 1780), Johannes Keller junior or Isaac Keller (Strasbourg, from about 1780), and Les Frères Keller (Strasbourg, from about 1790, F-Bayonne).[38]

During the last decade of the eighteenth century, a sixth key for C♯/G♯ appeared on French-made clarinets. J. X. Lefèvre initially advocated this closed key positioned for the left-hand little finger and had it added to his clarinet about 1790 by Jean Jacques Baumann (Paris).[39] The C♯/G♯ key was particularly useful for players since it produced an in-tune c♯[1], a note that was noticeably out of tune and muffled with the conventional forked fingerings: (12 4), (12 45), or (12 4 6).[40] In addition, intonation problems on five-key clarinets are more noticeable in the chalumeau register than in the clarinet register, where the forked fingerings are better in tune. In 1790, Baumann was only eighteen, but he certainly would have been capable of constructing a clarinet with a C♯/G♯ key. At least ten six-key clarinets by Baumann are known.[41]

The C♯/G♯ cross-key was usually mounted horizontal to the bore for correct placement of its tone hole and easy access to its touch by the left-hand little finger. Baumann added the C♯/G♯ by attaching a circular brass plate with screws, soldering a pillar to it, and mounting the key with a screw through a hole in its shank. A flat brass spring was riveted to the shank's underside. Many descriptions cite the use of a brass pillar as evidence for the later addition of this key, but nineteenth-century makers such as Baumann, Gentellet (Paris), François Amlingue, and Michel (Paris) preferred pillar mounting.[42] Other makers in England, Germany, and elsewhere during the nineteenth century often mounted the C♯/G♯ key in a block.

Expensive instruments were occasionally made of ivory. François Lefèvre (Paris) made a very fine example of an ivory ten-key C clarinet (ca. 1825, US-SD, 5931) with an ivory mouthpiece and gold-plated keys and ferrules. The additional five keys for f/c, E♭/B♭, C♯/G♯, B/F♯, and B♭/F are pillar-mounted. This instrument shows little use, looks impressive, and plays easily and in tune. Subsequent French nineteenth-century makers include Roche (Paris), Brelet (Paris), Bühner and Keller (Strasbourg), Courturier (Lyon), Printemps (Lille), and Tabard (Lyon). In 1817 Halary (Jean Hilaire Asté; Paris) made metal clarinets in high F and E♭ for military bands; he patented them in 1821.[43] They have a thin brass body, called a "skeleton model," on which soldered short tubes provide finger holes. Very few have survived from the early nineteenth century.[44]

In summary, eighteenth-century French makers were the earliest to design a four-key clarinet with an F♯/C♯ key. It was played in operas, chamber music, and solo music beginning in the 1750s. As the instrument became more popular, several makers offered five-key clarinets for military and wind bands. Paris was the leading music center, and many individuals throughout Europe performed the newest French music and purchased instruments. Scores of eighteenth-century clarinets were lost during the French Revolution when many possessions of the nobility were destroyed. Clarinet production by nineteenth-century makers increased dramatically by the 1820s when the clarinet was widely played in bands and orchestras. Michel Amlingue and his son François-Michel produced the widest variety, from the baroque three-key to the thirteen-key clarinet. Four of the most innovative French makers and inventors were Baumann, Simiot, César Janssen, and Iwan Müller who worked during the early nineteenth century. Their contributions are discussed later.

BELGIUM

Makers active in what is today Belgium made some of the earliest extant four-key instruments, the fourth key a small Ab/Eb positioned for R4. The first maker was Jean Baptiste Willems, who was active in Brussels from 1758 constructing clarinets with two, four, and five keys. However, Willems's son or a relative very likely made five-key clarinets as late as 1810.[45] An unusual four-key Willems D clarinet (ca. 1760, B-Bruxelles, 2560) illustrates a three-key baroque clarinet converted to a classical instrument by the addition of an Ab/Eb key. It consists of mouthpiece-barrel, middle joint with six finger holes, and stock-bell sections. Its third key (for E/B), now missing with only the spring visible, was mounted on the dorsal side for operation by the thumb. As on three-key clarinets, there are two finger holes for the little finger of either hand; the one for L4 is now plugged with wood. The stock-bell section is similar to those on other three-key clarinets; the added Ab/Eb key is mounted in a ring farther down than on typical four-key instruments, with the touch and shank of the E/B key positioned for L4.[46] The touch and shank of the Ab/Eb key are straight, resembling the A key.

The important maker Godfridus Adrianus Rottenburgh was active in Brussels from 1744 to his death in 1768. From 1772 until his death in 1803, his son, the maker and builder Fransiscus Josephus, advertised that his instruments were marked with "G. A." (his father's initials).[47] Like the Willems shop, the Rottenburghs constructed clarinets with two, four, and five keys. Two four-key clarinets and four five-key clarinets d'amour are extant.[48] A Rottenburgh four-key A clarinet (ca. 1765, GB-Cambridge) exhibits careful design and workmanship, resulting in pleasing proportions and a beautiful appearance. Its slightly later date is indicated by blocks for the E/B, S, and A keys, as well as an ivory ferrule on the upper end of the lower stock. It has a metal extension to elongate the E/B touch piece when tuning from Bb to A, and a straight touch for the Ab/Eb key.[49]

A four-key C clarinet (mid-1750s–early 1760s, NL, private collection) made in Brussels is stamped "[crown]/BRANDT" on each of its four sections and resembles Rottenburgh's clarinets in its use of a straight touch for the Ab/Eb key, no ferrules, and the convex shape of the upper tenon of its right-hand finger hole section. All keys are mounted in rings, and the mouthpiece-barrel has irregular notches for binding the reed to the mouthpiece (as found on a few of the earliest baroque clarinets) rather than the regular grooves found on mouthpiece-barrels of classical clarinets. Brandt may have been a maker working in the Rottenburgh shop or elsewhere in Brussels, or a dealer; perhaps Brandt was the name of a village or province close to Brussels. In any case, this is the only known example of an instrument with this stamp.

Two later four-key clarinets are extant, one by I. P. Lebrun (Brussels, ca. 1780s, B-Bruxelles, 2562) in B♭ and one by Speck (Grammont, ca. 1800, B-Bruxelles, 2299) in C with mouthpiece-barrel and stock-bell joints. The Lebrun clarinet is quite similar to the earlier Rottenburgh clarinets. In addition, there is an extant five-key C clarinet (B-Bruxelles, 926) by Lebrun.[50]

Five-key clarinet construction in the Rottenburgh shop from the 1770s varies. An early extant five-key B♭ clarinet (B-Bruxelles, 168) has mouthpiece-barrel and stock-bell sections, ivory ferrules, and a straight A♭/E♭ touch. It is probably earlier than another four-key example (B-Bruxelles, 2572) with separate mouthpiece and barrel sections and a bent or hooked A♭/E♭ touch, curved toward the little finger hole. Later Rottenburgh instruments and classical clarinets in general have the A♭/E♭ touch hooked toward the little finger hole, facilitating motion between this hole and the key.[51] Another five-key Rottenburgh clarinet (B-Bruxelles, 4363) in A is left-handed with the long shanks for the F♯/C♯ and E/B keys positioned on the right side.[52] Otherwise, it is identical to other Rottenburgh five-key clarinets.

A depiction of clarinets possibly linked to the Rottenburgh workshop appears in an interesting contemporaneous carved wooden panel (1765–80) from a rood screen previously in a church in west Flanders, now preserved in the Musée Gruuthuse in Bruges. Two clarinets cross diagonally over two oboes. Each has a mouthpiece-barrel, right- and left-hand joints, and stock and bell joints. Keys are not clearly shown (except for what appears to be an elongated key possibly for A–B trill), but the bulging, convex shape on the right-hand-joint upper portion of the top clarinet is similar to extant examples by Rottenburgh.[53]

In 1782, Jean Arnold Antoine Tuerlinckx founded the most important and prolific Belgian woodwind firm during the late eighteenth and early nineteenth centuries in Mechelen (formerly Malines). By about 1810, their woodwind and brass factories employed a workforce of forty which supplied instruments for several military and civilian bands. In 1827, Corneille Jean Joseph Tuerlinckx succeeded his father, who retired, and the firm continued until about 1840. A 1784–1818 *registre de comptabilité* (order book) documents all the woodwinds they supplied.[54] The Tuerlinckx firm made clarinets in G, F, E♭, D, C, B♭, A, and clarinets d'amour in F and G with from two to four corps de réchange. The higher pitched clarinets in G, F, E♭, and D were made for military bands; the C, B♭, and A for bands and orchestras; and the clarinets d'amour for orchestras and wind ensembles. Twenty-five Tuerlinckx clarinets with five to thirteen keys, three clarinets d'amour (one pitched in C), and two alto clarinets in F are extant.[55]

Later Belgian clarinets reflect the influence of contemporary German and French makers. For example, a six-key Tuerlinckx A clarinet (ca. 1815, D-Berlin, 5337) features additional finger hole joints for B♭, with an additional key for B♭/F. The F♯/C♯ key shank has a metal touch piece soldered to it curved toward the dorsal side and positioned for the thumb, similar to the thumb branch on Müller clarinets. This clarinet has a special shaped, decorative double half moon design at the tip of the extensions, positioned at the end of the touches for F♯/C♯ and E/B. Most Tuerlinckx instruments and clarinets by Nicolas Marcel Raingo (Mons, B-Bruxelles, 2569), Lebrun (B-Bruxelles, 2562, 926), and Speck (B-Bruxelles, 2299) during the eighteenth and early nineteenth centuries include these half moon designs. Additional makers active mainly during the nineteenth century in Belgium include Devaster (Leuven), Joseph Dupré (Tournai), Lebrun, Charles Joseph Sax (Brussels), and I. P. Steegmans (Mechelen). Sax was particularly skilled, making instruments for titled patrons, such as a thirteen-key ivory clarinet (1830, US-NY-New York-M, 53.223) with gold-plated keys, rollers, and lion heads engraved on each key head.[56]

GERMANY

By the 1760s in southern Germany, makers were constructing four-key clarinets with an A♭/E♭ key rather than an F♯/C♯ key, similar to the instruments by Belgian makers. The earliest were the lower-pitched clarinets d'amour made in A, A♭, or G by Johann Michael or Joseph Stinglwagner (Triftern), marked "I, S [stamped over T] W."[57] Unlike the soprano clarinet, the A♭/E♭ touch pieces on two four-key clarinets d'amour (A-Salzburg, 18/6, 18/7) by one of the Stinglwagners had a double wing or swallowtail shape so that it could be used by either right- or left-handed players.[58] An interesting B♭ clarinet (ca. 1790, GB-London-H, 243) by Joseph Stinglwagner features a double wing touch for the A♭/E♭ key, with the wing farthest to the left of R4 now partly filed down. The six-section boxwood instrument has mouthpiece, barrel, left- and right-hand sections, stock, and bell. Block mounting for the E/B key and horn ferrules suggest a late-eighteenth-century date.[59]

In 1782, Forkel cited the Dresden makers Carl Augustin Grenser and Jakob Friedrich Grundmann as among the best German makers of flutes, oboes, bassoons, and clarinets.[60] Both continued to make four-key clarinets as late as the 1790s. A four-key Grenser C clarinet (D-Leipzig, 1472) has small double holes side by side in a depression or cove for L3 and R4 as in eighteenth-century oboes. When the player masters sliding from one hole to the other, intonation is more exact for the semitones c♯¹/g♯² and f♯¹/c♯². This instrument, stamped "1777" on the stock-bell, is among the earliest dated German clarinets. Its boxwood body with ivory ferrules has four sections for the stock-bell, one finger hole section, barrel, and mouthpiece (now missing). The touch of the A♭/E♭ key gently curves upward for easy manipulation with R4.[61] Five Grenser five-key clarinets survive. Two more dated five-key clarinets by Grenser (1785 and 1796), are extant, as are instruments by Grundmann with three (1789), four (1775), and five keys (1795).[62] Christian Friedrich Riedel and Johann Christian Gehring constructed four-key clarinets that were destroyed during World War II. Riedel died in 1784. Gehring died in 1791; his four-key instrument was dated 1788.[63]

One of the earliest German woodwind makers to construct clarinets was Heinrich Carl Tölcke (Brunswick), who advertised bassoons, transverse flutes, clarinets, and recorders in 1751 in the *Braunschweiger Nachrichten*.[64] Not until nineteen years later did Tölcke again include clarinets, in two advertisements in the *Braunschweiger Nachrichten* in 1770 and 1772.[65] The two extant Tölcke classical clarinets appear to date from the early to mid-1770s. The earlier of the two is a very interesting five-key clarinet (ca. 1770, N-Trondheim, RMT 75/3) in five sections: mouthpiece, barrel, two finger-hole sections, and stock-bell. The sections are boxwood except for the ivory barrel and three well-executed ivory ferrules, including one that is half ivory and half wood on the upper tenon of the right-hand joint. The A♭/E♭ key is mounted in a large socket boss similar to those found on early English clarinets. Originally, this instrument had its F♯/C♯ and E/B keys, now mounted in blocks, on the dorsal side for R0. The original tone holes were filled and these keys relocated to the frontal side for L4. As a result, Tölcke's stamp on the stock-bell is displaced from its original position, where it was aligned with the stamps on the other sections.[66]

The second Tölcke clarinet (ca. 1775, US-MA-Boston, 17.1875), pitched in B♭, is similar to the example in Trondheim, with the same number of unmounted sections, a period or original wood mouthpiece, and an A–B trill key (see figure 2.6).[67] In the shape of the bell, ferrules, and socket boss for the A♭/E♭ key, it resembles clarinets by the English maker George Miller. Tölcke also includes a cranked F♯/C♯ key, similar to that found on many English clarinets from the early 1770s. Only the convex barrel and two scribe lines on the socket boss for the A♭/E♭ and E/B keys indicate continental construction. The unusual scribe lines on the stock-bell socket are similar to those on the four-key clarinet stock-bell illustrated in Castillon's article in the *Supplément à l'Encyclopédie* (1776). Tölcke left a raised ridge below the E/B key head as wide as the block that mounts this key on his two clarinets. This ridge appears to be a remnant of a ring that circled the entire bell found on earlier English instruments.[68] Tölcke probably made this B♭ clarinet specifically for the English market with a cranked F♯/C♯ key and an A–B trill key. The A–B trill brass touch is curved to the player's left in a distinctive manner that appears on the A–B trill key of a Hespe clarinet (ca. 1780, GB-Cambridge) made in Hanover.[69] Perhaps these clarinets were identical to the six-key clarinet reportedly owned by a player who passed through Berlin, mentioned by Castillon in his *Encyclopédie* article.

Köster describes the clarinet in the *Deutsche Encyclopädie*, the first German encyclopedia modeled on Diderot's *Encyclopédie*.[70]

> Clarinet, a wind instrument which has a softer tone than the oboe, and shriller than the flute; it is midway between the oboe and transverse flute. The facile military clarinets shriek more than a trumpet

particularly if they have a brass mouthpiece instead of a wooden one. Here, the discussion is about softer instruments like those handled by the new concert artists. A clarinet has a range similar to a string instrument but extends five tones lower; also it has generally come to be used in a relationship of a fifth [to the tonic pitch], since they [the clarinetists] would rather play the note b♭ than b♮, and find playing in the key of F easier than in C. In general there is no other instrument that gives the composer more trouble than the clarinet. When playing the chalmeau [register] a C clarinet goes up to e¹ and two tones lower than the violin. One cannot ascend above c³ or d³. Its keys help to produce semitones and its range has the best effect in the middle.[71]

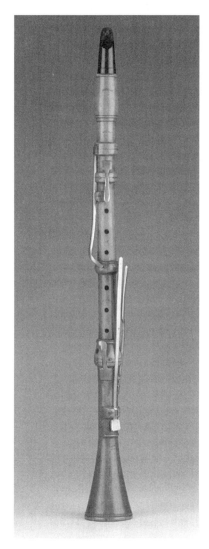

FIGURE 2.6   Six-key clarinet in B♭, Heinrich Karl Tölcke, Brunswick (ca. 1775, US-MA-Boston, 17.1875).

It is notable that the clarinet's tone is described as softer than the oboe and shriller than the flute. One may assume that the trumpet-like clarinets in the regiment were the shrill, higher-pitched F clarinets or the bright-toned E♭ clarinets. The metal mouthpiece (the earliest known reference) probably helped produce a brilliant tone quality. The softer instruments used by the new concert artists were undoubtedly the lower-pitched instruments in C, B♭, and A. Their similarity in compass to a string instrument (e.g., violin) was obvious since the clarinet often took the leading part in regimental bands. Cross-fingerings make the b♭ better in tune than b♮, which explains why players preferred F major to C major. Köster seems to be referring to transposing clarinets and the tonic note of F major when he states that there is a "relationship of a fifth." For example, when a B♭ clarinet plays in the tonality of E-flat major, the clarinetist transposes the part to F major to form a fifth between the nominal clarinet pitch and the transposed tonality. The "chalmeau" register is from e¹ down to the lowest note, e. This is the earliest German source to mention specific written pitches. Köster prefers the midrange, probably c² to c³, as having the best quality of tone; a somewhat cautious upper limit of d³ matches that of the majority of contemporary orchestral and chamber music. Although Köster does not specify, he is probably describing a five-key clarinet.

August Grenser and Heinrich Grenser use double holes for L3 and sometimes R4. In 1802, Koch refers to a double hole on good clarinets but only for the third finger.[72] Later German makers constructed double holes, such as a six-key Johann Gottfried Heinze (Leipzig) instrument (ca. 1810, D-Eisenach, I 142) with a double hole for L3. This boxwood clarinet with horn ferrules features an A–B trill key that, by this time, was becoming more popular in Germany. During the early nineteenth century, Carl Gottlob Bormann (Dresden) also made at least four clarinets with double L3 holes, some of which include an original C#/G# key to provide a fingering option to the player.[73] During the late eighteenth and early nineteenth centuries, three-key clarinets were inexpensive instruments. Two late three-key examples (both D-Nürnberg, 456, 150) are extant, with the third key positioned for L4.[74]

German makers employed corps de réchange shortly after they began to be used in Paris. For example, in 1780 the Detmold court orchestra had two B♭ clarinets with A corps, and two C clarinets without corps.[75] In 1783, a Koblenz court orchestra inventory included two A clarinets with B♭ corps, and a 1789 inventory (dated 1790) made note of two D clarinets with silver keys and corps.[76] In neither orchestra are there C clarinets with corps, although the notation "ohne Einsatzstücken" implies that a corps for B♮ was available. There are a few examples of D clarinets with corps for tuning to E♭.[77]

Some instruments with corps have a barrel and another mouthpiece for greater intonation accuracy. Most have sliding extension levers on the touches of the F#/C# and E/B keys. In 1793, the maker Friederich Gabriel Kirst (Potsdam) advertised "a B♭ clarinet of dark ebony wood with two joints, four mouthpieces, three barrels and silver keys" for six Louis d'or, obviously an expensive, deluxe model.[78] Löbel, in his popular 1796 *Conversationslexicon*, describes the clarinet as "a special instrument which is not tuned in all keys, but it must play certain pitches using either appropriate middle pieces or an entirely different clarinet. These include B♭, A and C clarinets etc. which match the given pitch."[79] One of the last appearances of a German clarinet corps de réchange is in an 1847 price list by the Dresden maker Samuel Gottfried Wiesner. He offered eleven-key B♭ clarinets with A corps in ebony with ivory ferrules and silver keys for sixty reichstalers; in boxwood with ivory ferrules and brass keys for thirty reichstalers; and in boxwood with horn ferrules and brass keys for seventeen reichstalers.[80]

Backofen illustrates a typical five-key German clarinet at the turn of the nineteenth century in a fingering chart in his *Anweisung zur Klarinette nebst einer kurzen Abhandlung über das Basset-Horn* about 1803. The instrument in five sections includes a dark wood mouthpiece (probably ebony), a barrel, two middle joints, and a stock-bell. The stock features a rounded swelling where the F♯/C♯ and E/B keys are mounted, and the bell opening is quite wide.[81] By 1811, Fröhlich was describing an instrument made in six sections with a divided lower stock and bell. He stated that the bell should be rather wide and somewhat convex so the lower range will be full and strong and the upper range easily played.[82] As for new instruments, Fröhlich reports that a sixth key (C♯/G♯) was added on the left-hand joint to correct the dull and impure g♯[2] or a♭[2] and that it also improved the corresponding c♯[1] or d♭[1]. A special key (A–B trill) on the left-hand joint next to the a[1] key is used to produce the b♭[1] trill.[83]

The F♯/C♯ key levers on German instruments of this period were usually straight rather than offset, as on English-made instruments; the few German instruments that featured an offset lever were probably made for export. A good example of a six-key B♭ clarinet (ca. 1800, US-MI-Ann Arbor, 615) by the celebrated maker Heinrich Grenser has five sections without a mouthpiece, ivory ferrules except for the bell, a C♯/G♯ key mounted on a wooden block, and large finger holes.[84] Most extant German-made six-key clarinets include this key rather than the A–B trill key favored by the English makers.

An unusual five-key Jaeger (Neukirchen) C clarinet (ca. 1830, US-SD, 125) features metal inserts in all finger holes. This clarinet suffered severe cracking through its finger holes. Very few clarinet makers used metal inserts, and they seem to have been more successful in the smaller finger holes of Sellner-system oboes by the Viennese maker Koch about 1825 and by later oboe makers.[85]

At the beginning of the nineteenth century, several makers added keys to the five-key clarinet to provide clearer intonation produced with cross-fingerings and to provide keys for cumbersome or difficult trills. In 1808, C. F. Michaelis published an article anonymously in the *AMZ* suggesting nine keys on the clarinet. Since many readers were wary of problems caused by complicated mechanisms, he mentions that after nine months only one key on his nine-key clarinet needed repair.[86] He did not describe the additional four keys, but they may have been G♯, E♭/B♭, C♯/G♯, and B♭/F as found on a nine-key instrument (ca. 1825, GB-Edinburgh, 106) by Johann Samuel Stengel (Bayreuth).[87] Another arrangement for nine keys is to substitute an f/c key for G♯ and a B/F♯ key for B♭/F, as found in an 1829 fingering chart by Gottfried Weber.[88]

The composer Louis Spohr promoted a more complicated clarinet. In the introduction to the 1812 edition of his Clarinet Concerto no. 1, he lists the improvements suggested by Johann Simon Hermstedt and other clarinetists and emphasizes that his highly technical concerto could not be properly performed without these amendments. In addition to the usual five keys, Spohr specifies (1) an E♭/ B♭ key for R1 for trilling d[1] to e♭[1] or a[2] to b♭[2], also called the B♭ key; (2) an f/c key for L2[89] for trilling e[1] to f[1] or b[2] to c[3]; (3) an A–B♮ trill key for R1 for trilling a[1] to b[1] or b♭[1] to c[2]; (4) a G♯ key for L1; (5) a B♭/F key for R3 for trilling a to b♭ or e[2] to f[2]; (6) a double hole for L3 or, preferably, a C♯/G♯ key to produce a pure c♯[1]; (7) a dorsal side hole for R0 to produce a b♮; and (8) curved touch pieces for the F♯/C♯ and E/B keys to allow the player to play b¹ and c♯² in quick succession.⁹⁰ Eleven-key clarinets by Heinrich Grenser feature all or most of the keys mentioned by Spohr but are usually lacking F♯/C♯ curved touches and a b♮ dorsal hole.⁹¹ Twelve-key clarinets with B/F♯ and B♭/F keys began to appear in Paris at the same time as the publication of Vanderhagen's tutor, about 1819. German makers immediately began to copy these instruments, and in 1824, Heinrich Backofen published a substantial tutor for the twelve-key clarinet.⁹²

In summary, during the 1760s and 1770s Johann Michael and Joseph Stinglwagner were the earliest German makers of four-key clarinets. Five- and six-key clarinets show fine workmanship by Tölcke, who was also active during the 1770s. During the late eighteenth century, August Grenser made both four- and five-key instruments, while Jacob Grundmann made three-, four-, and five-key clarinets. Other eighteenth-century makers include Wilhelm Hesse (Braunschweig) and C. F. Paulus (Neukirchen).⁹³ The writer Christian Friedrich Daniel Schubart claimed the best clarinets were made in Nuremberg, Munich, Hamburg, Berlin, and Vienna but unfortunately did not mention specific makers.⁹⁴ German influence on clarinet design during the eighteenth century is noticeable in similar instruments from Austria, the Czech Republic, Denmark, Italy, and America.

The most widely known and popular nineteenth-century German maker was Heinrich Grenser; twenty-eight clarinets with five to eleven keys survive from his shop.⁹⁵ Stengel continued his fine workmanship and made instruments with thumb keys based on Iwan Müller's clarinets. German clarinet makers during the early nineteenth century include Karl Adler (Bamberg), Backofen (Darmstadt), Johann Bischoff (Darmstadt), Joseph Ebner (Munich), Johann Floth (Dresden), Andreas Greve (Mannheim), Griesling and Schlott (Berlin), Hess (Munich), Adam Piering (Berlin), B. Schott's Söhne (Mainz), Schifferer (Passau), Max Stiegler (Straubing), and Streitwolf (Göttingen).

ENGLAND

There is ample evidence for the availability of clarinets in England by the mid-1750s. George Brown was the first to advertise clarinets for sale among other instruments in Jackson's *Oxford Journal* in 1754 and 1755. Thomas Underwood advertised clarinets in 1755 in the *Bath Journal* and in 1756 in the *Oxford Journal*.⁹⁶ These instruments may have been the baroque two- or three-key type or possibly the more advanced four-key design, probably imported from Germany, France, or Belgium. Further evidence of the clarinet's presence in England around this time is the 1753 wall stucco in the Upper Library of Christ Church, Oxford; it depicts eight "schalmeys" presumably intended to represent clarinets.⁹⁷ The lack of detail makes it unclear whether these are two-, three-, or four-key instruments.

During the last third of the eighteenth century, the income and spending power of England's large and expanding middle class were greater than that in any other European country. The demand for musical instruments helped strengthen woodwind businesses in London, and as a by-product of this healthy trade, musical instruments were available for export. In America, for example, the book dealer and printer James Rivington sold English-made pianos and a variety of woodwind, brass, stringed, and percussion instruments in New York City from 1773 to 1783.[98] In 1786, John Jacob Astor moved from London to open a music shop in New York City where he sold pianos and woodwinds imported from his brother George in England. During the 1790s, Longman and Broderip exported pianos and woodwinds, including clarinets, to Madrid. In 1795 the *Gazeta de Madrid* advertised "an English fortepiano, new, with three pedals in the modern style, built by one of the best makers, also a new clarinet, made in London, with the appropriate joints for raising or lowering the pitch."[99] It is not clear whether the novelty of this instrument was in its five or six keys or in its corps.

There is only one extant English four-key clarinet (late eighteenth or early nineteenth century, GB-Oxford, 413): an anonymous boxwood instrument in C with an A♭/E♭ key and narrow brass ferrules. It is similar to early-nineteenth-century instruments, with six sections for mouthpiece, barrel, two finger holes sections, stock, and bell.[100] The body and turned ring mounts resemble those of a five-key Kusder clarinet.[101] By far the most numerous extant clarinets are five- and six-key instruments made in London.

George Miller was the earliest English maker of the clarinet. He began to work in London about 1765, possibly having emigrated from Germany. Although he made other woodwinds, he specialized in the clarinet, of which there are eighteen instruments known with five and six keys and pitched in C, B♭, A, and high F.[102] The earliest and best-known English six-key clarinets (both ca. 1765, GB-Oxford, 4008, 4009) are a pair by Miller. One has a mouthpiece-barrel, two middle sections, and a stock-bell. The mouthpiece-barrel is in its original state as one integral section. The mouthpiece of the other is a replacement with a long tenon; an ivory ring reinforces the top of the cut-down barrel.[103]

Both Miller clarinets carry an early version of the English A–B trill key, positioned for L1 rather than R1 as on all subsequent instruments. Several factors suggest that the sixth keys on these Miller clarinets were later additions to the original keywork. The quality of the workmanship is lower than that for the other keys; the pivots for these left-hand keys are in the lower ring, where the A key is mounted; and the tone holes are level with the upper ring, which is flattened or cut away to receive the key head. All later English clarinets have a wooden ring or block on which to pivot the right-hand A–B lever below the block for the A key.[104] Several eighteenth-century English clarinets have the trill-key tone hole bored in the same ring as the S key. By the late eighteenth century, the S key was mounted in a block. These matching B♭ Miller clarinets were made for a wealthy gentleman named William Sharp.[105] A frequently reproduced painting (1779 to 1781) of the Sharp family by the German portrait artist Johann Zoffany shows musical instruments on a table, among which the bell of one of these clarinets is partially visible.[106] Both instruments have a wide ivory ring at the end of the bell and a boxwood body attractively decorated by either burning to simulate tortoise shell or stained in a tortoise-shell pattern.[107]

The earliest English clarinets are similar to Rottenburgh (Brussels) instruments. The finger hole sections are not completely cylindrical, and there is a slight downward taper and corresponding outward flare at the ends. The lever for the F♯/C♯ key, straight for its entire length, creates a sideways thrust at the bearing, as depicted in an engraving of a clarinet in an anonymous tutor about 1780.[108] On later English clarinets, to solve the thrust problem, an additional block was left turned on the body above the F♯/C♯ tone hole, with a slot in the swelling for the F/C finger hole to act as a guide for the key shank. On the earlier instruments, the middle of the F♯/C♯ shank angles to the left about 80 degrees for twelve millimeters before continuing straight.[109] This design places the touch piece conveniently for L4 and in close proximity to the E/B touch piece.

Thomas Collier probably worked for Charles Schuchart from 1753 and was established as his successor in 1765.[110] He made all types of woodwinds and was one of the few makers to date his clarinets. Six five-key clarinets pitched in C or B♭ are known.[111] An example (GB-Kneighly, 9110) stamped "London 1770" on its stock-bell is the earliest dated English clarinet, similar in design to Miller's instrument but without ferrules (see figure 2.7). The F♯/C♯ shank is straight and without a guide below the socket swelling or boss. Other early construction characteristics include the slightly curved end of the A♭/E♭ touch piece; a stock-bell and a mouthpiece-socket; the E/B, A, and S keys mounted in rings; and no guide for the F♯/C♯ shank below the socket swelling. Like Miller clarinets, it has very small tone holes (but slightly smaller than Miller's) on the right- and left-hand finger hole sections.[112] In general, the bore and tone holes are smaller and there is less undercutting on English instruments than on continental instruments, producing a lighter, more vocal timbre.[113] Instruments by Collier or similar to his were probably played by the earliest English soloist, John Mahon, when he performed one of his concertos in 1772.

By 1770, John Hale was lodging with and working for Collier. Hale began working as a key maker. He succeeded Collier in 1785 and continued to produce clarinets until 1804. There are twelve extant Hale clarinets with five to eight keys.[114] In addition, woodwinds stamped with Collier's name, such as a clarinet dated 1790 and an oboe dated 1791 made after Collier's death, are attributed to Hale.

A comparison of an early five-key Miller clarinet (ca. 1775, US-CA-Santa Monica) with a relatively common six-key Astor instrument (ca. 1810, US-CA-Claremont-R) reveals several differences. The Miller clarinet has smaller, round tone holes; smaller keys; and rings instead of blocks for mounting the keys. It has a smoothly turned swelling for R4 rather than a

FIGURE 2.7   Five-key clarinet in Bb, Thomas Collier, London (1770, GB-Kneighley, 9110)

sharply incurved one; a large boxwood ferrule on the upper part of the right-hand section rather than a smaller ivory ferrule; and an F#/C# shank offset by about 80 degrees instead of 60 degrees. The Miller clarinet has a small, thin, delicate block to guide this key rather than a thicker block; a more gradual flare of the bell; and an outward flare at the ends of the right- and left-hand sections. It also has a decoratively turned groove at the end of the bell and one ivory ferrule on the upper section of the stock-bell. The rings for mounting the S and A keys are very slightly rounded and do not have the center marks found on other early English clarinets. Later English clarinets often have thick brass wire underpinning below or above the pivot points of the S, A, and sometimes the E/B keys, crossing the grain of the wood to prevent cracks. This Miller clarinet does not include the underpinning, and its stamp depicts a unicorn rampant (standing upright). Only one other Miller clarinet (GB-Oxford, x42) has a unicorn rampant stamp. Several makers in London subsequently used the unicorn's head (an emblem of the British royalty).[115] Miller's probable German origin suggests the appropriation of a symbol similar to the lion rampant on several German instruments. Interestingly, a few woodwinds by Miller's contemporary Thomas Collier are marked with a lion rampant.[116] Byrne, however, suggests another maker made these instruments for Collier.[117]

The English maker Thomas Stanesby Jr. bequeathed his tools to his apprentice Caleb Gedney on the condition that he marry Stanesby's widow, the "late servant Catherine Gale"—a fairly common practice wherein an apprentice marries the surviving spouse and, unfortunately, often continues to use the late maker's stamp in order to command higher prices. Many extant woodwinds are stamped "STANESBY IUNIOR," a stamp assumed to have been used by Gedney.[118] Gedney is also identified as the maker of two clarinets in the collection of the music-loving squire Samuel Hellier.[119] Although a report has circulated that at least one Gedney clarinet survives in a private collection, the author has been unable to verify its existence.[120] A Wrede C clarinet (ca. 1815, US-DC, 275) has a barrel attributed to Stanesby Jr., but its shape suggests an early-nineteenth-century date. Furthermore, the barrel is stamped "STANESBY/JUNIOR" rather than the standard form of "IUNIOR" found on other Stanesby instruments, suggesting that it is a forgery.[121]

There are a few extant English clarinets with additional finger hole sections, as exemplified by a six-key Astor instrument (ca. 1800, GB-Oxford, 4) with two alternate finger hole sections for tuning from C to B♭. Perhaps a right-hand joint and another barrel for an extension to A (both now missing) existed, since there are additional compartments in the case.[122] English makers discontinued corps de réchange early in the nineteenth century, and some clarinetists preferred to carry three clarinets in C, B♭, and A completely assembled. Although few such sets are extant, there is one complete set of three Key clarinets (ca. 1830, GB-Edinburgh, 143–45) in C (twelve keys), B♭ (thirteen keys), and A (thirteen keys), with three alternate longer barrels to lower the pitch if necessary.[123]

The tremendous activity of a number of eighteenth- and nineteenth-century English makers, all located in London, explains the large number of clarinets and other woodwinds extant. The largest number of English eighteenth-century five- and six-key clarinets were made by George Miller, followed by Hale, Cahusac, Collier, Astor, Herman Wrede, Key, the Bilton firm, Goulding and Company, and D'Almaine and Company.[124]

Keys began to be added to the typical English six-key clarinet during the first decade of the nineteenth century, a development that can be traced through extant clarinets, patents, and tutors. The earliest extant eight-key clarinets (GB-Manchester, MPL 7; GB-Cambridge) are two by Hale.[125] The two additional keys for E♭/B♭ and B/F♯ provide flexibility for additional fingerings and a less muffled sound than the earlier cross-fingerings. John Hopkinson's clarinet tutor (ca. 1814) includes a fingering chart for an identical eight-key clarinet with an unusual convex barrel, a right-hand joint connected to its stock, and a separate bell (see figure 2.8).[126] His comments on fingering make it clear that these are recently added keys:

> To elucidate my remark on the Right Application of the Keys, particularly of the small ones newly invented, I must observe that as there are frequently various ways of taking the same note, in quick move-

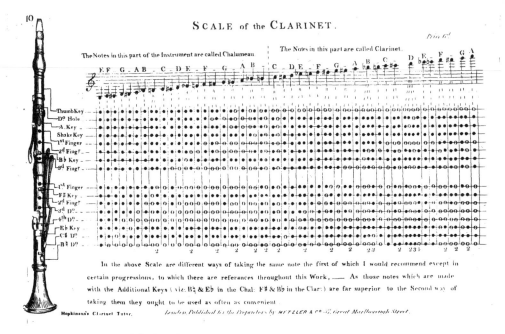

FIGURE 2.8   Eight-key clarinet, Hopkinson, *A New and Complete Preceptor* (London, ca. 1814).

ments whilst those are to be preferred which best suit the situation of the fingering in the preceeding & subsequent Passages, so in slow movements such must be selected as will produce the softest & most melodious tones.[127]

In 1812, Tebaldo Monzani applied for and received patent No. 3586 for an eight-key clarinet with a one-piece barrel and upper section and a one-piece lower joint and stock (see figure 2.9). A new key is specifically mentioned for a cross-G♯ on the left-hand joint; apparently the B/F♯ on the right-hand joint was not considered new. Although the drawing is not clear, it is assumed that the lever of an A–B trill key is present. Monzani lined the highest portion of the left-hand joint bore with metal, which explains the unusual convex shape of Hopkinson's barrel. However, the most important and lasting improvement the Monzani firm made was tenons covered with cork or cloth with chamfered or beveled ends on the mouthpiece and left- and right-hand joint tenons.[128] Instead of the cross-G♯, English makers used a side G♯ key; the one-piece right-hand and stock joint was adopted during the 1820s.

An eight-key clarinet (ca. 1815, US-CT, 3326,82) by the London firm of Monzani and Company matches Hopkinson's engraving, including the convex, metal-lined upper section of the left-hand joint, where a separate barrel usually is placed. This boxwood instrument with ivory ferrules has a right-hand section joined to its stock and a separate bell. Each joint except the mouthpiece has the serial number "1053"; and the word "patent" is stamped on the stock section, undoubtedly in reference to the 1812 patent. The Milhouse firm, publisher of Hopkinson's tutor, made clarinets with five, six, and eight keys. At least three clarinets (GB-London-H, 260; GB-Oxford, 4001; US-NY-Massapequa Park) have eight keys.[129]

During the early nineteenth century, Key occasionally made instruments in four sections: mouthpiece, barrel and left-hand section in one piece, right-hand section and stock in one piece, and bell.[130] A later Gerock nine-key English example in C (ca. 1821, GB-Edinburgh, 527) has a mouthpiece with a socket instead of a tenon; an ivory barrel; left-hand joint, right-hand joint, and stock in one section; round, flat key heads; and additional keys for the A–B trill, E♭/B♭, C♯/G♯, and B/F♯. The English players of the time began to adjust the pitch by extending the barrel to make the instrument longer rather than pulling out a long-tenon mouthpiece.[131]

By 1825 four extra keys were noted in a popular tutor, *Metzler's and Son's Clarinet Preceptor*, as the A–B trill, C♯/G♯, B♭/F or B/F♯, and E♭/B♭.[132] One year later, the well-known clarinetist Thomas Willman wrote a thorough tutor for the advanced and professional player with a fingering chart and an explanation concerning the thirteen-key clarinet.[133] Although the instrument differs somewhat from contemporary French thirteen-key clarinets, Willman's maker, Goulding and D'Almaine, incorporated some of the most important elements of their design. His instrument has the keys S, A–B trill, A, G♯, f/c, E♭/B♭, C♯/G♯, B/F♯ (fingered by R4), B/F♯ (fingered by R2), B♭/F, A♭/E♭, F♯/C♯, and two thumb branches for F♯/C♯ and E/B, all with flat, round key heads. Goulding kept an open finger hole for R4 rather than using the French-made F/C key. The speaker key has a wraparound key

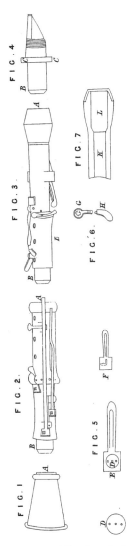

FIGURE 2.9 Nine-key clarinet, Monzani, British Patent No. 3586, 1812.

head, as found on French instruments, and the G♯ is a straight side key with its touch piece twisted toward the player's left for use by L1. Makers such as Key, D'Almaine and Company, and others made twelve- and thirteen-key clarinets with Willman's key arrangement, adding the French rollers between the touches of the F♯/C♯ and E/B keys, but not the thumb branches.

James Wood's Patents

James Wood succeeded Hale in 1804 and was active in London from about 1799 to 1832. In addition to clarinets and woodwinds, Wood constructed a number of black wood long-tenon mouthpieces that accompanied Goulding and Company clarinets and that bore a stamp on the reed side reading "I. WOOD FECIT."[134] His first patent, No. 2381 in 1800, was imaginative and specified several improvements for the five-key clarinet. He lined the bore of the barrel (which he called the socket or box) with a brass tube sixteen millimeters in diameter and twenty-six millimeters long for greater ease in tuning. The barrel slides onto a tenon of the left-hand joint. Wood illustrates these sections in his patent drawing and in John Mahon's fingering chart about 1803.[135] He uses small pipes or bushings of metal, wood, or other materials inserted into the tone holes and covered by keys in an effort to provide an airtight seating.[136] These round self-aligning or swivel key heads consist of a round key cover of "wood, bone, ivory, metal, brass or any metallick composition" that has a knob screwed to the top of each key head.[137]

In this patent, Wood states that he added a G♯ key to the "usual keys"— a seven-key clarinet, since the illustration includes an A–B trill for L1. The block to mount the A–B trill is far down the tube, between the first and second finger holes. The unusual G♯ key has a lengthy shank for R1 block mounted above the first finger holes. Interestingly, Wood's patent drawing has a right-hand joint combined with a stock section, a feature in Monzani's 1812 patent and not commonly found on English clarinets until the 1820s. A six-key B♭ instrument (ca. 1807, GB-Edinburgh, 933) with the mark of Goulding and Company includes Wood's first patent modifications, but without the G♯ key and with separate right-hand and stock sections.[138] The prolific London maker Key subsequently adopted Wood's improvement by using metal bushings (liners or sleeves) in tone holes beneath keys, and occasionally in finger holes.[139]

Wood received two additional patents for interesting innovations. His 1814 patent specifies metal tubes inserted into the middle and lower joints to prevent bore warping.[140] Wood became a partner in Goulding and Company about 1810, and they made and promoted his inventions.[141] His instruments must have made an impression in London, since the authority Charles Burney wrote approvingly in 1819 about the 1814 patent improvements. Burney mentions lining the bore with a brass tube and lining holes with "a soft metal pipe ground perfectly flat upon the surface, to which a stopper is screwed that renders the pipe air-tight."[142] A six-key Goulding, Wood, and Company clarinet (ca. 1815, US-SD, 2890) incorporates the patent features.

Wood's 1820 patent specifies that the E/B and F♯/C♯ keys overlap at the end of their touch pieces, enabling the player to slide easily between both keys with L4. Figure 1 of the patent shows the right-hand joint joined to the

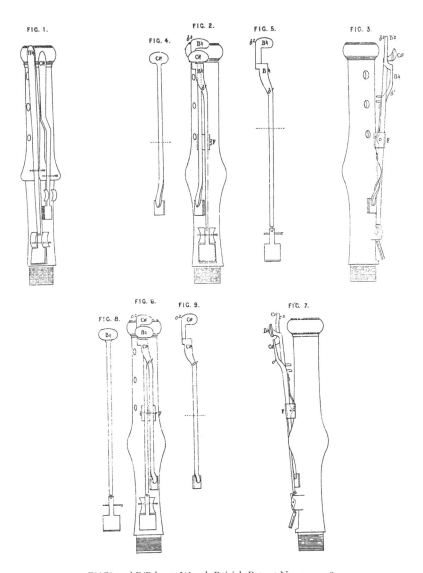

FIGURE 2.10   F♯/C♯ and E/B keys, Wood, British Patent No. 4423, 1819.

stock with normal pin-mounted E/B and F♯/C♯ keys (see figure 2.10). Wood's figures 2 and 3 show front and side views of the E/B and F♯/C♯ keys mounted on a metal saddle, attached with a screw. These keys' touches are wide and rounded so that the F♯/C♯ touch overlaps the E/B touch. When depressed, the F♯/C♯ touch presses against the E/B key shank and its key head closes. The F♯/C♯ key head is to the right of the E/B key from the player's viewpoint. Wood provides an alternative in his figures 6 and 7, with the E/B touch overlapping the F♯/C♯ touch. When depressed, the E/B touch presses against the F♯/C♯ key shank and its key head closes. The F♯/C♯ key head is to the left of the E/B key. This arrangement just preceded Janssen's rollers in Paris.

The highly successful teacher and flageolet maker William Bainbridge wrote enthusiastically about this improvement in 1823 without mentioning Wood by name.

> There are many very excellent Clarionet makers in London, and, unfortunately for the unwary, too many pretenders. One ingenious maker has lately obtained a patent for very important improvements on this instrument, particularly for facilitating the performance of music written in keys with sharps at the signature, by means of sliding keys, which render the hitherto difficult passage from A to B, C sharp, and D natural, easy.[143]

A well-made twelve-key Wood and Son clarinet (ca. 1825, GB-London-RCM, 326 C/10) features these patented keys. It is boxwood with ivory ferrules and a combined stock and lower section. Its keys, mounted in blocks and pillars with metal saddles, have cupped key heads (except the S key, which is flat).[144] Other examples with overlapping touch pieces are a six-key Wood B♭ clarinet (GB-Edinburgh, 938) and a six-key D'Almaine and Company C clarinet (GB-Edinburgh, 1846).

William Gutteridge's Patent

William Gutteridge, of Cork, Ireland, received a patent in 1824 for an ingenious key design specifying sixteen keys, including two extra levers to extend the range down to e♭ and d. His 1824 tutor describes a less complicated key arrangement on the lower joint with a range down to the usual lowest note, e. He asserts that his models date to 1813 but he was unable to continue owing to his service in a regimental band.[145] A fine boxwood B♭ clarinet with ivory ferrules and ebony mouthpiece following Gutteridge's design was made or sold by the London firm Clementi and Company about 1825. The instrument (GB-London-RCM, 248) has fifteen keys with round, flat key heads mounted in blocks and metal saddles. As specified in the tutor and patent drawings, two keys are on the dorsal side, one for playing b♭ and one as a speaker key.[146] The remaining keys are A–B trill, A, G♯, f/c, E♭/B♭, C♯/G♯, B/F♯, B♭/F, A♭/E♭ (2), F/C, F♯/C♯, and E/B. This is actually a thirteen-key clarinet with a separate b♭ key and an extra touch for A♭/E♭ (L4) that also closes E/B. The F/C shank is inserted into the wood and held up by a spring soldered to the underside of the shank; a round key head is soldered under the lever halfway down its length.[147] This key is similar to Müller F/C keys initially made about 1812.

Clementi and Company sold instruments and contracted with individuals and firms to make instruments to which they applied their name. For example, Charles Nicholson's improved flutes were made by Thomas

Prowse, but sold by the Clementi firm whose name is stamped on the instrument. It seems likely that the Prowse firm made these well-executed Gutteridge clarinets.

In summary, the most common extant English clarinets are the simple five- and six-key models. After 1800, many makers began offering instruments with additional keys, and during the 1820s, thirteen-key clarinets by Wood and others, as well as Gutteridge's exceptional fifteen-key instrument, were available. Only a few English firms, such as Goulding and Company, and Thomas Key adopted James Wood's design improvements. Makers produced thousands of clarinets and exported them to countries throughout the world. English clarinet makers were also very influential in America; until about 1850 the majority of American clarinets were based on English designs. The apogee of fine workmanship was the fifteen-key clarinet designed by Gutteridge and probably made by the Prowse firm.

AUSTRIA

Mathias Rockobaur, the earliest clarinet maker in Vienna, made oboe and bassoon reeds and repaired instruments from 1764. After his death in 1775, Johann Michael Rockobauer, a relative, continued the business until at least 1777.[148] There are no extant Rockobaur classical clarinets. Austrian clarinet makers began to make five-key clarinets during the 1780s; since few have survived, my conclusions are based on a small sample. Three anonymous five-key B♭ clarinets (1780–90, A-Graz-D, DM 6–8) tentatively attributed to Austrian makers are boxwood with horn ferrules. Each lacks a mouthpiece and barrel, has square rings for the S and A keys, and has a stock-bell with a wooden block to mount the E/B key head. In the same collection there is a boxwood stock-bell (A-Graz-D, DM 9) with a wooden block by Friedrich Hammig (Vienna) dated 1798.[149] Hammig made several types of wind instruments from 1791. A five-key Wolrath B♭ clarinet (ca. 1810, A-Graz-L, KGW 1.393) is boxwood and has horn rings, a separate mouthpiece, barrel, and stock-bell.[150]

Theodor Lotz, one of the most important and influential Viennese makers, lived in Vienna as early as 1772, when he performed clarinet solos at a Tonkünstlersocietät concert, and was employed by Cardinal Prince de Rohan until 1774.[151] He was evidently also a composer. In 1775, he wrote sixty-seven pieces for Prince Nikolaus Esterházy's wind band.[152] From 1778 to 1783, Prince Joseph Batthyány in Pressburg employed Lotz to play clarinet and viola.[153] In 1784, he moved to Vienna, where he was active as a player and a maker of clarinets, basset horns, and bassoons. Four years later, Lotz was appointed musical instrument maker to the royal court.[154]

Invoices from Lotz for 1782 to 1783 to the court orchestra indicate that he made clarinets for Anton and Johann Stadler pitched in C with corps (which are referenced as H Stücken or Mutationen) for tuning to B♮. Later invoices from Lotz for 1784 through 1786 indicate delivery of two more pairs of clarinets, one in C and another in an unspecified pitch.[155] The only extant example of a Lotz clarinet (ca. 1790, CH-Genève, 136) is a finely crafted boxwood five-key B♭ instrument with ivory ferrules in six sections: mouthpiece, barrel, two finger hole joints, stock, and bell. There is steel pinning below the S and A keys and across the bulge for mounting the three lowest keys; the key springs are anchored on the wood body. There are also extensions on the touches of the F♯/C♯ and E/B keys, and the finger hole joints are marked "B2," suggesting a second set of corps in B♭ (see figure 2.11). Lotz's bill for "Mutationen" suggests that different-sized finger hole joints were necessary to accommodate slightly varying pitch levels. There is an original blackwood mouthpiece stamped with the maker's name on the dorsal side, suggesting the player used a reed-below position. Lotz used a metal mount to reduce sideways motion of the E/B key head and metal guides for the F♯/C♯ key—characteristics of later Viennese makers. Wooden knobs replaced by metal guides or saddles are usually credited to nineteenth-century makers and testify to the forward-looking quality of Lotz's work.[156] The mouthpiece on this instrument and Viennese clarinets in general appears to have a slightly longer and narrower window slot than German or English mouthpieces. According to Ross, this instrument produces good intonation between the registers, with evenness of scale in the low register and the largest, thickest sound of any clarinet he had tested. The unusual dynamic range and sound quality may be due to its large bore size (between 15.0 and 15.05 millimeters).[157]

Raymund Griesbacher and his brother Anton were clarinetists in Haydn's orchestra at Esterházy from December 1775 to the end of February 1778.[158] From 1778 to 1781, Raymund played the basset horn in Count Palffy's wind ensemble[159] and from 1794 to 1800 was active at the Viennese court as a clarinetist and instrument maker. He may have worked with Theodor Lotz since his basset horns are very similar to Lotz's. In 1800, Griesbacher was appointed court supplier of musical instruments.[160] His extant instruments include seven clarinets with five to twelve keys.[161] A price list (ca. 1800) by Griesbacher guarantees correct intonation and includes a clarinet in B♭ with a corps for tuning to A and a third corps for tuning higher or lower. It is more expensive than a flute or oboe with corps de rechange, but less expensive than a bassoon, contrabassoon, or Russian bassoon. A basset horn with ivory ferrules is listed at the same price as a contrabassoon—a price one would expect for a large and complicated instrument.[162] In 1804, Joseph Rohrer described his clarinets as "not needing to fear comparison with any other instruments, and . . . they could be heard throughout Europe."[163] In 1807 and 1808, invoices from Griesbacher indicate he supplied the Viennese court with two boxwood B♭ clarinets with ivory ferrules, corps de rechange in A, two mouthpieces, and C boxwood clarinets with ivory ferrules for 150 gulden.[164] Within about seven years, the price of these instruments had increased considerably.

Pitch variation in Vienna and adjoining cities must have prompted the Viennese makers Lotz, Friedrich Lempp, Kasper Tauber, and Griesbacher to

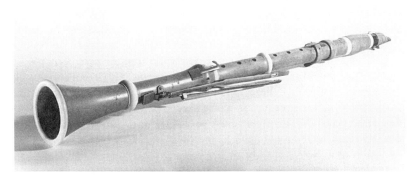

FIGURE 2.11 Five-key clarinet in B♭, Theodor Lotz, Vienna (ca. 1790, CH-Géneve, IM 136).

offer additional corps to tune to other pitches during the 1780s and 1790s. Makers asked buyers, especially those outside the area, to specify pitch. For example, in the *Wiener Zeitung* in 1789 Lempp advertised a clarinet in B♭ with an A joint for 4 to 6 ducats (18 to 27 gulden), but asked those from abroad to specify "Vienna pitch, Kammerton, or even French pitch, or to send me a tuning fork."[165]

Tauber was active as a maker from 1794 until his retirement in 1829. His extant instruments include seven clarinets with five and six keys.[166] Tauber, a student of Lotz in 1794 announced in the *Wiener Zeitung*, "He leaves it to experts to judge whether he flatters himself too much in asserting that his instruments are the same quality and purity [of intonation], and are even easier to play, than those of the late Mr. Lotz, the famous maker who employed him for many years."[167] An A clarinet (GB-Cambridge) is similar in appearance and large bore to Lotz's clarinet.[168]

Johann Baptiste Merklein was active in Vienna as a woodwind maker from 1799 to 1847.[169] An eight-key Merklein A clarinet (GB-Cambridge) is boxwood with ivory ferrules in the usual six sections but includes corps of two finger hole joints. The additional keys are mounted in metal saddles for the A–B trill and the cross keys for C♯/G♯ and B♭/F. Merklein includes larger tone holes at the bottom of the instrument in order to produce a fuller and louder sound in the chalumeau register.[170] An unusual five-key Merklein A clarinet (ca. 1815, A-Wien, N.E. 340) has two alternate finger hole joints with seven keys for tuning to B♭; with three keys on the common stock joint, this corp provides a total of ten keys. There are extensions on the F♯/C♯ and E/B keys, and the five additional keys are A–B trill, G♯, E♭/B♭, C♯/G♯, and B/F♯.[171] Professional players would find the additional keys on the B♭ clarinet useful. In Austria, corps were available until about the middle of the century: Uhlmann and Söhne was offering Mutationen in A and E♭ in a price list from about 1845.[172]

Stephan Koch was an outstanding Viennese woodwind maker from about 1809 until his death in 1828. His son Stephan Jr. continued producing woodwinds until about 1878. A superb twelve-key Koch C clarinet (ca. 1830, GB-Edinburgh, 81) with five stained, tiger-striped boxwood sections, a cocus wood mouthpiece, and right-hand joint combined with a stock is still quite conservative in appearance. Its keys are silver with round, flat key heads and rather thin, delicate touches and shanks. The unusual S key moves with a thumb lever conveyed to a front key by a ring mechanism concealed by a silver band.[173] The metal-lined barrel provides a tuning slide. All the keys are block mounted; the blocks for the shafts for the F♯/C♯ and E/B keys are lined with silver; and there are duplicate keys for E♭/B♭ for L4 and for the A♭/E♭ key, which is mounted in a silver saddle between the F♯/C♯ and E/B keys for L4. Müller's F/C key is noticeably lacking.[174] Other notable Viennese makers during the nineteenth century were Johann Tobias Uhlmann, who began work as a tradesman in 1810, and Johann Ziegler, who established his business in 1820.[175]

In Vienna during the late 1820s, there is evidence of more highly complicated key systems. In 1829, Stephen Edler von Keess stated: "Formerly clarinets were fitted with five keys that could not provide all the accidentals in the highest and lowest register. Now there are two corps de réchange (or replacement sections) which hold from nineteen to twenty-four keys, which provides the advantage of more accurate intonation throughout the range as far as the lowest E."[176]

Although the firms headed by Koch, Uhlmann, and Ziegler could have made clarinets with an advanced mechanism, they continued to make conservative clarinets without an F/C key, similar to Koch's instruments.[177] Keess may have been referring to Simiot's nineteen-key clarinet reported in a Munich newspaper,[178] since complex Viennese clarinets did not appear until Benedikt Pentenrieder's 1840 patent using crescent-shaped ring keys.[179]

In 1841, the Viennese writer Joseph Fahrbach extolled the virtues of Viennese clarinets and makers.

> The Viennese instruments have long been universally recognised as the best, and it may justifiably be maintained that apart from Vienna, no other city in the world has produced anything so thoroughly successful in this field. Since we are dealing here only with the clarinet, we shall restrict ourselves to mentioning the names ZIEGLER, UHLMANN, and KOCH, who have done outstanding work in improving the clarinet, and whose products we can highly recommend to all lovers of this fine instrument.[180]

Viennese clarinets by Lotz, Griesbacher, Merklein, Tauber, Ziegler, and Koch have an excellent reputation because they are well-crafted, fine-sounding instruments—qualities present in other Viennese woodwinds of the period such as flutes, oboes, and bassoons. Other makers and their successors in Austria made clarinets during the early nineteenth century, including

Doke (Linz), Franz Harrach (Vienna), Wolfgang Küss (or Kies; Vienna), Augustin Rorarius (Vienna), Schemmel (Vienna), Kriechbaum (Stockerau), and Johann Uhlmann (Vienna).

CZECH REPUBLIC

The emergence of the clarinet in Prague mirrored eighteenth-century developments in Vienna because of the cities' geographical proximity and strong commercial ties. The earliest report of the clarinet in Prague is a brief but important entry in a trilingual (Czech, Latin, and German) 1768 encyclopedia by J. K. Rohn. Here, the clarinet is described as having three to six keys. "The Clarinet [is] a pipe similar to the oboe but somewhat stouter, and below wider. [It has] a head or top, a middle piece, and a cup [bell] without a bottom. It generally has three flaps or keys, sometimes six. The feathers. Large mouthpiece with reed."[181]

This is also the earliest known published report of six keys. Rohn's instrument has mouthpiece-barrel, finger hole, and stock-bell sections. The sixth key may have been for the A–B trill, as found on eighteenth-century German clarinets. It is obvious that at least one maker was adding keys to the clarinet a decade before Castillon was amazed by a six-key clarinet. Rohn's feathers were probably used to clean the instrument after playing, as oboists do at present. No four-key clarinets made in Prague are presently known.

Franz Bauer (Beroun) made the earliest dated clarinet in the Czech Republic. A five-key 1789 clarinet (GB-Cambridge) is similar to German and Viennese instruments, with a stock-bell and extensions on the F♯/C♯ and E/B keys. Bauer or a successor may subsequently have worked in Prague from about 1803 to 1835.[182] Prague's earliest clarinet maker was Franz Doleisch, who made woodwinds from about 1781 until his death in 1806. His son Franz Jr. continued the workshop until 1812. An unmounted, stained-boxwood Doleisch B♭ clarinet (1793, GB-Cambridge) appears similar to Viennese examples, with barrel, two finger hole joints, stock-bell, wide ferrules with ornamental rings on the lower joint, and rings for the S and A keys. At 1.3 centimeters, the bore is closer to that of later Viennese instruments by Koch and smaller than the bores of most Grenser clarinets. Early-nineteenth-century makers from Prague include Franz Czermak Jr., Wenzel Horák, and Franz Ludwig.

DENMARK

The Finnish-born Peter Appelberg constructed the earliest Danish clarinets in Copenhagen from 1770 to 1807.[183] Appelberg played first clarinet in the Copenhagen court theater orchestra in 1762, and by 1770 he was playing a copy of an English clarinet in the court chapel orchestra described as "a sort of clarinet found and invented in London."[184] Perhaps this instrument was a five- or six-key clarinet with corps de réchange. In 1770, the court musician Hans Hinrich Jacobsen purchased an English clarinet from the Prince of Glouchester to play in the ballet *Den Franske Comoedie*.[185] However, the influence of German musicians and their instruments quickly appeared with the hiring of a wind octet of pairs of oboes, clarinets, horns, and bassoons in 1773. The clarinetists were Joseph Rauch of Bavaria and Albert Rauch of Saxony.[186] The only example of an Appelberg clarinet (in a private collection) shows a German-inspired boxwood five-key instrument with horn ferrules in six sections including a dark-wood mouthpiece.[187]

Appelberg's contemporary Friedrich Coppy, who was active as a woodwind maker in Copenhagen from 1784 to 1800, first advertised clarinets and flutes in 1785. In 1786, Coppy advertised that he made clarinets and flutes of grenadilla, ebony, and boxwood and in 1791 offered a pair of B♭ and A ebony clarinets for 100 reichsdalers.[188] According to the Copenhagen court orchestra's records, an ebony B♭ clarinet and an A clarinet were purchased from Coppy in 1791 for Joseph Rauch. In 1793, the court orchestra purchased two grenadilla clarinets in B♭ and A by Coppy.[189]

Jacob Georg Larshoff and Henning Andersen Skousboe were nineteenth-century makers in Copenhagen who experimented with the position of the C♯/G♯ key, presumably to achieve better intonation. Larshoff was an accomplished woodwind maker in Copenhagen from 1798 to 1834. He specialized in clarinets but also made flutes, oboes, basset horns,[190] and at least one basset clarinet. Skousboe, who was apprenticed to Appelberg, was active from 1804 to 1854[191] and produced a large number of woodwinds.

Both makers placed the C♯/G♯ key vertically or as a side key, mounting it into the wooden ring of the left-hand section for L4; the pad covered a tone hole on the right-hand section above the fourth finger hole. This configuration appears on an eight-key Larshoff C clarinet (ca. 1815, DK-Tåsinge, 17) and an eight-key Skousboe B♭ clarinet (ca. 1815, DK-Tåsinge, 9) with an additional corps for tuning to A.[192] Larshoff and Skousboe also mounted the C♯/G♯ key horizontally as a cross-key in the upper section ring. Examples are a seven-key A clarinet (ca. 1815, DK-Copenhagen-R, 28) with corps for tuning to B♭ and two twelve-key Skousboe B♭ clarinets (both ca. 1825, DK-Copenhagen-R, 44, 45).[193] Larshoff tried another approach by mounting the C♯/G♯ key horizontally as a cross-key with its end anchored in a wide wooden ferrule, its touch piece curled upward toward L4 so the end presses a lever opening a vertically mounted rectangular key head. An example of this mounting is found on a ten-key Larshoff A clarinet (ca. 1820, S-Stockholm, F.305).[194]

Larshoff received a patent in 1821 for a fifteen-key clarinet that could also be applied to basset horns. The instrument has six sections with keys for S, A–B trill, A, G♯, G♯ (operated by a touch for R1 that opened the G♯ key head), f/c for L2, f/c for R1, E♭/B♭, C♯/G♯, B/F♯, B♭/F, A♭/E♭, A♭/E♭ (operated by a touch for L4 opening the A♭/E♭ key head), F♯/C♯, and E/B. The patent drawings show the cross-keys for f/c, E♭/B♭, B/F♯, and B♭/F on what appears to be raised tone hole seatings, as used by the Grenser and the Griessling and Schlott firms.[195] Despite the ingeniously placed duplicate keys, this clarinet retains a conservative stance toward fingering. Larshoff explained in his patent that most of the additional keys were useful for trilling and he retained the finger hole for R4, rather than adopting Müller's F/C key. Larshoff's extant clarinets have five to sixteen keys.[196] The court orchestra commissioned Larshoff in 1825, 1826, and 1833 for eleven-key clarinets and a fourteen-key basset horn.[197] Other nineteenth-century Danish makers include Matthias Christian Brustgrün (Flensburg), Peter Groth (Fåborg), Hans Christian Hansen (Odense), Hendrik Jensen (Fåborg), Wilhelm Lund (Copenhagen), Heinrich Ludwig Rödel (Copenhagen), Rudolph (Copenhagen), Thorsen (Copenhagen), Henrik Adolph Weesch (Tranekær), and Wiborg (Copenhagen).[198]

ITALY

A 1781 list of tariffs for goods entering Florence includes a listing for clarinets.[199] At this time, clarinets were imported from Austria and Germany. Italian makers started producing clarinets during the 1790s; there are few extant eighteenth-century examples. Andrea Fornari, the first maker, submitted a document in 1791 to Venice's supervisory committee for protection as a maker of woodwind instruments and navigational and mathematical instruments. Among his list of "all wind instruments that I made myself, of my own invention, all improved" are clarinets in D and B♭ with corps de réchange in A, and flutes, bassoons, recorders, fifes, and chalumeau (*salmuò*) in different sizes.[200] It seems unusual that Fornari was still making rather old-fashioned instruments like recorders and chalumeaux, but there must have been some demand. The majority of his extant instruments are English horns and oboes, most dated from 1791 to 1832.[201] Only one clarinet is known: a five-key C clarinet (1806, D-Nürnberg, MIR 437) in six sections of boxwood with horn ferrules, blackwood mouthpiece, and five brass keys, each with a unique key head design.[202] The S and A keys are mounted in rings. Aside from the decorative key heads, Fornari designed an unusual A♭/E♭ key by anchoring the end of the key shank into a metal flange to act as a pivot and soldering a square key head a little less than halfway down the underside of the shank. Ivan Müller had used the same design for his important F/C key from about 1812, but its use on the A♭/E♭ key is unique to Fornari's instrument.

The earliest Italian instrument with a date is a five-key clarinet (I-Roma-M) in E♭ by Ermenegildo Magazzari (Bologna) with "1798" on the bell.[203] This boxwood instrument with horn ferrules is in six sections, including a dark wood mouthpiece. It appears similar to contemporary German instruments. There is no information on this maker, who may have worked during the late eighteenth and early nineteenth centuries. A low-pitch five-key C clarinet (ca. 1800, I-Roma-S) stamped "I. Biglioni" is attributed to Domenico Biglioni (Rome). It is in six boxwood sections with horn ferrules and a block for mounting the E/B key, marked with the pitch letter "C."[204]

Carobi (Clusone, northeast of Bergamo) made boxwood clarinets during the early nineteenth century with decorative carving on the bells and sometimes the stock joints. This type of decorative carving is usually found on recorders, flutes, and oboes; he is the only known clarinet maker to decorate his instruments in this manner. Unfortunately, information on this maker is scant; he was active in the early nineteenth century, about 1810 to 1830. A five-key example (ca. 1810, D-Nürnberg, MIR 436) has a carved vase of flowers on the frontal side of the bell (also stamped with the maker's name and city) and several trees on the dorsal side. The bell of a second Carobi B♭ clarinet (ca. 1810, I-Milano-MTS, FA/15) is more ornate, with a scene of Noah, his three sons, the ark, and the Latin motto "NOE VINUM BIBIT ET INEBRIATUR" (Noah drank wine and became drunk)—a reference to the story in Genesis 9:18–33. There is an additional carving of a tree with fruit on the lower stock.[205] An ornately carved Carobi clarinet bell (ca. 1815, US-SD, 4146) depicts eleven musicians sitting or standing behind a railing, a pipe organ, and three saints.[206] The rest of the clarinet is not extant.

Only three Italian makers are known to have constructed clarinets during the eighteenth century: Fornari, Biglioni, and Magazzari. Early-nineteenth-century makers include Berlingozzi (Siena), Bimboni (Florence), Bosa (Naples), Castlas (Turin), Lorenzo Cerino (Turin), Coselschi (Siena),[207] De Azzi (Venice), Giovannini (San Giusto), Koller (Trieste), Lesti (Ancona), Luvoni (Milan), Maruti (Fabriano), Carlo Mich (Tesaro),[208] Panormo (Naples), Pietro Antonio Piana (Milan), and Porporato (Volvera). Piana founded his firm in 1811 and continued until about 1842.[209] He made all types of woodwinds, was a large manufacturer and exporter, and made clarinets with between five and fourteen keys.[210] An eleven-key Piana clarinet (GB-Cambridge) reveals French influence in its use of finger touch extensions on the E/B and F♯/C♯ keys and a slanted position of a cross-B♭/F key. During the nineteenth century, the dealers Brizzi and Nicolai (Florence) imported Stengel (Bayreuth) instruments.

Spain

The clarinet arrived in Spain by the 1770s.[211] In 1785 and 1786, the makers Joseph Estrella and Fernando Llop (Madrid) advertised "clarinets" in the *Diario de Madrid*.[212] The earliest known Spanish clarinet is a five-key example (B-Liège, A 3104) in C by Luís Rolland of Madrid about 1800.[213] During the 1780s and 1790s, English clarinets were imported.[214] Later makers included José Claret (Madrid) and Leandro Valet (Madrid), both of whom exhibited brass clarinets at the Madrid Exhibition of 1827.[215]

The Netherlands

The baroque clarinet was played by the 1720s in Amsterdam but there is little evidence of clarinet making before 1800. Evidently, eighteenth-century players relied on instruments made in other countries such as Germany. Reynvaan describes a four-key clarinet (with an Ab/Eb key) and provides a fingering chart in his 1795 music dictionary, the only known fingering chart for the four-key clarinet with an Ab/Eb key. The engraving resembles German examples and includes a stock-bell section.[216] An anonymous four-key D clarinet (ca. 1780, NL-Den Haag, Ea 360-1933) is likely by a German, rather than a Dutch maker. It consists of a boxwood mouthpiece-barrel, finger hole section, and stock-bell. The stock-bell has a horn ferrule but the mouthpiece-barrel has an ivory ferrule and may be a replacement. There is an Ab/Eb key and a double hole for the seventh finger to play f♯/c♯2 by uncovering one of the double holes with R4. August Grenser (Dresden) and other German makers used the double hole for R4 on four-key clarinets.

The Christiani firm (Amsterdam) was the earliest Dutch firm to produce five-key examples by the first decade of the nineteenth century. A five-key Christiani clarinet (NL-Den Haag, Ea 8-1989) is similar to contemporary German instruments but includes curved and raised brass pieces on the ends of the touches of the F♯/C♯ and E/B keys to improve sliding between the touches. Other early-nineteenth-century Dutch firms include Birrer (Zofingen), Ludwig Embach (Amsterdam), Hanken (Rotterdam), H. van den Horn (Leiden), Johannes Imandt (Rotterdam), Theodor Lutz (Wolfhalden), and Otté (Groningen). A six-key Otté A clarinet (NL-Den Haag, Ea 52 x1952) includes a C♯/G♯ key and extensions on the touches of the F♯/C♯ and E/B keys like those made by the Tuerlinckx firm in Mechlin, Belgium.

Switzerland

Jeremias Schlegel, the earliest Swiss clarinet maker, was active in Basel from 1752 until his death in 1792. He apprenticed with his father Christian Schelgel and made all types of woodwind instruments, horns, and harps. At least five Schlegel clarinets with from five to seven keys are extant.[217] In a 1759 document, Schlegel announces that he makes "bassoons, oboes, transverse flutes, recorders, clarinets, chalumeaux, flageolets, harps, etc. and operates this business with great success."[218] In 1765, Schelgel and the German maker Tölcke advertised flutes for sale in two issues of the *Nürnbergische wochentliche Frag- und Anzeigenachrichten*.[219] In 1772, Schelgel sold pairs of flutes and clarinets to the Munich court,[220] and in 1773, the Wallerstein court purchased clarinets and bassoons.[221] Later property transactions indicate that he became prosperous.[222]

Schlegel produced a four-key clarinet d'amour (B-Bruxelles, 931) with an F♯/C♯ key, probably made for the French market. He also made one of the most beautifully designed and finely constructed extant eighteenth-century five-key B♭ clarinets (ca. 1775, D-Bonn, 137).[223] It differs from examples by his contemporary Tölcke in that it has a smooth bulge rather than a socket to accommodate the F/C tone hole and to act as a pivot for the shanks of long F♯/C♯ and E/B keys. This ebony instrument has ivory ferrules with an unusually large one on the upper part of the stock surrounding the F/C tone hole; the E/B key is mounted in a ring; and there is a decorative ring below the E/B key rather than the simple ridge characteristic of Tölcke instruments.

Schlegel made at least two five-key clarinets with ivory bodies in six sections including ivory mouthpieces. The first (D-Markneukirchen, 1041) has silver keys, black horn ferrules, and a nominal-pitch letter "C" marked twice on the body. The length of sixty-seven centimeters with the mouthpiece suggests a B♭ clarinet; the pitch has been tested at A = 415. However, the mouthpiece is a replacement made by Paul Ficker about 1900,[224] so these results may be unreliable. The second (DK-Copenhagen, CL 49) is in B♭, with silver keys, no ferrules, and a replacement grenadilla mouthpiece.[225]

Another eighteenth-century Swiss clarinet maker, M. Sutter (Appenzell), made a five-key clarinet (private collection) dated 1788. Like Schlegel, Sutter also advertised his instruments in a Nuremberg newspaper, but in 1787.[226] A document lists Joseph Anton Schuler as a clarinet maker in the old grinding mill in Dorfbach during the late eighteenth or early nineteenth century. A surviving Schuler five-key instrument (CH-Basel, 1950.27) is signed "Schwitz," indicating that he worked in modern-day Schwyz.[227] Nineteenth-century Swiss makers include Ammann (Alt St. Johann), Beltrami (Lugano), Georg Caspar Felchlin (Bern and Schwyz), Anton Fleischmann (Baden), Seelhoffer (Kehrsatz, Bern, Fribourg), Streulli (Horgen), and Thommen (Basel). Among Swiss makers, Schlegel was by far the most important and original. Later makers absorbed the influence of contemporary German and French makers.

AMERICA

In 1761, Gottlieb Wolhaupter was the first merchant to offer clarinets for sale, in an ad in the *New York Gazette*.

> Gottlieb Wolhaupter, living at the sign of the Musical Instrument-Maker, opposite Mr. Adam Vanderbert's, has just imported from London, a choice parcel of the best English box-wood: Where he continues to make and mend, all sorts of musical instruments, such as German flutes, hautboys, clareonets, flageolets, bassoons, fifes; and also silver tea-pot handles.[228]

Wolhaupter ran the same advertisement in the *New York Gazette* almost every week up until 1762. These instruments were probably three- or four-key rather than the advanced five- or six-key examples.[229] No other advertisement appeared in the *Gazette* until he moved to a new address in 1770, where he called himself David Wolhaupter, still making and mending the same instruments—minus flageolets and with the addition of "common flutes" (recorders) and bagpipes. Shorter ads continued until late 1775.[230] One could expect that by the 1770s Wolhaupter would have been offering copies of five- or six-key English clarinets, since many English clarinets would have been imported or brought by English bandsman and colonists. No American-made four-key clarinets are extant.[231]

In 1764, Michael Hillegas offered a variety of instrumental and vocal music and a large number of instruments, including clarinets, at his music store as advertised in the *Pennsylvania Gazette-Philadelphia*.[232] He did not offer clarinets again until 1774. James Rivington began advertising clarinet reeds in 1772 in the *New York Mercury*.[233] In 1779, he offered clarinets and other instruments as well as clarinet music. In 1774, Wells Stationary began advertising clarinet reeds and other merchandise in the *South Carolina and American General Gazette*,[234] and in 1781, a number of instruments were advertised in the *Royal Gazette-Charleston* as "just imported from London," including clarinets, clarinet reeds, and clarinet tutors.[235] John Jacob Astor of London established a music shop in New York City in 1786 and imported clarinets and a variety of other instruments to America from his brother George. In 1802, Astor sold his business to Michael and John Paff, but he continued to import and sell instruments as late as 1815.[236]

The earliest American clarinet maker was Jacob Anthony (Philadelphia), who initially advertised himself in 1772 in *Der Wöchentliche Philadelphische Staatsbote* as a maker and dealer who "makes flutes, recorders, oboes, clarinets, and fifes and improves old instruments."[237] Beginning in 1785, Anthony is found in the Philadephia directories as a turner and instrument maker, and from 1793 to 1804, both Jacob Anthony Sr. and Jacob Anthony Jr. are listed separately as makers. Anthony Jr. continued making instruments until 1811.[238]

Luckily, two five-key clarinets marked "Anthony/Philad." are extant. A fine example of an Anthony A clarinet (ca. 1800, US-DC-S) is modeled after German examples,[239] constructed of stained boxwood with ivory ferrules in six sections with a blackwood mouthpiece. Its F♯/C♯ key is straight, as on German instruments; the E/B key head is block mounted, and the A♭/E♭ key is mounted in a partially repaired German-style swelling. Another Anthony C clarinet (ca. 1800, US-MN) is similarly constructed of stained boxwood with ivory ferrules in six sections, a straight F♯/C♯ key, the E/B key head mounted in a block, and the A♭/E♭ key mounted in a swelling. This clarinet has a metal guide just above the F♯/C♯ key head similar to guides found on German or continental examples; there are springs soldered to the bottom of the keys; and the shape of the finger touch for the A♭/E♭ key is elegantly curved.

Heinrich Christian Eisenbrandt made clarinets in the German style, and after coming to America in 1808 he may have worked for Anthony. In

1811, Eisenbrandt established his own business, and in 1815 he moved to New York City. He traveled to Göttingen to work in his father's shop (Johann Benjamin Eisenbrandt) for two years and in 1819 returned to establish a firm in Baltimore, where he remained until 1849.[240] Heinrich Gottlob Gütter moved from Neukirchen in 1817 to the Moravian settlement of Bethlehem, Pennsylvania, where he established an instrument shop in 1819. Several five-key clarinets stamped with his name and "Bethlehem, Penn." were very likely imported from Gütter's family's firm in Neukirchen. They are stained boxwood instruments with horn ferrules, German-style short-tenon mouthpieces, straight F♯/C♯ key shanks, a block-mounted E/B key head, and a swelling for mounting the A♭/E♭ key on the stock.[241]

The firms of Graves (Winchester, New Hampshire) and Whitely (Utica, New York) made clarinets in the German or English styles, depending on the customer's preference. Some examples of the German style are a five-key Graves and Company C clarinet (US-SD, 5755); a five-key Whitely B♭ clarinet (US-MI-Dearborn, 71.70.30); and a ten-key Whitely D clarinet (US-SD, 5923) with the continental characteristics of a short-tenon mouthpiece, straight F♯/C♯ lever, and a swelling to mount the A♭/E♭ key.[242] A more typical American instrument (ca. 1830, US-DC, 65.729b) by Whitely is a five-key boxwood clarinet with ivory ferrules; characteristically English offset F♯/C♯ lever; small, long-tenon mouthpiece; waisted barrel; and sharp incurve of the mounting for the A♭/E♭ key. In addition, instrument dealers often imported instruments from France and England and stamped them with their own name. Examples include a five-key Godfroy E♭ clarinet (ca. 1818–21, US-SD, 4663) with the New York dealer and music publisher J. A. and W. Geib's stamp, and a six-key B♭ clarinet (ca. 1830, US-CA-Claremont, W233) of English origin stamped "G. E. Blake" (the Philadelphia dealer).

William Whitely made woodwinds in Utica, New York, from about 1810 to 1854. There are at least fourteen extant clarinets in D, C, and B♭ with five, nine, and ten keys.[243] Samuel Graves began making woodwinds in West Fairlee, Vermont, during the early 1820s. In 1827, he opened a shop with three partners in Winchester, New Hampshire, as Graves and Alexander. The firm, which became the first large-scale wind instrument manufacturer in America, used water-powered machinery to construct flutes, fifes, flageolets, and clarinets. From 1832, the firm was Graves and Company, and it continued to produce woodwinds until about 1845.[244] There are at least twenty-one clarinets by Graves and Company in E♭, C, and B♭, with five, six, eight, eleven, twelve, and thirteen keys.[245]

Early-nineteenth-century American clarinet makers include Ferris and Giffen (New York City), Firth Hall and Pond (New York City), Asa Hopkins (Litchfield, Connecticut), Harley Hosford (Albany, New York), Meacham and Meacham and Company (Albany, New York), and Edward Riley (New York City). Almost all their clarinets are modeled on English instruments, with the typical English-style socket boss on the lower stock with a sharp incurve and a small blackwood long-tenon mouthpiece. German-style instruments from the Klemm family of makers (Neukirchen) were exported to John George Klemm, who settled in Philadelphia in 1819.[246]

In summary, American clarinets made during the late eighteenth and early nineteenth centuries were mostly copies of English clarinets, but a few were copies of German clarinets. Since they were made in fairly large numbers, many survive today. American makers did not carry out genuine innovations in clarinet design until the twentieth century.[247]

Individual Contributors

SIMIOT

In 1808, the innovative maker Jacques François Simiot (Lyon) published an explanation of his clarinet improvements and a seven-key fingering chart,[248] making him the first important maker to construct and promote successful, high-quality instruments with more than five keys. An excellent example is a seven-key B♭ clarinet (ca. 1810, GB-Cambridge) of boxwood with ivory ferrules, a blackwood mouthpiece, and corps de réchange for tuning to A consisting of two additional finger hole sections and barrel.[249] Simiot added two keys to the normal five-key clarinet. On the left-hand joint, he added an A–B trill for L2; on the right-hand joint, a side B/F♯ key for playing the troublesome low b or trills (from b to b♭ or f² to f♯²) with R3 or R4. In addition, there is a double hole instead of a key for L3 to play the notes c♯¹ or g♯². There is an extension on the touch piece of the F♯/C♯ key and the A♭/E♭ touch piece is strongly curved to bring it closer to R4. Simiot's additional improvements include

> an ingenious circular ring mechanism (under a brass sleeve) for opening a speaker hole at the front of the instrument, where it is less susceptible to blockage by water. A brass tube in the thumb hole to retard the flow of saliva; a tuning slide of thin brass between barrel and mouthpiece. A mark [A] indicating the position to which the bell should be drawn out when using the corps for tuning from B♭ to A.[250]

During the 1770s, English and German makers made an A–B trill key with a long shank positioned for R1. Simiot's placement of this key was more efficient than the older design, since less finger motion was required. The B/F♯ key head was mounted adjacent to finger hole R2 on Simiot's 1808 instrument. Later Simiot instruments (ca. 1815, F-Le Mans) have a side key placed between R1 and R2, producing either b♮ (with the addition of R1) or b♭ (with R1 and R2).[251] Simiot also experimented with the placement of other keys. A boxwood-and-ivory seven-key model (F-Nice, 1875) includes keys for C♯/G♯ and B/F♯. Instead of the C♯/G♯ key being mounted in a saddle as on Baumann clarinets, "a rectangular brass base is screwed into a countersunk slot in the body and a thin metal pivot or tenon with a hole at one end is soldered to the base. The side of the key shank is threaded to receive a hinge screw passing through the tenon."[252] A nine-key Simiot B♭ clarinet (ca. 1815, F-Nice, C-135) includes the side B/F♯ key mounted between R1 and R2.[253] Like the 1808 instrument, this clarinet features a thin brass tube inserted in the barrel for tuning and a circular ring mechanism for opening the speaker hole on the front. All the key heads are flat and round, and the key levers end in a tapered point in the center of the head. Simiot flattened the left side of the stock joint to accommodate a F/C key rather than have the usual tone hole for R4, and he included an elegant A♭/E♭ key positioned at an angle for easier access by R4. "The end of the F/C key is mounted into a slot in the wood, the key cover is just above a bridge-shaped guide."[254] Simiot's adoption of an F/C key is indebted to Müller's F/C key on his thirteen-key clarinet, developed by 1812. Later Simiot clarinets feature hinged thumb levers as additional keys for the F♯/C♯ and E/B (examples in GB-Cambridge). His thumb hinge levers may have been a response to the Müller thumb keys, and he disapproved of rollers because he thought they moved too slowly.[255]

Simiot received a silver medal—the highest award given to a wind instrument maker that year—at the 1823 Paris Exhibition for his improvements to the bassoon and for "a clarinet in C that has the same qualities of sound as that of a clarinet in B♭."[256] A thirteen-key C clarinet (ca. 1823, GB-Cambridge) may have been the example awarded the silver medal in 1823. This instrument has four boxwood sections with ivory ferrules: barrel, left-hand joint, right-hand joint joined to the stock, and a bell. All the keys are pillar mounted, attached to the body on oval brass plates, with round, saltspoon key heads. The E/B key is on the dorsal side for R0 and a tuning slide of thin brass is inside the barrel. In addition, metal tubes inserted in the tone holes reduce the surface area to assure optimum closure of the pads. Simiot's position and mounting of the keys, except for the thumb hinge lever and the speaker key, were adopted by makers in Lyon, such as Tabard, Piattet, Brelet, and Louis Muller.[257]

Simiot's most advanced clarinet, produced in 1827, has nineteen keys. It is in B♭ (GB-Edinburgh, 115) with ebonized light wood in two sections, silver ferrules, and keys with cupped or salt-spoon key heads. The barrel is integral with the left-hand joint, the stock section is integral with the right-hand joint, the bell and blackwood mouthpiece are separate, and there is a corps de rechange in A consisting of a right-hand joint with an integral barrel pitched in A. After inserting the A corps the metal-lined stock section below the right-hand joint extends by means of a rack-and-pinion device. Simiot's 1808 circular ring mechanism to open the speaker hole at the front of the mechanism is included with a raised key seat for the key head. The keys are mounted to the body with plate-mounted pillars and screws and the tone holes and finger holes have silver bushes. This instrument is actually an elaborate thirteen-key clarinet with six additional touches. These are a thumb plate for the G tone hole for L0, two additional trill keys (for a¹ to b¹ and b♭¹ to b♮¹) for L2; a side B/F♯ key for L4, an A♭/E♭ for L4; and hinged levers for R0 to operate the F♯/C♯ and E/B keys. The F♯/C♯ and E/B keys are mounted high on round metal saddles to provide room for the extra lever and key head for an A♭/E♭ key. Metal loops at the end of the shanks of the F♯/C♯ and E/B keys are attached to the key heads to ensure that they close when the rack-and-pinion device is used. The instrument is stamped "Innové par Simiot."[258]

The Academie Royale approved this nineteen-key Simiot clarinet and his alto clarinet in 1827.[259] Simiot took the distinguished clarinetist Fréderic Berr to demonstrate his new instrument.[260] Later, he wrote a letter to the Institut Royal de France in 1828 stating that Berr and Mocker, the first clarinetists of the Théâter Italiens and the l'Odéon, were demonstrating the advantages of his instruments.[261] In an 1829 letter to Fétis published in the *Revue musicale*, Simiot claims to have made a twelve-key clarinet in 1803. Even though 1803 is quite early for a twelve-key clarinet, it is not difficult to believe that Simiot made one, considering his ability and innovative nature. Simiot also notes that in 1812, he began to make B♭ and A clarinets but without additional corps de réchange, asserting that all chromatic scales are playable on his instruments.[262]

Some makers close to Lyon favored doubled finger holes, probably because of Simiot's excellent work. For example, a seven-key Bouchmann clarinet (ca. 1825, US-NY-Massapequa Park) includes a doubled third finger hole. On a few instruments, Sautermeister (Lyon) mounted a side B/F♯ played by R1 or R2 instead of a C♯/G♯ key.[263] Simiot's son-in-law and student Tabard adopted the high, round metal mounts for the F♯/C♯ and E/B keys for a fourteen-key B♭ clarinet (ca. 1830, US-CA-Santa Monica), with an extra A♭/E♭ key for L4. Several other makers adopted Simiot's idea of mounting S to the front with a simple ring attached to the thumb lever to open the key head on the front side. Examples include a thirteen-key Schott clarinet (ca. 1825, NL-private collection) and a thirteen-key Printemps B♭ clarinet (1837, US-CA-Santa Monica). Only Koch seems to have copied Simiot's circular key ring mechanism for some of his clarinets such as a thirteen-key example (ca. 1830, GB-Edinburgh, 81). Baumann used Simiot's metal tuning slide inserted into the barrel in two thirteen-key clarinets (ca. 1825, US-CA-Claremont, W267; US-AK). The example at Claremont also has a thin brass tube in the thumbhole. Simiot's other key innovations were generally not copied beyond the region of Lyon.[264]

MÜLLER'S IMPROVEMENTS

The Russian-born musician and maker Iwan Müller made the most important and significant modifications to classical clarinet design during the first and second decades of the nineteenth century. No instruments survive with Müller's mark, so it seems likely that he employed others to make instruments that he designed and played. Simiot corresponded with Müller in 1803, and Müller constructed an eight-key clarinet while he was living in Russia.[265] By 1808, Müller had gone to Dresden, where he worked with the German maker Heinrich Grenser to construct an alto clarinet in F (called the "Müllersche Bassethorn") by applying a new system of sixteen keys to a basset horn and removing its four lowest keys (for d♯, d, c♯, and C).[266] In 1809, the Vienna correspondent for the *AMZ* reviewed a concert where Müller played his basset horn. He quotes Müller as stating that his improvements to the basset horn could and should be applied to the clarinet. The journal's editor, Johann Friedrich Rochlitz, also mentions the use of leather pads under each key head of Müller's basset horn, which minimized the rattling when the key levers were depressed, and a metal bell.[267] While Müller was in Vienna, he had the maker Merklein construct a soprano clarinet that he played at a concert in 1809 along with his Grenser alto clarinet. His alto clarinet was criticized for not having as full a sound as a basset horn but his clarinet is not described, so we can only speculate that it may have been a thirteen-key instrument with additional thumb levers.[268]

In 1811, Müller traveled to Paris, where he set up an instrument-making shop with the assistance of Marie Pierre Petit, a clarinetist and stockbroker, and Boscari, an amateur musician.[269] The first person to design a thirteen-key clarinet, Müller was particularly attentive to tone hole placement in the acoustically correct position for proper intonation. Müller's clarinet had eight keys in addition to the standard five keys—A–B trill key; G♯ placed under the A key; side key for f/c; cross-keys for E♭/B♭, C♯/G♯, and B♭/F; side key for B/F♯; and F/C key. There are two additional levers, operated by Ro—a shank (called a "branch") soldered to the F♯/C♯ lever and a lever that opened the A♭/E♭ key. The latter, pivoted at its midpoint with a piece of cord or a coiled spring at its distal end, is attached to the usual A♭/E♭ lever. This is an articulated key that, when the touch piece is pressed, acts upon another lever which lifts the key head. Müller's positions for the A♭/E♭ and G♯ keys are acoustically correct, a significant improvement over the design of earlier clarinets.

Müller provides engravings of slightly different clarinets in his *Gamme pour la nouvelle clarinette* (ca. 1812) and *Méthode pour la nouvelle clarinette et clarinette-alto* (ca. 1821; see figure 2.12). The main difference is the design of the important F/C key. In the *Gamme* the F/C key is articulated; that is, depressing the touch piece on one side of a metal pivot closes the key head on the other side of the pivot. In the *Méthode* the action is direct; that is, the F/C shank is attached below the tone hole and curves over it so that depressing the touch piece closes the key head (attached on the curved part of the shank) on the hole.[270] Makers during the 1820s (Lefèvre, Baumann, and Gentellet) kept the direct action of the F/C key by anchoring about 3 centimeters of its upper end, with a spring soldered underneath, in a metal plate above the touch piece. They retained Müller's curved shank but placed the key head at the lower end of the shank. Later makers all used a short and

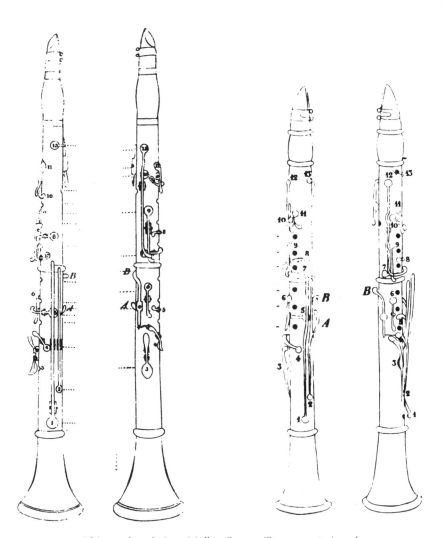

FIGURE 2.12   Thirteen-key clarinet, Müller, *Gamme* (Bonn, ca. 1812), and thirteen-key clarinet, Müller, *Méthode* (Paris, ca. 1821). Courtesy of the Bibliothèque Nationale and the New York Public Library.

straight F/C key either by anchoring the upper end, with a spring soldered underneath in a metal plate, or by mounting the upper end between two pillars. Müller's *Gamme* clarinet uses flat, round key heads. By the 1820s, Müller introduced pads of gut or leather stuffed with wool like an "elastic ball," as discussed in the *Méthode*. The pads required a round, hollow cup (called a salt spoon) soldered to the shank with the corresponding tone holes countersunk, leaving a raised wood rim for the pad to rest upon.

Müller also introduced a metal ligature with two screws to hold the reed to the mouthpiece, initially shown in his *Gamme,* as preferable to twine for its ease of adjustment and better appearance.[271] Another contribution is the one-piece construction of the lower sections used to mount the F/C key, proof that corps de réchange are not necessary. Müller wanted his clarinet to be "omnitonic," that is, playable in any tonality, freeing the player from the necessity of owning a whole set of clarinets.[272] In addition, the right-hand joint and stock in one piece accommodates the thumb lever for the A♭/E♭ key, positioned between R2 and R3.[273]

A rare example of an anonymous fourteen-key B♭ clarinet (ca. 1810, GB-Cambridge) is very similar in key layout to Müller's clarinet in his *Gamme* except that, on the former, all the keys are mounted in wooden blocks rather than metal saddles. There are four boxwood sections with horn ferrules, a thumb branch soldered to the F♯/C♯ key, an articulated key mounted on the dorsal side for Ro to open the A♭/E♭ key, and flat, round key heads as shown in Müller's *Gamme.*[274] Shackleton suggests that this instrument was a prototype of Müller's revolutionary thirteen-key clarinet.

In 1812, Müller presented his B♭ thirteen-key soprano clarinet and his alto clarinet (probably in E♭, although the report does not specify) to an eight-member commission from the Paris Conservatory for approval. They did not accept Müller's soprano clarinet but did approve his alto clarinet. The improved technical capabilities and intonation of his soprano instrument were recognized, but it was rejected on the grounds that with its sole use, the composer would be deprived of the individual tonal characteristics of clarinets pitched in C and A.[275] Writing in 1828, Gottfried Weber reports that this decision was reversed in 1814, and Müller's clarinet was approved for use at the conservatory.[276] In 1823, Müller exhibited his new clarinet at the Paris Exhibition and received a bronze medal.[277] The maker is unknown, but Müller's basic design for a thirteen-key clarinet without thumb keys was manufactured in Paris beginning in the 1820s. One of the first makers was François Lefèvre whose 1824 thirteen-key instrument (F-Paris, E.475, C.537) is made of boxwood with ivory ferrules in four sections. As with Müller's instrument, the keys are pillar-mounted with salt-spoon key heads, right-hand joint combined with the stock, and an F/C key.[278]

A very rare C clarinet (ca. 1830, D-Uhingen) by Karl Friedrich Adler (Bamberg) has all the keys depicted in Müller's 1821 *Méthode.* It is boxwood with horn ferrules in four sections and has a blackwood mouthpiece, brass keys mounted in wooden blocks, and round, flat key heads. The only difference between this instrument and the one depicted in Müller's tutor is a built-up key seat for the S key head and the use of blocks.[279]

One of the earliest advertisements for Müller's clarinets appears in Carl Almenräder's bassoon tutor *Abhandlung über die Verbesserung des Fagotts* (Mainz, 1822) published by B. Schott's Söhne. The Schott firm price list includes clarinets with five, nine, twelve, and fifteen keys, "the last after Iwan Müller's new invention."[280] By 1825, Schott appears to have discontinued soprano clarinets with more than twelve keys; their advertisement in the firm's

TABLE 2.1
Clarinets advertised by B. Schott Fils in 1825

Pitch of clarinet	Type of wood	Type of ferrule	Type of key	Number of keys
B♭	box	horn	brass	5
B♭	box	ivory	brass	6
B♭	box	ivory	brass	9
B♭ nouvelle invention	box	ivory	brass	12
B♭ nouvelle invention	box	ivory	silver	12
B♭ nouvelle invention	ebony	ivory	silver	12
B♭ avec cor en La	box	horn	brass	5
B♭ avec cor en La	box	ivory	brass	6
B♭ avec cor en La	box	ivory	brass	9
B♭ avec cor en La nouv. inv.	box	ivory	brass	12
B♭ avec cor en La nouv. inv.	box	ivory	silver	12
B♭ avec cor en La nouv. inv.	ebony	ivory	silver	12
C	box	horn	brass	5
C	box	ivory	brass	6
C	box	ivory	brass	9
C nouvelle invention	box	ivory	brass	12
C nouvelle invention	box	ivory	silver	12
C nouvelle invention	ebony	ivory	silver	12
E♭	box	horn	brass	5
E♭	box	ivory	brass	6
E♭	box	ivory	brass	9
E♭ nouvelle invention	box	ivory	brass	12
E♭ nouvelle invention	box	ivory	silver	12
E♭ nouvelle invention	ivory	ivory	silver	12
F	box	horn	brass	5
F	box	ivory	brass	6
F	box	ivory	silver	6
Alto clarinet	box	ivory	brass	14

periodical *Cäcilia* has twenty-seven models with five, six, nine, and twelve keys (the latter marked "nouvelle invention"), and one alto clarinet with fourteen keys (see table 2.1).[281]

Although there are no prices in this advertisement, it is assumed that the least expensive instrument was the small boxwood five-key F clarinet with horn ferrules. Ivory ferrules, silver keys, an ebony body, corps de réchange, and additional keys no doubt increased the cost. The fourteen-key alto clarinet probably featured Müller's additional thumb keys, which are also found on some thirteen-key clarinets.

Contemporary sources credit the following makers with constructing thirteen-key clarinets during the 1820s: Gentellet, 1820;[282] B. Schott's Söhne, 1822;[283] Brelet, 1823;[284] Johann Bischoff, 1824;[285] and Griessling and Schlott,

1825.[286] Extant clarinets by these makers typically do not include Müller's thumb key and thumb branch but do include his designs for the F/C key and the one-piece right-hand joint and stock, a fact that suggests players found the thumb keys awkward to manipulate.

Müller had an enormous influence on later makers, particularly in their design of pillar mounting, the F/C key, salt-spoon key heads with stuffed pads, and the metal ligature. Thousands of thirteen-key clarinets without thumb keys (subsequently known as simple-system clarinets) incorporated these improvements and were made in France and many other countries as late as the twentieth century. Furthermore, his clarinet was used as a model for several German and Austrian makers (e.g., Stengel and the firms of Mollenhauer, Kruspe, and Oehler) who developed distinctive clarinets during the nineteenth and twentieth centuries.

Janssen's Improvements

According to an 1824 report of the Paris exhibition, the clarinetist César Janssen worked to improve his instrument since 1806.[287] As in Müller's case, no instruments bearing his name are known, so he must have commissioned others to build clarinets according to his designs. At the 1823 Paris Exhibition, Janssen received honorable mention for his thirteen-key clarinets and was praised for the use of rollers or revolving cylinders attached to the end of the touches of the adjacent E/B and F♯/C♯ keys and A♭/E♭ and F/C keys. The rollers made it possible to create a smooth slur between $c♯^2$ and $d♯^2$ and between c^2 and $e♭^2$, a slur that was unobtainable on earlier designs. Francoeur notes that Janssen also improved the S key and the position of the keys on the upper joint.[288] In addition, he designed a depression in the tip of the S key's touch piece and similar depressions at the tips of other keys to permit the thumb and fingers to slide easily on and off the touches.[289] An early example of a thirteen-key Baumann B♭ instrument (ca. 1821, GB-Cambridge) is an extraordinary boxwood clarinet with ivory ferrules in six sections with separate right-hand joint and stock. It includes a corps de rechange in A with separate barrel, and all keys have depressions on the tips, or sides if they are cross-keys, for easier manipulation; it also has four very large rollers.[290] The earliest prizewinner of the premier prix at the Paris Conservatory to receive a thirteen-key clarinet was Pierre Hugo, a student of Louis Lefèvre, in 1825.[291] It seems likely that a few adventurous clarinetists were playing thirteen-key instruments based on Müller's design by the early 1820s.

Janssen's innovations were copied by a number of makers, particularly the rollers on bassoons and thirteen-key clarinets. Two thirteen-key Baumann clarinets (ca. 1825, US-CA-Claremont, W267; US-AK) have medium-sized rollers with wide touches. Stengel (Bayreuth) included rollers for F♯/C♯, A♭/E♭, and F/C on a thirteen-key D clarinet (ca. 1835, US-SD, 5827). It has two duplicate levers—a thumb lever for F♯/C♯ and a long A♭/E♭ lever for

L4—pillar-mounted keys, and G♯ crossing over the A key. Small, thin rollers were adopted by virtually every nineteenth-century French maker; the important Albert family in Brussels; and many German and British makers. Except for German- and Austrian-made clarinets, rollers disappeared with the slow rise of Boehm-system clarinets.

Many of the most innovative and important clarinet makers were active in France during the early nineteenth century, including Simiot, Müller, Baumann, Gentellet, and Janssen. The keywork and other characteristics developed by Müller and Janssen were used by dozens of later makers throughout the century. Their work was refined and altered during the development of the important Boehm-system clarinet by the Parisian maker Louis Auguste Buffet working with the clarinetist Hyacinthe Klosé during the 1840s. Specifically, the placement and design of the A, G♯, and F/C keys and touches by Müller and Janssen influenced Buffet's design. Boehm-system instruments have duplicate keys for the little fingers of both hands, so there is no need for rollers. Müller's desire to design a truly "omnitonic" clarinet was never realized, since composers, makers, and players chose to keep the distinctive tone color of the various clarinets and continued primarily to use those pitched in C, B♭, and A.

The Basset Clarinet

A basset clarinet is a clarinet in C, B♭, or A with an extension of notes below the usual limit of e to C. The keys for the lowest notes (below e) are mounted on the dorsal side of basset horns of the period. The history of the basset clarinet properly begins before the use of Anton Stadler's instrument to play Mozart's well-known works during the 1780s and 1790s. A list and description of extant basset clarinets is given by Shackleton and Rice in Lawson's *Mozart: Clarinet Concerto*, 84–90. Two instruments in A or A♭ have the angled shapes of basset horns: Mayrhofer (ca. 1770, D-Passau, 3160) and an anonymous eleven-key instrument (ca. 1790, F-Paris, 980.2.566).[292] Two anonymous seven-key instruments (ca. 1775, F-Paris, E.190 C.543; E 2194) resemble the clarinet d'amour, with their curved metal necks and slightly flared bells. Another is an anonymous curved eight-key instrument (ca. 1785, D-Berlin, 2886). None of these early basset clarinets could have been used to play Mozart's concerto or quintet, since they lack a fully chromatic scale of basset notes e♭, d, c♯, and C. However, any of these instruments may have been the initial design on which the Viennese maker Theodor Lotz based his instrument of the 1780s for Anton Stadler.

ANTON STADLER'S BASSET CLARINETS

By 1788, Lotz had completed clarinets in B♭ and A for Stadler with an extension of the D and C keys, as found on his basset horns. They were es-

sentially basset horns in B♭ and A. but because of their use in Mozart's concerto and chamber music, they were immediately called "Bass-Klarinett,"
probably to draw attention to their unique low range. The earliest evidence of
the use of the basset clarinet in Vienna is a 1788 concert program from the
Royal and Imperial Theater. "Herr [Anton] Stadler . . . in the service of his
majesty the Kaiser . . . will play a concerto on the Bass Clarinet. . . . Herr
Stadler will play a variation on the Bass Clarinet, an instrument of new invention and manufacture of the Royal and Imperial instrument maker, Theodor
Lotz. This instrument has two more low tones than the normal clarinet."[293]

In newspaper reports, Stadler always advertised his "newly invented"
clarinet with its extended range, full sound, and softer tone. The Berlin
Musikalischer Korrespondenz in 1790 reports Anton Stadler "has refined his
instrument and added notes at the bottom, so that e is no longer the lowest
tone, but rather the C a third under this. He also negotiates the c♯ and d♯ in
between, and those with special ease!"[294] Ernst Gerber repeats this description almost verbatim in his article about Stadler, with the addition of a key
for the note d, omitted in the description given in the *Musikalischer Korrespondenz*.[295] In 1790, Lotz gave the instrument a chromatic extension downward to include the notes d♯, d, c♯, and C, enabling Stadler to play Mozart's
concerto. Stadler's concert tour or series of tours ran from 1791 to 1795.
Poulin has reconstructed his appearances in various cities and the dates of
concerts from newspaper reports.[296]

Stadler's Berlin performance in 1792 was "brilliant, polished and precise," but he did not have the soft tone quality and tasteful delivery of the
well-known clarinetist Franz Tausch, then a Berlin resident. "Mr. Stadler has
also added several notes to his instrument by means of keys. However, the
gain, through the added keys, is not very great, because the instrument is almost overladen with keys."[297] This statement suggests that the writer had
never seen a clarinet with four long keys on the dorsal side to produce the
lowest chromatic notes.[298]

Poulin discovered three programs for Stadler's 1794 Riga concerts that
include an engraving of Stadler's basset clarinet (see figure 2.13).[299] On the
program, Stadler takes credit for the invention of his extended-range clarinet, although during the tour he also played basset horn. The engraving raises
some intriguing questions. The most obvious is the position of the mouthpiece, which would require the maxillary position of the reed against the
upper lip. Many scholars and players have assumed that Stadler played with
the reed-below position, but this engraving indicates the opposite. However,
this is not absolute proof of Stadler's normal playing position. Other interesting details are the vent hole in the "cross-pipe" or L-shaped section and
the vent holes in the flat section of the partly cylindrical bell. These holes
probably improved the intonation for the lowest notes, and in fact Hoeprich
reports this to be the case with his basset clarinet reproduction.[300] The S, A,
A♭/E♭, F♯/C♯, and E/B keys are visible in the engraving. One lever and four
blocks or indentions appear on the back of the instrument, suggesting

thumb keys for E♭, D, D♯, and C. This instrument must have carried the four basset keys needed to play Mozart's concerto, even though not all the keys are clearly shown. The neck is erroneously positioned away from where the clarinetist would play, which allows the engraving to fit above the program's selections.[301] The player would have to turn the neck 180 degrees in order to play the instrument.

Luckily, a 1795 letter survives that suggests that another maker may have made a basset clarinet. Stadler wrote to the Bremen theater director Daniel Schütte that he had commissioned the turner and maker J. B. Tietzel to build to his specification a "neue Art Clarinette d'amour" (new type of clarinet d'amour).[302] Furthermore, in the Riga engravings, the bell of Stadler's basset clarinet resembles the bulbous bells of many clarinets d'amour more than the round or oval metal bell of the basset horn or the flared bell of the normal soprano clarinet. No instruments by Tietzel have been traced.

In 1795, Anton Stadler performed concerts in Hanover, where he advertised he would play on a "clarinet of his own invention which differs from the ordinary clarinet by its different construction, a softer tone, and a range of four complete octaves."[303] It is not certain who made Stadler's instrument for this concert—Lotz, Tietzel, or another maker. The next day Stadler played both his basset clarinet and a basset horn at a concert in Hanover.[304] A year later, the writer J. F. von Schönfeld noted that in addition to the ordinary clarinet, the Stadlers played an instrument in Vienna called the "basset clarinet." "Stadler brothers, with the Imperial court orchestra are excellently skillful artists, both on the ordinary clarinet and the basset clarinet. The latter instrument is difficult to handle in its production of tone, the delicacy of expression, and the facility to have it perfectly under control."[305] It is possible that Schönfeld was referring to Stadler's basset clarinet, but the fact that he singled it out as more difficult to play than

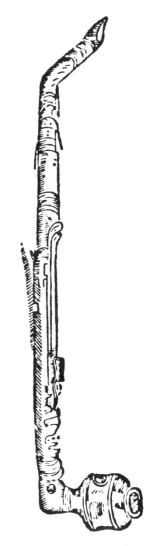

FIGURE 2.13   Engraving of a basset clarinet on a program for 21 March 1794 played by Anton Stadler in Riga (Latvian Fundamental Library, Riga).

the ordinary clarinet suggests that Schönfeld was referring to a basset horn, with its narrow bore. The modern small-bore basset horn is definitely more difficult to control than an ordinary clarinet, and this was probably true in the eighteenth century as well.[306] In addition, Stadler did not use the term "Baßetklarinet" in his newspaper advertisements.

Stadler continued to play his basset clarinet after his concert tour, as shown in a detailed description of an 1801 concert in Vienna.

> Herr Stadler, a great virtuoso on several wind instruments, presented himself at one of the concerts performed by amateurs in the Augarten. He played a clarinet with modifications of his own invention. His instrument does not, as is usual, run straight down to the bell. About the last third of its length, it is fitted with a transverse pipe from which the projecting bell flares out further. The advantage of this modification is that the instrument gains more depth by this means, and in the lowest notes, resembles the horn.[307]

This description fits Stadler's instrument in the engraving for his Riga program. The only questionable part is that the transverse pipe appears about three-quarters the length down the tube. In the engraving, the short L-shaped section connects to a bell about seven-eighths the length of Stadler's instrument. Of course, we should not expect complete accuracy in these descriptions.

Early-Nineteenth-Century Basset Clarinets

The Viennese maker Franz Scholl took over Lotz's workshop after his death in 1792. In 1799, Scholl advertised in the *Wiener Zeitung* that he had improved the clarinet and bassoon, and in 1800, he advertised an "Inventions-clarinet" that has "excellent playing qualities and a very lovely tone."[308] This clarinet may have been a basset clarinet. In 1803, Scholl's advertisement was more specific. "His clarinets (in B♭ or C) go 2 tones lower, namely to the low C, which always produced a good effect because one has the low tonic note for cadences. Moreover, his clarinets strongly recommend themselves by their good construction, by their pure tuning, and by a new manner by which the keys are mounted."[309] The new manner for key mounting was very likely metal saddles for the F♯/C♯ and E/B keys, as Lotz used. Unfortunately, none of Scholl's basset clarinets are extant.

Backofen mentions basset clarinets made in Vienna in his tutor (about 1803) as "a new and excellent invention now being made in Vienna that, like basset horns, have the low D and C. This much improves the clarinet, in addition is the great advantage of gaining the bass note C, which previously has been so lacking in the clarinet's favorite key of C, and it now has 3 full octaves which any clarinetist can easily play."[310] Like Scholl's instruments, Backofen's basset clarinets include keys only for D and C. His three-octave range must have been meant for the average player: Backofen knew that advanced players could play as high as g^3 or c^4, since these notes are included in his fingering charts for the five-key clarinet and nine-key basset horn.[311]

Even though Backofen was enthusiastic about the new instruments, he felt it necessary to add in the next paragraph: "For the present, I will pass over the many and important advantages of this previously mentioned new invention, and detail them at great length only when this clarinet has become more common."[312] Unfortunately, this was not to be the case, although there is another report of a maker advertising basset clarinets, and there are four extant instruments dating from around 1800 to 1840.

In 1806, Friedrich August Peuckert (Breslau) made a B♭ basset clarinet with the advice of the basset horn player Vincent Springer. In a newspaper report, Peuckert credits the invention to Springer. "Through the invention of the clarinetist, Mr. Springer of Amsterdam, I was able to construct entirely new type of B♭ clarinets that are slightly bent, descend to low C, have an outstandingly beautiful tone, and are finished in the highest perfection."[313] Although flutes and clarinets survive by Peukert, none of his basset clarinets are extant.[314]

Later extant basset clarinets include an eleven-key example in C by Johann Benjamin Eisenbrandt (Göttingen; ca. 1800, NL-Amsterdam) that is very similar to Stadler's instrument; a thirteen-key Strobach A clarinet (Carlsbad; ca. 1815, D-Hamburg, 1912.1562); a fifteen-key Jacob Georg Larshoff B♭ clarinet (Copenhagen; ca. 1830, CH-Zumikon); and a sixteen-key Johann Gottlieb Karl Bischoff B♭ clarinet (Darmstadt; ca. 1840, D-Darmstadt, Kg 61: 116).[315] Only the Eisenbrandt and Bischoff instruments include a fully chromatic register below e.

The Larshof B♭ basset clarinet is a very skillfully made straight boxwood instrument with ivory ferrules in four sections plus a blackwood mouthpiece (see figure 2.14). A second stock section has keys for A♭/E♭, F♯/C♯, and E/B, with rollers on the touch pieces of the F♯/C♯ and E/B keys so the instrument may be played like a normal clarinet. The upper part of the bell includes a tuning hole not visible in the photograph. Another tuning hole is in the tenon of

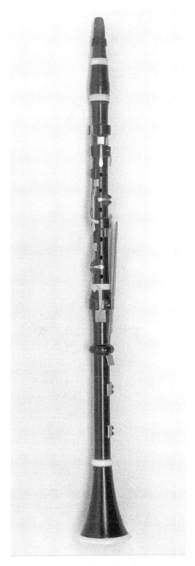

FIGURE 2.14   Fifteen-key basset clarinet in B♭, Jacob Georg Larshof, Copenhagen (ca. 1830, CH-Zumikon).

the stock section for the normal clarinet, but it does not appear in the tenon for the basset clarinet.[316] The fifteen brass keys are S, A–B trill, A, G♯, f/c (mounted on saddles, probably a later addition), E♭/B♭ (R1; probably a later addition), E♭/B♭ (L3), C♯/G♯, B/F♯ (probably a later addition), B♭/F, A♭/E♭, F♯/C♯, E/B, D, and C.

The nine basset clarinets discussed include five dating from the late eighteenth century, one from about 1800, and three from the early nineteenth century made in Germany, Austria, and Sweden.[317] Because the basset clarinet was expensive and more difficult to make than the ordinary clarinet, the demand was lower. Only a few players, such as soloists like Anton Stadler, would have been interested in these instruments. Basset clarinets are required only in Mozart's quintet and concerto for clarinet in A, the aria "Parto, parto ma tu ben mio" from *La Clemenza di Tito* for a B♭ basset clarinet, the Quintet fragment in B♭ (1790–91), and the second B♭ clarinet part to "Ah lo veggio" from *Così fan tutte*. After Mozart's death Stadler is known to have played his basset clarinet as an obbligato instrument in "Una voce al cor mi parla" in act II of *Sargino* (1803) by Ferdinando Paer. It is also likely that Stadler adapted other repertoire for playing on his basset clarinet.[318]

Conclusion

The evolution from the four-key classical to the thirteen-plus-key early romantic instrument was significant in the overall history of the clarinet. This era represented great experimentation, trial and error, and innovation from players and composers as well as makers. From about 1750 to 1780 in Germany and France, the four-key clarinet was a transitional instrument. The popular five-key clarinet began to replace it and the earlier two- and three-key instruments during the 1770s. By about 1780, the five-key clarinet had become the favorite throughout Europe. The six-key clarinet was first played during the 1770s, along with the five-key instrument. More than those of any other country, English makers of the late eighteenth and early nineteenth centuries exported their five- and six-key instruments to European countries and America; thus, the greatest number of surviving boxwood clarinets come from English firms.

James Wood, Jacques François Simiot, and Tebaldo Monzani created innovations in design that were adopted by only a few makers because of the difficulty of modifying tools and the added cost of construction. Basset clarinets or extended-range clarinets were offered by several late-eighteenth- and early-nineteenth-century makers but were never generally adopted by clarinetists because they represented an additional cost and composers did not require them.

The most popular instrument continued to be the five-key clarinet until about 1810; seven-, eight-, ten-, eleven-, and twelve-key clarinets gained in popularity after that time, and by the 1820s, the thirteen-key clarinet was the instrument of choice for the professional player. Metal clarinets were initially made by Halary and other makers during the early nineteenth century and became quite popular during the twentieth century. During the 1820s and 1830s, makers slowly adopted many of the innovations of Iwan Müller and César Janssen.

3

PLAYING TECHNIQUES

To appreciate the history of the clarinet it is essential to understand the evolution of its design and construction. It is equally important to be aware of how the clarinet was actually played and how composers wrote for the instrument. This is particularly pertinent for modern clarinetists interested in playing old or reproduction instruments. Thus, this chapter investigates six important aspects of playing techniques utilized during the eighteenth and early nineteenth centuries, namely compass, registers, and fingerings; embouchure and mouthpiece position; articulation; selection of a clarinet; transposition; and notation of parts and clefs. In addition, the unusual technique of using a mute is put in focus. Tutors and treatises, musical scores and parts, extant instruments, and pictorial sources inform the analysis.

Compass, Registers, and Fingerings

Parisian publications clearly show the evolution of the clarinet from a baroque two-key to a classical four-key clarinet. For example, Corrette includes the clarinet in a table of commonly used instruments and voices in his 1758 *Le parfait maître à chanter*[1] with a compass of f to c^3, equivalent to the two-key clarinet compass specified by Eisel in his treatise twenty years earlier. In his 1761 general encyclopedia Garsault describes a two-key F clarinet with a compass of f to e^3, which is slightly larger than the compass given by Corrette.[2] The pivotal year was 1764, when the clarinetist and composer Valentin Roeser explained how to write for a French four-key clarinet in his *Essai d'instruction à l'usage de ceux qui composent pour la clarinette et le cor*.

Roeser describes in detail the four-key clarinet compass in his treatise and divides it into three registers by means of a scale of notes (see figure 3.1). The first or fundamental register, from f to bb^1, he called the Chalumeaux (chalumeau); the second or overblown register, from b^1 to c^3, Clarinettes (clarinet); and the third, from $c\#^3$ to f^3, Aigûs (high).[3] Roeser's three-part

FIGURE 3.1   Four-key clarinet compass, Roeser, *Essai* (Paris, 1764), 3.

compass is the earliest explanation of the clarinet's registers and proved to be quite influential, since it was copied by almost all subsequent writers. Roeser also wrote a detailed description of each part of the compass.

> There are up to three types of sounds in the compass of the clarinet. The first, from the F in the small octave to the B♭ in the first octave [f to b♭¹] is called chalumeau because it is very sweet. The second, from the B natural of the first octave up to the C♯ of the third [b¹ to c♯³], is called clarion or clarinet because it is very sonorous and very brilliant. The third, which is from the D of the third octave up to F [d³ to f³], is called shrill because it is very loud and can't be played as softly as the preceding. That is why one ought never to use it in delicate passages. I could have shown some further semitones in the compass of the clarinet, but as these are very out of tune, I have considered it appropriate to leave them out.[4]

About five years later, Roeser published an important fingering chart for the French four-key clarinet corresponding to all the notes given in his *Essai* as well as four additional notes for f♯, b, g♯¹, and g³.[5] Francoeur wrote an informative treatise on how to write for wind instruments in 1772. He copies Roeser's names for the three parts of a clarinet compass from e to a³; adds one note above Roeser's *Gamme de la clarinette* to the high register, a³; and indicates most of the chromatic notes throughout.[6] In addition, Francoeur assigns two different, smaller compasses for a *premier dessus* (first part), from a to f³, and *second dessus* (second part), from f to c³ or e to d³. These smaller compasses were suggestions to composers and are similar to the tessituras or primary range of notes written for clarinets in many eighteenth-century French operas (see Chapter 4). Francoeur also lists six clarinets in G, A, B♭ or B♮, C, D, and E and gives each instrument smaller compasses for the first and second clarinet parts.[7] For the premier dessus, in every case the lowest note is c¹, while the upper note extends beyond his general description to g³ for clarinets in C and D. For the second dessus, the compass is f to c³ or d³, and for the D clarinet it is from e to e³. Incidentally, two 1765 concertos by the Bohemian composer Franz Pokorny for B♭ clarinet make use of compasses similar to Francoeur's. His Concerto in E-flat Major is designated "per il clarinetto primo" and the Concerto in B♭ Major is designated "per il clarinetto secundo." The compass of these works is c¹ to e³ for the E-flat concerto and f to c³ for the B-flat concerto.[8] Later composers of clarinet concertos, however, do not make use of Francoeur's division of compasses for two clarinets.

Although Francoeur lists a^3 as his highest note, the earliest fingering for this note appears in a fingering chart for a four-key clarinet in an edition of Corrette's flute tutor about 1773.[9] Two flute tutors by Corrette (ca. 1773) and Hotteterre (ca. 1775) include fingering charts for the four-key clarinet and oboe or bassoon fingering charts. At this time, woodwind players had to be proficient on several instruments, and these charts were helpful. Additional fingerings were added to the compass of the French four-key clarinet, such as $c\sharp^1$ by Castillon in 1776, and $g\sharp$ by Amand Vanderhagen in 1785 in his method for five-key clarinet.[10] Subsequent treatises show that these gaps in the scale were gradually completed and the upper compass extended for the five-key clarinet. In 1790, the Viennese theorist Albrechtsberger writes that a full chromatic scale from e to c^4, considered the present-day standard compass, was within the capabilities of the instrument and the player.[11] In Germany, Löbel's popular 1796 *Conversationslexicon* describes the clarinet's compass as wider in the low range than the oboe's compass, specifically from e to c^4 and d^4.[12] A later edition, titled *Conversations-Lexicon* (1814), revised the clarinet's compass to e to f^3 and criticized those who play to c^4 as excessive.[13]

In 1802, J. X. Lefèvre, in his widely used tutor, was the earliest clarinetist to designate fingerings for e to c^4.[14] The innovative French maker J. F. Simiot published a fingering chart for his seven-key clarinet along with a two-page explanation in 1808. In addition to the standard five keys, Simiot's instrument bore additional keys for an A–B trill and the note B/F$\sharp$. Surprisingly, Simiot's fingerings feature seven additional notes above Lefèvre's highest note of c^4, $c\sharp^4$ chromatically to g^4, simply to attract attention to his instruments.[15]

The fingerings used by classical clarinet players gradually became standardized during the early nineteenth century, although charts sometimes include suggestions for alternate fingerings that are more comfortable for awkward note combinations. Many instruction books merely duplicate fingerings that appeared in earlier charts.[16]

Between 1769 and 1830, tutors, instruction books, and fingering charts appeared for clarinets with four to fifteen keys. Several individual fingerings for notes on seven-, eight-, and nine-key clarinets are identical to those for the five-key clarinet. The additional keys beyond five were useful to trill from one note to another but were not used in slow passages due to questionable intonation and the unreliable operation of the keys. The development of eleven-, twelve-, and thirteen-key clarinets, which were used mostly by professional and advanced clarinetists, provided the opportunity for definite changes in fingering patterns and improvements to intonation. Clarinetists playing these instruments can use fingerings for five-key instruments, but by the 1820s, many composers were demanding more fluent technique in various tonalities. Makers such as H. Grenser, Baumann, and Koch constructed instruments with key touches shaped for easier manipulation in rapid passages and technically demanding music. As a result many players learned to play eleven-, twelve-, and thirteen-key clarinets and incorporated the new fingerings into their technique.[17]

Sources written in France account for the greatest number of fingering charts with twenty-four, followed by England (nineteen), America (eighteen), Germany (eight), Italy (three), the Netherlands (two), and Austria (one). Many of the French sources and one German source include more than one type of clarinet: for example, charts for five- and thirteen-key clarinets. Based on the numbers of charts and their origin, it is clear that the majority of fingerings were intended for English- or French-made clarinets. The American charts, all for the five-key clarinet, were mainly copied from English sources.

Basic fingerings are shared among all the charts. Despite the fact that some fingerings are country-specific, there is no evidence for a national school of clarinet fingering. Many later charts include several alternate fingerings for the same note and some of the English and French charts, modeled on *The Clarinet Instructor* (ca. 1780) and Vanderhagen's *Méthode* (ca. 1785), specify different fingerings for b and c$\sharp^1$ because of questionable intonation. French tutors such as Vanderhagen's *Méthode,* Blasius's *Nouvelle méthode* (ca. 1796), Vanderhagen's *Nouvelle méthode* (ca. 1799), and Michel's *Méthode* (ca. 1801) provide separate fingerings for the enharmonic or equivalent pitches g$\sharp^1$ and a$\flat^1$. In all the charts, the largest variety of fingerings occur above c^3; there are seventeen for d^3. Roeser offers an explanation in his *Gamme de la clarinette* (ca. 1769): "When one passes c^3 the scale is not standard, because everyone does it according to his own taste."[18] Froehlich confirms the lack of standardization for fingerings in his 1810–11 treatise.

> Due to the different construction and various manners of blowing of wind and reed instruments, there are no generally applicable rules of fingering. All one can do is give the usual fingerings and a critique on each tone, and, at the same time, to inform the student of the various manners in which the same tone can be fingered, in order to make the dark tones brighter and more sonorous, and to improve the bad ones. Consequently, one must really see to it that each player evolves the fingering for himself.[19]

The reed-below mouthpiece position used by German players apparently required an additional support or buttress finger, usually R3.[20] The German writers Backofen and Fröhlich added R3 on several fingerings in their tutors *Anweisung zur Klarinette* (ca. 1803) and *Vollständige Theoretisch-pracktische Musikschule* (ca. 1810–11). Castillon added the E/B key as a buttress fingering in his four-key fingering chart for the article "Clarinette" in the *Supplément à l'Encyclopédie* (1776). The use of this buttress finger affected the resonance and tuning of certain notes, helped to balance the instrument, eliminated unnecessary finger shifts, and facilitated smoother playing.[21]

A rare printed observation advising players on how to play difficult passages is found at the end of the third caprice of Anton Stadler's *Trois Caprices pour clarinette seule*, published about 1808. Stadler refers to alternate fingerings for a♯[1] and e♯[2] marked with an X in measures 17 and 18; because of questionable intonation, they were meant to be used in fast passages.

> If the normal a♯[1] fingering, i.e. b♭[1], seems to be too difficult at the first X mark, one may finger it like a b♮[1]. Open the long [F♯/C♯] key, the A key with the right forefinger, and open the third or g[2] finger. At the second X do not finger the e♯[2] like f[2] with the fork, but instead like f♯[2], adding the right little finger on the F/C hole.[22]

In other words, a♯[1] was fingered: SAL012/4567 F♯/C♯ E/B; e♯[2]: SL0123/56 F/C.

Five- and six-key clarinets were common from the 1760s through the 1830s; eight-, nine-, and eleven-key clarinets were played during the early nineteenth century. With the development of the twelve- and thirteen-key clarinets during the second decade of the nineteenth century and their use initially by professional players, the present-day compass of e to c[4] became firmly established. Fingerings became standard only after the mid-nineteenth century.

Embouchure and Mouthpiece Position

The French word *embouchure*, when applied to woodwinds, usually refers to the position and shape of the lips while playing; it also designates the mouthpiece of the clarinet or the head joint of the flute.[23] The earliest published instruction concerning embouchure appears in the fingering chart of an anonymous English tutor, *The Clarinet Instructor,* written about 1780 for the five-key clarinet. "Blow moderately strong the Chalumeau Notes, but for the Clarinet Notes the reed must be pinched with the Lips a little and blown a little stronger: yet be careful that the Teeth do not touch the Reed in blowing."[24]

The majority of eighteenth-century clarinetists played with the reed placed against the upper lip, explaining this author's sensible warning against impeding the reed's vibrations with the teeth. Vanderhagen, a Parisian clarinetist and flutist, offers additional embouchure directions in his important and detailed 1785 *Méthode*.

> I will say, thus, do not put the mouthpiece of the clarinet too high [into the mouth], but only up to the absence of the cut of the reed. . . . Support the mouthpiece on the teeth and cover the reed with the upper lip, in no case touching the reed with the upper teeth, because the upper teeth have to sustain and press on the upper lip in order to pinch the high tones. The lips of the mouth must close firmly for one not to lose air through the mouth.[25]

Here, Vanderhagen addresses two basic aspects of blowing: how far the mouthpiece is placed in the mouth, which affects response and tone, and the position of the lips around the mouthpiece that must be maintained in order to keep air from leaking while the player is blowing. Blasius repeats some of Vanderhagen's statements in his tutor about 1796 but is more explicit concerning the reed: "take good care that the mouthpiece nor the reed is touched by the teeth. It is necessary to support the mouthpiece on the lower lip to cover the reed with the upper lip, without the teeth touching any of it."[26]

Rather than covering only the upper teeth as Vanderhagen suggests, Blasius prefers to cover the upper and lower teeth with both lips in what modern players call the double-lip embouchure. This is the normal embouchure for the oboe and bassoon, and eighteenth-century clarinetists often played these wind instruments as well. Lefèvre also recommends the double-lip embouchure in his influential *Méthode*, written about 1802.[27] Writing about 1801, the clarinetist Michel differs with Blasius, suggesting that "one ought to rest the mouthpiece on the lower teeth, and cover the reed with the upper lip without ever allowing the upper teeth to touch it."[28] Of course, the width of the upper lip and the size and angle of the teeth contribute to an individual player's decision to use one or both lips.

These descriptions emphasize that clarinetists placed the mouthpiece and attached reed against the upper lip, contrary to the predominant present-day practice of putting them against the bottom lip—that is, the reed-above rather than the reed-below mouthpiece position. Each position affects the resonance, response, pitch, and articulation of notes differently. The majority of French and English clarinets from this period seem to require a reed-above position since the mouthpieces are small and must be rotated to align the maker's stamp with those on other sections.[29] Confirmation of the reed-above mouthpiece position appears in a number of treatises and tutors from the period. However, the body of evidence suggests that clarinetists were free to use either mouthpiece position.

A preference for one position or the other by players from different countries is evident in several published sources. For example, Roeser is the earliest to declare the French preference for the reed-above position in 1764. He advises composers not to write repeated sixteenth notes as one would do for the violin because "many repeated sixteenth notes are not employed on the clarinet since the lungs must substitute for the tongue stroke, due to the position of the reed under the roof of the mouth."[30] Roeser then illustrates repeated sixteenth notes played on the violin and a substitution of dotted half notes, quarter, and eighth notes for the clarinet. The tongue is not used to articulate; articulation is accomplished by aspirations of breath known as chest articulation. About five years later, Roeser depicts the reed-above position on the fingering chart for a four-key clarinet in his *Gamme de la clarinette*.[31]

It seems likely that the playing practices of clarinetists in Paris influenced visitors from other countries. For instance, a letter dated 31 August 1772 from Johan Miklin, music director in Linköping, Sweden, to the music historian A. A. Hülphers mentions large clarinets "used in concerts in Paris" and describes chest articulation similar to that mentioned by Roeser.

> The reed is not as on an oboe, rather over the oblong opening one puts and inserts a thin, flat wide reed. It is always stationary, is lightly pressed by the lips, but never touched by the tongue. One must so to speak puff out the wind, but it is not heavy or hard to play. The best and most accurate information about this you may obtain in Stockholm.[32]

Miklin's description of the lips pressing the reed suggests that the players used a double-lip embouchure. If the Swedish players were following current French practice then the use of chest articulation further implies the reed-above mouthpiece position. However, Miklin's description is not detailed enough to confirm this supposition.

Most French writers of subsequent methods for five- and six-key clarinets illustrate the reed-above mouthpiece position.[33] However, Pierre Bazin depicts an early example of the reed-below position in a 1780 portrait of Villement, which shows him playing a five-key clarinet with what appears to be a reed-below mouthpiece position.[34]

The Norwegian bandmaster Berg made the earliest recommendation for the use of the reed-below position in his 1782 treatise:

> If you want the clarinet to sound good, you must not put the mouthpiece too far into your mouth, as it must otherwise shriek like a happy goose. Instead, the reed is placed on the lower lip, and in this manner you force it with the breath to produce a pleasant sound and tone, using the tongue to separate the notes at your discretion.[35]

Berg emphasizes that a player may use the tongue to separate the notes using this type of mouthpiece position. When the tongue is used with the reed-above position, the feel and response are somewhat different.

A few years later, several German writers acknowledged or advocated the use of the reed-below position. About 1803, the German clarinetist Heinrich Backofen mentioned both positions but did not advocate one in particular. "By the way, whether it is better while playing to place the reed against the upper or lower lip—which clarinetists call on top or underneath—I have no preference. I have heard good people play in both manners. Here, what one is used to is most important."[36] Backofen's fingering charts illustrate a clarinet with a reed-above mouthpiece position. However, C. F. Michaelis makes a much stronger statement in preference for the reed-below position in an 1808 issue of the *AMZ*.

> In order for the clarinet to become a connoisseur's instrument . . . it is first necessary that one cease to play with the reed on top as the

French still do in their methods. Admittedly, one may then lose the extreme high register, but on the other hand, one gains—may I say—the entire instrument. Even the playing position is more difficult according to the former method and gives to the head a disagreeable angle of inclination. But, how is it possible to form a smooth and tender sound if one touches the fibrous reed with his teeth? In this way . . . a harsh sound must unavoidably issue forth.[37]

Michaelis was convinced that tone improved with the reed-below position. He also observed that the player had to hold the instrument at a wider angle, about 60 degrees away from the body, when using the reed-above position.

Two years later Joseph Fröhlich described the advantages and disadvantages of each mouthpiece position in his detailed treatise.

There are two ways of playing the clarinet, one, by having the reed on top, the other by having it on the bottom of the mouthpiece. In the latter, the player has more advantage in articulation with the tongue attacking, for example, in faster passages; but the disadvantage is that he cannot play with equal quality, nor with changes from high to low, as anyone who knows the nature of the clarinet can understand. In the first method, the tongue cannot be securely and precisely used; also, since there is a certain whistling of air, the tone cannot be correctly formed and does not achieve sonorous quality. And those who believe that without tonguing [i.e., with the reed-below position] no lively, energetic performance is possible, err the more, as they seem to misjudge the real goal of all instrumentalists, especially the clarinetist, which is to equal the singer.[38]

Fröhlich favors the reed-below position in this description, although he stresses that fine results may be achieved with the reed-above position and later cites an example of the excellent playing of the Würzburg court clarinetist Phillip Meissner. He notes that with the reed-above position, the tongue cannot be securely used and the tone quality does not achieve a sonorous quality. However, he illustrates the reed-above position in his fingering chart.

Additional evidence for the optional use of either mouthpiece position in Germany and neighboring countries is the rarity of maker's stamps on eighteenth-century clarinet mouthpieces made in Germany, Austria, and Bohemia.[39] An important exception noted by Hoeprich is a five-key B♭ clarinet (CH-Genève, IM 136) by Theodor Lotz, the maker of Anton Stadler's first basset clarinet. All the joints of Lotz's five-key instrument are stamped, including the mouthpiece, where the stamp is on the side opposite the reed. When all the stamps are aligned the clarinet must be played with the reed-below position.

The reed-below mouthpiece position became more popular throughout Europe during the late eighteenth and early nineteenth centuries, thanks to the influence of German virtuoso players. For instance, Fétis reports that during the 1780s, the virtuoso Josef Beer heard the sweet tone quality produced by a German clarinetist named Schwartz, which prompted him to change his style of playing (probably adopting the reed-below position).[40] The important German virtuoso and teacher Franz Tausch probably also used the reed-below mouthpiece position. Gerber describes his soft and colorful tone quality. "What versatility in gradation of tone! At one moment the low whisper of leaves borne along by the soft breath of the zephyr; at another his instrument soared above all others in a torrent of brilliant arpeggios."[41]

If Tausch did play with the reed-below position, he would have taught this method to his students at the Berlin Wind Conservatory, who included the well-known virtuosi and composers Bernhard Crusell and Heinrich Baermann. Yet, a fingering chart in Vanderhagen's *Methodé*, published about 1819, includes an engraving of a twelve-key clarinet used by Baermann during his highly successful 1818 concerts in Paris with the reed-above mouthpiece position.[42] However, this illustration may simply reflect the prevailing French taste rather than indicating how Baermann played.

The earliest writer to illustrate the reed-below position was the clarinetist and inventor Iwan Müller. Müller moved to Paris in 1811 in order to promote and build his instrument. His *Gamme pour la nouvelle clarinette*, published by Simrock about 1812, shows the first model of Müller's thirteen-key clarinet. Nine years later, Müller strongly advocated the reed-below position in his extensive and thorough method.

> There are several reasons . . . to prefer the reed supported by the lower lip: First, the right thumb becomes useful for fingering because it no longer is needed to support the clarinet. . . . Second, one has the advantage of being able to put a small piece of heavy paper over the lower teeth, and thus prevent the lip from becoming cut, as those who put the reed on top can scarcely avoid. Finally, the performer is not obliged to contract his muscles, and by so doing, to disfigure his facial characteristics [i.e. with the reed-above position], because the upper lip is too small to be able naturally to cover the teeth. This last reason is not the least; in fact, the performer ought to search carefully to avoid anything that might arouse a disagreeable or painful sensation in the listener.[43]

During the 1820s several leading French players, such as Franco Dacosta, Gabriel Péchignier, and Jacques Bouffil, adopted the thirteen-key clarinet[44] and may have been playing with the reed-above mouthpiece position. In the 1824 edition of his tutor, Backofen was particularly critical of players who adopted Müller's thirteen-key clarinet and played with the reed-above position because he believed that they could not use Müller's keys for the right thumb without disturbing the position of their mouthpiece.[45]

Subsequently, French authors of clarinet methods, such as Rybicki about 1826 and Vaillant about 1828, illustrated the reed-above position for the five-key clarinet and the reed-below position for the thirteen-key instrument. The Czech clarinetist Blatt published a bilingual German-French method in Paris about 1828 that illustrates the reed-below position in his charts for six-, nine-, and twelve-key clarinets. In his method of 1829, Carnaud noted both mouthpiece positions, preferring the reed-below but illustrating the reed-above for six- and thirteen-key clarinets.[46] In 1829, Fétis strongly advocated the reed-below position to the French clarinetist.

> In France, the oboes, flutes and bassoons leave nothing to be desired. The clarinet is less successfully cultivated, although we have many commendable artists for their talent. Our inferiority in this genre, in regard to Germany, is due to a vicious system that our clarinetists have adopted as far as the position of the reed in the mouth, where force is applied to the reeds. In Germany, where the clarinet is cultivated with much success, the mouthpiece of the instrument is placed in the mouth of the player in a way that the reed is placed on the lower lip; in France, it is the contrary and the reed is placed on top. The advantages of the German manner are evident; that the lower lip is much better in softness and smoothness then the upper, the tongue is not able to punctuate but compelled to go up with the French manner.[47]

Again, in 1830, Fétis asserted that "the German clarinetists are incontestably superior to the French." He admits the French play in a brilliant manner, but says they lack the sweetness and soft qualities of tone produced by the German players. Fétis attributes this lack of quality to the powerful and voluminous tone production of the French and their use of the reed-above position.[48] These criticisms must have prompted some French players to adopt the German reed-below position and tone production.

In England, most clarinetists played with the double-lip embouchure and reed-above mouthpiece position until about 1830, when mouthpieces became larger to accommodate longer reeds.[49] It is generally easier to use the reed-above position on small English mouthpieces than with larger German, French, or Austrian mouthpieces. The English soloist Mahon states in his tutor of about 1803 that "the Mouthpiece of the Clarionet must not be put so far in the mouth as the tying of the Reed, which must be upwards, the Teeth should not touch the Reed."[50] Hopkinson, an early English advocate of the reed-below position, wrote a tutor about 1814 stating, "Opinions vary considerably on the proper manner of applying the reed; foreigners play with it downwards, the contrary is practiced in England; for a Dilettante i.e. a non Professional Performer I must acknowledge I give the Preference to the first method."[51]

The famous English clarinetist Thomas Willman advocates both techniques in his method of 1826.[52] Subsequently, an anonymous author in *Metzler and Son's Clarinet Preceptor*, published about 1825, observes that "some play with the Reed pressing against the lower lip—but the general mode is the reverse—viz: the reed up."[53] American clarinetists also played with the reed-above position until about 1840 since the vast majority of their clarinets were modeled after English examples.[54]

Articulation

A rticulation, an essential element in delineating melodic lines and emphasizing the beginnings of phrases, is the separation of notes achieved by the player using the breath and chest along with the tongue. During articulation the tip or middle of the tongue may touch the reed or back of the mouthpiece, depending on the position of the mouthpiece. Eighteenth- and nineteenth-century composers did not always specify articulations such as detached (staccato) or connected (legato) notes; in these cases, the player decided the articulation. By the early nineteenth century, composers were using more articulation in printed parts in order to mark musical phrases, just as a writer creates sentences and paragraphs with the use of particular words, pauses, and punctuation marks.

About 1785 Vanderhagen wrote the earliest instructions about how to achieve articulation, utilizing two letters. When the notes are not marked with articulation (*coup de langue ordinaire*) the player should pronounce the voiced consonant "d"; for notes marked with short dots (*détaché*), the unvoiced consonant "t" is utilized. When slurring pairs of notes (*coulé*), Vanderhagen suggests the first of each pair be given a little more emphasis. A fourth marking, the wedge (*piqué*), is the shortest of the tongue strokes.[55] In order to sound these letters, the tongue moves to different positions, thereby creating the long or short articulation sounds. In one of his examples, Vanderhagen specifies three types of tonguing as legato, short staccato, and accented staccato (see figure 3.2).[56] Legato or slurring is a smooth motion between notes supported by a continuous air stream without articulation.

In the second edition of his tutor, written about 1799, Vanderhagen suggests "té" instead of the earlier-recommended "d," and "tu" instead of "t." Notes are marked to indicate the accented or short staccatos with either a vertical stroke, a wedge, or a dot. The vertical stroke on a downbeat indicates a longer and more marked staccato than the dot, which signifies a shorter and less accented articulation. If the vertical stroke does not appear on a downbeat, the note is played short, similar to the dot.[57]

FIGURE 3.2   Three types of tonguing, Vanderhagen, *Méthode* (Paris, ca. 1785), 8.

FIGURE 3.3   Throat articulations, Vanderhagen, *Méthode* (Paris, ca. 1785), 9.

During his discussion of slurred groups of triplets, Vanderhagen also advocates the use of the throat rather than the tongue: "to mark them off three by three, one must make the first felt by a small expression from the throat, not by a small tongue stroke. For the first [note], over-emphasised by a tongue stroke, would positively sound like [a piqué followed by a coulé]" (see figure 3.3).[58] Evidently, it was second nature for Vanderhagen to use either tongue or throat articulations while playing.

A third type of articulation, previously unmentioned, appears in contemporary English instruction books. An anonymous author implies that the diaphragm creates the articulation as air is expelled. A tutor of about 1785 shows the vertical stroke and dot as staccato marks, explaining that the notes "must be played in a very spirited and distinct manner." The duration of each note in the example is one-half its written value. The only distinction between the vertical stroke and dot staccatos is the word "soft" below the notes with dots above them.[59]

German writers also provide instruction concerning articulation. Backofen describes three means for articulating notes: with the tongue, lips (diaphragm), or throat. He favors the use of the tongue, since using the lips creates an "ugly grimace" (*hässliche Grimace*), and "even if the musician does not grimace when he produces the notes with the throat, there is something else that is unpleasant, the [glottal] stop in the throat that is audible with every note."[60] Backofen also describes two additional articulation markings not mentioned by Vanderhagen. "If, over several notes a tie is placed in addition to the dots . . . then they are somewhat separated by a gentle attack of the tongue, but the tone is in no way interrupted. More forceful attacks of the tongue in an uninterrupted melody are designated [with dashes under a tie]."[61]

Fröhlich advocates a diaphragm aspiration for clarinetists who play with the reed-above position. They "must pronounce an easy and light syllable 'ha,' which need only be done somewhat more strongly in the lower register, the performance of which can also be aided with the lips [diaphragm]. Those who play with the reed-below position can use the syllable tü or tu."[62] Fröhlich advises the reed-above-position players, when slurring a group of notes, to keep the lips slightly apart while pronouncing the "ha" syllable. A short staccato, notated with a wedge, is produced with the lips held together pronouncing "ha," and a softer staccato, notated with a dot or small line, is played with the lips held together, as when slurring.[63]

In summary, during the late eighteenth and early nineteenth centuries, composers wrote three types of articulation: the tongue stroke (using the

voiced consonant "d" and the unvoiced consonant "t"); the throat or glot-
tal stop; and the diaphragm aspiration (using "ha").

Selection of a Clarinet

During the 1760s and 1770s, clarinets were made in nine different nominal pitches of G (the pitch of the clarinet d'amour), A, B♭, B♮, C, D, E♭,
E, and F.[64] An orchestral player would most often need a B♭ clarinet with
corps de réchange or extra finger hole joints for tuning in A and a C clarinet
with corps in B♮. The higher-pitched clarinets and clarinets d'amour were
only occasionally required in orchestral and chamber music. Instruments in
different nominal pitches made it easier to cope with difficulties encoun-
tered in both fingering and intonation when playing music written in various tonalities with a four-key clarinet. According to Roeser, the tonalities
easiest to play were F and C major, and D and G minor.[65] Indeed, the author
has verified that works written in tonalities with more than one flat or one
sharp often present serious difficulties in both fingering and intonation of
the low register. Performing in other tonalities is possible but practical only
at slow speeds because of the awkward fingerings.

In his instructions to composers on the transposition of clarinets and
the easiest tonalities, Roeser writes a scale, identifies the nominal pitch of the
clarinets, and provides a corresponding scale on the viola or violin. He also
writes four-bar examples in a short score with the same notes written for
first and second clarinets, violin, and bass. Examples are given for clarinets
in A, B♭, C, D, and E.[66] Francoeur provides four-bar examples, identifies the
nominal pitch, and provides a short score with the same notes written for
first and second violins and a bass part. The nominal pitch of the transposing clarinets is written and indicated with a second clef in the margin, preceding the example written in treble clef. Francoeur suggests that the composer indicate the sounding pitch by using a clef in the margin but notes
that the clarinetist should play the notes as written.[67] His clarinets in G, A,
B♭, B♮, C, D, and E (which incorporate Roeser's) include a number, nominal pitch of each clarinet, written tonalities, and sounding tonalities.

Roeser also recognizes the different tonal qualities of differently pitched
instruments. For example, he states that the clarinet in G is the sweetest
type, and that the clarinets in D and E are more brilliant and sonorous than
the clarinet in A. The high-pitched instruments in E and F are only for special effects in loud orchestral scenes in operas. Francoeur and La Borde subsequently added two clarinets in B♮ and E♭ to his list.[68]

Table 3.1 shows the pitches of clarinets recommended by Francoeur for
different tonalities. It shows that the clarinetist almost always uses a part
written in the transposed tonalities of C and F major, the easiest to negotiate
when playing a four- or five-key clarinet. Roeser and Francoeur state that a
C clarinet may be used to play in the tonalities of B-flat and E-flat major, but

TABLE 3.1
Pitches of clarinets recommended for different tonalities by Francoeur (1772)

Example number[1]	Nominal pitch	Written tonality[2]	Sounding tonality[3]
1	G	C	G
2	D	F	D
3	A	C	A
4	E	F	A
5	B♭	C	B♭
6	C	B♭	B♭
6b	F	F	B♭
7	B♮	C	B
8	E	G	B
9	C	C	C
10	G	F	C
11	D	C	D
12	A	F	D
13	C	E♭	E♭
14	B♭	F	E♭
15	E	C	E
15g	B♮	F	E
16	A	G	E
17	C	F	F
17j	F	C	F
18	C	g	g
19	A	c	a
19k	D	g	a
20	A	d	b
21	B♭	d	c
22	C	d	d
23	A	g	e
24	B♭	g	F

1. These are numbered examples illustrating the recommended clarinets for specific tonalities in Francoeur, *Diapason général*, 26–30, 32–33. Letters refer to clarinets suggested in Francoeur's footnotes to these examples.

2. The clarinet part in Francoeur's example 8 (p. 27) was incorrectly transposed to G, a whole step too high. The clarinet parts in Francoeur's example 19 (p. 32) omitted the key signature of three flats.

3. Upper-case letters represent major tonalities; lower-case, minor.

the parts are technically more demanding. G major may be played on an A clarinet and is an easy tonality. In B-flat and E major, the B♭ and A clarinets, respectively, are used instead of the less common small F and E clarinets because, again, these high-pitched instruments are used only in the orchestra for very loud works.[69] According to Francoeur, E-flat major is a very difficult key to play in, and the composer rarely uses B major. For minor keys, the clarinetist usually plays in D and G minor, the parallel keys to F and B-flat major. The exceptions to the rule are G minor for the C clarinet and C minor for the A clarinet.[70] The clarinets most often played are pitched in A, B♭ or B♮, C, and D.[71]

In a letter to Hülphers dated 31 August 1772, the Swedish music director Miklin clearly states his preference for the tone quality of the lower-pitched clarinets (probably in B♭ and A):

> The larger clarinets, which are used in concerts in Paris, sound infi-nitely better than the clarinets [i.e. the two-key instruments] that are used at the regiments, as they don't screech so. But the larger ones are delightful, owing to the fact that one can so easily play forte and piano and the lower chalumeau notes. They have many long brass keys for both hands.[72]

In Paris, Miklin may have heard B♭ or A clarinets played in chamber music or operas by La Borde such as *Annette et Lubin* (1762) and *Gilles, garçon pein-tre* (performed in 1767). By the 1760s, these lower-pitched clarinets with four or five keys were gaining in popularity due to their mellow tone quality, greater flexibility of dynamics, and the lower notes within their compass.

Castillon wrote an important article in 1776 about the popular French four-key clarinet in Robinet's *Supplément à l'Encyclopédie*. His clarinet was pitched in A and had two middle joints or corps de réchange for tuning to B♭. Castillon supports Roeser and Francoeur's conclusions that the sound-ing tonalities of A and D major, played in C and F major, are the easiest tonalities in which to play technically demanding passages. In like manner, difficult passages on the B♭ clarinet in the sounding tonalities of B-flat and E-flat major are played in C and F major.

During this period most English clarinetists were not familiar with the A clarinet. The anonymous English author of *The Clarinet Instructor* (ca. 1780)—the first known tutor for the five-key clarinet—knew only clarinets pitched in B♭ and C.

> As Pieces of Music are composed in different Keys, in which Clar-inets can play in Concert with other Instruments; it is necessary to have two Clarinets, one a B.[-flat] the other a C. [T]he B.[-flat] Clar-inet must be used if the Peice [*sic*] is in the Key of E.[-flat] or B.[-flat] and the C. Clarinet if it is in the Key of F. or C. [I]n [these] four Keys, B.[-flat] C. E.[-flat] and F.[,] Pieces of Music most commo[n]ly are, when Clarinets join in Concert.[73]

This description as well as five others in similar English tutors help to doc-ument the fact that the C and B♭ clarinets were the most popular in England during the late eighteenth century.[74] This fact is supported by a large num-ber of extant English five-key C clarinets. However, the A clarinet was re-quired by a few composers working in England. In 1777 in London, Tom-maso Giordani was the first to use the A clarinet in the pasticcio *Le due contesse*, followed three years later by Antonio Sacchini in *Armida*. Furthermore, about 1789 the English composer Samuel Wesley refers, in his manuscript devoted to musical instruments, to three clarinets pitched in C, B♭, and A.[75] The A clarinet was infrequently used in England until after 1800.

By about 1799 in France, the D clarinet was no longer in use, according to Vanderhagen.[76] The normal practice, as reported by the clarinetists Blasius about 1796 and Lefèvre about 1802, was to use two clarinets with additional middle joints to change the pitch from B♭ to A and C to B♮.[77] Lefèvre advocates using these clarinets in every major (except G♭)and minor tonality. In a section concerning transposition in his tutor, he provides musical examples of all twenty-four major and minor tonalities divided among and written for the C, B♮, B♭, and A clarinets.[78] Table 3.2 shows the clarinets recommended by Lefèvre for different tonalities. He indicates that the clarinetist should be able to play in D, E-flat, and B-flat major as well as their parallel minor tonalities. Besides the use of the B♮ clarinet in E major, Vanderhagen specifies the use of the B♮ clarinet for B major, as well as the parallel tonalities of G-sharp and C-sharp minor.[79]

Writing in 1785, Vanderhagen makes a distinction between the B♭ and B♮ clarinets in his tutor by labeling them respectively "clarinette en Si" and "clarinette en Mi♯."[80] In the second edition of this tutor, he calls the latter clarinet the "clarinette en Mi majeur," evidently referring to its use in the sounding key of E major. "The clarinet in mi majeur has a corps in E which is put on the clarinet in C. . . . This clarinet is a semitone lower than the clarinet in C. . . . Consequently, it is necessary to play or write a semitone higher than for the violin."[81]

Toward the end of the eighteenth century, pitch letters were stamped on clarinets in order to distinguish between different corps. In 1800 the Italian writer Carlo Gervasoni explained that for convenience in playing in various keys, clarinets are marked on their middle joints as "Clarinetto in B fa" and "Clarinetto in E la fa" to indicate B♭ and B♮.[82] In 1813, Francesco Antolini gave a fuller explanation of these markings on the middle joints of the clarinets in C, B♮, B♭, and A.

> Note that the manufacturers are accustomed to mark each section of the clarinet with the letter of the key in which it is constructed. That in C carries the letter C, because the c^2 fingering actually produces the c^2. That in B♭ carries the letter B, because the fingering for c^2 actually produces the $b♭^1$. The corps in A carries the letter A. . . . Only the corps in B♮ is not named for the note produced by its c^2 fingering (which produces the said b♮), but instead, for the fingering for f^2 which produces e^2. It is marked by all manufacturers in this manner: = E. ♯ =.
>
> I believe that this distinction cannot have any other purpose than to prevent the confusion that could arise if this joint were marked with the letter B, between it and the clarinet in B♭, which is also

TABLE 3.2
Pitches of clarinets recommended for different tonalities by Lefèvre (1802)

Nominal pitch of clarinet	Sounding tonality	Written tonality
C or B♭	C	C or D
C or B♭	a	a or b
C or B♭	F	F or G
C or B♭	d	d or e
C	G	G
C	e	E
C or B♭	B♭	B♭ or C
C or B♭	g	g or a
C or A	D	D or F
C or B♮ or A	b	b, c, or d
B♮	g♯	A
B♮ or A	E	F or G
B♮ or A	C♯	d or e
B♮	F♯	G
B♮	d♯	e or b
B♮	C♯	D
B♮	A♯	B
B♮ or A	A	B♭ or C
B♮ or A	f♯	g or a
B♭	E♭	F
B♭	c	D
B♭	A♭	B♭
B♭	f	G
B♭	D♭	E♭
B♭	B♭	C
B♭	e♭	F
A	B	D
A	g♯	B
A	G♭	B♭
A	E♭	G

marked with the letter B. This confusion, however, would be avoided
easily if only the clarinet in B♭ were marked not merely with B
(which strictly speaking means b♮, not b♭), but as = B♭ =, and then
marking the piece in b♮ with B alone.[83]

Jeltsch reports the existence of a very rare B♮ corps stamped "E" with a C
clarinet by the Parisian maker Nicolas Viennen (F-private collection). A
corps de réchange in B stamped "E♯," corresponding to Antolini's description of 1813, is not known.

Although corps de réchange were made from the 1770s through the
1840s, few are extant. Because of the expense, only a few professional clar-

inetists owned a set of C and B♭ clarinets with corps. Only four complete sets are known today, made by the Parisian makers Baumann about 1800 and Roche (Paris) after 1802. All the sets include C clarinets with a common stock and bell and corps of a barrel, right- and left-hand sections for changing to a B♮ clarinet, and B♭ clarinets with a common stock and bell and corps for tuning to A. In the photograph by Ross of the Basel five-key set (CH-Basel, 1966.89), the clarinets are in a case but their mouthpieces appear to be missing.[84] The Paris five-key set (F-Paris, E. 980.2.118, E. 980.2.123) consists of C and B♭ instruments with corps for B♮ and A instruments. Each section of the six-key set (F-Le Mans) with a C♯/G♯ key and corps (but not the black wood mouthpieces) is stamped "C, H, B, and A" to indicate the nominal pitches of C, B♮, B♭, and A. The shared sections are the stock and bell of the C and B♭ clarinets. All sets have extensions on the key shanks for the E/B and F♯/C♯ keys.[85]

At this time in Germany, the use of corps de réchange for changing the tonality of the clarinet seems to have become less common. For instance, according to H. C. Koch in 1802, clarinets pitched in C, B♭, and A were employed in the orchestra and in Harmonie, with the B♭ instrument the most commonly played.[86] In his tutor about 1803, Backofen recommends the use of the B♭ clarinet to the student rather than, "like the French, a C clarinet," since it is a good compromise between the C and A instruments.[87] The writer Michaelis, however, prefers the A clarinet as the main instrument because it has the most beautiful tone quality of these three clarinets.[88] None of the German sources mentions additional middle joints.

One English author explains the popularity of the B♭ clarinet: "The C, B[♭], and A clarionets are those chiefly used in orchestras; of these, the B♭ is the favourite with both composers and performers, for the tone is more mellow than the C, and the instrument not so large, or difficult to finger, as the A clarionet."[89] Catrufo reported in 1834 that in France, three clarinets in C, B♭, and A replaced the use of corps.[90]

In summary, during the 1760s and 1770s the composer had as many as nine clarinets at his disposal. The preferred clarinet was easily playable in C or F major, although tonalities with up to three flats (E-flat major) were possible. By 1800, players could play in any tonality with the use of clarinets in C, B♮, B♭, and A. Some makers constructed sets of instruments with corps de réchange, and professional clarinetists recommended them. Beginning in the early nineteenth century, clarinetists and composers relied on three instruments, in C, B♭, and A. to play in an ever-widening palette of tonalites.

Transposition

In the 1760s, composers began to use the term "chalumeau" or "chal." to indicate that a particular passage written in the upper or clarinet register should be played an octave lower, that is, in the chalumeau register. Similarly, "clarinette" or "clar." is employed to indicate when transposition is to be discontinued and the notes are to be played in the normal manner. In addition to these terms, sometimes a line above the notes in the clarinet parts would indicate the beginning and end of the portion to be transposed. This convention of octave transposition avoids the need to write ledger lines under the staff for notes below e.

The earliest known musical example using these designations is Pokorny's 1765 Concerto in B-flat Major. In measures 143–48 of the first movement of the manuscript clarinet part, there are two variations of the notation. Originally, these measures were written in the treble clef, with the word "Shale" (an abbreviation for Shalumeau or Schalümo) at the beginning of the line to specify that the six notes of the first half of the measure, written as c^2 descending to e^1, are to be played an octave lower (see figure 3.4a). Most of the remaining notes of these five measures are written too low for this octave transposition. The first version in Pokorny's manuscript is crossed out and a second, with some changes in the choice of notes, is written in the bass clef, in the lower margin of the score next to the word "vi-de" (see figure 3.4b). The designation "Clarin" found at the beginning of this second version can only mean that these notes are to be played an octave higher, since most of them are below the compass of the clarinet. Interestingly, the second version of these five measures includes two low e's, a note that does not appear elsewhere in this concerto. Perhaps the e was omitted in the first version because of the questionable intonation of this note on clarinets of this period.[91]

Köster's definition of clarinet in the 1781 *Deutsche Encyclopädie* acknowledges octave transposition by stating that "when playing the chalmeau [register] a C clarinet goes up to e^1 and [descends] two tones lower than the violin,"[92] thus describing the notes from e to e^1 as chalumeau notes. Vanderhagen also identifies these notes as the chalumeau register suggesting that the student use them to test the playing response of the reed.[93] The earliest published explanation of the use of the word *chalumeau* to indicate transposition down by one octave appears in the first edition of a Dutch music

FIGURE 3.4   "Shale" and "Clarin" abbreviations in the manuscript of Pokorny, Concerto in B-flat major (1765), from Titus, "The Solo Music," 171.

dictionary by Reynvaan in 1789. "Whenever one finds this term written in a clarinet part, it denotes that one should play that passage, next to which it is found, one octave lower. This being the pitch of the chalumeau, and being done in order to prevent the use of the bass clef, which would otherwise have to be used."[94] Reynvaan's mention of the term chalumeau reflects the earlier German practice, as shown in Pokorny's 1765 Clarinet Concerto in B-flat Major.

Blasius was the earliest writer to explain both terms concerning octave transposition: "In clarinet music there is a word used called *Chalumeau*. This word means to transpose or to play a passage one octave lower. When music is written under the word *Clarinette*, the clarinetist plays the notes as written."[95] At this point in his tutor, Blasius gives a one-line example using both terms and the actual sounding notes when transposed.[96] A few years after Blasius's tutor was published, Backofen explained octave transposition by equating the use of the bass clef for the lowest notes of the basset horn, written g to C but sounding an octave higher, with the use of the term "chal." for the clarinet.[97]

Aside from octave transposition, the earliest published evidence that players transposed their parts at sight from the sounding pitch is in Francoeur's 1772 treatise. He states that in the absence of other clarinets, the composer can use the C clarinet to play in all major or minor tonalities, but he must avoid difficult passages in the minor tonalities.[98] In his instrumentation treatise of about twenty years later, Vandenbrœck proposes the use of the C, B♮, B♭, and A clarinets for many of the same tonalities given by Roeser and Francoeur. He also explains the usual practice of French composers:

> Nevertheless, most composers omit all the flats and sharps of the key signature [and] the musicians are [therefore] obliged to know all the key signatures and their transpositions. We have musicians who find themselves very embarrassed when it is necessary to transpose, and others for which it is not troublesome, because they had made it a frequent habit.[99]

Writing about 1801, Michel prefers to play the B♭ clarinet, transposing when necessary because "it is lower by one tone than [the clarinet] in C, which introduces the necessity of transposing in order to correspond in unison to the violins, but this slight inconvenience disappears in front of all good musicians, who find an advantageous compensation in its more beautiful and vigorous tone and much more facility in fingering."[100] Michel must have been referring to the technical facility of playing the B♭ clarinet when transposing in tonalities with more than one flat. He also observes the usefulness of the C clarinet: "it is good, however, to know how to play in all the pitches with one clarinet in C because of sharp and flat modulations that one can encounter in a piece of music."[101] Michel's comments imply that professional clarinetists usually played as much as possible with the C clarinet, refraining from the use of corps de rechange. The scarcity of extant corps, especially those for the B♮ clarinet, substantiates this viewpoint.

An English author writing about 1830 was convinced it was necessary to have three clarinets in C, B♭, and A, particularly when one was requested to transpose parts for the convenience of singers.

> What then must be the situation of the instrumentalist, when a vocalist turns round in an orchestra, requesting the song to be played in F (the key Miss Paton has sung it in), or in E with four sharps, or even D with two sharps? (Catalani's key.) Were it not for the C or A clarionets being ready at hand, and the aptitude of the performer at transposition, the result must be anything but harmonious. Singers ought to be aware of this.[102]

In summary, a number of eighteenth- and early-nineteenth-century composers use the terms "chalumeau" to start transposition an octave lower and "clarinette" to revert to playing the notes in the original octave. Francoeur, Vandenbrœck, and Michel advocate the transposition of music by the use of several clarinets. Clarinets pitched in B♭ are preferred in flat tonalities and those in C for sharp tonalities, although instruments pitched in A and B♮ are also considered useful for transposing in sharp tonalities. By the early nineteenth century, three clarinets—in C, B♭, and A—were considered essential for transposing many tonalities required by a composer or a singer's transpositions.

Notation of Parts and Clefs

Several eighteenth-century composers specify the clarinet in scores as an optional instrument. The earliest examples include a Symphony in E-flat Major by Johann Stamitz from a collection called *La melodia germanica*, published in 1758 by Venier (Paris), the title page of which states that "in place of clarinets, one may play [the parts] with two oboes, flutes or violins."[103] Rameau indicates an alternate use of oboe for the clarinet parts in the autograph score to *Les Boréades*, his 1764 *tragédie en musique*.[104] In fact, many eighteenth- and early-nineteenth-century opera scores contain the clarinet in C and oboe parts on one line, although in some scores the clarinets emerge as a distinct voice in short solo sections. By the 1780s it is unusual for the flute to be named as an alternate instrument for the clarinet, as found in Framery's 1781 opera *L'infante de Zamora*, a parody of Paisiello's 1774 *La frascatana*.[105] On 30 September 1786, Mozart sent to his friend Sebastian Winter several works for performance by the court orchestra of Duke Joseph Maria Benedikt of Fürstenberg at Donaueschingen. One of the works was Mozart's Piano Concerto in A Major, K. 488, about which Mozart wrote: "The Concert in A includes two clarinetti—If you should not have two clarinetists at your court, a good copyist could transpose these parts into the appropriate keys in which the first part is played by a violin and the second part by a viola."[106] The practical nature of Mozart's advice is obvious and in other works clarinet parts, when players were not available, were un-doubtedly transposed and played on substitute instruments.

Even though Roeser, Francoeur, and Castillon advise the composer to indicate which tonality is required for the clarinet at the beginning of a piece, in fact there was a mixture of practices, no single one of which pre-vailed until the 1830s.[107] Composers used four distinct notation methods in scores and clarinet parts: (1) using a clef to indicate transposition; (2) trans-posing the part but not indicating the nominal pitch; (3) writing a direction for transposition in the part; and (4) not indicating a transposition but in-structing or expecting a copyist to transpose the part or the clarinetist to transpose by sight.

Rameau was the earliest composer to use clefs to indicate transposition for the two and three-key baroque clarinet. In the Entrée section of the sec-ond act of his *Acante et Céphise* (1751), he uses two clefs at the beginning of the section: a treble clef in F major followed by a soprano clef in D major.[108] The players use an A clarinet to play the treble clef part in F major; the com-poser or score reader reads the part with the soprano clef in D major for convenience when viewing it in relation to other parts. Later in act 2, D clar-inets in the aria "L'amour est heureux" are provided with transposed parts using two clefs: a treble clef in C major followed by an alto clef in D major.[109] The transposed part with a treble clef in C is played on a D clarinet, whereas the alto clef indicates the untransposed notes in relation to the other parts in the D major score.

A later example of clef notation, probably for the five-key classical clar-inet, appears in *Orione* (1763), J. C. Bach's first opera written in England. In the D major overture, Bach transposes parts for the first and second D clar-inets but notates the music with an alto clef (see figure 3.5). At the beginning of the parts is the pitch indication "in D." Each part is transposed for a D clarinet, and presumably the players were comfortable playing the music with the alto clef notation. These technically simple parts are limited in compass from c^1 to g^2 and c^1 to e^2 and were played on D clarinets by read-ing the part with a treble clef and playing in C major. The use of the alto clef is very rare and does not occur in later works by Bach.[110] However, during the nineteenth century G. Weber (1829) and F. Bellini (1844) recommend the alto clef for clarinet transposition.[111]

Italian composers were among the first to use different clefs to indicate transposition. For example, the earliest appearance of the tenor clef in clar-inet parts is in Matia Vento's first London opera, *Demofoonte* (1765).[112] In a recitative and the duetto that follow the E-flat major aria "Misero pargo-letto," there are two clarinet parts written with tenor clef in F major (see fig-ure 3.6). The parts are transposed and carry a key signature appropriate for the B♭ clarinet, one whole step lower than flutes, oboes, and violins. How-ever, Vento did not indicate the nominal pitch of the clarinet as Bach had done in *Orione*, which suggests that players were trained to play tenor clef parts on B♭ clarinets. In 1766, Vento again uses the tenor clef to designate B♭

FIGURE 3.5   Alto clef notation in Bach, *Orione* (London, 1763), first clarinet part.
Courtesy of the University of California at Berkeley, Music Library.

FIGURE 3.6   Tenor clef notation in Vento, *Demofoonte* (London, 1765), 1, clarinet parts. Courtesy of the University of California at Los Angeles, Music Library.

clarinets in five arias, all in E-flat major (transposed to F major), in *Sofon-isba.*

Soprano clefs are occasionally used in operas to indicate the transposition required for A clarinets. Examples include Salieri's *Tarare* (1787) in an A-flat major aria transposed to F major, and Paer's *L'intrigo amoroso* (1795) in an A major aria transposed to C major.[113] In the autograph score of *Tancredi* (1812), Rossini uses both a soprano clef in the margin of the score and a treble clef at the beginning of the clarinet parts in the E major "Aria Amenaide." This aria is transposed for A clarinets.[114] The first clef is used by the score reader and the second by the players,[115] a reversal of order from Rameau's *Acante et Céphise*. Gossett mentions that the clarinet parts are marked "Clarinetti in Alamiré" (clarinets in A) but suggests the clarinets for this aria are actually pitched in C because of the indication "Clarinetti in C" in the parts of another version of the opera.[116] Of course, it is possible that in later versions performed during the 1820s or 1830s, clarinetists could have played the part on a C clarinet, particularly a thirteen-key instrument. The clarinetists in the earliest 1812 performances, however, would likely have used five-key A clarinets.

Francoeur's use in 1772 of seven clefs (baritone, tenor, mezzo-tenor, mezzo-soprano, alto, soprano, and French violin) in his transposition examples was mentioned earlier in the section on clarinet selection. However, these clefs are meant as an aid to the composer and are not recommended for use in playing parts. Kollmann represents the German and English practices when he states that the G clef is used for clarinets.[117] Backofen, who was exposed to Italian and French practices when he traveled to various courts throughout Germany, states that the treble clef is used for the C clarinet, but suggests that composers think (and transpose) parts in the tenor clef for the B♭ clarinet and in the discant or soprano clef for the A clarinet.[118] Catrufo writes in a later treatise that "the B♭ clarinet uses the treble clef but the composer must be able to write for it by using the tenor clef," and for the A clarinet "the treble clef is used but the composer must be able to write for it by using the soprano clef."[119] In his examples, Catrufo uses tenor clefs followed by treble clefs transposed for B♭ instruments. Additional writers who mention the identical practice and sometimes suggest the use of additional clefs include P. Gianelli (1820), G. Weber (1829), and Seyfried (1837).[120]

Italian composers and others who studied in Italy use the tenor clef for B♭ clarinet parts in many scores of opera and stage works. Published in London, Paris, and Milan, they range chronologically from Vento's *Demofoonte* in 1765 to Donizetti's *Maria Stuarda* in 1834. Works that have at least one aria or section where the tenor clef is used include J. C. Bach's Vauxhall song "Cruel Strephon will you leave me" (1766); Vento's *Sofonisba* (1766); Grétry's *Céphale et Procris* (1775); Piccinni's *Roland* (1778); Paisiello's *La serva padrona* (1781), *La Passione di Gesù Cristo* (1783), *Il barbier di Siviglia* (1784), *Le roi Théodore* (1786), *Le marquis Tulipano* (ca. 1789), *Nina* (1789), *I zingari in Fiera* (1789), and *Elfrida* (1792); Sacchini's *Dardanus* (1784); Bianchi's *La villanella rapita* (1789); Salieri's *La cifra* (1789); Sarti's *Les noces de Dorine* (1789); Paer's *L'intrigo amoroso* (1795) and *L'agnese* (1809); Cimarosa's *Il matrimonio segreto* (1792)[121] and *Gli orazi e i curiazi* (1796); and eleven operas by Isouard, from *Les confidences* (1803) to *Joconde* (1814). From the number of examples of the tenor clef found so far, it appears that its use to indicate transposition was not uncommon in French and Italian scores.

In the majority of these works, the tenor clef indicates a transposition for a B♭ clarinet. However, in manuscripts of Paisiello's *I zingari in Fiera* (1789) and Salieri's *La cifra* (1789), the clef indicates a transposition of a minor third lower for the A clarinet. To complicate analysis, some composers retain the key signature of the aria in the transposed tenor clef clarinet parts. Three examples by Paisiello are in the manuscript scores of *Il barbier di Siviglia* (1784) and *I zingari in Fiera*, and in the printed score of *Le roi Théodore* (1786).

The musicologist John Rice suggests that Salieri in *La cifra* uses the tenor clef to indicate that the clarinet parts are played an octave lower.[122] While this is possible, the clarinet part-writing in the aria Rice cites seems more appropriate for playing at pitch. In this example, Salieri changes his mind and writes the tenor clef over treble clef signs on the first page of the accompaniment to the recitative "Alfin son sola" (see figure 3.7).[123]

It has also been suggested that Paisiello uses the tenor clef to indicate a transposition of one octave lower[124]—probably an incorrect assumption. In the manuscript of his oratorio *La Passione di Gesù Cristo* (1783), act 1 includes an extended clarinet solo part in the tenor clef rather high in its tessitura. At one point in act 1 the notation "8va: sopra" (an octave higher) is indicated for a trio of two clarinets and bassoon.[125] However, Paisiello may have used this notation simply to avoid ledger lines. The remainder of his clarinet parts in the tenor clef, although rather high in tessitura, fit into the instrumental texture and were played in the written octave, since a low d¹ is written in one solo passage, which cannot be played an octave lower.[126]

One example of the tenor clef in symphony parts to indicate B♭ clarinets was written by the Polish composer Jakub Pawlowski in his Symphony in B-flat Major, written during the second half of the eighteenth century. Jan Pronak wrongly assumes that the tenor clef indicates that the parts are to be played an octave lower and explains in his revisional notes that the parts are transposed an octave higher and notated in the treble clef.[127] The tenor clef is also used for the B♭ clarinet in several chamber works. For example, in the clarinet parts of a *Concertone a violini, viola, clarinetto obbligato, corni, violoncello et contrabbasso* by Giuseppe Gherardeschi, dated 1784, and a *Concertone per più strumenti obbligati* by Giuseppe Sarti, the tenor clef is written in the margin of the work and the treble clef is written in the transposed B♭ clarinet parts.[128] Palese uses the tenor clef for the B♭ clarinet in three duets for flute and clarinet about 1823, and Pietro Bottesini uses a soprano clef for

FIGURE 3.7 Tenor clef notation in Salieri, *La cifra* (1789, MS).

the A clarinet in his *Divertimento per clarinetto con accompagnamento di due violini, viola e violoncello* about 1827.[129]

The second notation method, transposing the clarinet part but not indicating the nominal pitch, occurs in many works using the tenor as well as treble clefs. La Borde wrote clarinet parts in A, B♭, C, and E in the overture and four arias of the Paris opera *Annette et Lubin*. The score indicates that the A-flat major overture is written in F major for C clarinets. In an E-flat major aria in act 7, clarinets in the treble clef are clearly transposed to F major, one step higher, to be played on B♭ instruments.[130] A D major aria in *Annette et Lubin* is transposed to F major, to be played on A clarinets, and an E major aria is transposed to C major, for E clarinets doubling the first and second flutes.[131] This interpretation of the transposition in *Annette et Lubin* is verified by a set of published parts for clarinets.[132] Similarly, Floquet did not indicate the nominal clarinet pitch in *L'union de l'amour et des arts* (1773). He includes several arias in D major transposed into C major for D clarinet; arias in E major transposed into F major for B♮ clarinets; and one duo in A major transposed into C major for A clarinets.[133]

The transpositions of these parts follow the recommendations by Roeser in 1764 and Francoeur in 1772. It is important to note that La Borde or his copyists must have been confused as to how to transpose clarinet parts. In the A-flat major overture to *Annette et Lubin*, the clarinet parts are written in F major but are clearly meant to be played on a C clarinet. Perhaps this is one reason Roeser wrote his instrumentation treatise in 1764.

An example of the modern practice of indicating nominal pitch and the absence of any pitch indication for transposed parts is found in Gossec's *Missa pro defunctis* (1760), published in Paris in 1780 as the *Messe des morts*. The overture specifies parts for "Clarinetti G" (clarinets d'amour), and two other sections call for "Clarinetti B" (B♭ clarinets). In two sections of the *Messe des morts*, the tonality of the clarinets is omitted where instruments in B♭ and C are required.[134]

The third notation method, writing a direction for transposition in the part, is evident in several examples. Charlton notes this practice in his dissertation after examining thirty-one French operas written from 1768 to 1788.

> In the overture to Gretry's *L'amitié à l'épreuve* (1770), which is in D major, the instruction appears as for a C instrument with a key signature of two sharps, "en ut" refers not to the proposed key of the clarinet but of the clarinet part. A D instrument was intended, as was also the case in Floquet's *L'union de l'amour et des arts* (1773). A dance movement in D major, p. 38, requires oboes in unison with clarinets; these are given on one stave of music, in two sharps. The instruction reads, "Clarinettes comme les hautbois en ut." Similarly, on p. 85 clarinets in B♭ on their own stave in E major are labeled "en fa." Comparable labeling systems may be seen in Cherubini's *Démophoon* [1788] and in many scores of all kinds after 1789.[135]

Other examples of this practice appear in Sacchini's *L'Olympiade* (1777), where an E-flat major aria carries the instruction "clarinette en fa," indicating transposition for B♭ clarinet; and in Sacchini's *Dardanus* (1784), where an F major aria is marked "clarinette en ré," indicating transposition for an A clarinet.[136]

Writing during the 1790s, Cherubini uses two methods to indicate nominal pitch. In *Lodoïska* (1791) an A-flat major aria is transposed into B-flat major and marked "clarinettes en fa." Another aria in C major transposed for B♭ clarinets is marked "clarinette in si♭," using the modern method to indicate nominal pitch. In another G major aria in *Lodoïska*, the B♭ clarinet part is marked "Clarinetti in Mi Min" and transposed into F major; the same transposition occurs in another aria, where the part is marked "Clarinette in Mi♭."[137]

The fourth notation method is not to indicate transposition but to instruct or expect a copyist to transpose the part or the clarinetist to transpose at sight. The earliest examples are found in the 1756 Paris ballet *Célime* by Chevalier d'Herbain. Clarinet parts are notated in the overture, in a short fanfare in D major, and in an E-flat ariette marked Presto. Cucuel suggests that these parts are for the D and B♭ clarinets, apparently basing this assumption on the transposition tables in Francoeur's treatise.[138] In at least one published version of *Célime*, there are additional cues for C clarinets, but no parts. For example, there are cues for horns and clarinets in an F major hunting scene, and a C major air in 6/8 near the end of the ballet includes the cues (indicated in pen) "petts flus et hb: cors et clars." Cucuel found parts only for transposed F clarinets in the Bibliothèque de l'Opéra, so perhaps D and B♭ clarinets were not available for some performances.[139]

The best-known scores previously thought to have been written for C clarinet appear in Gluck's eight Paris operas.[140] By applying Roeser's and Francoeur's recommendations to the key signatures of the arias, it is obvious that clarinets in C, B♮, B♭, or A were played except in *Iphigénie en Aulide* (1774), which may be performed entirely on a C clarinet.

By the 1840s, the modern practice of using the treble clef for all clarinets, transposing the parts, and indicating the nominal pitch was standardized in most countries except Italy. Carl Czerny, in his *School of Practical Composition*, published in London in 1839, advocates use of the treble clef adopted by many later writers on the subjects of composition and instrumentation.[141]

The Mute

The muting of woodwind instruments is found initially in scores from the first half of the eighteenth century. For instance, muted flutes and oboes are required in Handel's oratorio *La resurrezione* (1708), and muted bassoons are required by Zelenka in his oratorio *Gesù al Calvario* (1735).[142] Page notes that "the sound of muted woodwinds are [*sic*] linked in several works to the theme of funerals or burials. By the nineteenth century muting wind instruments was understood to produce a sound which represented the emotion of sorrow."[143] For instance, F. D. Weber writes that the clarinet, oboe, and trumpet could be muted "in pieces with a very sorrowful and soft sentiment."[144] Muted wind instruments also have an association with the heavenly or spiritual, as heard in the quintet "L'innocence et l'amour" in Spontini's opera *Milton* (1804); or the feeling of distance in the march in act 2, scene 5, of Spontini's opera *Fernand Cortez* (1809).[145]

The earliest documented use of a clarinet mute is in the funeral march in C minor in the finale of act 2 of Paer's *Achilles* (1801). Oboes and clarinets play the march with mutes (*con sordini*).[146] Three years later, Spontini specifies muted clarinets in *Milton*. The method of muting is not specified; all that can be deduced is that muting neither affected the instrument's compass nor softened it too much when it was combined with other instruments. Indeed, Spontini began an E-flat major quintet in *Milton* with a passage for muted B♭ clarinets, oboes, and muted E♭ horns, and includes clarinet solos with and without a mute.[147] At the beginning of the second act of Spontini's *Fernand Cortez*, clarinets, oboes, and horns are marked "sourdine" in the autograph score.[148] Spontini gave more precise instructions in the printed score of *Fernand Cortez* to "enclose the end of the instrument in a bag of leather."[149] Hector Berlioz uses this identical method at the end of the cantata *La mort d'Orphée* (1827) for B♭ clarinet and later adapted this section for his mélologue *Lélio ou Le retour à la vie* (1831–32), scored for A clarinet. The instruction in the score states that the instrument may be put in a cloth or leather bag.[150] It may be assumed that the players of Paer's *Achilles* muted their instruments with a leather bag.

Cotton or wool was also recommended for muting in the instruction books by J. C. Fischer (ca. 1773–76, ca. 1780) for the oboe, by H. Domnich (ca. 1807) for the horn,[151] and by F. D. Weber for winds in general.[152] At least three small pear-shaped English wooden mutes dating from the late eighteenth or early nineteenth century are associated with an oboe (ca. 1800, GB-London-RCM)[153] by Goulding, Wood and Company, and with oboes (ca. 1800, GB-Oxford)[154] by William Milhouse, London.

During the eighteenth century, J. A. A. Tuerlinckx made a type of clarinet mute initially recorded in a 1784 Flemish instrument register: "For eight clarinets with four A pieces, two D pieces, two mute, 105 gulden."[155] Apparently four of these instruments are pitched in B♭ and supplied with corps de réchange for tuning to A; two are pitched in E♭ with corps in D, and two clarinets have mutes. In 1785, Tuerlinckx supplied twenty-three B♭ clarinets with A *corps en sourdine* to a Mr. Van Geurik.[156] Clarinets in A and B♭ made with mutes are listed until 1789.[157]

Nothing precise is revealed about these mutes in the register, but it is possible that they were wooden and similar to those that have survived with oboes in England. However, a suggestion as to the nature of some mutes appears in a 1791 article by an anonymous German author, who was quite impressed with the sound of the muted clarinet. He exclaims, "How moving is the tone of this instrument above the others, when its loudness is moderated through its bell (that is, through the peculiar mute belonging to it)?"[158] The sound of the lowest notes on a clarinet may be affected by a globular-shaped bell, as found on the clarinet d'amour, and a few clarinets d'amour pitched in C and A have globular bells. In fact, one surviving C clarinet (B-Bruxelles, no. 2597) by the Tuerlinckx firm includes a globular-shaped bell. Thus, it is possible that the Tuerlinckx firm sold globular bells as mutes.

A clarinet mute was used at a time when composers and players were sensitive to small differences in timbre and tone color. It never became standardized in orchestral scores, and directions in the scores of the early nineteenth century indicate that a bag of cloth or leather was usually used as a mute.

Conclusion

With the exception of the use of the mute, the playing techniques discussed in this chapter, became essential aspects of the teaching curriculum at music conservatories during the early nineteenth century. With the gradual adoption of the thirteen-key clarinet and later designs of clarinet systems after 1820, there were fewer differences in playing between large cities. By about 1840, the compass (e to c⁴), the four registers, and fingerings were standardized in method books. The use of a single- or double-lip embouchure remained the choice of the player, but during the nineteenth century the reed-below mouthpiece position was adopted by the majority of players, with the exception of many Italian clarinetists. After 1840, three clarinets—in C, B♭, and A (without corps de rechange)—were generally accepted in the orchestra, and higher-pitched clarinets in E♭, F, and A♭ continued to be used in military bands. During the eighteenth and early nineteenth centuries, transposition was a necessity for the orchestral clarinetist and to this day players continue to transpose C clarinet parts on B♭ clarinets, resulting in the loss of the special timbre of the C clarinet. Soprano and tenor clefs were used by many composers to indicate A and B♭ clarinets. By about 1840, most composers had adopted the treble clef in writing for all types of clarinets. Finally, owing to the awkward fingering of the classical clarinet in remote tonalities and the poor intonation of many notes in the low register, the earlier instrument was superseded by thirteen-key clarinets. These improved instruments allowed greater ease of fingering and made more accurate intonation possible.

4

MUSIC FOR THE
CLASSICAL CLARINET

The purpose of this chapter is to investigate the utilization of the classical clarinet in the music literature written from 1750 to 1830 with an emphasis on unpublished or infrequently discussed works from the late eighteenth century. The chapter is organized by genre—opera and concert arias; choral music; concertos; orchestral music; and chamber music—and within each genre, by composer. Because the literature is substantial, only a selection of composers and titles is included. The intent is to characterize in each genre the use and evolution of writing for the clarinet regarding range, tonality, prominence of the part, and instrumentation. Individual composers' subsequent use of the clarinet, changes in writing for the instrument, and importance and significance within the genre are discussed. Selections illustrate the musical and technical requirements that composers and players demanded of the instrument as it evolved in design and construction. The form and harmonic content of works are not analyzed for the majority of works.

With the dissemination of instrumentation treatises such as Roeser's (ca. 1764) and Francoeur's (ca. 1772) and the increase in the number of players who specialized in the clarinet during the 1760s, composers in Paris became aware of the capabilities and unique tone color of the four-key clarinet. At the same time, in London and throughout Europe, makers introduced five-key clarinets that were eagerly accepted by both players and composers. Even though contemporary flute and oboe players could play in more tonalities and were more fluent in fingering and technique, clarinetists played an instrument with a distinctive tone quality, more extensive range, and wider scope of dynamics. Beginning in the 1770s, soloists such as Josef Beer in Paris and John Mahon in London performed at public and private concerts, greatly enhancing the popularity of the instrument. During the 1780s Beer, Michel Yost, Mahon, Anton Stadler, J. M. Hostié, and many other soloists performed clarinet concertos in London, Paris, Vienna, and other cities in Europe and Russia. The introduction of the clarinet into wind ensembles of pairs of clarinets, horns, bassoons, and sometimes oboes during the 1740s through the 1760s was also a significant factor in the rapid dissemination and acceptance of the clarinet. It was swiftly adopted by military and Harmonie bands and became the leading melodic wind instrument in most large cities throughout Europe, America, and Scandinavia by the 1780s. In addition, clarinets appeared in Harmonie and wind ensembles in special instrumental numbers in operas, the most famous of which is the stage band in Mozart's *Don Giovanni* (1787). Solo concertos began to appear in the 1750s, and by the 1790s, there was a flood of published works. Chamber music with strings, keyboard, and winds appeared during the 1760s and, during the 1790s, clarinet sonatas with keyboard accompaniment.

An English author of an instruction book for the five-key clarinet about 1781 states:

> The Growing repute of this Instrument, may it is presumed, make a new set of Instructions, very acceptable at present, when the Clarinet is considered as the life of every martial band; and as an indispensible [sic] accompaniment to other wind instruments in concerts, where its tones, judiciously managed, are exhilarating and animating beyond almost any other. And though it may have some disadvantages as a solo instrument, yet a judicious player may make it something more than barely agreeable, even without an accompaniment.[1]

During the last quarter of the eighteenth century and the beginning of the nineteenth, many composers approached the clarinet cautiously, limiting its range to that of the oboe, c^1 to d^3. Notes below c^1 on some clarinets, particularly English instruments, were muffled and softer than notes in the clarinet register. In addition, cross-fingerings in the chalumeau register for eb^1, $c\#^1$, and b were difficult to play smoothly in rapid passages and out of tune, particularly in comparison to analogous fingerings on the flute and oboe. About 1806, Marsh advised in *Hints to Young Composers of Instrumental Music*: "In some few symphonies there are both hautboy and clarinet parts, in which the latter are set the lowest of the two, as the compass of the clarinet can be extended six notes below that of the hautboy; but these notes, being very weak, are only proper to being used in mere accompaniment."[2]

Players, who were often also composers, were familiar with these problems and coped with them according to the physical characteristics of their clarinet. For example, two leading clarinet soloists during the 1770s — Beer, a Bohemian, and Mahon, an Englishman — both composed concertos to display their five-key instruments to greatest advantage. In his Second Concerto Mahon limits the clarinet solo part to a compass of e^1 to g^3, while in his First Concerto Beer freely uses the lowest range of the instrument, writing from e to e^3. The difference in writing is due to a combination of factors: the style of composition, differences in clarinet construction, and differences in embouchure and blowing techniques. In particular, Mahon's English-made clarinet sounds more restrained in the chalumeau register because of its small tone holes, bore configuration, and small mouthpiece, while Beer's

German- or French-made instrument is fuller sounding in the chalumeau register because its tone holes, bore, and mouthpiece are larger.

Every classical clarinet possesses a deep-sounding chalumeau register from e (a sixth below the lowest note of the flute and oboe) to f^1. Its most outstanding quality, however, is the beauty of its clarion register, a twelfth above the chalumeau register, from b^1 to c^3. In 1785 Vanderhagen wrote, "The beauty of the clarinet lies in its dulcet tone; that is the main thing, and even a mediocre performer can delight the listener with this instrument."[3] During the 1780s, Schubart enthusiastically described its warm, sensual sound: "Its character symbolizes the melting sentiments of love—it is the tone of the passionate heart. . . . The tone is so mellifluous, so languishing; and he who knows how to bring out the medium timbre, is sure to conquer every heart."[4] Albrechtsberger characterizes the clarinet as "closest [in sound] to the human voice,"[5] and Koch writes in his *Musicalisches Lexikon*, "The Clarinet is a woodwind instrument admirably distinguished by its pleasing tone."[6] Grétry, a prolific composer for the clarinet in his Parisian operas, associates its sound with sadness: "the clarinet expresses sorrow. . . . Even when executing cheerful airs, it still mixes in a shade of sadness. If one could dance in prison, I would do so to the sound of the clarinet."[7] By the 1790s the clarinet was so well liked and admired that Reichardt, in the third edition of Löhlein's violin treatise, described Stradivari violins as having "a strong, penetrating clarinet-like tone."[8]

Although most clarinets made between 1770 and 1830 had five keys, some composers wrote concertos for particular soloists who owned the most advanced instruments. Examples include Mozart's quintet (1789) and concerto (1791), written for Anton Stadler, who owned a basset clarinet with keys extending the compass four notes lower than the soprano clarinet; it would have been at least a nine-key instrument. Ludwig Spohr wrote his First Concerto (1808) and Second Concerto (1810) for Johann Simon Herm-stedt, whose eleven-key clarinet Spohr describes in his published preface to the First Concerto. In 1811, Carl Maria von Weber wrote his clarinet Con-certino and First and Second Concertos for Heinrich Baermann, who played ten- and, later, twelve-key clarinets. Shortly afterward, at least three com-posers wrote concertos specifically for Müller's thirteen-key clarinet: Reicha in 1815 (now lost); G. A. Schneider in 1816; and Riotte in 1818.[9]

Even though several eighteenth-century composers featured the dis-tinctive low or chalumeau register in solo concertos, only a few, such as Nic-colò Isouard and Spohr, made use of this register in opera and orchestral music during the first decade of the nineteenth century. With the develop-ment and availability of the more powerful and versatile thirteen-key clar-inet during the 1820s and 1830s, composers began to use the chalumeau reg-ister freely. An early and effective use of this register is the overture in Weber's 1821 opera *Der Freischütz*. Another musical characteristic that became more common in opera and orchestral works is the use of extended chromatic passages and leaps of more than one octave.

Identifying the type of clarinet originally played in a particular work is sometimes problematic. For example, music written during the 1750s or 1760s could have been intended for baroque two- or three-key or classical four- or five-key clarinets. By the 1810s many advanced and professional players had ten-, eleven-, twelve-, and thirteen-key clarinets.

Opera, Concert Arias, and Choral Works

This discussion presents a general outline of the use of the clarinet in opera during the late eighteenth and early nineteenth centuries by the most significant opera composers.[10] Choral works discussed here include cantatas, oratorios, and works for solo voice or chorus and orchestra. The parts are generally limited in scope but occasionally there are prominent clarinet solos, such as the solos in Joseph Haydn's *Creation*. The most important works that established the clarinet as an indispensable part of the orchestra occur in opera, a genre that to date has not been thoroughly investigated.

Composers for the baroque clarinet such as Telemann and Johann Valentin Rathgeber use a clarino writing style, characterized by repeated notes, arpeggios, triadic figures, and an avoidance of notes below c^1. Stylistically, it is identical to trumpet music. The French composer Rameau also writes in this style in the overture to his 1751 opera *Acante et Céphise*. However, in ten of the thirteen movements with the clarinet, Rameau pairs two clarinets with two horns, with and without stringed accompaniment, constituting a preclassical style that emphasizes diatonic melodic lines.[11] Rameau is also the first composer to associate clarinets and horns with hunting, such as in "Un chasseur" (A hunter) in act 2 of *Acante*. Throughout the eighteenth century and into the nineteenth, many composers used the clarinet-horn combination and a hunting-call theme in opera, concertos, and wind music.[12]

Operas were often only one part of a lengthy program that frequently included instrumental solo works, vocal solos, ballets, plays, and other types of entertainment. In London, for example, a performance would often be a double bill with a main piece, usually a play, followed by an hour-long afterpiece, often an opera or pantomime. The capability of the singers was a most important consideration for the opera composer, who often fashioned each aria to a singer's individual abilities. Published English opera scores often included the singer's name at the beginning of his or her aria to emphasize the singer's importance.

Our understanding of clarinet use in opera derives mostly from analysis of scores, a task complicated by the variety of publication practices at the time. In Paris, publishers made full opera scores available immediately after the first performance. In London, the publication of most full scores stopped after 1762.[13] Instead, as a cost-saving measure, they published vocal scores of selected numbers with three to four staves and limited instrumental cues.[14] Occasionally, separate parts were published for winds, including the clarinet. In many operatic centers, such as Berlin, Dresden, Milan, and Naples, operas were generally not published, but scores and parts were circulated in manuscript copies. As a result, the historical record is clearest and easiest to obtain for French operas. Further obscuring the practices of composers active in London is the loss of the majority of manuscript full scores by fire during the eighteenth and nineteenth centuries in the two main or patent theaters, Covent Garden and Drury Lane.

Johann Wendelin Glaser

Glaser, the cantor and music director of the Wertheim court from 1743 to 1783,[15] was the earliest German composer to use the clarinet and horn combination in the orchestra. Of 310 cantatas, Glaser includes clarinet parts in just 10, dating from about 1748 through the 1770s or 1780s.[16] Although the majority of Glaser's manuscripts were destroyed during World War II, ten measures of a clarinet and horn melody were found in the 1756 cantata "Alles was Odem hat, lobe den Herrn," reproduced by Treiber. Glaser gives the leading part to a C clarinet in the lively first phrase, four measures long; the horn answers for two measures, then the clarinet plays a closing four-measure phrase (see figure 4.1).[17] The compass, from g^1 to c^3, is entirely in the clarinet register, and although the excerpt is very short, the jaunty tune, range, and 3/8 meter remind one of the hunting-call tradition. This simple part could have been easily played on a three-key clarinet, although a four-key instrument may have been available. Treiber notes that when Glaser uses clarinets and horns together they produce a charming effect with a solo voice part. The full instrumentation of "Alles was Odem hat, lobe den Herrn" includes

FIGURE 4.1   Glaser, "Alles was Odem hat, lobe den Herrn" (1756), from Treiber, "Kantor Johann Wendelin Glaser," 66 ex. 17.

a four-part choir, strings (violin, viola, and cellos or bass), organ, two flutes, two horns, three clarinets, two trumpets, and timpani.

Glaser includes the clarinet in another cantata, "Ihr müsset gehasset werden" (1760s or 1770s), with a separate, single part for B♭ clarinet (marked "Toni: B:") in a da capo aria in 3/8 along with parts for solo E♭ horn, cello, bassoon, and organ with a figured bass part. This cantata is one of the earliest works to designate a nominal clarinet pitch. The clarinet's compass is limited from f^1 to c^3 and was probably played on a German four- or five-key clarinet. Since the manuscript of the clarinet part is in a different hand from the other parts, it was probably added for a later performance. This simple part, however, is more diatonic than the part in "Alles was Odem hat, lobe den Herrn" and is not written to evoke the hunt.

JEAN BENJAMIN DE LA BORDE

La Borde was one of the first opera composers to write for the classical four-key clarinet. He studied composition in Paris with Rameau and made a successful debut as a stage composer at fourteen. Cucuel discovered La Borde's earliest use of the clarinet in *Gilles, garçon peintre, z'amoureux-t-et-rival* (1758), with clarinets in D and B♭.[18] In the E♭ major overture, there are transposed parts for B♭ clarinets. The tessitura or part of the compass primarily employed is mostly restricted to the clarino register: the first clarinet plays f^1 to f^3, while the second has greater latitude, from g to c^3, but only occasionally ventures into the chalumeau register. Transposed parts for B♭ clarinets appear again in scene 10, in E♭ major, where the first clarinet has the same compass but the second is restricted to a range of e^1 to b♭^{2}. In all these sections, the clarinets join horns, strings, and continuo to fill in the harmony. A final C major quartet has transposed parts for D clarinet, c^2 to e^3 and c^1 to c^3, including a larger orchestra of two horns, two oboes, strings, and continuo.[19] The Comédie Italienne clarinetists Gaspard Procksch and George Thomas François Flieger performed this opera six times in 1758. These clarinetists also played eighteen performances of Rameau's *Acante et Céphise* between 1751 and 1762.[20]

In the 1762 pastorale *Annette et Lubin*, La Borde specifies clarinets pitched in E, C, B♭, and A in three arias and the overture; parts for the E, B♭, and A clarinets are transposed in the score.[21] La Borde was among the earliest composers to require four differently pitched clarinets in one work, although the players would have used corps de rechange with two finger hole joints to change the B♭ clarinet to A. He was also one of the few composers to specify the higher-pitched E clarinet when most composers preferred the D clarinet.[22] Clarinets in La Borde's parts are in unison throughout with oboes, flutes, or violins without independent solos. The largo aria "Quelle frayeur vient me saisir!" in scene 7, act 1, uses B♭ clarinets as a predominant tone color, initially to double the violin parts and pianissimo with oboes when the voice solo enters (see figure 4.2). The "très doux" indication at the beginning of the movement implies that La Borde intended the clarinet timbre

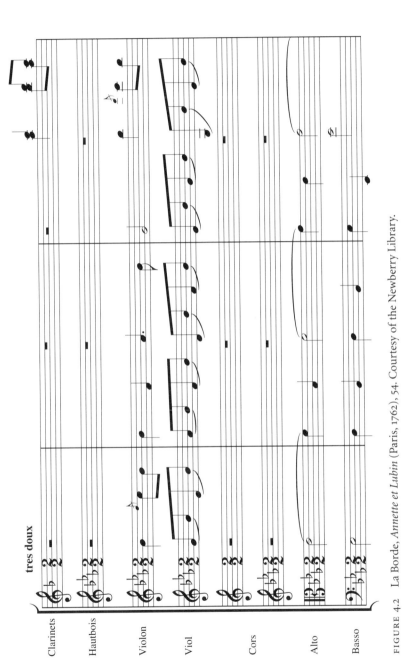

FIGURE 4.2 La Borde, *Annette et Lubin* (Paris, 1762), 54. Courtesy of the Newberry Library.

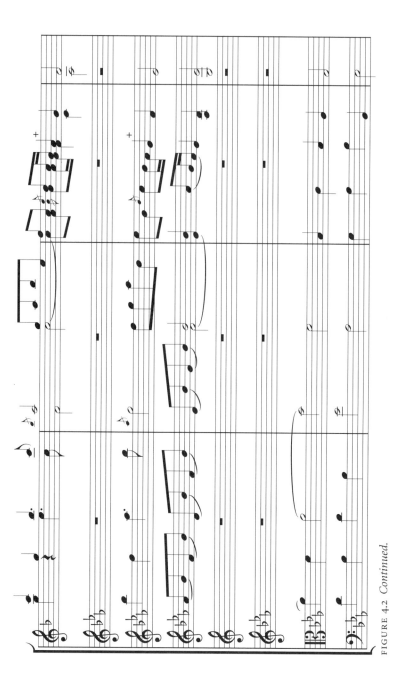

FIGURE 4.2 Continued.

to add a sweet sound to the ensemble. Both clarinets' tessitura is primarily in the clarino register, and the overall compass is very limited—from f¹ to d³ for the first clarinet and from a to b♭² for the second.

The next year La Borde used D clarinets, transposed in the score, and C clarinets in six sections and the overture of *Ismène et Isménias*. Initially performed in 1763, it was quite successful: it received twenty-three performances and was revived in 1770.[23] The clarinet parts double the oboes, are often paired with horns, and are mostly restricted to the clarino register. For example, in the overture, the first clarinet plays g¹ to f³, but the second clarinet has a larger compass of g to d³. Later, in a G major minuet, D clarinet parts are transposed to F major, and in act 2, C clarinets are used in a section with a chorus. In act 3, C clarinets appear in the introductory "Marche des Peuples" and a chorus, where the first clarinet has arpeggio figures and a wide compass of c¹ to f³.[24] Four years later La Borde used only the A and E clarinets in six sections of the 1767 *Amphion*, a *ballet pastorale héroïque*.[25] In the score, the A and E clarinet parts are transposed into C major and are quite limited in compass, primarily doubling the oboe parts. La Borde's clarinet parts were most likely played on four-key French clarinets with an F♯/C♯ key, as described by Roeser in 1764. According to M. F. Beche in a 1788 manuscript, it was about 1767 when clarinets and horns were added to the King's Chapel for use in choral works.[26]

THOMAS AUGUSTINE ARNE

The use of the clarinet in opera orchestras in London began immediately after its use in Parisian opera by La Borde. Arne, an English composer and violinist, was the leading figure in English theatrical music during the mid-eighteenth century. He uses the clarinet sparingly in three operas to set the mood or to add color to the orchestration. At the beginning of his opera *Thomas and Sally, or the Sailor's Return*, first performed in 1760, Arne prominently features a Harmonie quartet of two clarinets and two horns in a manner not unlike the "Un chasseur" scene in Rameau's *Acante et Céphise*. Quartets of winds or Harmonie were familiar to the English gentry, who employed their own bands, but the English public would have considered it an enjoyable novelty.

The spirited overture in 3/8, played by two clarinets and two horns in C, is the best-known work of the hunting-call genre (see figure 4.3). In addition, Arne provides precise written directions for the timing and placement of the instruments; "Half the following Symphony is play'd behind the Scenes at the further end. Then the Horns & Clarinets come on Sounding the Crest of the Symphony several Huntsmen follow & last of all the Squire."[27] The entrance of the horns and clarinets on stage is marked "Enter" and coincides with the eighth-note pick-up by the first horn in measure 17. A noticeably dramatic effect is achieved when clarinets and horns walk onto the stage playing the second half of the overture, followed by several huntsmen and

FIGURE 4.3 Arne, *Thomas and Sally* (London, 1761), 6. Courtesy of the Clark Library, University of California at Los Angeles.

the Squire, a tenor. Immediately, the Squire sings a rousing song, "The echoing horn," accompanied by the clarinets and horns. Here, the horns double the tenor while the clarinets play a third below. In the refrain, an oboe replaces a clarinet, and violins, cellos or basses, and tenor and bass singers enlarge the ensemble. Arne's writing in the first sixteen measures consists of a tune simple enough for both the horn and clarinet players to memorize, but he requires a wider compass than La Borde: g^1 to a^2 for the first clarinet and g to g^2 for the second. These clarinet-horn quartets subsequently became quite popular during the 1760s and 1770s in London at the pleasure gardens of Marylebone, Ranelagh, and Vauxhall.[28]

A little more than a year later, Arne featured the clarinet-horn quartet again at the beginning of act 2 of *Artaxerxes* (1762) in the aria "In fancy our hopes and fears." Although the clarinets begin with the same melodic material as the overture to *Thomas and Sally,* its meter is 2/2. It is more ornamented with trills and exhibits a lyrical stepwise four-measure phrase, while the horns answer, accompanied by a string ensemble of two violins, one viola, and a continuo of harpsichord and cello to strengthen the bass line. The tenor soloist, a Mr. Peretti, enters after the introduction (see figure 4.4).[29] The musical effect of the similar theme is quite different from that evoked by the bouncy horn-call aria in the overture to *Thomas and Sally.* During the second half of this aria, the clarinets double the first and second violin parts, respectively, as shown by the indications "Uniss Col Primo" and "Uniss Col Secondo." The compass—g^1 to c^3 for the first clarinet and d^1 to c^3 for the second clarinet—places a greater emphasis on the clarino register than in *Thomas and Sally.*

C clarinets are again required in act 3, in the F major aria "Water parted from the sea," sung by a Mr. Tenducci.[30] The orchestra consists of two clarinets, two horns, two bassoons, violins, "violetta" (viola), and continuo. Both clarinet parts continually double the violin parts, usually paired with bassoons, and do not have solos. Although the clarinetists play almost continuously, the compass from g to bb^2 is wider for the first and only slightly more restricted for the second from g to g^2. There are two trills: from a^1 to b^1 for the second clarinet in "In fancy our hopes and fears," and from bb^1 to c^2 (twice) for the first clarinet in "Water parted from the sea." This latter trill, like the a^1 to b^1 trill, is playable without a trill key but clumsy to manipulate. It must have been obvious to both players and makers that a trill key for these notes would be very useful, since by the mid-1770s English makers had added the A–B trill to clarinets.[31]

In *The Fairy Prince* (1771), Arne begins the E-flat major da capo duet "Seek you Majesty" with two clarinets playing a four-measure phrase in thirds, followed by bassoons before canonic entrances of the two soprano soloists, a Master Wood and a Miss Brown.[32] Two violins and a continuo group of cellos and/or basses and bassoons come in at the entrance of the second singer. Although the three- to four-part vocal score indicates clarinet parts in the same tonality as the other instruments, B♭ instruments were

FIGURE 4.4 Arne, *Artaxerxes* (London, 1762), 86. Courtesy of the Clark Library, University of California at Los Angeles.

very likely played. The transposition of the E-flat major key of the aria a whole step up to F major, a tonality much easier to negotiate, supports this assumption. Furthermore, the E-flat major part includes very awkward trills from g^2 to ab^2 and ab^2 to bb^2 that are playable a major second higher on Bb clarinets. Near the end of the duet in measure 73, the indication "with the Voices" suggests that the clarinets doubled the voice parts for the next twenty-four measures with strings, bassoons, and continuo to close the duet. The compass of the clarinet parts, including this last section, is g^1 to d^3 and f^1 to bb^2, which is more restricted than in the two earlier operas. In each of these three operas, Arne uses the clarinet always with horns, achieving a distinctive blend of tone qualities.

FRANÇOIS-JOSEPH GOSSEC

Gossec, who was originally from the Netherlands, championed the clarinet in Paris. He became familiar with the Mannheim symphonic style during Johann Stamitz's tenure as director of La Pouplinère's orchestra from 1754 to 1755, and when Stamitz left, Gossec succeeded him as director of the orchestra.[33] Gossec wrote a "Missa pro defunctis" in 1760 that was initially performed in 1761 and published in 1780 as the *Messe des morts*. Here he specifies and transposes parts for clarinets in G (clarinets d'amour) in the introduction, clarinets in Bb in nos. 3, 8 ("Tuba mirum"), and 19; and clarinets in C in no. 22 ("Pie Jesus").[34] His writing for the clarinet exhibits aspects of both the older baroque reliance on arpeggios and repeated notes and the newer choice of diatonic lyricism usually given to the oboe or flute. For example, chorus no. 3 exhibits smooth and stepwise writing with the entrance of the first and second Bb clarinets doubling the soprano and contralto soloists (see figure 4.5). Gossec often pairs the clarinets with two horns in Eb, doubling oboes or the first violin. The range is even more limited than in La Borde's operas: g^1 to d^3 for the first clarinet and f^1 to bb^2 for the second. In the "Tuba mirum," Gossec utilizes an offstage wind band consisting of one Bb clarinet; two Eb trumpets or horns; and alto, tenor, and bass trombones. The single clarinet, which was presumably loud enough to balance the brasses, plays triadic, trumpetlike figures within a one-octave range, c^2 to c^3.

Gossec subsequently uses the clarinet in his moderately successful 1774 opera *Sabinus* and in the 1782 *Thésée*.[35] His greatest contribution was in the use of the clarinet in his symphonies and chamber music, and in many works, beginning in 1790, for chorus and band celebrating the French Revolution.

JOHANN CHRISTIAN BACH

Johann Christian was the youngest son of Johann Sebastian Bach. After writing operas for theaters in Turin and Naples in 1762, he composed two operas for the King's Theater in London, where he made his home.[36] Bach

FIGURE 4.5   Gossec, Chorus no. 3, *Messe des morts* (Paris, 1780), 9. Courtesy of the
Newberry Library.

was among the earliest champions of the clarinet in England, using it in ten
operas as well as additional cantatas, arias, and songs through the 1770s. His
first London opera, *Orione, o sia Diana vendicata*, initially performed in
1763, makes use of clarinets in D in one version of the outer movements (Allegro con brio and Allegro) of a three-movement overture; in B♭ in no. 4 (act
1) and no. 21 (act 2); and in C in no. 10 (act 1).[37] It includes an unusually full
instrumentation with the usual string section in addition to pairs of oboes,
bassoons, and horns; and in the overture and selected numbers he uses pairs

FIGURE 4.5   *Continued.*

of flutes, clarinets, and "tallie" (tenor oboes or English horns) in F. The music historian Charles Burney described the well-received opera enthusiastically:

> Every judge of Music perceived the emanations of genius throughout the whole performance; but were chiefly struck with the richness of the harmony, the ingenious texture of the parts, and, above all, with the new and happy use he had made of wind-instruments: this being the first time that clarinets had admission in our opera orchestra.[38]

One version of the D major overture printed parts includes clarinets "in D." He wrote the D clarinet parts with an alto clef, but the players transposed the parts by performing them in C major using a treble clef. By playing in C major all the difficulties in fingering and intonation of the D major parts were solved (see figure 3.5).[39] Fanfarelike figures predominate in the clarinet parts in four measures of the first movement; six measures of the third movement feature clarinets alone, predominantly in thirds. These passages are very restrained and comprise conjunct parts within small intervals of a fourth or a sixth. The clarinets' compasses are correspondingly small, from c^1 to g^2 and c^1 to e^2.

There are transposed parts for B♭ clarinet in the E-flat major aria "Ferma cudello sdegno" (act 1, no. 4); and parts in "Di quest' alma desolata" (act 2, no. 21) marked "Clarinetti in B" (B♭). Parts for both arias, which simply double the violins and supply harmonic support, are limited to two octaves or less: f^1 to d^3 and e^1 to $b♭^2$; c^2 to c^3; and e^1 to a^2. The C clarinets included in the C major aria "Andrò dal colle al prato" (no. 10) have a broader compass of b to c^2 and g to c^2 and support the flutes and violins throughout by playing the same part an octave lower.

Subsequently, Bach wrote for the clarinet in *Zanaida* (1763); the pastoral *Menalcas* (1764); *Adriano in Siria* (1765); *Carattaco* (1767); a revision of Gluck's *Orfeo ed Euridice* (1774); *La clemenza di Scipione* (1778); and, for a commission from Paris, *Amadis des Gaules* (1779). In addition, Bach received a commission to write an opera for the 1772 name-day celebrations for Elector Carl Theodor in Mannheim. In that richly scored work, *Temistocle*, he specifies three D basset horns marked "clarinetto d'amore." A second opera for Mannheim, *Lucio Silla*, followed in 1775; it included clarinets and, in one aria, D basset horns marked "clarinetto d'amore."[40]

Bach uses the clarinet to provide special orchestral color in one to three arias out of an average of twenty per opera.[41] D clarinets appear in the overtures to *Orione* and *Amadis des Gaules*, but in the majority of Bach's subsequent works he specifies only C and B♭ instruments. Usually clarinets have a few brief solos in slow arias with pairs of horns and bassoons. Occasionally they appear in allegro arias, paired with flutes or tailles but not oboes. It seems likely that the clarinetists also played oboe since in some operas these instruments are not simultaneously required. However, in Mannheim additional wind players must have been available, since *Temistocle* combines basset horns with oboes, and *Lucio Silla* has basset horns and clarinets.

Bach also uses the clarinet in three cantatas: *Endimione* (1772), *Amor vincitore* (1774), and *Cefalo e Procri* (1776). In *Endimione*, there are B♭ clarinets with two horns and strings in act 1, no. 4, and C clarinets with two flutes and strings in act 2, no. 12. In *Cefalo e Procri*, C clarinets play with two flutes, two horns, and bassoon. The clarinets mainly double the flutes with short solos.[42]

Bach's cantata *Amor vincitore* (1774) includes a clarinet obbligato part to Alcidoro's aria "Quest selve gia d'amore." Two movements of this work feature solo parts for flute, oboe, clarinet, and bassoon written for four virtuoso performers: Karl Weiss (flute), Johann Christian Fischer (oboe), Josef Beer (clarinet), and Georg Wenzel Ritter (bassoon). The first performance was in 1774 at Carlisle House in London, followed by a benefit performance for Fischer and a private performance before the British royal family.[43] The sprightly allegro maestoso introduction to the aria features solo flute, oboe, B♭ clarinet, bassoon, both B♭ horns, and strings in primarily an accompaniment role (see figure 4.6). This writing is similar to that found in the popular symphony concertante, a type of concerto that features two or more solo instruments with orchestral accompaniment. Brief solos pass from one woodwind to the other, and the clarinet, still restricted to a narrow compass of b♭ to g², accompanies with repeated sixteenth notes and Alberti bass figuration.

Matia Vento

Vento received training in Naples and had a number of successful operas presented in Milan, Rome, and Venice. He became a popular opera composer in London after the production of his first opera, *Demofoonte*, performed at the King's Theater in 1765. Coincidentally, Bach's 1765 *Adriano in Siria* was performed at the same time in the Haymarket Theater with B♭ clarinets, but only in one aria.[44]

In *Demofoonte* Vento uses B♭ clarinets in two arias—an E-flat major "Misero pargoletto" and a "Recitativo" transposed to F major and followed by a "Duetto" transposed to C major. The orchestra includes violins, viola, basso (cello and harpsichord), and horns in F and E♭. There are separate parts for flutes, and one movement requires oboes. Vento's clarinet parts use a tenor clef, which indicates transposition of a whole tone played on the B♭ clarinet. This is evidently based on an Italian tradition of using clefs to indicate transposition of wind instruments, specifically the horn, trumpet, and clarinet (see chapter 3). His clarinet parts in *Demofoonte* are restricted in compass from f¹ to b♭² and e¹ to g² and include technical demands similar to those required in several of J. C. Bach's operas. The clarinet parts double the flutes and fill in the harmony with a one-measure solo for both clarinets in thirds.

Vento again specifies the B♭ clarinet in his opera *Sofonisba*, given at the King's Theater in 1766. The orchestra includes two bassoons not specified in the short score to *Demofoonte*, and two arias with clarinet have tenor clef parts marked "Clarinetti an B♭." However, Vento's autograph score shows B♭ clarinets specified in five E-flat major arias, each using tenor clefs with transposed parts.[45] The latter suggests that Vento preferred to use clarinets more frequently in his operas than J. C. Bach. Unfortunately, additional evidence to support this statement is lacking, since the autograph scores of most of Vento's operas are lost. As in *Demofoonte*, flutes or violins duplicate the clarinet parts and support the inner parts of the score. However, the compass is

Allegro maestoso

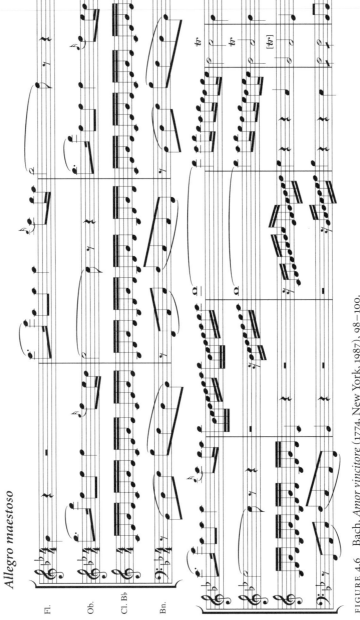

FIGURE 4.6   Bach, *Amor vincitore* (1774, New York, 1987), 98–100.

slightly wider—b♭^{1} to a^2 and c^1 to e^2 for the first aria, and b♭^{1} to c^3 and g to g^2 for the second.[46]

Vento uses the clarinet in only one later opera: *La vestale*, performed in London at the King's Theater in 1776. One aria, in E-flat major, has the same instrumentation as *Demofoonte*, including parts for B♭ clarinets printed with tenor clefs but engraved "Clarinetti E♭." The clarinets double the flutes with an overall compass for both of c^1 to b♭^{2}.[47]

ANDRÉ-ERNEST-MODESTE GRÉTRY
AND ÉTIENNE JOSEPH FLOQUET

More-demanding clarinet parts begin to appear during the 1770s—earlier in France than in England because of composer interest and the greater availability of players. In the operas, Grétry requires several differently pitched clarinets, solo clarinet passages, and clarinet parts in multiple arias and instrumental sections. Born in Liège, Grétry spent his professional life as a composer in Paris where he made important contributions to the opéra comique and enjoyed unparalleled success from 1769 until the French Revolution.[48] He continued to write operas, some of which were successful, and several popular choral and band works.

Grétry uses the clarinet throughout his career in at least twenty-four of his sixty-seven operas. Initially, in *Le Huron* (1768), he writes simple parts for the D clarinet with restricted compasses of g^1 to c^3 in only one aria and in a later march with horns, oboes, and piccolos. A printed note before the aria states that oboes may be substituted for clarinets, as Rameau had done earlier in *Les Boréades*.[49] In his next three operas, Grétry uses lower-pitched clarinets, but in only one aria each. *Les deux avares* (1770) includes C clarinets doubling oboes; *L'amitié à l'épreuve* (1770) has D clarinets in the overture and B♭ clarinets doubling the violin parts with horns in E♭ in another aria. The compasses in the latter opera are still rather narrow and completely avoid the chalumeau register by using e^1 to e^3 and f^1 to d^3. The chorus in act 3, scene 6, of *Zémire et Azor* (1772) has more extensive parts, where B♭ clarinets pair with horns in E♭, bassoons, and three singers at the back of the theater. The compass for both clarinets is c^1 to d^3.[50]

One year later Floquet, a contemporary of Grétry's, staged his first theatrical work, a 1773 *ballet-héroïque* titled *L'union de l'amour et des arts*. Highly successful, it was performed sixty times up to 1774.[51] Floquet uses D, C, B♭, and A clarinets in fifteen sections (arias and instrumental numbers) plus the overture—more than any previous composer.[52] The clarinets are often paired with horns, restricted in range, and sometimes double the oboe parts. We may ask why this composer uses clarinets to such an extent. By the early 1770s, players adopted Parisian four-key clarinets, which provided a technical facility greater than that achievable on earlier two- and three-key clarinets. Furthermore, Floquet was a violist who played in the Opéra orchestra and probably learned the capabilities of these four-key instruments from the players themselves. Seven years later, Floquet again uses four clarinets in C, B♮, B♭, and A in eight sections of his 1780 opera *Le siegneur bienfaisant*.[53] All the clarinets have technically rather limited parts, and all, aside from the C instruments, are transposed in the score.

Grétry's *Céphale et Procris* (1775) was performed in Versailles after the premiere of Floquet's successful *L'union de l'amour et des arts*. Perhaps in response to Floquet's work, Grétry requires D, C, B♭, and A clarinets in eleven sections and the overture. However, the clarinets' compass of c^1 to d^3 or e^3 is slightly wider than in Grétry's previous operas, and for the first time both tenor and treble clefs appear for the B♭ instrument in different arias.[54] Grétry continues to use the clarinet in as many as ten to thirteen different arias in *Les mariages samnites* (1776); *Colinette à la cour* (1782); *L'embarras des richesses* (1782); *La rosière républicaine* (1794); and *Anacréon* (1797). More demanding but limited-range solo clarinet passages appear in *La caravane du Caire* (1783), *Panurge dans l'île des lanternes* (1785), *Guillaume Tell* (1791), and *Elisca* (1799). *Guillaume Tell* begins in a most unusual manner with a solo C clarinet playing the "Rhans des vaches," an evocative Swiss call with a limited compass of g^1 to a^2. Nine additional sections require C or B♭ clarinets in simple, rudimentary parts.[55] During the 1760s and 1770s, French four-key clarinets were played in Grétry's and Floquet's operas. By the early 1780s, French five-key clarinets were available.

JOHANN AGRICOLA, CHRISTIAN CANNABICH, GEORG VOGLER, AND JOHANN REICHARDT

The use of the clarinet in operas written in Prussia began late in the 1760s. Agricola was musical director of the Opera in Potsdam under Frederick the Great. His *Amor e Psiche* (1767) includes parts for the clarinet that the writer Hiller in 1769 considered a novelty:[56]

> It is a rarity to notice clarinets with a prominent part in the theater orchestra. An intelligent composer knows how to make use of everything available to him at his epoch, and there is no doubt that this penetrating and powerful instrument, if handeled by skilful people and with care, should hold an important position among wind instruments. Up to now, it has perhaps only served to make tolerable the tone of a military fife and the noise of the drum.[57]

Hiller was alluding to the use of the clarinet in military bands; he was probably unaware of its use in an earlier opera. At about the same time in Mannheim, Cannabich and Vogler used the clarinet in ballet music. Cannabich selected clarinets in A and horns in D in four sections and C clarinets in one section for *Le rendes-vous, ballet de chasse* (1769). Vogler requires B♭ and A clarinets in two sections of his *Le rendez-vous de chasse* (1772). Both composers wrote parts with limited ranges of one to one and a half octaves that did not descend below f^1.[58] Cannabich also used B♭ and A clarinets with oboes or flutes and D horns in four sections of the ballet music for *Médée et Jason* (1772).[59] German four- or five-key clarinets were probably played in the works of Agricola, Cannabich, and Vogler. Twenty-six years later, the Berlin composer Reichardt freely used C, B♭, and A clarinets throughout his opera *Der Geisterinsel* (1798), with prominent passages for B♭ clarinets and horns and for clarinets and bassoons, as well as one solo at the beginning of the third act.[60] Five-key clarinets were played in this opera.

Christoph Willibald Gluck

The important Bohemian-Austrian composer Gluck uses the clarinet in all his Paris dramatic operas from the 1774 *Iphigénie en Aulide* through the 1780 *Echo et Narcisse*.[61] All the clarinet parts in the scores are written in C rather than transposed, but an analysis of the key signatures according to Francoeur's list of clarinets suggests that *Orphée et Eurydice* (1774), *Alceste* (1776), and *Armide* (1777) used C, B♭, and A or B♮ clarinets.[62] *Iphigénie en Aulide*, *Iphigénie en Tauride* (1779), and *Echo et Narcisse* utilized C and A clarinets. One short section in the autograph of *Orphée et Eurydice* introduces clarinets in G (clarinets d'amour).[63] Furthermore, the intonation difficulties players experienced in the low register suggest that they chose B♭ clarinets to play in E-flat major and A-flat major, and A clarinets to play in E major. In addition, accuracy of intonation is important in these works because the clarinets often double the flute, oboe, or violin parts. In most of his operas, Gluck requires clarinets in usually eight to nine sections, with as many as thirteen in *Cythère assiégée* (1789).[64] The parts usually stay within a two-octave compass of c^1 to c^3, at most a to e^3, and were played on French four- or five-key clarinets.

Tommaso Giordani

Giordani was another Italian composer working in London who wrote for the clarinet. His earliest use of the clarinet is in three concert arias published in London in 1772. The collection *Three Songs and a Cantata Sung by Mrs. Weichsel at Vaux Hall* includes one aria, "Balmy music leads the gale," quite similar to the concert arias by J. C. Bach. The scoring is for two violins, B♭ clarinets, B♭ horns, bassoon, and basso continuo of harpsichord with cello or bass. The clarinet parts of this B-flat major aria have a wide compass of c^1 to c^3 and c^1 to a^2, and the clarinets sometimes double the horns.[65] Two more arias appear in *A Collection of Favourite Songs Sung by Mrs. Weichsell at Vaux-hall*, in which the instrumentation is the same as for the previous aria.[66] Both B♭ clarinets have a slightly higher tessitura in the first aria, e^1 to e^3 and c^1 to c^3, but a more restricted compass for the second, g^1 to c^3 and $f\sharp^1$ to c^3.[67]

Giordani adapted J. A. Hasse's opera *Antigono* in collaboration with Vento and Tommaso Traetta in 1774. In the B-flat major da capo aria "Sventurata in tanti affanni," B♭ clarinets, B♭ horns, strings, and continuo have short but effective parts.[68] Identical instrumentation appears one year later in the da capo aria "Quanto è dolce quanto è grato!" from the 1775 pasticcio opera *La marchesa giardiniera*.[69] The writing is idiomatic and effective in blending the clarinet and horn timbres. Both parts are very restricted in compass, c^2 to c^3 and g^1 to a^2, and played on English five- or six-key clarinets. Later in the opera, a B-flat major overture from *Artaserse* (probably based on the overture from Hasse's opera) includes very simple C clarinet parts along with two horns in B♭ and a solo bassoon.[70]

In 1777, Giordani made the earliest use of the A clarinet in London in the pasticcio *Le due contesse*, an adaptation of Paisiello's *Le due contesse*. Two A clarinets, two A horns, and bassoon begin the A major aria "In van sperar dovrebbe," in which the most prominent orchestral tone color is the clarinets' clarion register, although the range is limited to a^1 to d^3 and d^1 to b^2 (see figure 4.7).[71] Giordani's choice of this clarinet was not only for the convenience of the player but also for the warm tone color contributed by the A clarinet, described by Francoeur in 1772. The performers very likely played on French or German four- or five-key A clarinets. English clarinets may have been played, but none from this period have survived.

Giovanni Paisiello

The important opera composer Paisiello was one of the earliest to write for the classical clarinet in Italy. D Clarinets are in the finale to act 2 of *I scherzi de amore e di fortuna*, first performed in Naples in 1771.[72] A four- or five-key German or French clarinet would likely have come to Italy by the 1770s because Italian clarinet makers began working only during the 1790s. In 1775, Paisiello wrote for C or B♭ clarinets in one aria of the second version of *Socrate imaginario* for a Naples performance, and he wrote for B♭ and A clarinets in four arias of *Il gran Cid*, first performed in Florence.[73] The next year Paisiello received and accepted an invitation from Catherine II of Russia to become her *maestro di cappella* in St. Petersburg for three years. In 1777, his opera *Nitteti* played in St. Petersburg with clarinets in D, C, and B♭.[74] Most of his operas performed in St. Petersburg include the clarinet, namely *Lucinda ed Armidoro* (1777), *Achille in Sciro* (1778), *I filosofi immaginari* (1779), *Il Demetrio* (1779), *Il matrimonio inaspetto* (1779), *La finta amanto* (1780), and *Alciede al Bivio* (1780).[75] Two B♭ clarinets appear in two arias in *La serva padrona* (1781), performed at the czar's palace.

From 1776 to 1784, while Paisiello was employed at the Russian court, Catherine II established a time limit for opera performances of one and a half hours. As a result, Paisiello's musical characterization sharpened, his orchestration became more colorful, and his melodies acquired greater warmth. Furthermore, scholars have found discernible traces of Paisiello's style in Mozart's important operas *Le nozze de Figaro* and *Don Giovanni*.[76] For example, Paisiello's first aria for Figaro, in his *Il barbier di Siviglia* (1782),

FIGURE 4.7 Giordani, *The Favorite Songs in the Comic Opera of Le due contesse* (London, 1777), 6. Courtesy of the Bodleian Library.

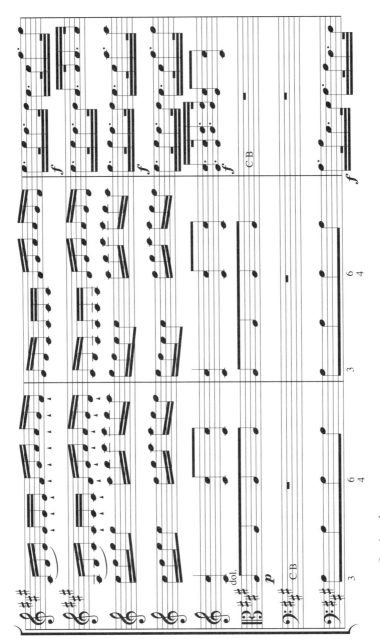

FIGURE 4.7 *Continued.*

132

FIGURE 4.7 *Continued.*

makes use of melodies similar to Figaro's cavatina "Se vuol ballare" in Mozart's *Le nozze de Figaro* (1786). Count Almaviva's cavatina in Paisiello's opera is reminiscent of Cherubino's arietta "Voi, che sapete" in Mozart's opera. There are also similarities between Paisiello's touching portrayal of Rosina and Mozart's Countess, particularly in the latter's E-flat major aria in act 3. Paisiello's comparable aria (no. 13) is also in E-flat major, and clarinets and bassoons accompany this sensitive heroine in both composers' works.[77]

Il barbier di Siviglia, first performed at the St. Petersburg court in 1782, was highly successful and retained its popularity until the 1820s. It was first performed in Vienna in 1783 and in Naples in 1783. In *Il barbier*, Paisiello carefully specifies B♭ clarinets in just one number in each of acts 1, 2, and 4, paired with the first violins, bassoons, or horns. He reserves the clarinet's warm tone color for certain characters and stays within a compass of c^1 to c^3.[78] For example, in no. 16 (act 3), solo clarinet and bassoon introduce Rosina's aria "Gia riede prima vera," mainly in alternating thirds (see figure 4.8).[79] Directly following this aria is an unusual "cadenza moderato" section for the soprano Rosina, B♭ clarinet, and bassoon. The text, "La parad dolendo del mio cor," uses long held notes to blend the two winds and voice, and the clarinet is given a rudimentary Alberti bass accompaniment without notes below c^1 (see figure 4.9).[80]

Paisiello continues to prominently employ the clarinet in his operas. *Il re Teodoro in Venezia* (1784) includes B♭ and C instruments in six sections.[81] He writes even more extensive B♭ and A clarinet parts in eight sections of a very popular comic opera, *Nina*, first performed in Vienna in 1789. In Paisiello's subsequent operas, initially produced in Naples, clarinet use varies. For example, in *I zingari in fiera* (1789) one aria specifies only the A clarinet; C and B♭ clarinets appear in five sections of *Elfrida* (1792). A modern edition of *Elvira* (1794) opens with a night party in a castle garden with music performed by clarinet and guitar soloists, two oboes, two bassoons, and two horns. The clarinet plays in its clarino register while the guitar performs the Alberti bass accompanying part, similar to that given to the clarinet in *Il barbier*.[82]

WOLFGANG AMADEUS MOZART

Mozart's works are without doubt the most important contributions for the clarinet in opera. He wrote for the clarinet in the ballet *Les petits riens* (1778) and in eight operas dating from 1781 to 1791.[83] In Mozart's 1785–86 instructions to his English student Thomas Attwood, he advises, "The Clarinette must always be written in C or in F."[84] He recommends these tonalities since they are the easiest to finger and the least troublesome in intonation for the five-key clarinet. A table of transposition illustrates four clarinets in C, B♮, B♭, and A with the comment, "The Clarinett is very useful instead of the oboes when the Key has a number of Flats or Sharps."[85] Indeed, Mozart usually follows his own advice by writing for the clarinet in C and F major, in the tradition of earlier composers and of Francoeur's advice

No. 16 Andante con moto

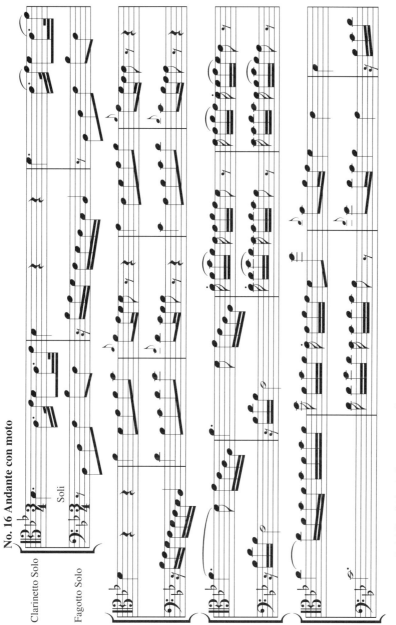

FIGURE 4.8   Paisiello, "Gia riede prima vera," act 3, no. 16, *Il barbier di Siviglia* (1782, MS), fols. 26–28. Courtesy of the Honnold Library of The Claremont Colleges.

FIGURE 4.9   Paisiello, "La parad dolendo del mio cor," act 3, *Il barbier di Siviglia* (1782, MS), fols. 46–47. Courtesy of the Honnold Library of The Claremont Colleges.

in his 1772 treatise. For example, the E major numbers of *Idomeneo* (the chorus "Placido è il mar" and the aria "Zeffiretti lusinghieri") and *Così fan tutte* (the trio "Soave sia il vento" and the rondo "Per pietà") call for B♮ clarinet with the parts transposed to F major. Occasionally, Mozart's choice of clarinet is determined by its tone color, as in the Kyrie in D Minor, K. 341/368a, where A clarinets in four flats play instead of C clarinets.[86]

Les petits riens, K. Anh. 10, performed in Paris in 1778, has six sections that include B♭ and C clarinets, but Mozart wrote only the overture and no. 12. His clarinet writing is similar to that in other French works of the 1770s,

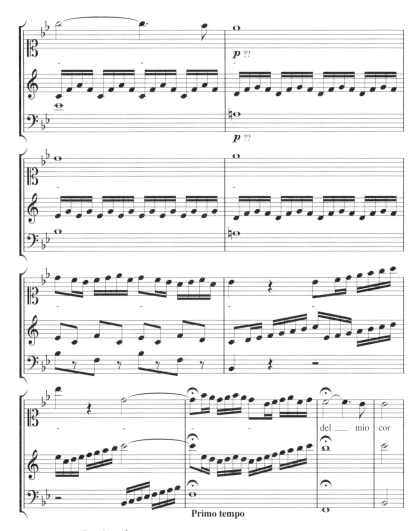

FIGURE 4.9 *Continued.*

staying within a limited compass of as little as an octave, c¹ to c², to an octave and a sixth, e¹ to c³.[87] He wrote his next opera in 1780 for the instrumentalists of the famous Mannheim Kapelle, who had recently left Mannheim with the new elector, Karl Theodor, to live in Munich. *Idomeneo* (1781) uses A, B♭, B♮, and C clarinets, and the writing is more challenging technically, beginning in the overture where A clarinets play a number of awkward accidentals in eighth notes (d♭, e♭, g♭, and a♭²). The compass is widest in the overture, a♭ to d³ and a♭ to g².[88] Jacob Tausch and Franz Wilhelm Tausch performed these parts on five-key B♭ clarinets with corps de réchange for tuning in A, and C clarinets with corps for tuning in B♮.

While living in Vienna during the 1780s, Mozart was particularly sensitive to the clarinet's special tone color in relation to the text of the arias and its dramatic impact. The brothers Johann and Anton Stadler, who both played the basset horn, played the clarinet parts. In *Die Entführung aus dem Serail* (1782) C, B♭, and A clarinets play in nine numbers and the overture, and in act 2, no. 10, two basset horns in F combine with flutes, oboes, bassoons, and horns. In act 2, no. 15, Belmonte's adagio 4/4 aria, "Wenn der Freude tränen fließen," is followed by a change to a faster allegretto 3/4 tempo. Oboes drop out and pairs of B♭ clarinets with bassoons, and B♭ horns play with a simple yet uplifting effect (see figure 4.10).[89] In act 3, no. 17 (Belmonte's aria "Ich baue ganze auf deine Stärke"), the second clarinet has an Alberti bass figure in triplets that includes a written b.[90] Although Mozart's clarinet writing is technically similar to Paisiello's in *Il barbier*, the clarinet is given greater prominence within the woodwind choir, and Mozart's orchestration is fuller and more complex.

In the one-act comic opera *Der Schauspieldirector* (1781), Mozart makes good use of C and B♭ clarinets. First and second clarinets effectively accompany no. 3, a vocal trio ("Ich bin die erste Sängerin") with Alberti bass sixteenth-note passages to low g.[91] Mozart's careful and deliberate use of the clarinet's tone color is more evident in *Le Nozze di Figaro* (1786). After using A clarinets in the overture, he waits until no. 6 to include B♭ clarinets with the introduction of an important new character, Cherubino. According to Kozma, an excited voice line, a flowing legato orchestral movement, and the enticing timbre of the clarinets leading in the accompaniment distinguish Cherubino from the emotional level of previous numbers. The winds consist of B♭ clarinets, bassoons, and E♭ horns without oboes and flutes.[92] In the trio that follows, clarinets remain along with oboes to provide color to the orchestration. Mozart excludes the clarinets until the dramatic introduction of the Countess at the beginning of act 2. Warmth is supplied by the combination of clarinets, bassoon, and horns in act 2, no. 11, "Porge amor qualche ristore."[93] In the following arietta, the orchestration includes solo flute, oboe, B♭ clarinet, and bassoon with two E♭ horns and strings, the latter playing pizzicato throughout. The clarinet provides an introduction to Cherubino's aria, act 2, no. 12, "Voi che sapete," with a chromatically ascending motif on the words "Donne vedete d'io l'ho nel cor" (see figure 4.11).[94] Five additional numbers in act 2 require C, B♭, and A clarinets.

In *Don Giovanni* (1787), Mozart requires C, B♭, and A clarinets in ten numbers and the overture; he increases the compass of clarinet parts in the adagio section of the finale, act 1, no. 13, "Protegga il giusto." Here, the first B♭ clarinet, when accompanying a trio of voices, uses the entire chalumeau range in arpeggios from e to e¹ and f to f¹ (see figure 4.12).[95] In his last three operas, Mozart uses the clarinet more freely, relying on the flexibility and virtuosity of the Stadler brothers and their specially made basset clarinets with an extension of two notes to the low register. For example, in *Così fan tutte* (1790), seventeen numbers and the overture require C, B♮, B♭, and A

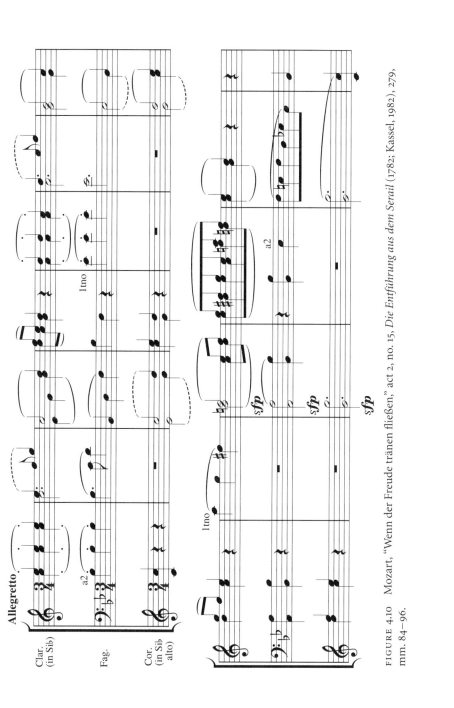

FIGURE 4.10 Mozart, "Wenn der Freude tränen fließen," act 2, no. 15, *Die Entführung aus dem Serail* (1782; Kassel, 1982), 279, mm. 84–96.

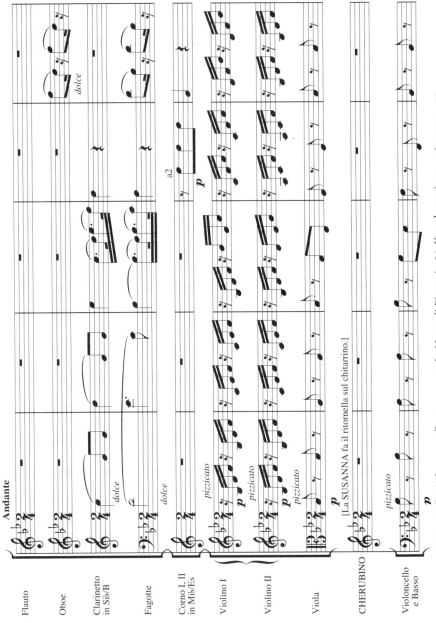

FIGURE 4.11   Mozart, "Voi che sapete," act 2, no. 12, *Le Nozze di Figaro* (1786, Kassel, 1973), 175–76, mm. 1–20.

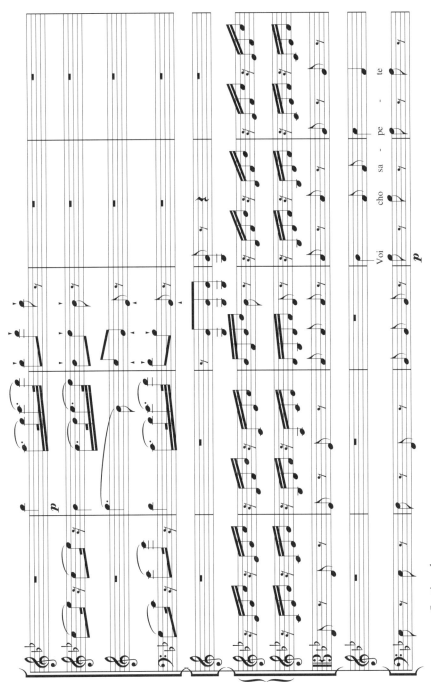

FIGURE 4.11 Continued.

141

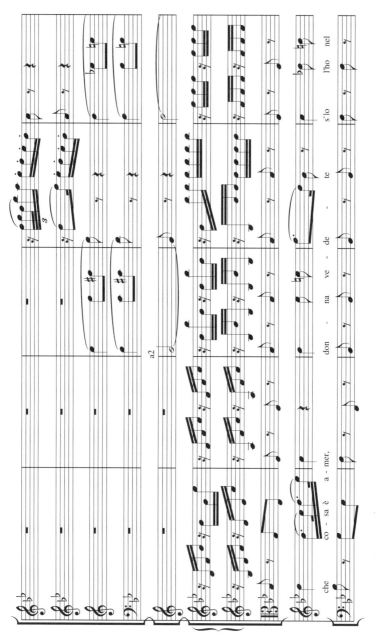

FIGURE 4.11 Continued.

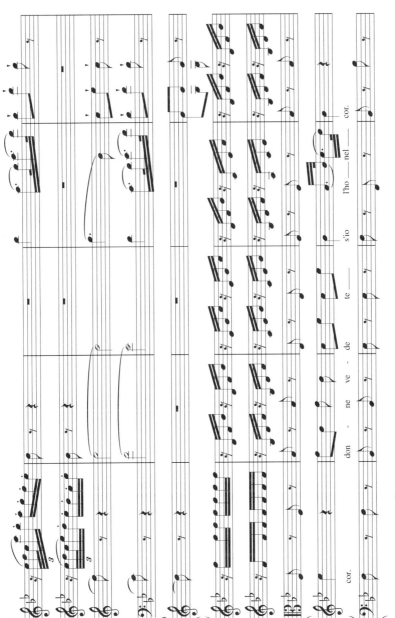

FIGURE 4.11 *Continued.*

FIGURE 4.12   Mozart, "Protegga il giusto," act 1, no. 13, *Don Giovanni* (1787, Kassel, 1968), 201–2, mm. 257–64.

clarinets. In the act 2, no. 24 aria "Ah lo veggio," two measures appear in the bass clef to avoid ledger lines and include two low Ds, which could not be played on a normal-range B♭ clarinet.[96] In Mozart's two last operas, *Die Zauberflöte* and *La clemenza di Tito* (both 1791), he reduces his use of the clarinet to save it for special dramatic moments or obligato solos. In *Die Zauberflöte,* seven numbers and the overture use C and B♭ instruments. Number 9 demands delicacy and accurate intonation from the Stadler brothers. An instrumental march marked "sotto voce" features some remarkable tone colors: solo flute doubled by two basset horns in F with two bassoons; horns in F; alto, tenor, and bass trombones; and strings.[97] In *La clemenza di Tito,* Mozart writes for C and B♭ clarinets in seven numbers and

Adagio

FIGURE 4.13   Mozart, "Parto, parto ma tu ben mio," act 1, no. 9, *La clemenza di Tito*
(1791, Kassel, 1970), 104–5, mm. 26–39.

the overture. In addition, there are two extensive and exacting solos written
for Anton Stadler. The aria "Parto, parto ma tu ben mio," act 1, no. 9, includes a florid obbligato part marked "Adagio" for a B♭ basset clarinet with
written Ds and one C (see figure 4.13).[98] A second extended obbligato part
calls for basset horn in F in the aria "Non più di fiori," no. 23.[99] Mozart's flexible writing for clarinet, basset clarinet, and basset horn unfortunately does
not appear in any subsequent composers' works.[100]

WILLIAM SHIELD AND STEPHEN STORACE

Shield includes B♭ clarinets in his popular 1782 afterpiece *Rosina*. Limited
parts in the overture, no. 5, and no. 6 are in F major. In measures 67–69
of the 4/4 allegro overture, the clarinets play three bars of exposed whole
notes trilling c^3 and c^2 that accompany a melody in thirds played by both
horns.[101] In order to successfully perform this trill, the first clarinetist very
likely played an English six-key clarinet with an A–B trill key. In *Robin Hood,
or Sherwood Forest* (1784), Shield includes a section ("The Call to Dinner")
scored for clarinet and horn quartet that recalls the hunting scene in Arne's
Thomas and Sally.[102] Fiske also notes Shield's contrasting use of clarinets and
oboes in the song "Through circling sweets."[103]

Storace was a leading opera composer in the 1790s. The afterpiece *No
Song, No Supper* (1790) was one of his most popular operas and was printed
in full score. Storace utilizes C and B♭ clarinets in three numbers. The fifth
aria, "With lowly suit," opens with a short, five-measure clarinet solo doubled an octave lower by strings beginning in measure 3. The part is limited
to g^1 to c^3. Fiske notes that in the manuscript score an oboe doubles the clar-

inet part, but the vocal score is marked "Clarinett Solo." This suggests that although the preferred instrument was the clarinet, if none was available the part could be played on the oboe.[104] The finale to act 1, no. 8, "How often thus I'm forced to trudge," begins with a 4/4 aria featuring short solos for each of six singers and ends with a 3/4 chorus. Since the oboes are tacit until the end of the work, these musicians could have played the two C clarinet parts that double the chorus. Surprisingly, in act 2, the duet "Thus ev'ry hope obtaining" begins with a solo for both B♭ clarinets written in thirds for two measures without any accompaniment. However, the compass is very limited, c^1 to $b\flat^2$ and c^1 to f^2.[105]

FERDINANDO PAER

Paer uses C, B♭, and A clarinets in nine sections of his *L'intrigo amoroso* (1795), produced in Venice. There are two clarinet solos, including one where the clarinetist is on stage. In *Sargino* (1803), premiered at the Dresden court theater, he writes for C, B♭, and A clarinets and includes a technically challenging part for solo clarinet in "Una voce al cor mi parla" in act 2. It requires a compass from c^1 to f^3 and several arpeggios on B♭ clarinet.[106] Paer requires C, B♭, and A clarinets in twelve sections of *L'agnese* (1809), premiered at the Teatro Ponte d'Altaro in Parma. The larghetto aria of act 1, scene 9, includes a virtuoso clarinet part with thirty-second notes and chromatic scales and a broad compass from g to e^3. This last aria may have been played on a ten-key clarinet.

JOSEPH HAYDN

Haydn's late oratorio *The Creation* (1798) makes masterly use of the five-key clarinet. Number 9, "With verdure clad the fields appear," is delicately scored for solo clarinet and bassoon in octaves with string accompaniment. He is sensitive in the subsequent interplay among flute, horns, soprano solo, horns, and bassoons. The trio, no. 26 ("Achieved is the glorious work"), reveals Haydn's idiomatic writing for all the woodwinds and vocalists and his careful attention to orchestration and tone color. Clarinets doubled by the first flute begin this charming section, and the winds (two each of flutes, B♭ clarinets, oboes, bassoons, and E♭ horns, along with a contrabassoon) blend seamlessly with two soloists (see figure 4.14).[107] Haydn directed this famous oratorio with vocal and orchestral ensembles numbering from 32 to about 200. Some of the larger performances, with an orchestra of 120, included three choirs of woodwinds and horns (marked Harmonien I, II, III), the players of which doubled the parts marked "tutti." In the passages marked "solo," only the players of the first Harmonie performed.[108]

Other works in which Haydn cautiously uses the clarinet are *L'anima del filosofo* (1791), *Die sieben letzten Worte* (1796), and the *Theresienmesse* (1799). Lawson notes that Haydn's clarinet writing is freer when he is com-

FIGURE 4.14 Haydn, *Die Schöpfung* [The Creation] (1798, Leipzig, ca. 1879), 238–39, mm. 1–13.

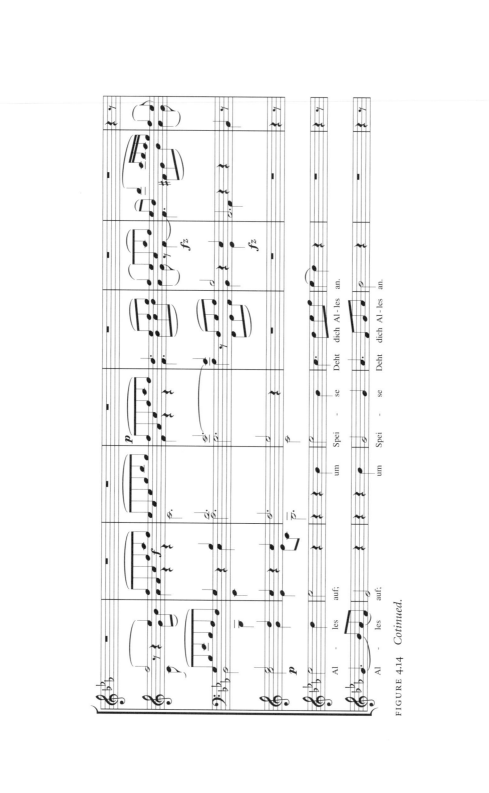

FIGURE 4.14 *Cotinued.*

posing in Vienna than in London. A particularly beautiful section for C clarinet appears in the *Missa in tempore belli* (1796), and there is a brief but dramatic solo for B♭ clarinet in the *Missa sancti Bernardi de Offida* (1796).[109] A newfound confidence in the instrument is demonstrated by Haydn's writing throughout *The Seasons* (1801), the *Schöpfungmesse* (1801), and the *Harmoniemesse* (1802).[110]

Niccolò Isouard

Isouard was one of the most influential *opéra comique* composers in Paris during the early 1800s[111] and was the earliest opera composer to use the entire "normal" range of the clarinet, e to g³. This appears in the first act of *Rendez-vous bourgeois* (1807) in a G major arpeggio (g¹ to g³, then down to e) played on a B♭ clarinet. One of the earliest appearances of a low e in a second B♭ clarinet part occurs in the first act of Isouard's *Lulli et Quinault* (ca. 1812).[112] Isouard wrote for B♭ and C clarinets as a standard part of the woodwind choir in at least eighteen operas published from 1802 to 1816.

Carl Maria von Weber

Weber's most famous and influential opera is *Der Freischütz*, finished in 1821. Thirteen numbers and the overture require clarinets in C, B♭, and A. He makes full use of the compass from e to d³; in addition, there are many short solos and much unison writing for both clarinets. Weber writes in A major or E major throughout the opera. A long clarinet solo in the overture features decrescendos and crescendos in the clarinet register, beginning with the fortissimo entrance marked "con molta passione." Weber skillfully leads to a memorable eight-bar melody over a subdued string section and seven measures of an urgent clarinet melody (see figure 4.15). At this point, flute, clarinet, and bassoon repeat the eight-bar melody in octaves. Later in the overture, the clarinets sustain long chalumeau-register notes over pianissimo strings that build to a crescendo and then decrescendo. The overture ends triumphantly in fortissimo and includes an energetic rendering of the eight-bar melody by the strings and flutes.[113] Weber's writing for the clarinet was a model for many later romantic composers. Clarinetists initially played this work on German eleven-key clarinets.

Concertos

At least a hundred composers wrote clarinet concertos during the eighteenth century, and the instrument's popularity increased during the early nineteenth century.[114] Titus reports that about 85 percent of all the concertos he examined were written for B♭ clarinet; others were written for A and C clarinets.[115] Almost 70 percent of the concertos are in B-flat major,

FIGURE 4.15   Weber, *Der Freischütz* (1821, New York, 1977), 11–12.

and about 15 percent are in E-flat major.[116] The earliest composers of concertos were Johann Stamitz for the B♭ clarinet (1754–55), Michael Haydn for the A clarinet (1764),[117] and Carl Stamitz for the C clarinet (ca. 1771). During the 1770s, clarinet concertos began to be popular concert items in Paris, London and other cities. Starting in 1780, composers and players wrote many clarinet concertos, culminating in the masterpieces of Mozart, Spohr, and Weber. Between 1770 and 1830 a number of symphony concertantes or concertos for two clarinets; clarinet and bassoon; or oboe, clarinet, and bassoon with orchestra were also popular, particularly in Paris.[118] Well-known examples include Carl Stamitz's Concerto for Two Clarinets or Clarinet and Violin, the Concertante for Two A Clarinets by Heinrich Backofen, and the Concerto for Two Clarinets by Franz Krommer.[119]

JOHANN STAMITZ

The important Mannheim composer Johann Stamitz visited Paris from 1754 to 1755 and conducted the orchestra at the palace of the wealthy arts patron La Pouplinière, who employed clarinetists. As a result, the Mannheim orchestra added clarinets in 1758 and officially listed them after July 1759.[120]

In 1936, the Stamitz biographer Peter Gradenwitz discovered a manuscript in the Thurn and Taxis Archive of Regensburg, the title page of which reads: "Concerto a 7 Stromenti/Clarinetto Principal Toni B/Violino Primo et Secundo/Corno Primo et Secundo in B/Alto Viola et Basso/del Sign.

FIGURE 4.16   J. Stamitz, Concerto (1754–55, Mainz, 1967), first movement, mm. 39–47.

Stamitz."[121] Written in three movements—Allegro moderato, Adagio, and Poco Presto—it is the earliest known concerto for the B♭ clarinet. Gradenwitz attributes this work to Johann Stamitz on the basis of several stylistic characteristics and the orchestration.[122] Subsequent researchers also attribute this work, his only clarinet concerto, to Johann.[123] Newhill suggests that Stamitz wrote this concerto during his 1754–55 Paris visit for Gaspard Procksch, a clarinetist in La Poupliniére's orchestra.[124]

The concerto's clarinet solo part is technically challenging. For example, the compass, e to f♯³, is larger than previous concertos. There are frequent wide leaps, chromatic passages in the clarinet register, sixteenth notes, and then triplet sixteenths, followed by thirty-second notes (see figure 4.16). The rococo, lyrical style is freer than that of works written for the baroque clarinet. Furthermore, Stamitz writes for the instrument's full range, with frequent use of the chalumeau register in arpeggio passages, diatonic lines, and wide intervallic leaps. The second movement begins on a sustained note c³ (as do the second movements of some Molter concertos), from which flows a singing melody in the clarino register (see figure 4.17). The third move-

FIGURE 4.17   J. Stamitz, Concerto (1754–55, Mainz, 1967), second movement,
mm. 5–12.

ment, written in 3/8 and marked Poco presto, includes broken arpeggios,
which are typical of many later eighteenth-century works for the clarinet.
Noteworthy is a low e, part of a two-octave leap to e^3 (see figure 4.18). The
frequent appearance of $c\sharp^2$ and b^1 in chromatic passages suggests that this
work was written for a four- or five-key clarinet. Even though the typical instrument used by orchestral players during the 1750s had two or three keys,
it seems likely that a soloist would have used a clarinet with one or two additional keys for a concerto of this technical difficulty.[125]

MICHAEL HAYDN

In 1764 Michael Haydn, the younger brother of Franz Joseph, wrote a nine-
movement Divertimento in D, ST 68, that was one of the earliest works
written for the clarinet in Salzburg, the earliest solo work for A clarinet, and
Michael Haydn's only work for solo clarinet.[126] It is not a full concerto but
is scored for solo clarinet in A (movements 5 and 6); solo trombone, probably an alto in D (movements 7 and 8); two each of flutes, oboes, bassoons,
horns, trumpets; violins, violas, and cellos, and bass. In movements 5 and
6—an Andante in 3/4 and an Allegro spirituoso in 4/4—the A clarinet has
a technically difficult part equivalent to a concerto for a single instrument.
The compass of movements 5 and 6 is from e to d^3, beginning with a lyrical
melody that makes free use of the chalumeau register and leads to a leap of e
to g^2 (see figure 4.19). In the theme's recapitulation, the leap extends upward
from e to $b\flat^2$ in measure 94. In movement 6, accented eighth notes produce
a forceful, jaunty tune that includes many leaps of one and a half octaves—
for example, c^3 to f^1 and c^3 to e^1 (see figure 4.20). The chalumeau register
continues to be freely used, and a number of accidentals are required; the re-

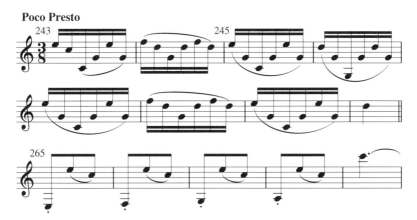

FIGURE 4.18   J. Stamitz, Concerto (1754–55, Mainz, 1967), third movement, mm.
243–50, 265–69.

curring c$\sharp^2$ and e$\flat^2$ suggest the use of a five-key clarinet. In the no. 9 finale,
marked Presto, the clarinet appears in one sixteen-measure arpeggio from g
to c^3, followed by two solo bassoons and finally the solo trombone. Birsak
believes a virtuoso on a five-key clarinet played this work but questions the
availability of a player of this caliber in Salzburg. He suggests that Haydn
probably wrote it before his arrival there in 1763.[127]

Münster suggests an alternative origin for this work, or at least the two
virtuoso clarinet movements, in his description of Haydn's seven-movement
Serenata, ST 407 (1785), which includes two virtuoso movements for the D
trumpet. According to Münster, Haydn wrote the majority of his works for
the Salzburg court; several Austrian and Bavarian monasteries (St. Peter's at
Salzburg, Michaelbeuren, and Herrenchiemsee, among others) also commissioned works from him. Thus, even though Haydn's divertimento is designated "Salzburg," the virtuoso clarinet movements may have stemmed
from a previous commission by a monastery.[128]

Franz Xaver Pokorny

Two concertos that do not approach the high technical level of Haydn's
divertimento are by the Bohemian composer Pokorny. He wrote them
for players at the Oettingen-Wallerstein court, and they are unusual for
the designations on the autographs: "Concerto per il clarinetto primo" and
"Concerto per il clarinetto secundo" (the latter dated 1765).[129] Both concertos specify B$\flat$ clarinet in three movements, the first in E-flat major and the
second in B-flat major. In these works Pokorny follows an earlier practice of
writing for first and second horn players by staying within a higher range, c^1
to e^3, for the first clarinetist and a lower range, f to c^3, for the second. He
is the only composer of the period to follow this procedure, although the

FIGURE 4.19   M. Haydn, Divertimento in D (Budapest, 1965), fifth movement, mm. 23–38.

Parisian composer and theorist Francoeur notes this practice in his 1772 treatise on instrumentation.[130] The First Concerto has two flutes, two horns, strings, and continuo, the flute parts serving to highlight the higher tessitura of the solo part. The Second Concerto has two horns and strings, emphasizing the sound of the chalumeau range of the solo part.

The clarinet parts of these concertos are moderately difficult. The first has a few accidentals, such as bb^2, $f\#^2$, $c\#^2$, $c\#^3$, and there is one eb^2 in the third movement, a Presto. The Second Concerto features the most interesting musical themes and an attractive use of the chalumeau register in the first movement (see figure 4.21). Here Pokorny effectively contrasts the difference in tone color between the clarinet and chalumeau registers by alternating musical phrases with a measure between them. Although Pokorny requires eb^2 in the second movement and $c\#^2$ in the first movement of the Second Concerto, both concertos are suitable for a German four-key instrument with a doubled finger hole for R4, similar to clarinets made by the Dresden makers August Grenser and Jakob Grundmann.

Carl Stamitz

Stamitz was one of the most prolific of the composers from Mannheim. He wrote ten concertos and one double concerto or symphony concertante for two clarinets (or clarinet and violin), all for Bb clarinet except the Concerto no. 1, which is for C clarinet.[131] In 1770, Stamitz moved to Paris

Allegro spiritoso

FIGURE 4.20   M. Haydn, Divertimento in D (Budapest, 1965), sixth movement, mm. 40–52.

and in the following year became court composer and conductor for Duke Louis of Noailles. There he began composing clarinet concertos for the clarinetist Josef Beer. As soloist, Beer played these concertos for the first time at Concerts Spirituels in 1771 and 1772.[132] He continued to perform concertos at twenty-one concerts from 1772 through 1779, presumably those by Stamitz, of his own composition, and by other unidentified composers.[133] Catalogs of the Sieber firm (Paris) in 1777–79 and 1782 list five Stamitz solo clarinet concertos, and it is possible that Beer performed most or all of these concertos at Concerts Spirituels.[134] Stamitz received a 1786 commission, which Beer may have initiated, from the Berlin court for a clarinet concerto.[135] Concerto no. 6, published in 1793 or 1794, was the result, composed jointly by Stamitz and Beer.[136]

Kaiser established the numbering of the Stamitz concertos in approximately chronological order.[137] Table 4.1 correlates Kaiser's numbering with the Sieber printed concerto numbers and with Boese's numbering; the latter system has been generally adopted by writers and publishers.[138]

A good example of Stamitz's writing for the clarinet is a three-movement concerto in E-flat major for the B♭ clarinet, cataloged as no. 11 by Kaiser but known as no. 9 from Boese's work and a published edition.[139] The orchestral accompaniment includes two flutes, two horns, and strings. His

FIGURE 4.21   Pokorny, Konzert in B-dur (Wiesbaden, 1958), first movement, mm. 31–46.

lyrical writing appears in the first theme of the Allegro first movement, which stresses expressive melody in the clarino register interspersed with triplets and chromatic sixteenth-note runs (see figure 4.22). Technical demands are limited almost entirely to the clarino register, although the total range is f to d³. The second and third movements were adapted from a viola d'amour concerto and are quite idiomatic for the five-key clarinet. A simple melody in ABA form begins the second movement, an Andante moderato marked "Aria"; the tessitura falls between b¹ and c³. The third movement, a 6/8 Rondo alla Schas, begins with a lively tune leading to some characteristic broken arpeggios in the chalumeau register and an effective but not difficult leap from c¹ to b♭² (see figure 4.23). Stamitz's hunting-call tune in measures 149–64 is identical to a ten-measure "Ton pour le Débuché" (Call to Market), printed on a plate that includes hunting calls and that is reproduced in the 1762 *Encyclopédie*.[140]

John Mahon

Mahon was an important and popular eighteenth-century English clarinetist, basset hornist, violinist, and composer. He made his debut performances in 1772 playing a clarinet concerto, likely his own First Concerto, at the Holywell Music Room in his hometown of Oxford. Subsequently, he performed concertos in London, 1773 to 1800; Oxford, 1773 to 1778; and Cambridge, 1786 to 1789.[141] By 1777, he had moved with his clar-

TABLE 4.1
Numbering of Stamitz Concertos

Sieber, 1777–82	Boese, 1940	Kaiser, 1962
No. 1	No. 4	No. 1
No. 2	No. 5	No. 2
No. 3	No. 6	No. 3
No. 5	No. 7	No. 4
No. 6	No. 8	No. 5
	No. 11	No. 6
	No. 3	No. 7
	No. 1	No. 8
	No. 2	No. 9
	No. 10	No. 10
	No. 9	No. 11

inetist brother William to London. John Mahon also performed a number of concerts in Dublin, Edinburgh, Dundee, and Belfast from 1781 to 1821.[142]

In 1775, Mahon performed his Second Concerto at the Haymarket Theater, for which an advertisement reads "After Part II of Catches and Glees, Concerto on Clarinet with variations on the Wanton God by Mahon."[143] Mahon played this concerto again during his first performance in Belfast in 1786. The advertisement mentions "Concerto Clarionett with the Airs of How oft Louisa and the Wanton God; composed and to be performed by Mr. Mahoon [*sic*]."[144] Mahon may have written several concertos for his own use but only the Second Concerto survives in published editions. The London publisher Welcker initially listed a Mahon concerto in his 1774 catalog,[145] likely the First Concerto, which does not survive. Two copies of the

FIGURE 4.22   C. Stamitz, Konzert in Es-dur (Hamburg, 1953), first movement, mm. 52–65.

FIGURE 4.23   C. Stamitz, Konzert in Es-dur (Hamburg, 1953), third movement, mm. 130–38.

Second Concerto published by Bland in London exist, one dated 25 March 1786.[146]

The title page of the second concerto indicates that it may be played by "Clarinett, Hoboy, German Flute or Violin," a practice of interchangeability common to the baroque period that continued until the end of the eighteenth century.[147] This surely would have increased sales. It is the earliest surviving concerto by a British composer and was available, probably in manuscript, in New York from the music dealer James Rivington in 1779 and 1780.[148]

The Second Concerto, which uses an accompaniment of string orchestra without additional winds, is written in F major but transposed to G for B♭ clarinet, a tonality found only in this concerto.[149] The clarinet's compass is limited to e¹ to g³, and the tessitura is primarily c² to c³.[150] In the first movement, the themes are quite short, and there are many scalar passages. The theme of the second movement, an Andante, features a lyrical flowing style and the characteristic "Scotch snap" in the charming tune "How oft Louisa" as part of the melody (see figure 4.24).[151] The third movement, a 6/8 Rondo, features a jaunty theme elaborated by sixteenth-note passages, all in the upper range. Mahon played this work on an English five-key clarinet.

Josef Beer

Beer, a Bohemian, was the earliest internationally known clarinet soloist. He popularized the German playing style, which is characterized by a

FIGURE 4.24   Mahon, Concerto no. 2 (London, 1989), second movement, mm. 1–8.

soft expressive tone quality and brilliant technique. As a young man, he studied the horn and trumpet, and at fourteen he became a trumpeter in the Austrian militia. After enlisting with a French militia band in 1763, Beer moved to Paris to play with the Garde du Corps and was inspired to learn clarinet after hearing one. Within four months, he became an excellent player. He was employed by the Duke of Orléans from 1767 to 1777. The Prince of Lambesc employed Beer from 1778 to 1779 and 1781 to 1782.[152] He came to the attention of the Parisian public through many successful performances of several concertos by Carl Stamitz at Concerts Spirituels from 1771 until 1779.

Beer toured extensively in many countries, including the Netherlands, England, Italy, Bohemia, Germany, Austria, Poland, and Russia. In England, he initially performed a concerto (composer unnamed) at the King's Theater in 1774.[153] After performing in England for several months, it seems likely that Beer returned to Paris with an English five-key clarinet or subsequently purchased a German five-key instrument, since Fétis credited him with the "addition" of a fifth key.[154] In Paris, he performed a new concerto of his composition, and he performed his concertos and concertos written by others, perhaps including Carl Stamitz, at four concerts in 1777, two in 1778, and five in 1779.[155] Fétis relates that while passing through Belgium on his way to the Netherlands, Beer heard Schwartz, a regimental musician from Kaunitz, whose soft, expressive tone made such an impression on him that he worked for months to modify his own.[156] It is likely that to this end Beer adopted the reed-below position, turning his mouthpiece so that the reed pressed against the lower lip.

In 1780 and 1781, Beer gave concerts in St. Petersburg and Moscow for Empress Catherine II and her family. He performed another concert in 1782 before he left for Warsaw with his student Franz Dworschack. After two successful concerts, Beer returned to St. Petersburg in 1782 and played in concerts, operas, and table music at the Russian court. By 1783 Beer had received a playing contract, but he obtained permission to travel to Berlin in 1784 and to Moscow in 1785 and 1788 to give concerts. In 1791, Beer participated in a public subscription concert at the house of the restaurateur Ignaz Jahn in Vienna. Beer played several works, sharing the concert with the singer Madame Aloysia Lange and Mozart, who played a concerto on the fortepiano. In 1791, Beer resigned his position; in 1792 he traveled to Berlin to become a chamber musician for Frederick William II, king of Prussia. Over the next four years, Beer visited Copenhagen, Weimar, Gotha, Vienna, and Prague. In 1808, he played a concerto in Vienna, and in 1809, at sixty-five, his performance was overwhelmingly praised at the Gewandhaus in Leipzig. Beer remained at the Prussian court until his death in 1812.[157]

Beer wrote three concertos and cowrote one with Carl Stamitz. Breitkopf and Härtel published two B-flat major concertos and listed them in their Supplement 16 for 1785–87. In 1807, Kühnel (Leipzig) published another B-flat major concerto by Beer as op. 1.[158] Its classical style, however, suggests that it was composed during the 1780s, as does the use of a Russian theme for the third movement, a Rondo. Although the writing is very idiomatic, Beer's concerto is more technically challenging than any previous concertos. The overall compass is three octaves and a minor third, from e to g^3; the first movement makes extensive use of the chalumeau register, with leaps of two octaves or more and many technically challenging thirty-second-note runs (see figure 4.25). The audience must have been astonished and delighted with Beer's extensive use of the chalumeau register in the first movement.[159] Beer's second movement stays entirely in the clarinet register with a simple melody. The Rondo, "Thême Russe," features a catchy theme later presented a second time in A minor, with sixteenth-note runs in the chalumeau register for sixteen measures (see figure 4.26).[160] It is likely that Beer used this theme after hearing it during his first visit to Russia in 1780. During the early nineteenth century, Beer probably played his later works on a clarinet with more than five keys.

Mozart

M ozart wrote his superb Clarinet Concerto, K. 622, in 1791 for Anton Stadler, a celebrated clarinetist and basset horn player who had lived in Vienna since 1773 with his brother Johann Nepomuk Stadler, also a skilled clarinetist and basset horn player. Anton and Johann initially performed as clarinet soloists in Vienna at concerts for the Tonkünstlersocietät in 1773 and 1775.[161] By 1780, Count Carl of Palm in Vienna was employing both brothers, and in October, they were hired by the Piaristen religious order of Maria Treu. In 1781, Anton entered the service of Prince Dmitri Galitzin, the Russian ambassador to Vienna.[162] Both brothers played the clarinet on a freelance basis in Vienna's theater orchestra from 1779 and were officially appointed in 1782.[163] They also played in the Imperial Harmonien or wind band from 1782[164] and played the basset horn.

From about 1787, Anton Stadler owned B♭ and A clarinets with an extended compass to low C, and Mozart wrote music specifically for these in-

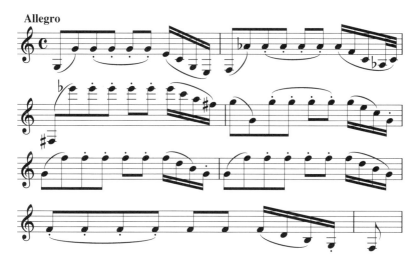

FIGURE 4.25   Beer, Concerto no. 1 (London, 1978), first movement, mm. 318–25.

struments. Stadler's first performance using his extended-compass clarinet was at Vienna's Burgtheater (Court Theater) in 1788. This lengthy concert billed Stadler as the featured performer in "a Concerto on Bass Clarinet played by Stadler" and in "Variations on the Bass Clarinet played by Stadler, a newly invented and manufactured instrument by the Royal and imperial instrument maker, Theodor Lotz. This instrument has two tones lower than the ordinary clarinet."[165] Stadler's first basset clarinet, the name now used to describe this extended-compass instrument,[166] was constructed by Lotz and probably pitched in Bb, with the notes d and C operated by the right thumb, analogous to the lowest or "basset" keys on contemporary basset horns. The concerto Stadler played may have been one that he wrote or perhaps the solo part of the manuscript concerto attributed to Josef Michel with cadenzas that include basset notes (d and C), written on slips of paper attached to the end of each of the three movements.[167] The variations could have been from one of three works for clarinet alone Stadler published during the early nineteenth century.

FIGURE 4.26   Beer, Concerto no. 1 (London, 1978), third movement, mm. 1–8.

The autograph of Mozart's Clarinet Concerto is lost, and the earliest printed editions present a musical text that was altered for an A clarinet with a normal range to low e. Breitkopf und Härtel (Leipzig) initially published the Clarinet Concerto in 1801; three other editions essentially identical to each other followed about 1802 by Jean André (Offenbach), Sieber (Paris), and Pleyel (Paris).[168]

To reconstruct the original musical text of Mozart's concerto, the researcher must consult the autograph of a sketch for the Clarinet Concerto for G basset horn and a review of the Breitkopf und Härtel edition of the concerto. In the Rychenberg Stiftung at Winterthur, Switzerland, there is a twenty-four-page, 199-measure draft of a concerto for G basset horn, probably written in 1791. It consists of eight staves scored for basset horn, violins, violas, flutes, horns in G, and bass; missing are the bassoons that would be used in the A Major Clarinet Concerto. Since it is a sketch, Mozart wrote the entire solo part but only sections of the violin and bass parts. Had he finished the sketch, Mozart would have filled in the inner voices. Without major differences, the musical material of the draft parallels over half of the first movement of the A major concerto. Beginning in bar 180, the notation of the bass line accompanying the solo part in G and D is a whole step higher, in E, indicating that Mozart was already conceiving the work in its later version for A basset clarinet.[169] The basset horn draft includes three notes below e—d, C♯, and C—and suggests the availability of an instrument with three basset keys. Mozart's change of instrument and key to A substantially changes the color relationship of the solo instrument to the orchestra. The tonal characteristics of the string section and the use of a different set of horn crooks contribute to this change.[170]

A review of the 1802 Breitkopf und Härtel edition of the concerto cites several passages altered from the original manuscript and includes the following comment:

> Finally, the reviewer feels obliged to say that Mozart wrote this Concerto for a clarinet encompassing low C. Thus, all of the following passages in the principal voice must be transposed from the lower octave. [here follow references in the score to seven changes in the first movement] . . . and similarly very many passages have been transposed or altered. [At this point in the score are references to three changes in the second movement and four changes to the third movement.] . . . However, since clarinets encompassing low C are among the rarer instruments at present, thanks are due to the editors for these transpositions and alterations, although they have not improved the Concerto. Perhaps it would have been just as well to have it published in the original version and to insert these transpositions and alterations in smaller notes.[171]

In addition to the passages cited in the review, Dazeley, Kratochvíl, Hess, Hacker, and Sheveloff suggest several additional passages for reconstruction

FIGURE 4.27   Mozart, Concerto for Basset Clarinet, K. 622 (Vienna, 1997), first movement, mm. 115–23.

based on melodic shape and orchestration.[172] There are two editions for clarinet or basset clarinet as well as a complete score for the basset clarinet in the *Neue Mozart Ausgabe*. The Hacker edition includes "basset" notes in smaller print,[173] and the edition by Weston is based on an early and important arrangement of the Clarinet Concerto for piano quintet (piano, two violins, viola, and cello) by Christian Friedrich Gottlieb Schwencke, published by Böhme in Hamburg between 1799 and 1805.[174] Schwencke owned a handwritten copy of the clarinet concerto, according to a catalog of his possessions auctioned after his 1824 death.[175] It is quite possible that he based his edition on this manuscript copy rather than on printed editions. Weston's edition includes considerably more ornamentation and added notes than any edition, presenting the concerto in a manner more consistent with early-nineteenth-century practices.[176]

The concerto's three movements (an Allegro in 4/4, an Adagio in 3/4, and an Allegro in 6/8) are ideally suited to the instrument and bring out its lyrical tonal qualities in the themes. Mozart carefully balances the orchestral color of flutes, bassoons, and horns against the clarinet's various registers. In measures 115–23 of the first movement, Mozart makes effective use of the obvious change in quality between the clarinet and chalumeau registers of the clarinet with alternating phrases in a dialogue (see figure 4.27).[177] Basset clarinet versions of Mozart's Clarinet Concerto use a range from C to g³, and some passages are written in bass clef, although the notes sound an octave higher. With this wider compass, the melodic line is not interrupted or transposed as it is in the early printed editions. An excerpt from the first movement provides an appropriate example (see figure 4.28).

The second movement, an Adagio, begins with a sublime melody in the clarino register. The third-movement rondo, an Allegro, begins with a playful theme and is a virtuoso vehicle for the soloist from the instrument's lowest C to g³ (see figure 4.29). Mozart's concerto remains the most important eighteenth-century concerto and the finest work in the entire repertoire.

Another concerto surely written for Anton Stadler and his basset clarinet is Franz Xaver Süssmayr's 1792 Concerto in D Major. Only one incom-

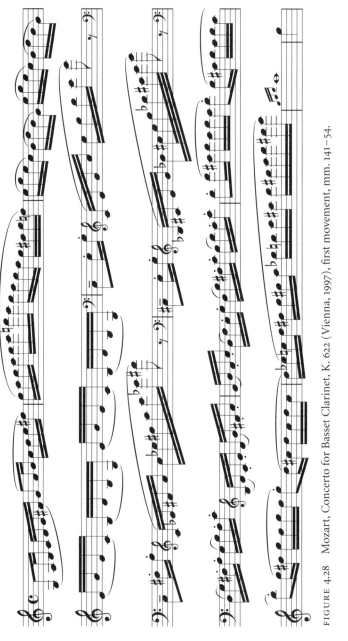

FIGURE 4.28   Mozart, Concerto for Basset Clarinet, K. 622 (Vienna, 1997), first movement, mm. 141–54.

FIGURE 4.29   Mozart, Concerto for Basset Clarinet, K. 622 (Vienna, 1997), third movement, mm. 301–11.

plete movement survives in manuscript, but it shows an astoundingly large compass, c to c[4].[178] Poulin discovered that in 1794 Stadler performed the entire concerto at a performance in Riga.[179]

Franz Wilhelm Tausch

Tausch was an important virtuoso clarinetist, composer, and teacher. He studied with his father, Jacob Tausch, a church musician in Heidelberg. In 1766, Jacob was asked to join the Mannheim court orchestra, and he taught the clarinet to his son.[180] In 1770, the eight-year-old played before the court and was made a student member of the court orchestra.[181] In 1778, Prince Carl Theodor left Mannheim for Munich to become the elector of Bavaria, and the court orchestra, including the Tausches, left with him. Jacob remained as the first clarinetist with the court orchestra until his death in 1803.[182] Franz, still in the student position, was given permission to tour as a soloist in 1780 and 1784. In 1785, he was promoted to a full position in the court orchestra, but in 1789 he left to perform in the private orchestra of the queen of Prussia in Berlin, where he stayed for two years.[183] After spending a year in St. Petersburg, Tausch returned to Berlin in 1792, where he remained for the rest of his life. In 1805, he founded a Conservatory for Wind Instrumentalists in Berlin, where he taught a number of students who later became prominent musicians, including Heinrich Baermann and Bernhard Crusell. Tausch's greatest influence came from his years of teaching at the conservatory.

Tausch's extant solo works are two solo concertos (1796 and ca. 1815) and two symphony concertantes for two clarinets (1800 and ca. 1817). The First Concerto, published in 1796, is technically demanding, with a compass from f to f^3 and most of the technical and melodic material presented in the clarino register.[184] The chalumeau register is featured in the first and third movements, but not as extensively as in Beer or Mozart's concertos. Tausch performed concertos in Berlin from 1803 to 1815.[185] Gerber praised his playing, and Fétis considered him to be on the same level as Beer and Stadler, having at the same time more charm and softness in his playing. Clinch believed, on the basis of the wide leaps and fast repeated notes in his works and his "soft caressing tone and stylish delivery,"[186] that Tausch played with the reed-below mouthpiece position.

The First Concertante, published in 1800, includes two solo parts that are technically equal to each other. For example, near the end of the first movement both parts ascend to g^3, the second in imitation of the first, with runs and arpeggios just as difficult. It is likely that Tausch wrote this work for Beer and himself, and they performed it in Berlin.[187] In an article written in 1808, Michaelis criticized this particular passage, written in octaves to high g^3, as unplayable. He mentions that Mozart seldom ascends as high as f^3 and only once to g^3, and that the passage could not be played with a reed used to produce a soft tone.[188]

Tausch's Second Concerto, published in 1819, attains the technical virtuosity of the most difficult concertos of the time by Spohr and Weber. The concerto is in three movements: a brilliant Allegro, a very short Adagio, and a Polonaise in 3/4. Tausch was very fond of leaping up to g^3 and of passages in broken octaves—features that do not appear to the same extent in any other clarinet concerto of the period.[189] In this first movement, there are two measures of leaps to g^3, and the last three eighth notes are g–g^3–e. This is followed by a chromatic run from e to g^3 and then by quarter notes to c^4; at the end of the movement, there are more octave leaps, an enormous leap downward from a♭^{3} to f, and more octave leaps, ending in a quarter-note passage to b^3.[190] Tausch is known to have discussed clarinets in 1811 with his student Bernhard Henrik Crusell, and it seems likely that a professional clarinetist and teacher would have played his own concerto on the most advanced clarinet he could obtain, an eleven-, twelve-, or thirteen-key model.[191]

BERNHARD HENRIK CRUSELL

Crusell was a Finnish clarinetist, composer, and noted soloist who lived most of his life in Sweden. In 1788, he played the clarinet in a military band at Sveaborg; in 1791 he was transferred to Stockholm and left the army. From 1793 to 1833, he was a clarinetist in the court orchestra.[192] In 1798, he was able to travel to Berlin, where he studied with Tausch for a few months. Afterward Crusell gave concerts in Berlin and Hamburg before returning to Stockholm. The AMZ favorably reviewed one of the Hamburg concerts; in fact, in more than fifty subsequent concert reviews, not a single negative comment can be found.[193] In 1803, Crusell traveled to Paris, where he performed and took clarinet lessons from Lefèvre and composition lessons from Henri-Montan Berton and Gossec. In Paris, Crusell played or purchased a mouthpiece by Amlingue and six-key C, B♭, and A clarinets by Baumann.[194] In 1811, Crusell visited Germany, where, in Leipzig, he arranged for the publication of his compositions by Kühnel; in June, he visited Tausch in Berlin, and the two discussed clarinets. Later in June, he visited a former benefactor in Leipzig, and in July he visited the Grenser shop in Dresden, at which time he purchased an instrument.[195] Crusell's Grenser B♭ clarinet (S-Stockholm, 43554) has eleven keys and corps for tuning to A with eight keys.[196] In 1822, Crusell visited Germany for almost four months, going to the firm of Wiesner, Grenser's successor, and Bormann in Dresden. He purchased clarinets from both firms.[197]

Crusell's solo works include three published concertos: in E-flat, op. 1 (Leipzig, 1811); in F minor, op. 5 (Leipzig, 1818); and in B-flat major, op. 11 (Leipzig, 1828). He also published the Variations for Clarinet and Orchestra on *Goda gosse glaset tom*, op. 12 (1804), and a Concertante for Clarinet, Bassoon, Horn and Orchestra, op. 3 (Leipzig, 1816).[198] Crusell's op. 5 and Weber's Concerto in F Minor (1811) are among the few nineteenth-century concertos in this tonality.[199] Crusell's works possess spontaneous lyric melodies consisting of a three-note descending diatonic pattern of half-note pulses, or a three-note outline, either ascending or descending, of the tonic triad.[200] The upper compass of his works is limited to g³, but the tessitura is consistently wide, making use of the entire chalumeau and clarino registers. The articulation in his works is quite diverse, and Dahlström believes that Crusell played with the reed-above mouthpiece position until sometime after 1800, when he changed to a reed-below position.[201] The technical virtuosity required and the demands of tone and color in these works are equal to those of any clarinet concertos written before the Spohr works.

Louis Spohr

Spohr wrote four clarinet concertos for the virtuoso Johann Simon Hermstedt, the first three for B♭ clarinet (op. 26, 1808; op. 57, 1810; and F minor, 1821) and the last for A (E minor, 1828).[202] In 1808, Duke Günther Friedrich Karl I of Sondershausen commissioned a clarinet concerto from Spohr for Johann Simon Hermstedt, who was employed in the Duke's Harmoniemusik. At the end of January 1809, the First Clarinet Concerto in C Minor, op. 26, was completed, and it was published in 1812.[203] Spohr's reaction to Hermstedt's request is in his *Autobiography*.

> I willingly accepted the proposition. Because of the great technical dexterity that Hermstedt had in addition to his beauty of tone and validity of intonation, I felt full freedom to abandon myself to my imagination. After I had acquainted myself with the techniques of the instrument with Hermstedt's help, I quickly went to work and completed it in a few weeks. Thus originated the C Minor Concerto

(published by Kühnel a few years later as Opus 26), with which Hermstedt attained such great success on his concert tours. Essentially, he is indebted to it for his reputation. I took it to him myself on a visit to Sondershausen at the end of January 1809, and instructed him in the manner of performance.[204]

The resulting concerto furthered the careers of Hermstedt and Spohr and enlarged the clarinet's technique with its technically challenging runs, similar to violin passages, some ascending to b♭³, b³, and c⁴, the highest notes of the clarinet range. In the preface to the 1810 edition, Spohr felt obliged to explain the difficulty of the clarinet part.

> I herewith present to clarinetists a concerto, composed over two years ago for my friend, Music Director Hermstedt in Sondershausen. Since at that time, my knowledge of the clarinet was pretty nearly limited to its compass, so that I took too little account of its weaknesses and wrote some passages that, to the clarinetist at first glance, may seem impossible of execution. However, Mr. Hermstedt, far from asking me to alter these passages, sought rather to perfect his instrument and by constant application soon arrived at such mastery that his clarinet produced no more jarring, muffled or uncertain notes.[205]

The preface also states that the clarinetist must own an eleven-key instrument in order to perform the concerto and describes the instrument in detail. By the beginning of the nineteenth century, Hermstedt very likely owned a clarinet more advanced than the typical five-key instrument. The first performance of the Concerto no. 1 in 1809 utilized an orchestra of one hundred with Spohr conducting. It was a resounding success, and Hermstedt used it often on his concert tours.[206]

This three-movement concerto begins with an Adagio introduction followed by an Allegro theme repeated by the clarinetist at the initial entrance. The long introduction and serious nature of this work play an important part in the early-romantic style of this concerto. Although it is in the fundamental key of F major for the B♭ clarinet, the music requires a nimbleness of finger technique not found in any previous or contemporary concertos. The technical display after the opening ten-bar theme is demanding and awkward to play (see figure 4.30).[207] Spohr also demands control of dynamics from pianissimo to forte, facility with chromatic scales, leaps to c⁴, and arpeggios throughout (see figure 4.31). Spohr's harmonic modulations are within the boundaries of the time: E-flat major for the principal thematic section, to B-flat for the secondary thematic section, to F for the development section. However, his transitions between these tonalities are chromatic, with a bass line that proceeds by half steps in order to establish a cadence.[208] After the recapitulation section moves to E-flat, a modulation in the orchestra brings the work to C major, and after much technical display

FIGURE 4.30   Spohr, Concerto no. 1 (Boston, n.d.), first movement, mm. 23–40.

FIGURE 4.31 Spohr, Concerto no. 1 (Boston, n.d.), first movement, mm. 70–85

FIGURE 4.32   Spohr, Concerto no. 1 (Boston, n.d.), third movement, mm. 30–38.

the movement ends gently with chromatic eighth notes and arpeggios with a diminuendo. The second movement, an Adagio in A-flat major, features a simple clarinet melody and written-out embellishments with a subdued string accompaniment. The third movement is a Rondo vivace that uses the same tonal scheme as the first movement; it is technically demanding, including many leaps and some awkward trills (see figure 4.32).

Spohr's Second, Third, and Fourth Concertos are as demanding for the soloist as the First Concerto. For example, the highest notes of the compass appear in all his concertos and concert pieces. These include c^4 (once in Concerto no. 1, twice in Concerto no. 2), b^3 (once each in Concerto no. 3 and Concerto no. 4), and $b\flat^3$ (twice each in Concerto no. 3 and Concerto no. 4). However, all four Spohr concertos and two of the concert pieces include optional *ossia* passages that provide easier versions of difficult or high notes.[209] Spohr's contributions to the technical development of the clarinet include his use of the instrument's wide dynamic range on a single sustained note in fast and slow movements. For example, the initial measures of Concerto no. 3 require a pianissimo whole-note entrance for three bars with a crescendo to forte; a few bars later, the opposite effect is required, with a forte whole note for three bars and a decrescendo to piano.[210] Spohr was also the first composer to use effectively the chalumeau register in stating a theme at the opening of the second movement in Concerto no. 2.[211] In addition, his use of rapid staccato on a single pitch in the third movement of the Concerto no. 2 is a technique employed by many subsequent composers.[212]

Hermstedt played these concertos and many others in concert tours to Gotha, Leipzig, Hildburghausen, Erfurt, Nuremburg, Dresden, Prague, Berlin, Göttingen, Hamburg, Kassel, Breslau, Frankfurt, Vienna, and Amsterdam, and he participated in music festivals throughout Germany.[213] He was a successful soloist, praised for his abilities. For example, Backofen states in the second edition of his *Anweisung* that "Hermstedt surpasses all others in his mastery of difficulties and through his highly expressive delivery."[214]

Backofen specifically mentions Hermstedt's performance of Spohr's works. Along with the Weber concertos, Spohr's four concertos are the most important in the nineteenth-century clarinet repertoire.

CARL MARIA VON WEBER

Weber wrote his Clarinet Concertino and two concertos for Heinrich Baermann in 1811, two years after Spohr finished his First Concerto. Baermann attended the School for Military Music in Potsdam from 1798 to 1804 and played in the band of the Royal Prussian Lifeguards.[215] There he studied with the virtuoso Josef Beer and in 1805 was sent to the newly opened Conservatorium for Wind Instrumentalists in Berlin, where he studied with Franz Tausch. Thus, Baermann had the advantage of studying with two of the most prominent clarinet soloists of the time. After the French defeat of the Prussians in 1807, Baermann left the army band and went to Munich to look for employment. He was engaged to play as first clarinetist in the court orchestra, and the Kapellmeister, Peter von Winter, wrote a three-movement concertino for Baermann and Peter Legrand, the orchestra's principal cellist. In 1809, Baermann returned to Berlin, where he purchased a ten-key clarinet at the shop of Griessling and Schlott,[216] to apply for a position, but he was unsuccessful and returned to Munich. Early in 1811, Baermann visited Darmstadt and began important friendships with two composers, Carl Maria von Weber and Giacomo Meyerbeer, who subsequently wrote works for him. Following Baermann's return to Munich, Weber arrived there shortly after beginning a short tour and wrote his concertino in three days. The performance was highly successful, and other wind players in the orchestra requested concertos from Weber, but he completed only a concerto for bassoon. The success of the concertino was so great that King Maximilian commissioned two more full-scale concertos for Baermann. Weber completed the First Concerto in F Minor and the Second Concerto in E-flat Major, and both were performed soon thereafter. Although Baermann played both in his subsequent tours through Europe and Russia, his favorite was the Concerto in F Minor, which he played more often than the Concerto in E-flat Major.[217]

Contemporary press notices often compared Baermann's and Hermstedt's playing. After Hermstedt gave a concert in Munich (Baermann's home), the *Zeitung für die elegante Welt* reported: "'Our' Baermann is the first of all clarinetists and remains it, but we think highly enough of Hermstedt not to call him second, for his is a very great artist."[218] Weber, who knew both personally, commented in his diary:

> Hermstedt played twice very beautifully. A thick, almost stuffy tone. Surmounts tremendous difficulties, sometimes completely against the nature of the instrument, but not always well. Also pleasing delivery. Has many strings to his bow, which is all to the good. But lacks

the uniform quality of tone which Baermann has between the high and low notes, and his heavenly tasteful delivery.[219]

From these criticisms and a comparison of the Spohr and Weber concertos, it appears that Hermstedt was the more technically proficient of the two performers, but Baermann may have surpassed him in tonal flexibility and interpretation.

The concertino begins with a serious C minor Adagio ma non troppo introduction. The clarinet enters dramatically with piano entrance on a long held b♭2 and immediately takes center stage. Weber skillfully incorporates the wide compass of the instrument into his theme, including leaps from f to a2 and e to a2 and many dynamic contrasts. A simple sixteen-measure Andante theme in the clarino register features Baermann's ability to leap, followed by a Poco più vivo section with a technical display of sixteenth notes and rapid articulation. A slower variation on the theme appears in flowing triplets, followed by a second variation presented "con fuoco" in sixteenth notes spanning a compass of e to d3. An orchestral interlude followed by a Lento section explores the unusual tone color created by an eight-bar theme presented in the chalumeau register over divided violas. The concertino triumphantly ends with a final Allegro section in 6/8 full of technical display, with a theme marked "con passione."

The First and Second Concertos follow the normal three-movement pattern of sonata-allegro first movement, songlike slow movement, and rondo finale. However, within these formal conventions Weber achieves many unusual effects, since his inclination was toward freer forms, as shown in the concertino and the *Konzertstücke* for piano and orchestra.[220] For example, the Concerto in F Minor begins with a serious-sounding theme initially presented by the cellos and highlighted by timpani. Weber's harmonic progressions and theatrical scoring raise anticipation even before the soloist begins. As in the concertino, the clarinet enters pianissimo on a held b♭2. Weber makes skillful use of legato and different articulations throughout the registers while presenting the theme in triplets.[221] After a brilliant display of runs, trills, and a trill on f♯3 resolving to g3, the movement ends after a pianissimo leap from e♭2 to f♯ to fade away on g. The C major second movement presents a beautiful theme under murmuring strings followed by an active fortissimo sixteenth-note section. A new effect appears when the clarinet plays a somber hymn over three-part harmony in the horns.[222] The movement quietly ends with the return of the first theme. The third-movement Rondo features lighthearted themes and technical display. Weber uses the entire compass of the clarinet, from e to g3, in a very idiomatic and natural manner.

After an orchestral introduction of fifty bars, the soloist begins the Concerto in E-flat Major with a three-octave leap from f3 to f that sets the mood for the virtuosity and brilliance of the entire movement (see figure 4.33). After a display of virtuosity near the end of the movement, the clarinet is given three declamatory motives in sixteenth notes, ascending from the low-

FIGURE 4.33   Weber, Concerto no. 2 (New York, 1958), first movement, mm. 50–54.

est notes, f and e, to quarter notes on f^3, a^3, and bb^3.[223] The free-form second movement, a Romanze in G minor, begins after an introduction by pizzicato celli over violas in thirds. The clarinet solo is a simple vocal line that becomes more elaborate and dramatic as the movement progresses. After a modulation to a short section in G major featuring a leap from e to g^3 followed by an ab^3, there is an almost operatic section in C minor marked "Recitativo ad lib." After a few measures, the clarinet line becomes more agitated, and the orchestra interjects chords while the clarinet answers. After a long held note, a brilliant written-out cadenza leads back to the movement's G minor theme (see figure 4.34). The last-movement rondo is marked Alla polacca and includes a polonaise rhythm created by a combination of the eighth-note orchestral accompaniment and the sixteenth notes of the soloist. There are several passages where the clarinet is alone that emphasize the soloist's agility in runs and leaps. For example, the clarinet exchanges the melody for obbligato sixteenths in measures 143–47, while the flute plays the melody. The end of the movement features the clarinet in a whirlwind of repeated sexlets, bringing the concerto to a spectacular end (see figure 4.35).

Orchestral Music

The clarinet entered the orchestra during the 1750s primarily as an optional instrument that was replaceable by the oboe or flute. Since clarinets were not widely available until the 1780s and 1790s, its status did not markedly improve until Mozart's symphonies of the 1780s. The clarinet finally achieved parity with the flute and oboe in Beethoven's symphonies of the first decade of the nineteenth century.

The amateur musician John Marsh comments on the introduction of the clarinet into symphonies during the mid to late eighteenth century in his *Instructions and Progressive Lessons for the Tenor* (London, ca. 1810–20):

On the introduction of the Symphonies of Bach, Abel, Richter, Stamitz, &c., about 50 years ago. For want of ripienos, the hautboy

FIGURE 4.34 Weber, Concerto no. 2 (New York, 1958), second movement, mm. 63–73.

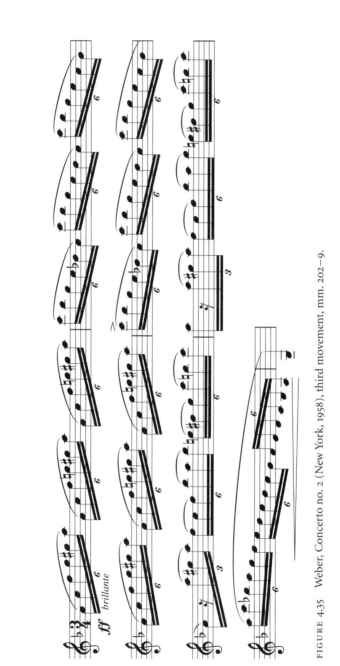

FIGURE 4.35   Weber, Concerto no. 2 (New York, 1958), third movement, mm. 202–9.

parts were, at first, played as such [i.e., ripienos] and doubled or tripled, as they used to be; but this making but an indifferent substitute for the real instruments intended, military bands were gradually introduced, which not only afforded a better substitute for the Hautboy, in the Clarinet, but also supplied the Horn parts and assisted the violoncellos with their bassoons.[224]

The earliest symphonies to include the clarinet are three by Johann Stamitz (no. 1 in D major and nos. 3 and 5 in E-flat major)[225] published by Venier (Paris) in 1758 as part of a collection of six works by several composers.[226] Its title page implies a preference for clarinets, stating, "Instead of clarinets one may play [the parts] with two oboes, flutes, or violins."[227] The D Major Symphony includes nontransposed parts in D major that were likely played on D clarinets in C major; parts for the E-flat major symphonies would have been played on B♭ clarinets. The D major symphony features clarinets and horns are in the first (Presto), third (Minuetto), and fourth (Prestissimo) movements. The compass, transposed to C major, is restricted to b to c^3 in the first movement and c^1 to c^3 in the third and fourth movements. In the first movement, the clarinets double the string parts and appear with horns in six-bar repeated phrases. In the Trio section of the second Minuetto movement, there is a solo section of eight bars. The compass of the clarinets in Symphony no. 3 expands somewhat, ranging from f^1 to f^3.[228] There are clarinets in twelve measures of the first movement, an Allegro assai, but they do not reappear in the rest of the symphony. Two- or three-key clarinets were played if French four-key clarinets were not available.

Gossec was one of the earliest composers in Paris to write for the classical four-key clarinet in an orchestral work. His Symphony in D Major, written in 1761 and published by La Chevardière in the 1762 collection *Symphonie periodique à piu stromenti*, no. 38, contains clarinet parts.[229] Optional clarinet parts are included in op. 4 (1758) and op. 5 (1761–62), and op. 8 in E-flat, F, and E-flat (1765).[230] Gossec specified clarinets in later works: Symphony no. 5 of op. 12 (E-flat, 1769),[231] a symphony in F (1776–77), and Symphonies nos. 1 and 3 of op. 13 (F major, 1786–92; 1782–84).[232] In 1774 either the op. 8 or op. 9 symphony was performed at the Oxford Holywell Music Room, where John Mahon and his brother William were very likely the clarinetists.[233]

Later in Mannheim, the composers Christian Cannabich and Ignaz Fränzl included clarinets in some of their symphonies during the 1760s and 1770s, and they published many works in Paris. Cannabich included D and B♭ clarinets in twelve symphonies, using them more after 1778.[234] Fränzl's Symphony in F Major (1767 or earlier) has C clarinet parts in all but the second movement. It is similar in style to Stamitz's symphonies, with the clarinet primarily doubling the strings and filling in the harmonic texture.[235]

Charles Barbandt, an oboist at the court of Hanover from 1735 to 1751, arrived in London in early 1752 and announced a benefit concert in Hickford's Great Room at which he performed one of his songs, two symphonies, and two concertos.[236] In 1756, his Great Concerto with Clarinets, French Horns, and Kettle Drums was performed at the Little Theater in the Haymarket between acts of Barbandt's oratorio *Paradise Regained*.[237] In 1760, the same work was performed at the Haymarket Theater, now entitled Grand Concerto on Clarinets and French Horns, after a performance of a play titled *Universal Prayer*.[238] Classical four- or five-key clarinets may have been played in these works.

The astronomer and musician William Herschel was among the earliest English composers to utilize the classical clarinet in a symphony. In 1762 and 1763, Herschel was the director of the Leeds subscription concerts, and it is likely that he composed eleven of his twenty-four symphonies for these concerts. He composed Symphony no. 18 in E-flat Major and Symphony no. 20 in C Major in 1762, according to the holograph scores, and Symphony no. 22 in A Minor in 1763. The scores do not include clarinets, but there are two clarinet parts in Herschel's hand for these three symphonies.[239] It is possible that clarinets were played in the 1760s or added during the 1770s or 1780s. If they were played during the 1770s, the performers probably played English five- or six-key clarinets in these works. Other English composers who used clarinets in their symphonies during the 1760s were Thomas Alexander Erskine, the Sixth Earl of Kelly, in his Periodical Overture no. 17 in E-flat Major (1767), performed in Edinburgh;[240] and François-Hippolyte Barthélemon in his *Six Simphonies*, op. 3 (1769), and *Six Overtures*, op. 6 (1775), performed in London.[241]

J. C. Bach used the clarinet in five orchestral works written during the 1770s: Symphony in B-flat Major (Paris, 1773), op. 9/21, no. 1; Symphony-Overture in E-flat Major, Hummel no. 28/Bremner no. 44 (1773); Symphony in E-flat Major (1774), op. 14, no. 2; and Symphony Concertantes in C Major (1775) and E-flat Major (1770s).[242] The clarinet writing of the last work includes about a two-octave compass, c^1 to c^3 and a to bb^2, with two identical short solos of eight measures and bassoons and horns in an accompaniment role. Maunder points out the idiomatic clarinet writing and the fact that $c\sharp^2$ is required in measures 135 and 137 of the first movement, implying the use of an English five-key clarinet.[243] Maunder's assumption is plausible based on the large number of surviving five-key English instruments dating from the 1770s. The remaining clarinet parts in the symphonies and symphony concertantes are written in a similarly restrained manner.

Among the several court orchestras in Germany that employed clarinetists is the small court of Count Philipp Karl Domenicus at Wallerstein. Franz Xaver Pokorny wrote orchestral works that included the clarinet while employed at Wallerstein from 1754 to 1770. In 1771, he joined the Kapelle of the Prince of Thurn and Taxis in Regensburg, where he stayed until his death. Pokorny took manuscripts of his earliest symphonies and two clarinet concertos written for the Wallerstein ensembles to Regensburg, where they remain in the Hofbibliothek.[244] A Symphony in E-flat Major (ca. 1760) includes two B♭ clarinets; seven subsequent symphonies were written for the Regensburg court Kapelle with clarinets: three in D major, two in E-flat major (one dated 1767), and two in B-flat major (both dated about 1770).[245] The D major symphonies call for German four- or five-key D or A clarinets, while the remaining symphonies are meant for B♭ instruments. Baron Theodor von Schacht was another Regensburg court composer. Schacht includes the clarinet in at least seven symphonies in D, F, E♭, B♭, and C (1772–73, 1779) and one Symphony Concertante in E-flat Major (1783).[246]

The Czech composer Wenzel Pichl was a violinist and assistant director in the private orchestra of Bishop Adam Patachich at Nagyvárad, Grosswardein (now Oradea, Romania). After the dissolution of the orchestra in 1769, he became the music director for Count Ludwig Hartig at Prague and, about 1770, first violinist of the Vienna court orchestra. An A Major Symphony composed by Pichl in 1769 includes clarinet parts probably written for four- or five-key clarinets in A.[247]

Mozart

Mozart calls for the clarinet in only four of his forty-one symphonies and in the orchestral work *Mauerische Trauermusik* (Masonic Funeral Music), K. 477 (479a). The reason is that until about 1790 clarinetists were not generally available in many orchestras. In Vienna, there were no orchestral clarinetists until 1782, and there were none in Salzburg or Linz until the nineteenth century.

The earliest of Mozart's five works to include the clarinet is the Symphony in D Major, "Paris," K. 297 (300a), completed in 1778 and premiered the same year by the orchestra of the Concerts Spirituels; Sieber published it in 1779.[248] The clarinet parts are written for A clarinet with a limited compass of c^1 to c^3 featuring only short passages without accompaniment. The clarinetists in Paris played French four- or five-key instruments, but the presence of e♭^{2} and c♯^{2} in the first clarinet part argues for a five-key instrument.

In July 1782, Leopold Mozart requested a symphony from his son for the ennoblement celebrations of Sigmund Haffner. Wolfgang finished the work that year, and the Salzburg orchestra perfomed it. In 1783, Mozart wrote to his father requesting that he send the music of the "Haffner" Symphony, K. 385, to Vienna for a performance. Mozart reworked the score and added pairs of flutes and A clarinets in the first and last movements, primarily to reinforce the tuttis.[249] The parts are technically easy but require a wider range than the "Paris" Symphony, from f to b♭^{2}.

Mozart completed the Symphony in E-flat Major, K. 543, in 1788. It is one of his few orchestral works without an oboe pair and contains his most well known soloistic use of two clarinets in the trio section of the third movement. Here the first B♭ clarinet plays a melody based on an actual

FIGURE 4.36   Mozart, Symphony in E-flat, K. 543 (Kassel, 1961), mm. 1–8.

ländler tune echoed in two measures by the flute, and accompanied by the second clarinet with an Alberti bass line in the chalumeau register (see figure 4.36).[250] This passage is the earliest example of a full and extensive chalumeau range, e to c^1, in an orchestral or operatic work. The public must have instantly recognized Mozart's ländler tune and would surely have appreciated his sensitive and skillful clarinet writing.

Mozart completed the Symphony in G Minor, K. 550, in 1788. In a second version, there are two B♭ clarinets with rewritten oboe parts to accommodate the addition of the clarinets. Although the clarinet parts are more demanding technically then those in the "Paris" and "Haffner" Symphonies, they do not provide a prominent solo role such as that in the Symphony in E-flat Major, K. 543.

Haydn

Haydn used the clarinet from 1793 in five of his last six symphonies written in London. In these works, the clarinet had not yet achieved the importance of the flute or oboe. However, Haydn skillfully adds B♭ clarinets for their contribution to color in Symphony no. 99 (1793), where the range is g^1 to c^3 and f to c^3. In Symphony no. 100 (1794), Haydn reserves C clarinets for only the second movement, an Allegretto, as part of a full Janissary band. Haydn writes for A clarinets in Symphony no. 101 (1794) that are largely buried in the texture and doublings. Although absent from the Andante movement of Symphony no. 103 (1795), B♭ clarinets are important to the wind sound and occasionally have prominence in the first movement. The A clarinet parts of Symphony no. 104 (1795) are rather cautious and conservative.[251]

Beethoven

Beethoven's greatest contribution to clarinet literature is his orchestral music. In his nine symphonies, he gave the instrument memorable lyric

FIGURE 4.37   Beethoven, Symphony no. 8, Menuet movement, clarinet part, mm. 49–65.

solos and technically adroit passages and paired it, usually with the bassoon or horn, to form distinctive orchestral tone colors. The solos became more frequent and important beginning with the Third Symphony in E-flat Major, "Eroica" (1804), with parts for the B♭ clarinet. The slow movement of the Fourth Symphony (1806) features long cantabile solos—a new texture, since earlier works feature clarinets in pairs.[252] In the later symphonies such as the Sixth (1809) and the Eighth (1812), Beethoven requires more control of dynamic and tonal resources, particularly in the clarino register. Beethoven's remarkably emancipated writing in the Minuet of the Eighth Symphony reveals his familiarity with clarinet technique (see figure 4.37). Here the clarinet floats above an accompaniment of horns and strings on a cantabile melody in the second register, reaching a pianissimo high g³ at the end of the solo. The flexibility, range of dynamics, and upper limit of g³ in this part suggest the influence of the accomplished clarinetist Joseph Friedlowsky.[253] Even with this example in the Eighth Symphony, writers such as Gottfried Weber in 1829 were still recommending an upper limit of c³ or d³ for orchestral players.[254]

Beethoven's use of C clarinets in the D minor Scherzo of the Ninth Symphony (1826) indicates his desire for a particular tone color.[255] In his orchestral works, Beethoven demanded from clarinetists a radical increase in volume and endurance, control of a number of articulations and dynamics, and the ability to play in a wide range of tonalities.[256] Due to Beethoven and other composers, the clarinet was an essential addition to the woodwind choir after 1800. His influence was important along with that of the many inventors, players, and makers who were independently contributing to the development of the clarinet.

Chamber Music

Beginning in the second half of the eighteenth century, a substantial number of chamber works appeared, many written for talented amateur players and performed in private concerts in wealthy or noble homes in London, Paris, Vienna, and other European cities. In Paris, musicians performed chamber music at musical salons before a public concert. The composers who gained entry to the salons performed their own works, and their published compositions often included a dedication to a gifted amateur musician. Some publications indicate the composer as a member of a resident private orchestra financed by the royal princes and the *fermiers généraux* (farmers general).[257]

SOLO WORKS

During the eighteenth century, published music for clarinet alone rarely appears aside from studies in method books and tutors. The earliest is a collection of opera airs, overtures, dances, and other songs called *Nouveaux recueils pour une clarinette seule d'ouvertures, morceaux de chant, airs de danse, et autres airs agréables*, chosen and arranged by Abraham and published about 1789.[258] Abraham, a clarinet teacher and composer who arrived in Paris in 1788, was a member of the Théâtre des Delassements Comiques orchestra in 1790. According to Fétis, he was employed by several music dealers to arrange overtures and airs for various instruments.[259] Whistling and Hofmeister listed eleven separate Abraham clarinet solos in their 1817 *Handbuch*.[260]

The *Nouveaux recueils*, written for the amateur player, consists of thirty airs numbered 30 through 60, with one to three selections per page. The majority of the music was adapted from popular operas by Berton, Stanislas Champein, Nicolas-Marie Dalayrac, Grétry, and La Borde, and airs by Abraham, d'Antonio, and Rameau. A note on the title page states that everyone should find this collection very easy to play since all the airs were previously performed.[261] The music is not demanding and lies within a comfortable compass of c^1 to e^3, with most pieces restricted to an octave or more. An exception is a Gavotte from Grétry's *La rosiére de Salency* (1773), the second section of which includes a number of leaps over one octave and downward slurs of up to an octave (see figure 4.38).[262] By the early nineteenth century, technically demanding solos were being published, such as Vanderhagen's *Air de danse de Chimène* (1807–11), a three-page solo with variations based on an air from Sacchini's opera *Chimène* (1784).[263]

FIGURE 4.38   Abraham, *Nouveaux recueils pour une clarinette seule* (Paris, ca. 1789), 20. Courtesy of the Bibliothèque Nationale, Paris.

Anton Stadler published three works in Vienna for clarinet alone during the first decade of the nineteenth century: *Trois caprices pour la clarinette seule* (ca. 1808), *Trois fantaisies ou potpourris pour la clarinette seule* (ca. 1809), and *Variations sur differents themas favorites pour la clarinette seule* (ca. 1810).[264] Like Abraham's solos, they consist of operatic airs, popular songs, and a theme followed by variations. The first and second are dedicated to Stadler's patron and pupil Count Jean Charles d'Esterházy de Galantha. Stadler dedicated the third to Leopold Offenheimer, probably a Viennese amateur. The three caprices are much more technically demanding than the other two solos, with many thirty-second-note runs and leaps of over one or two octaves. The other two solos are much more appropriate for the amateur and average clarinetist. A good example of the theme and variation movement is the song "Der Dudler" from the *Variations sur differents themas*. A simple folk melody begins the variation and is followed by two increasingly difficult variations that require a compass of e to f³ (see figure 4.39). It is very possible that Stadler played these solos during his many concerts and tours from the late 1780s through the first decade of the nineteenth century on one of his basset clarinets, making use of the instrument's additional lower range. Dozens of solos were written by Blasius, Devienne, Lefèvre, Michel Yost, Étienne Solère, and Vanderhagen, among others, many published during the early nineteenth century.[265]

DUETS

Duets for clarinets were among the most popular chamber music works beginning in the late 1760s. They consisted of original works and adaptations of popular songs and opera arias republished in tonalities comfortable for amateurs. Duets are almost always found as study material in tutors and method books and are among the earliest works that can be directly associated with the classical clarinet. David Randall found that 111 composers wrote 1,408 duets, most of which have not been located.[266]

William Bates wrote the earliest clarinet duets in his *Eighteen Duettino's for Two Guittars, Two French Horns, or Two Clarinetts*, published in London

FIGURE 4.39   Stadler, *Variations sur différents themas* (Vienna, ca. 1810), "Der Dudler." Courtesy of the Musikarchiv Stift Melk.

about 1769. Bates was a composer and singing teacher and wrote a number of works for London theaters and pleasure gardens.[267] Each duet, entitled "Duettino," consists of two short movements in C major with a compass of c^1 to c^3 for the first clarinet and c^1 to a^2 for the second; the tessitura lies mainly in the clarino registers, c^2 to c^3 and e^1 to g^2.[268] Randall mentions the sole use of $f\sharp^2$ for cadencing many of the A sections in the dominant tonality of G major. These duets exhibit simple diatonic scale and arpeggio pas-

FIGURE 4.39   *Continued.*

sages similar to those found in the anonymous *Airs a deux chalumeaux* (1717–22).[269]

Roeser was the earliest composer in France to write clarinet duos. His *Gamme de la clarinette avec six duos pour cet instrument*, published in Paris about 1769, consists of a fingering chart for a four-key French clarinet with the fourth key for F♯/C♯ and five pages of music. All the duets are bipartite in form, vary in length from one to five lines, and are mostly stepwise and diatonic. Although the chart provides fingerings from e to g³, the largest compass is f to d³ and is found in one example, and only one duet requires both clarinets to play f to c³.[270] Three subsequent publications with a fingering chart for a four-key clarinet, identical to Roeser's instrument, include popular melodies such as "La Furstemberg" and marches or arias from operas by Grétry and Pierre-Alexandre Monsigny, among others.[271]

In 1770, the composer and philosopher Jean Jacques Rousseau received a request for church music and a blank music book from the Marquis de Beffroi. Rousseau responded that the music book did not have enough space to allow him to fulfill the marquis's request, but he would send some pieces for the marquis's amusement.[272] These pieces were a duet in four movements for two clarinets within a compass of g to d³ for both clarinets, technically accessible to amateur players.[273] About 1770, C. P. E. Bach wrote a Duet for Two Clarinets (H. 636) with two movements, an Adagio e sostenuto and an Allegro. The overall compass for both clarinets is g to d³, and the musical material is well written and interesting.[274]

Gaspard Procksch published four collections of twenty-five duos for two clarinets in 1773 and 1774.[275] Unfortunately, these works are lost, but his

Primo

FIGURE 4.40   Procksch, *VIIIᵉ recueil*, op. 11 (Paris, 1776), no. 23, first and second parts, 8.

eighth collection of duos for clarinets or horns is preserved. Bignon published this work under Procksch's given name as the *VIIIᵉ recueil contenant 38 airs en duo pour deux clarinettes ou deux cors de chasse*, op. 11, about 1776. On the title page, Procksch identifies himself as the first clarinetist for the late Prince de Conti, who died in 1776.[276] Some of the duets are very demanding. For example, no. 23, an Allegro ma non troppo, has a compass of g to g³ for the first part and g to e³ for the second (see figure 4.40).[277]

During the 1770s and 1780s in Paris, Roeser, Abraham, and Vanderhagen published many editions of opera arias arranged for two clarinets. Roeser's first collection of airs from comic operas arranged for two clarinets (1774), with an optional keyboard accompaniment, is listed in the *Journal de musique* published by Le Menu.[278] Abraham copied all of these duets from Roeser's publication into small part books as the first of a series of thirty-two collections totaling 661 duets published from about 1778 to 1785.[279] Vanderhagen and other composers in Paris continued to arrange airs from operas as clarinet duets and occasionally wrote original music.[280] Many duets composed during the early nineteenth century used original compositions, notably those by Crusell,[281] Lefèvre,[282] Stadler,[283] and Yost.[284]

Secondo

FIGURE 4.40   *Continued.*

Published duets for clarinet and bassoon appeared in the 1780s. The bassoonist Franz Anton Pfeiffer composed two duets for violin with an alternate part for B♭ clarinet and bassoon or cello. Published duets are also available from Devienne,[285] François-Joseph Garnier,[286] François René Gebauer (ca. 1796),[287] Karl Andreas Goepfert (1821),[288] and Franz Tausch. Beethoven's Three Duets for Clarinet and Bassoon, WoO 27, exist in numerous editions but are now considered of doubtful authenticity.[289]

SONATAS AND SOLOS WITH KEYBOARD ACCOMPANIMENT

Clarinet solos called "sonata," "duo," or other designations with keyboard accompaniment appeared during the 1790s.[290] The earliest sonatas featured clarinet and an unfigured bass line played on a harpsichord or piano, the keyboardist filling in the harmony with the right hand, according to the conventions of the time. An optional cello or bassoon could double the bass line. For practice and performance at home, it was equally possible to play these sonatas with an accompaniment of simply a cello or viola, as suggested by Claude-François Buteux in his 1836 *Méthode de clarinette*. Buteux also suggests in an unattributed "Sonata Pastorale": "To make it easier for the teacher who does not know how to play the cello or viola well, because these sonatas are to be played on a B♭ clarinet, one lowers the cello and viola by a tone and plays the clarinet part as written."[291]

In his *Méthode*, Buteux incorporates six sonatas by his teacher, Lefèvre, and other unattributed sonatas and various pieces with treble and bass lines in the same key. There are also indications of arco, pizzicato, and tremolo, and some use of the alto clef. However, by the early nineteenth century, most published sonatas included piano parts written for both hands, and sonatas for clarinet with an unfigured bass line disappeared.

Gregorio Sciroli

From 1747 to 1757, the Neapolitan composer Sciroli wrote intermezzos, farsettas, and full-length comic operas for small theaters in Naples, Palermo, and Rome. For the next ten years, he wrote serious opera in northern Italy for theaters in Bologna, Milan, Pisa, and Venice. The large amount of his surviving church music suggests that he held a church position, possibly in Genoa. The 1769 supplement to Breitkopf und Härtel's thematic catalog lists incipits of his six trios for two violins and bass.[292]

About 1770, Sciroli wrote the earliest sonata for clarinet, possibly after a visit to Milan, where Mozart wrote his 1771 Divertimento, K. 113, for two each of B♭ clarinets, horns, and bassoons. The title page reads "Sonata/Clarinetto/et/Basso/Del Sig: Gregorio Sciroli."[293] Sciroli wrote for B♭ clarinet and a single basso continuo line in three movements (Allegro moderato, Lento, and Allegro in 3/8) with a compass from e^1 to d^3 and a light, cantabile melodic line.[294] He chose a limited compass so it would also be appropriate for the flute or oboe, where the range would be d^1 to c^3.[295]

Jean Xavier Lefèvre

The important French clarinetist and soloist Lefèvre wrote the earliest published sonatas for clarinet with unfigured bass, printed in 1793–94 by Janet (Paris) as *Trois grandes sonates pour clarinette et basse*, op. 12.[296] The Allegro moderato first movement of the First Sonata for B♭ Clarinet, written in C major, is remarkable for its technical demands. The entire compass is utilized, from e to g^3, although the highest note is part of a short cadenza in the first movement; the clarinetist is almost always playing, and breaths have to be taken at points in the phrases that do not disturb the flow of the notes; in addition, there are several chromatic passages in the upper register. Lefèvre distinguishes between three types of articulation: short, sharp staccato, marked by a dash; a semi-sharp staccato, marked by a dot; and a portamento marked by a dot and a slur. Clearly, this is a work for a virtuoso. In both the Adagio second movement and the short Rondo third movement the clarinet plays continuously. The second movement demands a wide compass of e to d^3, while the Rondo is restricted to the clarino register and requires rapid staccato throughout.[297]

Anton Eberl

In 1800, the Viennese composer Eberl wrote the earliest sonata for clarinet with an independent piano part as the second of two sonatas published in St. Petersburg.[298] The solo is for B♭ clarinet in three movements; an unusual feature is a separate bass line with arco and pizzicato indications that differ from the keyboard part. The work may be played without this part, but according to Voxman, it is definitely worth including.[299] Balássa and Mead prepared two detailed harmonic and formal analyses of this sonata.[300] As found in several early clarinet sonatas, the piano part in the first two movements is quite ornate and brilliant, while the clarinet part is technically undemanding. The clarinet part in the third movement has some sixteenth-note runs in G major and C major. Eberl uses an extensive compass from e to d^3 in the first and third movements and accompaniment figures in the chalumeau register.

Weber

The finest of the early solos and the most outstanding of the nineteenth century is the *Grand duo concertant* (1815, published 1816), J. 204, by Weber. Weber very likely wrote it for Hermstedt, who had requested a concerto in 1812.[301] It is possible that Weber began the piece as a concerto and rewrote it for clarinet and piano. This work is unusual in exhibiting a balance of thematic and melodic importance between both instruments. The clarinet part is easily as demanding as that of most concertos and includes leaps of over two octaves, with a compass of e to a^3. In addition, it is technically very demanding for the pianist, who must play in rapid thirds and sixths in the third movement. Weber did not conceive this work as a sonata with a sustained and developed musical argument, but rather as a dramatic presentation of instrumental character performed by two virtuosi.[302]

Weber completed the second and third movements in 1815, and later he and Baermann played a "duo" for clarinet and piano, probably these two movements, for the king and queen at the Nymphenburg in Munich. In 1816, the first movement was completed.[303] Rochlitz, a friend of Weber's, wrote a positive review in the *AMZ* after Schlesinger published the work in Berlin in 1818:

> The work consists of a fiery, continual stream in an Allegro in E-flat; and an exceedingly tender but by no means effeminate Andante in C minor. The third movement is a merry and in part piquant Rondo in E-flat, in which the entire movement mixes with manly cheerfulness, a deep seriousness and melancholy reminiscences that are wonderful and richly effective.[304]

After a brilliant opening in the first movement, Weber makes excellent use of the clarino register in two eight-bar phrases that effortlessly descend to

FIGURE 4.41   Weber, *Grand duo concertant*, first movement, from *Masterworks for Clarinet and Piano* (New York, 1951), 2.

the chalumeau (see figure 4.41). Weber's notable technique of pairing the clarinet and piano in many rapidly moving notes adds to the excitement and dramatic tension. The second movement, Andante con moto, begins with a soft, meditative melody that rapidly becomes theatrical in its gestures and dynamics. Altogether, it is a satisfying movement to hear and perform. The rondo third movement begins quietly with the clarinet and piano playing many sixteenth-note runs. Arriving at a D-flat major episode, the clarinet states an urgent theme over "thunderous piano tremolos."[305] A calming effect comes with the rondo theme in the bass, gradually leading back to the main theme in the chalumeau register. The combination of sixteenth-note runs and large leaps is the most demanding moment of the work (see figure 4.42).

Early-nineteenth-century sonatas and solos include three sonatas by Johann Vanhal (1801, 1803, 1810); one by Friedrich Heine (ca. 1803); Paul Struck's *Grand duo*, op. 7 (1804);[306] Franz Anton Hoffmeister's Six Duos (1807–12);[307] Ferdinand Ries's Sonata, op. 29 (1809) and *Sonata sentimentale*, op. 169 (ca. 1812);[308] Giocchino Rossini's Variations, 1809;[309] Carl Maria von Weber's Seven Variations (1811) and *Grand duo concertant* (1815–16); and works by François-Adrien Boieldieu (ca. 1810), Franz Danzi (1817–18), Archduke Johann Rudolph (1822), and Felix Mendelssohn (1824).[310] Optional violin solo parts were included in all the earliest sonatas by Eberl, Vanhal, Heine, Struck, and Weber (*Grand duo*) in order to increase sales.[311]

TRIOS

During the 1770s and 1780s C. P. E. Bach, Gassmann, Vanhal, and Wagenseil wrote the earliest trios. They utilized a variety of instrumental combinations, including clarinet, horn, and bassoon; clarinet, violin and

FIGURE 4.42   Weber, *Grand duo concertant*, third movement, from *Masterworks for Clarinet and Piano* (New York, 1951), 8.

basso continuo; and clarinet, bassoon, and basso continuo. These composers were working in London, Paris, and Vienna, where performances were common in homes and public venues.[312]

Florian Leopold Gassmann

The Bohemian composer Gassmann studied in Italy, probably under Padre Martini, and by 1757 had become a successful opera composer in Venice. In 1763, he returned to Vienna as a ballet composer and successor to Gluck. He wrote a Trio for Solo Clarinet, Obbligato Horn, and Bassoon in D major during the late 1760s or early 1770s for A clarinet, D horn, and bassoon.[313] The four movements—Andante, Minuet, Adagio, and Allegro—

are in a gallant style, with the leading melodic line given to the clarinet. The early use of an A clarinet is notable. Its restricted tessitura is almost entirely in the clarino register, and the trio's compass is f¹ to d³. The clarinet is paired throughout in thirds or sixths with the bassoon and horn.

Later trios for clarinet, horn, and bassoon include those by F. R. Gebauer (ca. 1799 and ca. 1804),[314] Devienne (ca. 1805),[315] Frédérick Duvernoy (early nineteenth century), and Crusell (ca. 1814).[316]

Georg Christoph Wagenseil

The Viennese court composer Wagenseil began publishing works for harpsichord in 1740 in Germany and became one of the more widely known composers of his day through his many publications by firms in Amsterdam, London, Paris, Vienna, and cities in Germany. His works were performed at Concerts Spirituels and various Parisian salons, including the Prince of Conti's, between 1759 and 1781. In 1765, he received a twelve-year *privilège générale* for publishing music.[317]

Wagenseil wrote a Sonata for Clarinet, Violin, and Basso Continuo, WV 580, that dates from the early 1770s.[318] Throughout this work, Wagenseil gives leading parts to the clarinet and violin, with an entirely accompanimental harpsichord continuo. The moderately difficult clarinet part utilizes a compass of g to d³, although most of the passages are in the clarino register. The designations "Chal." (chalumeau) and "Clar." (clarinet), indicating an octave-below transposition and a return to written pitch, respectively, are given several times in the first and third movements—the earliest known use of these terms in chamber music to indicate octave transposition. The presence of c♯² and d♯² suggests that the work was meant for a four- or five-key clarinet.

Johann Baptist Vanhal

Vanhal was a Bohemian violinist and composer who moved to Vienna sometime before 1761. He gave instrumental and singing lessons and established himself as one of the city's leading composers. After two years of traveling and studying in Italy, he declined an offer to become Kapellmeister of a private court in Dresden and moved back to Vienna. Vanhal's new patron was Count Erdödy, and he continued to live in Vienna. More than 270 publications of his were issued in Vienna, along with works in other cities.[319]

In 1775, an advertisement in *Almanach Musicale* announced Vanhal's *Six trios pour une clarinette, violon et basse*, published by Chevrardiere (Paris).[320] A later edition of this work, published by Le Duc about 1781, includes B♭ clarinet parts; trio no. 2 is for the C clarinet.[321] The clarinet parts are only moderately challenging, usually staying between c¹ and c³ within an overall compass of g to e³. They are charming and within the grasp of moderately advanced players of the five-key clarinet.[322]

Carl Philipp Emanuel Bach

Bach wrote the Six Little Sonatas, H 516–21, for clarinet, bassoon, and harpsichord continuo during the 1770s after he assumed G. P. Telemann's position as music director for five churches in Hamburg. Alternate versions appear as part of eleven subsequent works dating from the 1770s and 1780s.[323] A keyboard virtuoso, Bach gives the harpsichord a brilliant and leading part that simply doubled or echoed the clarinet and bassoon throughout. The clarinet part, however, is a brilliant contrast to that for the bassoon, making frequent use of the high register from c³ to f³, its entire compass ranging from c¹ to f³. This work includes a technically demanding part for a four- or five-key clarinet.[324] Bach's subsequent works with the clarinet in duets and pieces for wind band contain parts that are not as virtuosic.

Wolfgang Amadeus Mozart

Mozart composed his finest clarinet chamber works for the clarinetist Anton Stadler. The "Kegelstatt" Trio, K. 498, for B♭ clarinet, viola, and piano, was written in 1786 and first performed at the home of Francesca von Jacquin, with Stadler playing clarinet, Mozart on viola, and Jacquin on piano. Artaria (Vienna) published the first edition of the trio in 1788 with title page instructions that harpsichord or piano could be played, and that the clarinet part could be played on the violin.[325] André's 1793 edition has a printed piano part with no other parts above it, apparently an eighteenth-century practice, and separate parts for "violino, o clarinetto" and viola.[326] The violin or clarinet part was meant for the violin, since it is not transposed for a B♭ clarinet, and passages such as the triplet arpeggios in the third movement beginning with f and e and later arpeggios are transposed an octave higher or to other notes of the arpeggio. It is not known how many subsequent editions provide a separate B♭ clarinet part.

The first movement, an Andante in 6/8, has all the clarinet's melodic writing in the clarino register with a compass of e¹ to c³. It does include, however, some difficult chromatic passages in the first movement for the player of a five-key instrument, beginning with the initial entrance of the clarinet. The second movement is a short, joyful Minuet, followed by a serious C minor Trio, and ending with a buoyant clarinet melody in E-flat major. The third movement, Allegretto, features extensive solos for both clarinet and viola with arpeggios in the chalumeau register beginning on f and e. However, the most prominent part of the third movement is for the piano, which approaches the virtuosity of a concerto. Although all three movements are similar in terms of tempo, Mozart perfectly integrates the trio with beautiful melodies having subtle blends and contrasts. The work becomes ever more inspired as it reaches its conclusion.[327] Although later trios were composed for clarinet, viola, and piano, most composers chose to write for clarinet, cello, and piano, since the clarinet and cello have a better balance of compasses.

Beethoven

Beethoven wrote his Trio for Piano, Clarinet and Cello, op. 11, in 1797–98 after moving to Vienna. Mollo (Vienna) published the first edition in October 1798 with a title page suggestion of the violin as an alternate for the clarinet.[328] The first movement, Allegro con brio, provides a fine balance between the clarinet and cello and a brilliantly written piano part. The clarinet plays mainly in the clarino register, with a sixteenth-note run in one measure going down to e. The second movement, Adagio, provides an opportunity for the clarinet and cello to play fine cantabile melodies while the piano plays a delicate accompaniment. The third movement is a theme with nine variations based on the aria "Pria ch'io l'impegno" from Joseph Weigl's popular *L'amor marinaro*, introduced at Vienna's Hoftheater in 1797.[329] It features brilliant piano writing while the clarinet and cello exchange melodies frequently and effectively. In this work, Beethoven uses the clarinet as a vehicle for expressing both dramatic and lyrical qualities.[330]

Other Composers

Later notable trios include one for A clarinet, viola, and cello by Johann Nepomuk Fuchs (1808), Haydn's successor at Esterháza; and the Trio for Clarinet or Violin, Cello, and Piano, op. 28 (1810), by Ferdinand Ries, a student of Beethoven.[331]

QUARTETS

Quartets for clarinet with strings (usually violin, viola, and cello) were the most popular type of chamber music for clarinet during the late eighteenth and early nineteenth centuries. Tuthill identified over fifty works and Rau investigated about 300 works by ninety composers, mostly quartets.[332] A glance through the works in Whistling and Hofmeister's 1817 *Handbuch* and its ten supplements (1818–27) indicate that a large number were published,[333] particularly in Paris. These quartets are among the popular chamber works performed in the Parisian salon concerts during the late eighteenth century. Carl Stamitz, Cannabich, and Johann Kuchler were the earliest quartet composers, and all were published during the 1770s. Sieber published Stamitz's *Six quatuor a une clarinette violin alto et basse*, op. 8, in 1773. A note on the title page states that the clarinet part may be played on oboe or violin, and the viola part may be played on horn.[334] Number 4 of op. 8 is in three movements: Allegro, Andante, and Rondo. It is a work full of pleasing melodies with a limited compass of d^1 to d^3. Cannabich wrote two very charming quartets (1774) for oboe or clarinet, violin, viola, and cello or bassoon. His work and the quartets of Kuchler (1774) are similar to the Stamitz works in their high tessitura and limited compass of g^1 to d^3 and c^1 to c^3.[335]

Later quartets include those by Blasius (1782, 1782–84, ca. 1788, and ca. 1799); Georg Friedrich Fuchs (1788–91); Michel Yost and Johann Christoph Vogel (ca. 1789);[336] Pichl (ca. 1790);[337] Charles Bochsa (ca. 1795);[338] Paul Struck (ca. 1795); Charles-Simon Catel (ca. 1796); Mozart (transcriptions of K. 317d, K. 374, K. 496, and ca. 1799);[339] Hoffmeister (ca. 1802);[340] Franz Krommer (ca. 1802, 1811, 1814, and 1816); Karl Andreas Goepfert (ca. 1803 and 1818);[341] Lefèvre (ca. 1805);[342] Johann Nepomuk Hummel (1808); Crusell (1811, 1817, and 1823); and Iwan Müller (1817–18).[343] By the 1780s and 1790s, these works become technically demanding, with a freer use of the entire range from e to d³, rapid changes of registers, and Alberti bass figurations. In addition, Michel and Vogel's quartets require A and B♭ clarinets, and Bochsa requires C and B♭ clarinets. The quartets are on the same level of virtuosity as Lefèvre's 1793 sonatas. The most well known are the works by Krommer and Crusell because of their high quality, romantic style, and availability in modern editions.

QUINTETS WITH STRING QUARTET

Quintets for clarinet with a string quartet were a rare combination during the eighteenth century. Tuthill records only sixteen works.[344] The earliest example is Mozart's famous quintet written for Anton Stadler and his basset clarinet in 1789. About 1802, André published the quintet for a clarinet without the extension of notes below e.[345]

Mozart's four-movement quintet (Allegro, Larghetto, Minuetto, and Allegretto con variazioni) is the jewel of the clarinet's chamber music repertoire. The balance between all the stringed instruments and the clarinet is ideal, and musical ideas pass easily from one instrument to another. In fact, the quintet is chamber music in the truest sense, since there is no trace of the concertante style that is so common in works for clarinet and strings.[346] In the first movements of subsequent quintets by Backofen, Weber, and Baermann, the clarinet plays in many more measures and there is an increased use of sixteenth notes and triplets in the clarinet part.[347] Mozart makes effective use of the chalumeau range of the clarinet, although most of the important melodic material is in the clarino register. The second movement is especially notable for its flowing, lyrical theme. Because the autograph is lost, several musicologists have made suggestions for reconstruction of the original text.[348]

Later quintets for clarinet and strings include those by Backofen (ca. 1804),[349] Neukomm (ca. 1809), Joseph Küffner (1815),[350] Weber (1815),[351] Andreas Romberg (ca. 1818),[352] Krommer (ca. 1819),[353] Anton Reicha (ca. 1820), and Heinrich Baermann (1821 and 1825–29).[354] Six quintets by Backofen, Sigismund Neukomm, Joseph Küffner (ops. 32 and 33), and Krommer make use of the unusual combination of B♭ clarinet, one violin, two violas, and cello, mixing the low timbre of the violas and cello with the higher timbre of the violin and clarinet. Weber's brilliant Quintet, J. 182, is the most well known of these works. This four-movement work consists of an Allegro, a Fantasia-Adagio, a Menuetto capriccio–Presto, and a Rondo–Allegro giocoso. Weber wanted to show off Baermann's technical skill and agility and his control of dynamics, tone and phrasing, particularly in the Fantasia. In the second movement, a dramatic contrast appears in chromatic scales marked "*ff* possible," followed by the same scale pianississimo from e to c³. The Menuetto capriccio is an engaging "rhythmic tour de force" with short, Schubertian modulations. In this work, scales are important motives throughout and provide a theme for the final rondo.[355] Although the strings are purely accompanimental, this work delights as a virtuoso showpiece. The clarinet compass is from e to a³ with technical demands equal to those of Weber's Concerto in E-flat Major.

QUINTETS WITH PIANO

Two important quintets with piano, oboe, clarinet, horn, and bassoon were written by Mozart (1784) and Beethoven (1796–97). Mozart was the earliest composer to use this combination, and his Quintet in E-flat Major, K. 452, was completed in 1784 and performed at the Burgtheater in Vienna the same year.[356] Mozart specifically mentioned it in a letter to his father. "I composed two Grand Concertos and then a quintet that was extraordinarily well received;—I myself think it's the best I've written in my entire life.—It is written for 1 oboe, 1 Clarinetto, 1 Corno, 1 fagotto, and the Piano forte;—I so wished you could have heard it!—and how beautifully they played it!"[357] Anton Stadler and other members of the Vienna court orchestra took part in this performance. The work begins with a stately Largo introduction, followed by movements titled Allegro moderato, Larghetto, and Rondo allegretto. Mozart balances the importance of each instrument throughout the quintet quite skillfully. He constantly contrasts the timbre of the four wind instruments against that of the piano by writing short motives, often two-bar phrases, and passing them from one instrument to the other to create a rich panoply of tone colors and an ingenious unity.[358] The third movement ends with an unusual written cadenza that skillfully tosses short motives among all the instruments. The clarinet part stays within a limited tessitura of c¹ to c³ although g and f are required in the third movement.

Beethoven modeled his Quintet in E-flat Major, op. 16, on Mozart's quintet; they have the same tonality, scoring, and structure, but Beethoven's piece does not have the elaborate finale seen in the last movement of the Mozart.[359] A Grave introduction is followed by an Allegro, ma non troppo; Andante cantabile; and Rondo, Allegro, ma non troppo. Beethoven contrasts each wind timbre with the piano in the introduction and writes longer themes than Mozart. The piano often states the themes answered by the winds, with greater emphasis on the harmonic function of the wind ensemble. This work is less varied and subtle than Mozart's but larger in framework, with a broader tonal scheme, with many pointers to the dramatic music he would subsequently write.[360] The clarinet compass is e to d³, and there is a greater use of the chalumeau register than in Mozart's quintet. The first performance of Beethoven's quintet was in 1797 at the house owned by the restaurateur Ignaz Jahn, with the Viennese clarinetist Josef Bähr playing a five-key clarinet.[361]

WIND QUINTETS

The earliest wind quintets for flute, oboe, clarinet, bassoon, and horn appeared at the beginning of the nineteenth century. They probably developed from Harmonie ensembles such as the Imperial Harmonie used at the Vienna court of Joseph II from 1782, consisting of two each of oboes, clarinets, horns, and bassoons.[362] A precursor to the wind quintet is Antonio Rosetti's Quintet in E-flat Major, written about 1781 for flute, oboe, clarinet, English horn, and bassoon.[363] Nikolaus Schmitt and Giuseppe Maria Cambini wrote the earliest examples of the wind quintet.[364] The most well known are the twenty-four quintets by Reicha, opp. 88, 91, 99, and 100, published from 1817 through 1820, and the three sets of nine quintets by Danzi, opp. 56, 67, and 68, published from 1820 through 1824.[365] These works are in an early-romantic style, with demanding parts for all instruments that make a virtue out of contrasting timbres. They were popular items at Parisian salon concerts. The Reicha and Danzi works were performed on twelve- or thirteen-key French clarinets.[366]

Conclusion

The most significant and important period of musical activity for the clarinet was between 1760 and 1830, during which three important developments occurred. First, there evolved the classical and early-romantic styles of composition; second, a modern orchestral idiom appeared; and third, composers, players, and makers cultivated the technical and tonal capabilities of the clarinet. Outstanding individual performers often served as an impetus to the musical imagination of composers, such as Gaspard Proksch and Johann Stamitz; Josef Beer and Carl Stamitz; Anton Stadler and Mozart; Johann Hermstedt and Spohr; Heinrich Baermann and Weber; and Josef Bähr or Joseph Friedlowsky and Beethoven. In turn, makers and players contributed additional keys, design modifications, and construction changes to the clarinet.

This chapter touches on only a modest selection of significant works in order to illustrate the gradual change in musical style from the rococo period of Johann Stamitz though the classical period of Carl Stamitz and Mozart to the early-romantic period of Weber and Beethoven.

5

THE CLARINET
IN PERFORMING
GROUPS

Harmonie

Wind bands or Harmonie, with pairs of oboes, horns, and bassoons, became a popular form of entertainment throughout Europe in royal and aristocratic households beginning in the 1720s in Germany. The main function of Harmoniemusik was to provide background music at dinners, social events, and public and private concerts. Beginning in the 1750s, some Harmonie consisted of two clarinets and two horns. In England, clarinet and horn bands performed at plays between acts. For example, in 1754 the *London Public Advertiser* announced: "By particular Desire, between the Acts, will be introduced several pieces for Clarinets and French horns." In the same year, a "Benefit for Mr. Solinus and Mr. Leander" was announced, with pieces for clarinets and horns between the acts.[1] Beginning in the 1760s, clarinet and horn bands regularly played at pleasure gardens in London. In addition to theater work, several English musicians played three nights a week from May until September in summer pleasure-garden concerts between six and ten or eleven o'clock. For example, songs from Arne's opera *Artaxerxes*, which includes clarinets and horns, were heard in 1762 at Ranelagh. Later that year "Music in Four Acts" was performed, along with several "favourite songs" and works by Handel. An announcement declared: "Between the acts the French Horns and Clarinets will play favourite pieces in the Garden."[2] Vauxhall, Ranelagh, and Marylebone were the most important of the thirty-eight gardens offering summer concerts.[3]

In Paris, clarinets and horns played in 1753 at he home of the wealthy *fermier générale* La Pouplinière.[4] In 1763, the Prince de Conti, Louis-François de Bourbon, formed a Harmonie around a nucleus of experienced players previously employed by the late La Pouplinière. Gaspard Procksch, Simon Flieger, and Charles Duport played clarinets.[5] During the 1770s, some Harmonie sextets expanded to octets by addition of pairs of clarinets and oboes.

By 1768, the clarinet-horn combination had become so popular in Paris that the writer Antoine Terrasson lamented the decline in popularity of his favorite instruments, the vielle (hurdy-gurdy) and musette.

> But in spite of all that [improvements, music], the vicissitude of human things which influence instruments as they do everything else in life have caused a bit of a decline in the [popularity of] vielles and musettes. Especially as clarinets, horns and other loud instruments have expelled theorbos, lutes and bass viols, which (in the feeling of all true connoisseurs) were with the harpsichord the only instruments capable of supporting and nourishing the harmony.[6]

There is considerable Harmoniemusik from the Wallerstein, Donaueschingen, and Regensburg courts in southern Germany, but comparatively little from northern Germany. Relatively few important works were composed in the Low Countries, and few original, significant compositions appeared in England and France. Harmoniemusik in Italy was concentrated in areas under the influence of the Austrian empire and several composers wrote for Harmonie in Moravian towns in America.[7] Harmoniemusik was also found throughout Scandinavia. Mozart and Beethoven wrote its most outstanding works in Vienna.

Haydn initially wrote for the clarinet while employed as Vice-Kapellmeister for Prince Paul Anton Esterházy in Eisenstadt. A five-movement Divertimento, H II: 14 for two C clarinets and two C horns, was completed in 1761. Haydn wrote conservatively, generally using arpeggio figures and limiting the range to two octaves at its widest, c^1 to c^3. During the repeats, the clarinet parts were ornamented.[8] Another Divertimento, H II: 17 for two C clarinets, two C horns, two violins, two violas, and basso, dates from 1761 to 1765 during Haydn's employment by Prince Esterházy in Eisenstadt. The clarinet parts are similar to the previous work in their restricted range and arpeggios.[9] After the prince's death in the 1790s, Haydn moved to London and wrote several marches for military band that included clarinets.

Music for octets began to appear during the 1770s. The bassoonist Ernst Eichner is the earliest composer of an extant Harmonie octet, with pairs of oboes, clarinets, horns and bassoons. Two octets are extant, one published by Bérault (Paris), the other in manuscript (1773) in the British Library. Both works were probably intended for military use, since each begins with a march.[10]

A Harmonie octet was established at the Copenhagen court in 1773. The clarinetists, Joseph Rauch of Bavaria and Albert Rauch of Saxony, were employed at the theater and opera orchestra.[11] Another court that retained a Harmonie from 1778 to 1783 was that of Cardinal Prince Joseph von Batthyány at Pressburg, where the clarinetists were Theodor Lotz (Lots) and Michael Bum (Pum, Pomp, or Bumb). The composer Johannes Sperger wrote forty-two wind partitas for the Pressburg court with five to eight parts each.[12]

Of the hundreds of extant works, the most well known are by Mozart. Mozart's earliest use of the clarinet is in the Divertimenti K. 113 (1771), K. 186 (1773), and K. 166 (1773). The Divertimento K. 113 was written for a small orchestra of winds and strings and is discussed here because of its close association chronologically with the Divertimenti K. 186 and K. 166 and the use of the same wind instruments.

The first version of K. 113 was written in Milan in 1771; it is scored for two B♭ clarinets, two E♭ horns, and a string ensemble of two violins, viola, cello, and bass. The title of the autograph score is "Concerto ò Sia Divertimento à 8 in milano nel Mese Novemb: 1771."[13] The second version is a wind score for pairs of oboes, English horns, and bassoons; the date and place of composition are not noted, but it was likely completed in Salzburg after the Mozarts returned in March 1773.[14] Hausswald believed the sextet to be an addition to the first version and published a cumulative score of pairs of oboes, clarinets, English horns, bassoons, horns, and strings.[15] Blazin suggests this musically incomplete sextet was meant to substitute for the clarinets and horns; he based his argument on the frequent doubling of the clarinets with the oboes; there is much less doubling in the Divertimenti K. 186 and K. 166.[16] In fact, the clarinets also double the English horn parts in the second movement, Andante, and fourth movement, Allegro, but the horns offer a substantial foundation for harmonic support. Thus, clarinets could have been omitted in the cumulative second version of K. 133 without serious loss to the composition. Based on the dating of paper types, it is likely that Mozart wrote the sextet wind score during the first half of 1773 after he returned to Salzburg, even though all the wind instruments in the second version of K. 113 were likely available in Milan and Salzburg.[17] Although clarinets were not available in Salzburg's court orchestra, they were present in Salzburg's Feldmusik, a military band.

The clarinet parts for the first version of K. 113 are limited in their technical demands and compasses, e^1 to d^3 and c^1 to d^3, and no use is made of the chalumeau register. A chromatic passage for the second clarinet in the fourth movement (mm. 41–42) includes $c\sharp^2$ and $d\sharp^2$, suggesting the use of a four- or five-key instrument. Blazin mistakenly states that Mozart "imbued the clarinet with a trumpet-like character." Despite the occasional use of triadic themes paired with horns, there is much diatonic and chromatic writing for clarinets in the classical manner.

It is likely that the Divertimento in B-flat Major, K. 186, was written in Salzburg in March 1773, just before the Divertimento in E-flat Major, K. 166, dated 1773.[18] Both include a large wind complement of pairs of oboes, B♭ clarinets, English horns, horns, and bassoons. The large scoring is unusual for Harmonie ensembles, but Mozart wrote for smaller and larger combinations. Neither work exceeds the compasses of K. 113, and although short solos for the clarinets are found in the first movement of K. 166, there is less chromatic writing than in K. 113. Most of the thematic writing consists of melodic thirds played by oboes and English horns, and the clarinets are simply part of the texture. The bassoons usually play together on a single bass line.[19]

Interest in wind music and the establishment of the Kaiser's eight-member Harmonie in 1782 provided impetus for Mozart's important Harmonie works. These are the Serenade in E flat Major, K. 375 (1781), for a sextet of two B♭ clarinets, E♭ horns, and bassoons; the Serenade in C Minor, K. 388 (1782), for two oboes, two B♭ clarinets, two E♭ horns, and two bassoons; and the Serenade in B-flat Major, K. 361, or "Gran Partita" (probably 1781–82). Mozart wrote his father that he had put considerable care into composing the K. 375 serenade with the hope of bringing his Harmonie-musik to the attention of the court.[20] However, in 1782, his new composition was out of date because the emperor established his Harmonie as an octet of pairs of oboes, clarinets, horns, and bassoons. Mozart then spent part of summer 1782 composing the Serenade in C Minor and adding a pair of oboes to his sextet Serenade in E-flat. This course of action was also fruitless, because the emperor desired to hear mainly transcriptions of operas and ballets rather than original music. Mozart tried to impress the court with a transcription of *Die Entführung aus dem Serail*, but this also failed because Johann Went, an oboist in the Emperor's Harmonie, completed his transcription before Mozart had finished his.[21]

The Serenade in E-flat Major, K. 375, prominently features chromatic passages, fluent passing of melodic material between the clarinets and bassoons, and solos for all eight instruments. The compass for both clarinets is wide, g to e♭³ and e to c³, with both the clarinet and the chalumeau registers employed frequently.[22] The Serenade in C Minor, K. 388 (1782), is a superb example of an octet for winds written in four movements. An intensely serious work, it is imbued with the emotional tensions Mozart typically invests in that key. The clarinet's compass is slightly more restricted in this work, g♯ to b♭² and g to g² (see figure 5.1).[23] This work is inappropriate for the relaxed background music that was the normal role of Harmoniemusik and may have been written for a special occasion.[24]

According to the diary of Count Karl von Zinzendorf, at least one of Mozart's octets was performed in 1783 in Vienna's Augarten by the Imperial Harmoniemusik (Kammerharmonie) or "Des Kaisers stehenden acht blasenden Tonkünstler," as they were called on the program announcement. The performers were the clarinetists Anton and Johann Stadler, the oboists Georg Tribensee (Triebensee) and Johann Vent (Went), the bassoonists Wenzel Kauzner and Iganz Trobney (Drobney), and the hornists Jakob Eisen and Martin Rupp.[25]

Perhaps the finest work for Harmonie is Mozart's Serenade in B-flat Major, K. 361, written in 1781–82 (the dating is based on paper-type analysis).[26] It is a monumental work in seven large-scale movements: a largo introduction to a Molto allegro, two Menuetti with second trios, a Romanze, a theme-and-variations Andante, and a Molto allegro finale. The Serenade in B-flat Major is scored for an impressively large combination of thirteen in-

FIGURE 5.1 Mozart, Serenade in C Minor, K. 388 (Leipzig, 1878), mm. 1–16.

FIGURE 5.1 *Continued.*

struments: two oboes, two B♭ clarinets, two F basset horns, four horns (two in F and two in low B♭), two bassoons, and contrabass (see figure 5.2). The pair of horns in different nominal pitches allows fuller support in different tonalities. For greater depth and to balance the four soprano woodwinds, Mozart adds a string bass.[27] Although all the instrument pairs have solo passages, both clarinets are prominent throughout, primarily in the clarino register, and skillfully balanced with the lower notes of the basset horns. The overall compass for the clarinets is g to e^3 and g to c^3.[28] There are also many individual solos for the first clarinet, oboe, and bassoon. The first performance of this work was probably in Anton Stadler's Akademie at a benefit concert in Vienna's Burgtheater in 1784.[29]

A description of Stadler's concert the next year specifically mentioned this work and gave high praise to Stadler's playing and Mozart's composition.

> My thanks to you brave virtuoso! I have never heard the like of what you contrived with your instrument. Never should I have thought that a clarinet could be capable of imitating a human voice so deceptively as it was imitated by you. Indeed, your instrument has so soft and lovely a tone that no one who has a heart can resist it, and I have one, dear Virtuoso; let me thank you! I heard music for wind instruments today by Mr. Mozart, in four movements—glorious and sublime! It consisted of thirteen instruments, four horns, two oboes, two bassoons, two clarinets, two bassethorns, a contrabass and at each instrument sat a master—oh, what an effect it made—glorious and grand, excellent and sublime![30]

Other outstanding works for Harmonie are Beethoven's Octet in E-flat Major, op. 103 (1792; revised in 1793),[31] and Krommer's *Harmonie-Musik*, with optional string bass (1808–10).

Military Bands

During the seventeenth century, military wind bands in Germany had two treble shawms, a tenor shawm, and a curtal. By the first quarter of the eighteenth century, two oboes had replaced the shawms, and two French horns were being used to reinforce the inner voices, adding a new tone color.[32] Military bands added clarinets during the 1750s and 1760s and introduced them into many countries around the world. This section describes the introduction of the clarinet into military bands in England, America, France, Prussia, Austria, Spain, Sweden, Norway, and Finland.

FIGURE 5.2   Mozart, Serenade in B-flat Major, K. 361 (Leipzig, 1878) first movement, mm. 1–6.

ENGLAND

Early pictorial evidence from London appears in a 1753 line drawing by James Maurer titled "A View of [the] Royal Building for his Majesty's Horse & Foot Guards." Maurer illustrates a band of two horns held at shoulder level, two bassoons, two oboes, and two clarinets preceding "his majesty's horse & foot guards."[33] The drawing is vague, but the longer instruments were probably two- or three-key clarinets.

In England, bands with clarinets were recognized during the early 1760s, and oboes or clarinets became the leading treble wind instruments. Lieutenant Colonel W. Phillips traveled to Germany to engage a band for the First Battalion of the Royal Artillery in 1762. The first two "Articles of Agreement upon which the musicians for the Royal Artillery Band were engaged in Germany in 1762" state that:

> (1) The band to consist of eight men, who are capable to play upon the violoncello, bass, violin and flute, as other common instruments.
> (2) The regiment's musick must consist of two trumpets, two French horns, two bassoons and four hautbois or clarinetts; these instruments to be provided by the regiment, but kept in repair by the head musician.[34]

Farmer mentions that ten instruments are noted although only eight men were in the band. The trumpets may have been used primarily to announce regiment formations rather than as an integral part of the military band.[35] For flexibility, Colonel Phillips was looking for musicians who could play a variety of instruments.

Cavalry regiments had their own bands, which performed when dismounted. Richard Hinde describes these bands in *The Discipline of the Light Horse* (1778):

> In the year 1764, his Majesty thought proper to forbid the use of brass side drums in the Light Cavalry, and in their place to introduce brass trumpets, so that each troop has one trumpet, who when they are dismounted, form a band of music, consisting of two French Horns, two clarinetts and two bassoons, and also one fife to a regiment: but when mounted the trumpets only are found.[36]

Gardiner reports that in 1778 the clarinet was still new to some military musicians. "Half a dozen lads of the militia were sent up to London to be taught various instruments to form a military band. The German master Baumgartner put into their hands a new instrument called a 'clarionet' which, with its fiery tone, was better adapted to lead armies in the field of battle than the meek and feeble oboe."[37] According to Parke, the bands of the regiments of guards about 1783 consisted of an eight-part Harmonie for pairs of oboes, clarinets, horns, and bassoons. "They were excellent performers on their several instruments, were hired by the month, and were well paid. They were not attested, and were exempt from all military duties except that of the King's Guard."[38] The fact that these performers were professionals indicates that the most prestigious military bands accepted only the best musicians.

In 1783, the Honourable Artillery Company band had four clarinets, two horns, two bassoons, and a trumpet. By 1785, a new band for the Coldstream Guards had arrived under the direction of Christopher F. Eley from Hanover; it had twelve players—four clarinets, two oboes, two horns, two bassoons, trumpet, and serpent.[39] In London, military music became increasingly popular at the pleasure gardens, particularly during the wars with France (1792–1806). Beginning in 1783 at Vauxhall, a band of drums, fifes, horns, and clarinets performed while strolling the gardens after the regular concert.[40] From 1790 to 1816, Vauxhall featured the Coldstream Guards, formed by the Duke of York for his regiment.[41] Military music was also played at Ranelagh when an unspecified band played between the "acts" of the concerts in 1798; between 1799 and 1802, the "City Corporation Band" played "in full Uniform, several Military Pieces, composed expressly for the different Corps of Volunteers," on the nights when there was "a Grand Mask'd Ball."[42] A similar occasion at the Brighton Royal Pavilion about 1826, illustrated by John Nash, shows King George IV's Household Band of about twenty musicians in uniform led by the clarinetist Christian Kramer, who is not in uniform (see figure 5.3). The band is in front of the organ pipes; alongside the clarinetist, a timpanist is ready to play, and a percussionist holds a tambourine. Only a flutist and a few other clarinetists can be clearly distinguished in this charming illustration.[43]

AMERICA

The earliest reference to military wind bands in America is a 160-member "Band of Music" of the Freemasons in Philadelphia in 1755.[44] Three years later, in New York a call appeared in 1758 for wind players to staff a regiment band for General Lacell. "Any performers on the Hautboy, French Horn, Clarinet, or Bassoon, who are willing to engage themselves for five or six months; will meet with good encouragement by applying to the Commanding Officer of General Lascell's Regiment at Amboy."[45]

During the 1760s and 1770s, the clarinet was included in bands with several British Regiments of Foot. For example, in 1762 the 17th Regiment performed a regimental march that included a clarinet; in 1767 a concert with horns and clarinets was performed by the 13th Regiment; in 1774 clarinets were purchased for the 15th Regiment; and in 1777 a clarinet was purchased for the 58th Regiment.[46] The band of the 64th Regiment was very active in Boston, participating in concerts at the Concert Hall and the Coffee House from 1771 through 1774.[47] The band of the 4th Regiment (active in America from 1774 to 1780) participated in a funeral procession in 1774 that featured "Clarinets, Hautboys, Bassoons, French horns, Trumpets, Kettle Drums,

FIGURE 5.3   John Nash, "Music or Concert Room," from *The Royal Pavilion at Brighton* (ca. 1826), a close-up view of the band. The Minnich Collection, The Ethel Marison van Derlip Fund, The Minneapolis Institute of Arts.

&c., &c."[48] Later advertisements for band clarinet players appeared in 1777 and 1778; in 1779 "two French horns, two clarinets, two hautboys, one bassoon, wanted to compleat the band on board the General Pattison, Private Ship of War."[49]

FRANCE

In 1762, the French Guards (Gardes-Françoises) regiment established an official military band in Paris, the same year as the "Articles of Agreement" in London. The maréchal di Biron, then colonel of the regiment, obtained authorization from King Louis XV to form a band of sixteen musicians: four each of oboes, clarinets, horns, and bassoons. Hardy mentions a 1763 ordinance and identifies this band with the Swiss Guards.[50] A contemporary observer, Turpin de Crissé, verified that there were sixteen musicians attached to the regiment of the French Guards independent of the drums and fifes used by the regiment. He mentions that drums and trumpets were used to announce troop maneuvers and that horns, clarinets, and bassoons were admitted into the infantry's regiments, following a 1766 ordinance.[51] The French Guards band increased to twenty-four in 1788 and to thirty-two in 1789.[52]

The Parisian Guard Band became a civic organization and increased from forty-five members to seventy-eight in 1790; in 1792, it was reduced to fifty-four when some members had to accompany troops. It can be seen from the parts copied for individual works that bands were expanding their instrumentation. A 1794 program of the Institut National de Musique included a Catel overture, for forty-nine bandsmen with fourteen clarinets, and the Lesueur *Scène patriotique*, for sixty-two players with twenty clarinetists.[53] Commissioned to serve under the National Guard, the Musique Municipale de Mans had one F clarinet and ten C clarinets in 1799.[54] During the early nineteenth century, French composers wrote for C clarinets and the higher-pitched F clarinet—for example, Vanderhagen's *Symphonie militaire* (1811–12) for C clarinets, F clarinets, F flutes, C horns, C trumpets, bassoons, serpents, trombones, bass drum, and cymbals.[55] According to Kastner, in 1814 B♭ clarinets were recommended for use in bands instead of C clarinets.[56] A few years later, the government made this recommendation official. An 1823 ministerial disposition decreed that all C clarinets in military bands would be replaced with B♭ clarinets.[57]

GERMANY

There is no exact date for the introduction of the clarinet in German military bands, since their composition varied from regiment to regiment. The instrument was certainly available and sought after by individual bands, as shown in a 1763 Kassel newspaper advertisement: "The Hessian Life-Dragoon-Regiment desires a military musician who can play oboe, flute, and clarinet and who can furnish good recommendations; such a person should report to the regiment of Kirchhayn."[58]

The clarinet was part of a small military band with fifes and drums in Potsdam during the 1760s, as Hiller sardonically mentioned in a 1769 article describing the use of the clarinet by Agricola in his opera *Amor e Psiche* in 1767.[59] However, archival documents establish that Frederick the Great's artillery band included eight members with clarinets only by 1779. Over time, the instrumentation of the band varied. Some eighteenth-century manuscript military marches in Berlin called for two B♭ clarinets, two oboes, two bassoons; two B♭ clarinets, two oboes, B♭ trumpet, and bassoon; or two B♭ clarinets, two horns or B♭ trumpets, and two bassoons.[60] The Prussian military music corps included C clarinets and F basset horns before the middle of the nineteenth century. After 1850, the usual instruments were B♭ clarinets and E♭ basset horns or alto clarinets.[61]

TURKISH OR JANISSARY BANDS

An important early-eighteenth-century development was the adoption by European bands of percussion instruments from bands of the Sultan of Turkey's elite troops (Janissaries) such as cymbals, triangle, tambourine, long or Turkish drum, and Turkish crescent or "jingling Johnny." In turn, by the 1770s, these bands had added the clarinet. Burney reports two German military bands stationed in Ghent, Belgium, in 1775, one of which was a Harmonie octet played by hired nonmilitary musicians; the other was a Turkish band played by soldiers.

> There were two bands attending every morning and evening, on the *Place d'Armes*, or parade. The one was an extra-band of professed musicians, consisting of two hautbois, two clarinets, two bassoons, and two French horns; the other were enlisted men and boys, belonging to the regiments; the number of these amounted to twenty. There were four trumpets, three fifes, two hautbois, two clarinets, two tambours de basque, two French horns, one crotolo, or cymbal, three side-drums, and one great kettledrum. All these sonorous instruments, in the open air, have a very animating and pleasing effect.[62]

Evidence of Turkish bands in England is found in an anonymous engraving about 1790 titled "The Band of a Regiment of Guards entering the Colour Court, St. James's Palace" and showing a band in three parts. The first has one trumpet, two horns (one obscured by the drum major), bassoon, serpent, and three clarinets or oboes. This is followed by a percussion section of two boys beating a small timpani and a triangle and three "Africans" in "Oriental" uniform playing the cymbals, long drum, and tambourine. The third part has about twelve fifers and drummers playing snare or side drums.[63]

Austria

During the 1760s in Salzburg, the infantry regiment of Count Josef Colloredo had a band of two fifes and two clarinets.[64] According to a 1766 "Zirkular-Reskript," the grenadier band (Grenadiers-Compagnien) had two each of clarinets, fifes, and drums.[65] A two-part 1769 "Specification" indicates two bands: a Harmonie of nine musicians playing two types of horns, four oboes, and two bassoons at French pitch (A = ca. 410), and a field music (Feldmusik) of fifes, trumpets, and 2 three-key D clarinets with corps for tuning to C built at French pitch (A = ca. 410).[66] A 1776 grenadier band inventory lists clarinets along with fifes, trumpets, and drums.[67] A third Turkish band is documented by an 1804 inventory as having three C clarinets (one by Johann Merklein).[68] The 1804 inventory also lists a Harmonie attached to the regiment with two clarinets, one oboe, three bassoons, and two horns. Five-key clarinets in C and B♭ with corps in A were purchased respectively from Merklein and Johann Engelhard.[69]

In 1781, Christoph Friedrich Nicolai observed "curious military music" in Vienna consisting of two shawms, two clarinets, two French horns, one trumpet, two bassoons, one drum, and a large drum. The curious aspect of the band probably referred to the large drum beaten on both sides in the Turkish manner.[70] The account book of the Viennese Hoftheater for the year 1782/83 indicates a payment to the conductor Franz Tyron for a "band of artillery music" for performance of Mozart's *Die Einführung aus dem Serial*. This document shows the assistance of military bands in new music productions and the influence of Turkish bands on Viennese orchestration.[71] In 1791, Prince Liechtenstein established a "Turkish" band with two fifes or flutes, a trumpet, tambourine, triangle, and drum as an addition to his wind octet.[72] In 1796, Schönfeld described a Turkish band in Vienna with oboes, bassoons, horns, clarinets, trumpet, triangle, piccolo, a very large drum, an ordinary drum, and a pair of cymbals.[73] Early-nineteenth-century Austrian military bands used high F and C clarinets. In 1816 Beethoven wrote a military march that included these instruments.[74] An 1820 document in the Kriegsarchiv in Vienna indicates a military band of twenty-five, including one F clarinet, two C clarinets, and two basset horns.[75] By the 1840s, the Austrian military wind band included B♭ clarinets and E♭ alto clarinets.[76]

SPAIN

In 1769, a grenadier band in Madrid, similar to that in Salzburg, consisted of two clarinets, two fifes, and a drummer. The *Toques de guerra* by Manuel Espinosa included a march entitled "La marcha de granaderos," with fifes a fifth higher but often in unison with the clarinets.[77] This appears to be the earliest documented date for the introduction of the clarinet in Spain. Ten years later, the poet Iriarte mentions the "military" clarinet in his poem *La música* (1779).[78]

SWEDEN

The Royal Lifeguards in Stockholm had adopted the clarinet by the 1760s. In 1773, Hülphers reported that "military music was notably improved in the Royal Life-Guard by Privy Counsellor Count Fersen when he was Colonel, with the addition of clarinets and Turkish or janissary music which consists of specially made drums and cymbals. Similar additions were made to other regiments."[79] Norlind states that Count Fersen was still a colonel in the Life Guards during the 1760s, and he assumes that clarinets were introduced to the regiments during this time.[80]

During the 1770s, military bands with clarinets were established in smaller cities in Sweden. Letters from Johan Miklin, director of music in Linköping, to Hülphers describe these bands. In 1772, Miklin wrote a letter to say:

> Apart from this I have four students of my own that are going to be organists, in addition to these four I recently hired musicians for Sodermanland's infantry regiment, where Colonel Baron von Siegroth

is establishing a group of musicians consisting of ten persons, namely three oboists, two hornists, two bassoonists, two clarinetists, and one trumpet.[81]

A second 1772 letter reports that "Colonel Siegroth, now at the infantry in Sormanland, has with my help acquired ordinary field music such as oboists, waldhorn, one trumpet, two bassoons, two clarinets, and has even recently acquired in Stockholm the previously mentioned Janissary instruments, which cost him more than 60 pläter."[82] In his last letter, Hülphers goes on to describe the clarinets:

> I don't believe clarinets were in use in Sweden until 1762 or '63. The first time I heard them was in Malmö in 1766; the larger ones, which are used in Paris, sound infinitely better than the same clarinets that are used at the regiments, as they don't screech so. But the larger ones are delightful owing to the fact that one so can easily play forte and piano and the lower chalumeau notes. They have many long brass keys for both hands.[83]

The clarinets used in these early Swedish regimental bands probably had four or five keys and may have been higher-pitched D or E♭ instruments with a brilliant tone. "Many long brass keys for both hands" on the larger clarinet suggests a six-key instrument in C or B♭ with the long F♯/C♯ and E/B keys and an A–B trill key, probably an English or German clarinet.

NORWAY

According to a 1766 directive from the Oslo city music director Andreas Thomaesen Holthe, clarinets, along with the horn and trumpet, were introduced in the military field music that accompanied troops.[84] Music teachers taught many instruments including the clarinet. For example, the music director of Kristiansand, Lorents Nicolai Berg, writes of teaching the clarinet and several woodwind, brass, and string instruments in his 1782 treatise *Den første prøve for begyndere udi instrumental-kunsten* (The First Instructions for Beginners in Instrumental Art). Berg wrote a fingering chart for the less expensive three-key clarinet specifically for the beginner, but also described a five-key clarinet, which must have been the standard instrument.[85] Thus, we may assume that many clarinetists at this time in Norway learned on a simple clarinet and that, if they became advanced or professional players, they would purchase a five-key instrument.

FINLAND

The clarinet found its way to Finnish regiments at about the same time they appeared in Sweden. Colonel de Carnall, director of the royal regiment band at Pori, wrote to the regiment from Stockholm in 1771: "I sent to the regiment a while ago a clarinet player who I had encouraged to learn the instrument. I have bought two clarinets that cost 12 Plåter each."[86] As a result, de Carnall's band increased to twenty-four; in 1777, they purchased two more clarinets and trained two clarinetists. Four years later, three more volunteer players were taught the clarinet, and in 1795, eight clarinetists were sent to Pernaja for six months to study with Sergeant Fredrik Lindfors. By 1800, the band had increased to thirty-six players and in 1808, there were as many as eight clarinetists.[87]

South Africa

The Dutch East Indian Company (Vereenigde Oostindische Compangie) governed the Cape of Good Hope in South Africa from 1652 to 1795. Their earliest band had "12 Hautboisten" or German musicians of the Regiment of Württemberg during the summers of 1787 and 1788. This band may have included clarinets. The earliest documentation of the use of the clarinet is during the period 1803 to 1806 in a slave band of clarinets, horns, and bassoons at the farm of Jacob van Reenen in South Africa.[88]

Church Bands

In many churches, an organ was too expensive for the congregation, so parishioners supported the choir by playing instruments. One of the earliest examples of a clarinet in a church band was at the East Church in Salem, Massachusetts, on Thanksgiving Day, 1797. The band played in the church gallery with a bass viol, violin, clarinet, and viola.[89] In England, during the early nineteenth century at Winterbourne Abbas, six miles from Dorchester, three performers played in the church gallery: J. Dunford, a thatcher (clarinet), W. Dunford, a shepherd (bass), and R. Tompkins, a farm laborer (flute). An 1809 parish register for Walkeringham, Nottinghamshire, indicates that a bassoon and clarinet were bought to support parish singers.[90] The use of instruments in church galleries to support singers continued until about 1840 in America, when the instruments were replaced by reed organs.[91] In some English villages church bands continued to play until about 1881.[92]

Orchestras

Among the earliest German orchestral clarinetists were Joseph Flügel and Theodor Balthasar Klein, who played in the Cologne orchestra from 1748 until 1773.[93] It is likely that at some time during this period these players adopted the classical clarinet. In Paris, established orchestras hired musicians who could play the clarinet on a per-service basis when needed for performances. For example, the Paris Opéra hired clarinetists to play parts in Rameau's operas in 1749 and in 1751 to 1753. Because the clarinet was not a commonly played instrument during the 1760s, players did not appear in the list of regular orchestral personnel at public institutions such as operas and court orchestras. For example, in Paris some operas performed at the Comédie-Italienne required clarinets through the 1780s, but regular clarinetists were not listed on the orchestral roster. Two anonymous clarinetists were paid in 1767 for a revival of La Borde's *Gilles, garçon peintre*, but payments for clarinetists were not made for performances of Grétry's *Le Huron* (1768) and *Les deux avares* (1770), even though each opera features clarinets in one movement. This suggests that the clarinet parts were played by other orchestral musicians.[94]

At the same time in Paris, the classical clarinet was introduced into the orchestras of wealthy individuals who could afford to hire musicians for their entertainment. Private salon concerts were maintained on a regular basis by La Pouplinière, La Haye, the Prince de Conti, Prince de Monaco, Prince de Rohan, Baron D'Ogny, the Baron de Bagge, the Prince de Guéménée, the Duke d'Aiguillon, the Maréchal de Noailles, the Duke d'Orléans, Count d'Albaret, the Marquis de Branca, and the Marquis de Seignelai.[95] These patrons could afford clarinets and horns as part of a wind band, and they were used in orchestral works when needed.

Players of classical clarinets were initially hired in court orchestras in Cologne (1748); Mannheim (1758);[96] Würzburg (1760);[97] Zweibrücken (1760);[98] Coblenz (1769);[99] Mainz (1774);[100] Paris, Royal Chapel (1769);[101] Ansbach (1770);[102] Münster (1770);[103] Copenhagen (1774); the Paris Opéra (1774); the Turin opera (1780); the Munich court (1781);[104] the Viennese court (1782);[105] Bentheim (1783); Mecklenburg (1783); Pressburg (1783); Regensburg (1783); Stockholm (1783);[106] Naples, Teatro San Carlo (1786); Berlin court (1788); London, Haymarket Theater (1790);[107] London, Professional Concert (1793); London, Opera Concert (1795);[108] and Dresden (1795).[109] By 1800, most of the major court, opera, and theater orchestras in Europe and Scandinavia included the clarinet.

Conservatories and Music Schools

The role of the music school and conservatory was important in training military and professional clarinetists. Many conservatories were founded during the late eighteenth and early nineteenth centuries throughout Europe. In Paris, the General Council in 1792 created a free music school for the Parisian National Guard. This school trained 120 boys and young men in sixty battalions of the National Guard. The pupils were between ten and sixteen years for beginners and between eight and twenty for those with previous music instruction.[110] A 1793 payroll list shows nine clarinet teachers among the staff, including Jean Xavier Lefèvre as music master; Corporal

Jean Meric; four first-class teachers; and three second-class teachers.[111] In 1795, the National Convention established the Conservatoire de Musique with 115 teachers, 19 of whom taught clarinet, for 600 pupils.[112]

Many music schools were founded during this time, including those in Potsdam (School for Military Music, 1798), Berlin (Conservatory for Wind Instrumentalists, ca. 1805), Würzburg (1804), Coburg (1805), Koblenz (1805), Milan (1808), Naples (1808), Aschaffenburg (1810), Prague (1810), Cologne (1811), Passau (1812), Stuttgart (1812), Breslau (1815), Graz (1815), Vienna (1817), Innsbruck (1819), London (1822), Linz (1823), Milan (1824), The Hague (1826), Hamburg (1827), and Klagenfurt (1828).[113] The clarinet teachers of these schools taught many eager students, and during the nineteenth century several other schools were founded throughout Europe and America.

NOTES

1. Color or grain pattern is not an accurate indicator of wood used in construction, since many clarinet bodies were stained; exact material identification is often possible only by scientific analysis.

2. Rendall, *The Clarinet*, 46.

3. The well-known instrument maker Rudolf Tutz notes these characteristics in Carroll, "Anton Stadler's Contributions," 27.

4. The earliest writer to indicate these registers was Berr in his 1836 *Méthode*, 7.

5. See Rendall, *The Clarinet*, 37.

6. See Shackleton, "Clarinet," *NGDMI*, vol. 1, 391.

7. Only two clarinets known to the author feature curved key heads that close into the wood surface: an anonymous French five-key ivory clarinet (ca. 1820, US-MA-Boston-C, 89) and a seven-key clarinet (ca. 1825, US-SD 5949) by Bouchmann. For a photograph of the Boston Symphony instrument see "BSO Collection Reinstalled," 1. Curved key heads are also found on walking-stick clarinets.

8. During the early twentieth century, five-key boxwood clarinets were on sale in England, imported from Markneukirchen by Theodor Stark. See Poole, "A Catalogue of Musical Instruments," 31.

9. Backofen, *Anweisung zur Clarinette* (1824), 13 and frontispiece. Early examples of integral thumb rests are found on a five-key anonymous ivory instrument (early nineteenth century, US-DC, 443), possibly of English origin; a six-key C clarinet (ca. 1820, NL-Den Haag, 1939 24) by Schürer; a nine-key A clarinet (1830–40, GB-London-RCM, 325 C/9) by the Jehring firm; a ten-key D clarinet (ca. 1830, US-SD, 5923) by Whitely; and an eleven-key D clarinet (ca. 1825, US-MA-Newton Centre) by the Grenser firm.

10. An unusual example, a thirteen-key C clarinet (ca. 1830, F-Le Mans) by François Lefèvre, has a recessed or cut-down ivory ferrule, which could serve as a thumb rest on the lower part of its left-hand joint. This instrument may have been later modified but still presents an alternate method of supporting the clarinet.

11. At least two eight-key clarinets (GB-Manchester, MPL 7) by Hale are extant. See Ross, "A Comprehensive Performance Project," 209; Waterhouse, "RNC Collection," http://www.mcm.ac.uk/library/hwm1.htm.

12. In 1805, Claude Laurent was the earliest maker to use metal plates screwed to the body of crystal glass flutes and pillars in order to mount keys. See Waterhouse, *The New Langwill Index*, 225.

13. Dibley, *Historic Musical Instruments*, 11.

14. Strong waxed thread or silk twist was recommended by Fröhlich, *Vollständige Theoretisch-pracktische Musikschule*, 10.

15. Halfpenny, "Clarinet Mouthpieces."

16. Castillon, "Clarinette," 451, trans. Halfpenny, "Castilon and the Clarinet," 334.

17. See the 1780 Pierre Bazin portrait of the clarinetist Villement showing a clarinet with a separate barrel and a blackwood mouthpiece. Reproduced by Hoeprich, "Clarinet Reed Position," 51; Ross, "A Comprehensive Performance Project," 227. A 1784 invoice to the Donaueschingen court specifies a clarinet mouthpiece made of dark ebony. See Hamann, "Eine interessante Aufführungsanweisung Mozarts," 139.

18. Shackleton, "The Development of the Clarinet," 24; Shackleton, "John Hale," 26.

19. See Rice, "Clarinet Fingering Charts," 25. A book entitled "The Clarinet Tutor" was advertised by Longman, Lukey and Co. in 1772; see *Catalogue of Vocal and Instrumental Music*. Thus, this tutor or an earlier version of it may initially have been published in 1772. Furthermore, a clarinet tutor (probably published by Longman, Lukey and Co.) was advertised in *Rivington's New York Gazette* beginning in 1773. See Anderson, *Music in New York*, 25; Corry, Keller, and Keller, *PACN*.

20. Shackleton, "Clarinet," *NGDMI*, 391; Shackleton, "The Development of the Clarinet," 24.

21. Waterhouse, *NLI*, 145.

22. Monzani, "Clarionets and Flutes," illustration page. A nine-key Monzani clarinet (ca. 1809, GB-Cambridge) with two knobs on either side of the mouthpiece base is very similar to that shown in the patent.

23. A mouthpiece belonging to a clarinet by Saget (ca. 1815, F-Le Mans) illustrates that at least one continental maker adopted a variation of these knobs.

24. A clarinet (F-Le Mans) by Muller includes a mouthpiece with a short table stamped on the frontal side and a second mouthpiece with a long table stamped on the dorsal side. Shackleton illustrates eighteenth- and early-nineteenth-century mouthpieces in "Clarinet," *NGDMI*, 396, ill. 7, a–d.

25. "La nouvelle manière d'attacher l'anche sur le bec, a l'aide d'un anneau, est préférable à celle de le faire avec une ficelle: d'abord, l'anneau nous donne la grande facilité d'ôter et de remettre dix fois l'anche sur le bec, pendant qu'un autre, avec sa ficelle, ne le ferait à peine qu'une seule fois: en second lieu, on peut souvent, par le seul moyen des deux vis, la mettre comme elle doit être, et lui donner l'ouverture convenable, et de plus, le bec est beaucoup plus élégant avec l'anneau au'avec la ficelle." Müller, *Méthode*, 23.

26. An 1821 concert review in the *Berlinerische Nachrichten* mentions that the German soloist Hermstedt played on a silver mouthpiece with a metal ligature. However, his mouthpiece may have been blackwood or ebony with silver rails, tip, and table, similar to modern inlaid mouthpieces. The review was quoted by Birsak, *Die Klarinette*, 46, and the mouthpiece mentioned in the *Wiener Allgemeine Musikalische Zeitung* 1821, no. 91, col. 721, according to Eberhardt, "Johann Simon Hermstedt," 136.

27. See Streitwolf, "Verkauf," 24.

28. "Nachrichten," *AMZ* 34 (1832): 871. Streitwolf's price list (ca. 1830–35) advertised mouthpieces of ebony, grenadilla, or ivory. Invoices also include mouthpieces

of hardened tin for use in the Sondershausen wind band. See Eberhardt, "Johann Simon Hermstedt," 137; Birsak, *Die Klarinette*, 46.

29. In 1838, the Samuel Graves firm of Winchester, New Hampshire, offered pewter mouthpieces as a more expensive option—$1.00 or $1.12½—besides cocus or ebony—$.50. See Eliason, "Letters to Marsh and Chase," 45.

30. American examples with pewter mouthpieces include a Graves five-key C clarinet (US-SD, 5755); a Graves six-key B♭ clarinet (US-CA-Claremont, W64); and a five-key C clarinet (US-NY-New York-M) stamped "John Ashton, Boston," probably made by Graves. European clarinets with pewter mouthpieces include a Goulding six-key C clarinet (US-SD, 1355) and a Streitwolf thirteen-key B♭ clarinet (GB-Edinburgh, 979).

31. The clarinet is drawn with the long shanks for F♯/C♯ and E/B on the right side (from the player's viewpoint) of the instrument. This may have been intended to portray a left-handed instrument with the left hand positioned on the lower section, or it could simply be an error by the engraver.

32. "Tel est l'instrument avec lequel le Sieur Baërmann, musicien du Roi de Bavière, a fait tant de plaisir à Paris. Il avait de plus ajouté à sa Clarinette, une pompe d'environ six lignes, qui prenait dans le milieu du Baril, qui pour cet effet, était partagé en deux, et donnait la facilité de s'accorder en allongeant le baril par le moyen de la pompe qui, ne laissant presque point de vide, empêchait l'eau de s'y amasser comme cela arrive quand on est trop haut et qui'il faut tirer le Baril pour baisser. Il est facile d'ajouter ce petit appareil aux Clarinettes à douze Clés, et même aux Clarinettes anciennes; mais il faut alors un Baril plus long. Le luthier prendra ses dimentions à ce sujet en racourcissant du premier corps ce qu'il est obligé de donner au Baril." Vanderhagen, *Nouvelle méthode* (ca. 1819), fingering chart page. Vanderhagen identified the clarinet in this engraving as the instrument played by the soloist Heinrich Baermann while he performed in Paris during 1817 and 1818. The tuning slide is "la pompe" in the "Baril à la Baërmann." Lawson reproduced this engraving in *The Early Clarinet*, 28–29; see also Weston, *Clarinet Virtuosi of the Past*, 132–34. François Baumann made a clarinet with a similar mouthpiece (D-München-S) that includes a divided barrel and tuning slide. The author thanks Jean Jeltsch for information.

33. Examples include a Bouchmann seven-key C clarinet (US-SD 5949)and two Baumann thirteen-key C clarinets (US-CA-Claremont, W145; US-AK). For the Bouchmann clarinet, see Libin, *Clarinets*.

34. Smith, *Reed Design*, xi.

35. Of thirteen early-nineteenth-century English clarinet reeds (GB-Cambridge), seven are stamped "BILTON," four "D WITTON," and two "WITTON" (probably a dealer). Reeds were also available from dealers in different lengths to suit different mouthpiece dimensions. The Edinburgh firm J. and R. Glen received clarinet reeds from Small and Co. in 1840, presumably cut for English mouthpieces. In 1846, Glen received two dozen clarinet reeds from the London firm Bilton, cut in "French length." See Myers, *The Glen Account Book,* 27, 95.

36. *Catalogue of Vocal and Instrumental Music.*

37. For example, in a 1768 letter, Samuel Hellier, who employed clarinetists, wrote to John Rogers "I have sent you a Box by the Woverhampton coach will be down on Wednesday: The Messiah . . . and some cane to make clarinet reeds when wanted but not for hautboys." See Young, "The Shaw-Hellier Collection," (1993), 163–64.

38. Backofen, *Anweisung zur Klarinette* (ca. 1803), 3–4. See Kohler, "J. G. H. Backofen's *Anweisung*," 9–10; cf. Baines, *Woodwind Instruments*, 300.

39. Malot, *L'art de bien faire*, 4, ill. C.

40. Young described most of these instruments in *4900 Historical Woodwind Instruments*.

41. See Powell, *The Keyed Flute*, p. 180. For identification and dating of English hallmarks, see Fallon, *Marks of London goldsmiths and silversmiths*.

42. See, for example, Kreitzer, "Serial Numbers and Hallmarks," 168–80. Clarinets with serial numbers include a nine-key instrument in C by Monzani (no. 70, ca. 1809, GB-Cambridge) and a six-key C clarinet by Monzani (no. 1053, ca. 1814, US-CT-New Haven, no. 3326.82).

43. Examples include a five-key E♭ clarinet by Firth, Hall, and Pond, no. 1861 (US-CT-New Haven, no. 3300.71), and two instruments by Hanken: an eleven-key clarinet in high A or G, no. 1199, and a fifteen-key B♭ clarinet, no. 2022 (NL-Den Haag, nos. Ea15-1949 and Ea662-1933). For a photograph of the Firth, Hall, and Pond instrument see Renouf, *A Yankee Lyre*, 22–24.

44. The author is grateful to Jean Jeltsch for information.

45. Antolini, *La retta maniera*, 19 n. 2.

46. Byrne, "John Cramer," 512.

47. Examples by the Key firm include GB-Edinburgh, 80, 1681, 2452 and US-SD, 2839. Cf. Luke, "The Clarinets of Thomas Key," 37.

48. See Dibley, *Historic Musical Instruments*, 121.

49. Stradner, "Zur Stimmtonhöhe," 83, 85; Stradner, "Stimmtonhöhe," 287.

50. Ross, "A Comprehensive Performance Project," 252.

51. Haynes, "Pitch Standards," 476.

52. Ibid., 472–76.

53. Ross, "A Comprehensive Performance Project," 214–15. The pitch of the Miller A clarinet is recorded as A = ca. 435; see Dibley, *Historic Musical Instruments*, 73.

54. An unusual two-tier wooden case (ca. 1790, GB-Cambridge) with a cloth lining held a five-key clarinet in B♭ by Theodore. Its lower level includes spaces for joints appropriate for a clarinet d'amour or alto clarinet.

55. Marcuse, "The Instruments of the King's Library," 34–35.

56. Myers, *The Glen Account Book*, 24.

CHAPTER 2

1. Alterations are often visible on the tenons, inside the finger holes, and in the keys' workmanship. Evidence that manufacturers added keys to clarinets appears on extant instruments and in the records of the Edinburgh firm of J. & R. Glen. In 1846, the London Bilton firm included a charge of 12 shillings to Glen for "adding 3 Keys in boxes & tubes to alter 3 Clarinets." See Myers, *The Glen Account Book*, 95.

2. Shackleton, "The Development of the Clarinet," 17.

3. For example, the clarinetist Lefèvre made an uncorroborated attribution of keys in his influential *Méthode* (1802). He states that Mr. Friz [Fritz] added keys for E/B, F♯/C♯, and A♭/E♭. Lefèvre, *Méthode*, 1. In 1808, the maker Simiot embellished Lefèvre's account by stating that this "discovery" by Fritz was made in 1760. Simiot, *Tableau*, prospectus page. Other than these statements by Lefèvre and Simiot, there is no evidence to suggest that the Brunswick clavichord and organ maker Barthold Fritz (1697–1766) invented these keys or even made clarinets. Later in the century, the lexicographer François Joseph Fétis attributed the addition of an unspecified fifth key (probably A♭/E♭) to the well-known eighteenth-century clarinet soloist

Josef Beer, who performed many concerts in Paris during the 1770s. Although Beer probably performed on a five-key clarinet, there is no other evidence to support that he was responsible for the addition of a fifth key. See Fétis, *Biographie universelle,* vol. 2, 99. Subsequently, dozens of writers repeated these assertions by Lefèvre and Fétis as fact without verifying the accuracy. At present, there is no evidence to credit Fritz with contributing to the clarinet or the addition of a fifth key to Beer.

4. Corrette, *Le parfait maître,* 20; Eisel, *Musicus Autodidaktos,* 76–79, Garsault, *Notionaire,* 647.

5. "Depuis quelques années les *clarinettes* ont beaucoup pris à Paris, & on y en fait de très bonnes. Ce sont des instrumens à anche, longs à-peu-près comme un hautbois, mais leur diametre est beaucoup plus fort & il est égal par-tout; de sorte qu'on n'a besoin que d'une seule perce pour travailler cet instrument intérieurement. L'anche des clarinettes n'est pas comme celle des bassons ou hautbois, ce n'est qu'une mince platine de canne attachée avec de la ficelle à la partie supérieure de l'embouchure, qui, animée par le souffle, donne à cet instrument un son singulier: dans les bas c'est le son du chalumeau; & dans les hauts, qui ne sont point des octaves comme dans les autres instrumens à vent, mais des quintes au dessus des octaves, il a le son d'une trompette adoucie. Les clarinettes jouées avec goût & intelligence font un bel effet dans les symphonies, elles sont même très agréables à entendre en *quatuor avec des cors de chasse.* Tout l'art de l'ouvrier consiste à accorder cet instrument avec beaucoup de soin & d'exactitude, pour que les hauts tons aient la quinte double parfaitement juste. Les deux petites clefs placées au sommet de la clarinette doivent être dans leur véritable point de situation. On a ajouté depuis peu deux autres clefs à la patte ou derniere partie des clarinettes, qui font que cet instrument auquel il manquoit un ton dans l'ordre diatonique (savoir le *B-fa-si naturel*) est devenu complet, & qu'en même-temps il a tous les sémitons, du moins entre les mains des habiles jouers; jusqu'a présent cet instrument *ne s'étoit joué qu'en ut & fa,* quoiqu'il ait cependant beaucoup plus d'étendue que le hautbois." Du Moutier, "Faiseur," vol. 1, 439–40. This dictionary was given a *privilege du roi* on 22 August 1764, as noted on page XVIII. The author would like to thank Jean Jeltsch for a transcription from the *Dictionnaire portatif* and Thierry Boucquey and Thomas MacCracken for help with the translation.

6. Jeltsch and Watel, "Maîtrises et jurandes," 23, 25; Waterhouse, *NLI,* 242. Amlingue's activity is documented in the Paris archives. A three-key Amlingue low-pitch (A = ca. 385 Hz) C clarinet surfaced in 2002 in a French collection; it appears to have been made early in his career during the 1760s or 1770s. The author thanks Xavier Sallaberry for information on Amlingue.

7. Wachmann, "Clarinet Woodworking," 45–47.

8. See Becker, *History of Instrumentation,* 22; Bartenstein, "Die frühen Instrumentationslehren," 99–101.

9. Roeser, *Essai,* 10 n. *. The author thanks Thierry Boucquey and Thomas MacCracken for help with the translation.

10. For an illustration and dating, see Rice, "Clarinet Fingering Charts," 23–24, pl. V.

11. Corrette, *Méthode,* 55; Hotteterre, *Méthode,* 24; *Principes de clarinette,* 1; Abraham, *Principes,* 2.

12. This information is from documents in carton Y 5005/B, Archives Nationales. See also Gérard, "Inventaire," 196; Waterhouse, *NLI,* 132. The author thanks Jean Jeltsch for information.

13. Gétreau, *Aux origines*, 751. Two five-petal flower marks also appear on the dorsal side of the right-hand section and the stock-bell. The author thanks Jean Jeltsch for information. In correspondence with the author, Denis Watel believes the Geist clarinet to be pitched in D.

14. Dealers in Paris (1977–79) and Tours (1994) sold both instruments. The author thanks Joseph Moir and Denis Watel for information and Jean Jeltsch for a photograph of the Champlain clarinet.

15. Castillon, a Swiss musician and professor of mathematics in Berlin, wrote nearly six hundred articles concerning music in the five-volume supplement to the *Encyclopédie*. See Hardesty, *The Supplément to the Encylopédie*, 133.

16. Robinet, *Suite*, 144, pl. 4. These engravings are in Halfpenny, "Early English Clarinets," pl. VIII.

17. See Ross, "A Comprehensive Performance Project," 182–83; for an illustration of the Rottenburgh clarinet see Dullat, *Klarinetten*, 266, Abb. 161.

18. Castillon, "Clarinette," *Supplément à l'Encyclopédie*, vol. 2, 450–51. Cf. trans. in Halfpenny, "Castilon on the Clarinet," 334–35. The author thanks Thierry Boucquey and Thomas MacCracken for help with the translation.

19. Francoeur is the first to mention corps de rechange when he states that the B♮ clarinet is the same as the B♭ upon substituting corps. *Diapason général*, 24.

20. There are two later, crudely made anonymous four-key clarinets constructed about 1800 with an F♯/C♯ key. The first (SF-Helsinki, F 224) is a B♭ clarinet reported by the museum to be from the town of Loppi in northern Finland with five sections of an unidentified wood with horn ferrules, a separate mouthpiece, barrel, and bell. The author thanks Joseph Moir and the curators of the Helsinki Museum for information. The second four-key instrument (US-NY-New York-M, 89.4.900) has six fruitwood sections with mouthpiece, barrel, and bell. The shank of the F♯/C♯ key is sheet metal formed in a channel, as found on some three-key clarinets. All the key springs are attached to the wood and its E/B key is mounted in a ring rather than a block. According to the Crosby Brown catalog, this instrument came from Sweden. See *Catalogue of the Crosby Brown Collection*, vol. 1, 138.

21. The stock-bell of the Michel clarinet survives in Berlin. The author thanks Tom Lerch of the Berlin Museum and Jean Jeltsch for information.

22. See Jeltsch and Watel, "Maîtrises et jurandes," 27; Waterhouse, *NLI*, 62, 242, 263.

23. Sachs, *Sammlung*, 292.

24. Vanderhagen, *Méthode nouvelle*, 2–3.

25. For a photograph, see Giannini, *Great Flute Makers of France*, 41, ill. 25d.

26. See Ross, "A Comprehensive Performance Project," 225–26; ills. 99–100. Two boxwood five-key French clarinets similar to Martin Lot's made during the late 1780s or early 1790s are a Roberty B♭ clarinet (GB-Cambridge) and a C clarinet (US-CA-Claremont, W118) stamped "Naust." Both have ivory ferrules and one-piece stock-bells.

27. Blasius, *Nouvelle méthode*. Later French tutors that illustrate clarinets with a combined stock-bell include one by Vanderhagen (ca. 1799) and Michel (ca. 1800). The Vanderhagen and Michel tutors are reprinted in P. Lescat and J. Saint-Arroman *Clarinette: Méthodes et traités-dictionnaires*.

28. Lefèvre, *Méthode*, pls. 1–4.

29. Young, *4900 Historical Woodwind Instruments*, 5; Watel, "Michel et François Amlingue," 16–21; Jeltsch and Watel, "Maîtrises et jurandes," 26; Rousselet, "La foire," 28. The author thanks Xavier Sallaberry for information.

30. Watel, "Michel et François Amlingue," 19.

31. Crusell recorded his purchases from Amlingue on 2 June and from Baumann on 14 September 1803 in his diary in the Kungliga Biblioteket, Stockholm, Dahlström, *Bernhard Henrik Crusell*, 75, 278; Watel, "Michel et François Amlingue," 17. The author owns a five-key C clarinet (ca. 1820) marked "AMELINGUE," and a seven-key basset horn (ca. 1775) marked "AMELINGUE A PARIS" was purchased by the Musée de la Musique in Paris in 2002 at auction.

32. See Young, *4900 Historical Woodwind Instruments*, 4, Y5. Extendable keys include a shank made in two overlapping parts so the touch piece can be extended for ease of fingering. Extensions on both the E/B and F♯/C♯ keys became fairly common during the eighteenth and nineteenth centuries.

33. Bessaraboff, *Ancient European Musical Instruments*, 100, 317.

34. Bragard and De Hen, *Musical Instruments*, 192.

35. Simiot, "Correspondance," 541.

36. Jeltsch and Watel, "Maîtrises et jurandes," 22–23; Jeltsch, "'Prudent à Paris,'" 150–52; Giannini, "A French Dynasty," 7–10.

37. Prudent employed at least eight workers; Jeltsch, "'Prudent à Paris,'" 140. Extant Prudent clarinets include a five-key example (late eighteenth century, NL-Amsterdam) and a seven-key E♭ clarinet (ca. 1830, I-Milano, MTS-FA/13). For a photograph of the latter, see Bizzi, *La collezione,* 131; and see Jeltsch, "'Prudent à Paris,'" 147. A four-key clarinet by Prudent (Paris, 1780s) with an added key for A♭/E♭, partially obscuring the maker's stamp, was available from the dealer Jean Michel Renard in 2002.

38. The author thanks Denis Watel for information about Proff and extant clarinets by Trotochot, Porthaux, Boisselot aîné, and Keller; and Xavier Sallaberry for information about his clarinet by Les Frères Keller .

39. Lefèvre, *Méthode*, 1 n. 3. A contemporary of Lefèvre, Vandenbrœck knew of the C♯/G♯ key and states that Lefèvre's discovery was very necessary for making the instrument more perfect and true in intonation. See Vandenbrœck, *Traité général*, 45.

40. See Rice, "Clarinet Fingering Charts," 31.

41. Young, *4900 Historical Woodwind Instruments*, 16; see also Jeltsch, *La clarinette à six clés*, 5. A six-key Baumann clarinet (ca. 1800, US-CA-Santa Monica) should be added to Young's list.

42. On a ten-key François Amlingue B♭ clarinet (ca. 1820, GB-Cambridge), the right-hand section has a side C♯/G♯ key in a saddle so that the touch piece is between R2 and R3, with the key head close to the first finger hole. Shackleton states that with additional fingers down on the holes of the right-hand joint the notes produced with this key are in tune. For a photo of the Amlingue clarinet, see Watel, "Michel et François Amlingue," 18.

43. Halary described the instruments in an 1817 letter and provided a report of four instruments submitted to the Académie des Beaux-Arts in ìRapports sur 4 instrumens de musique, présentée à l'académie des Beaux-Arts, par monsieur Halary. Rapport fait . . . 19 Juillet 1817." The author thanks Jean Jeltsch for a transcription of the letter and the report. See also Waterhouse, *NLI*, 157.

44. Examples include anonymous metal five- and six-key E♭ clarinets (both ca. 1820, GB-Cambridge), the latter with an extra thumb lever attached to the F♯/C♯ lever, and an A–B trill key, perhaps made for the English market. Others are a Halari eight-key metal B♭ clarinet (D-München-S, 10201) associated with a Russian cavalry

band, and a thirteen-key Streitwolf E♭ clarinet (ca. 1830, D-Biebrich, Kl. 2). See Seifers, *Die Blasinstrumente*, 42; Heckel, "Holz und Metall"; and Dullatt, *Klarinetten*, 227, Abb. 145.

45. Young, *4900 Historical Woodwind Instruments*, 257; Waterhouse, *NLI*, 430. Paul Raspé, Conservatoire Royale librarian in Brussels, suggested the existence of two makers who stamped their instruments "J. B. WILLEMS," the first dying before 1777 and the second probably in 1809. See Ross, "A Comprehensive Performance Project," 184.

46. Mahillon, *Catalogue descriptif*, vol. 4, 346; Ross, "A Comprehensive Performance Project," 188–90.

47. Waterhouse, *NLI*, 337.

48. Young, *4900 Historical Woodwind Instruments*, 192.

49. Shackleton illustrates this instrument and mouthpiece in "Clarinet," in Sadie, *New Grove*, 2d ed., fig. 7; "Clarinet," in Sadie, *NGDMI*, vol. 1, 392, ill. 3(e), 396, ill. 7(a); *Made for Music*, no. 96; Shackleton, "The Development of the Clarinet," 23, fig. 2.5.

50. Waterhouse, *NLI*, 228, 378; Ross, "A Comprehensive Performance Project," 201–2, 332–33.

51. See Ross, "A Comprehensive Performance Project," 173, 179; Young, *4900 Historical Woodwind Instruments*, 192, nos. Y6, Y4.

52. Nicolas Raingo (ca. 1800, B-Bruxelles, 4363), Heinrich Grenser (1806–13, D-Ingolstadt-S, 2704), and Pezé (ca. 1810, US-MA-Newton Centre) made later examples of left-handed five-key clarinets. For a discussion of the Grenser clarinets, see Weber, "A Symmetrical Pair," 31–34.

53. For a color photograph see Vermeersch, *Musiques et son*, 34, where the panel is incorrectly dated ca. 1700.

54. Preserved at the Brussels musical instrument museum.

55. Waterhouse, *NLI*, 405; Van Aerde, *Les Tuerlinckx*, 112, 162–79; Young, *4900 Historical Woodwind Instruments*, 245–46.

56. Libin gives a color photograph in *Musical Instruments*, n.p.

57. The author is grateful to Andreas Masel for information on the Stinglwagners; see also Waterhouse, *NLI*, 387.

58. Birsak, *Die Holzblasinstrumente*, 46, nos. 18/6, 18/7; 114.

59. For photographs see Carse, *Musical Wind Instruments*, pl. VII(a); Jenkins, *Musical Instruments*, pl. 15, no. 84, where its maker is listed as Walch.

60. *Musikalischer Almanac*, 204–5. Forkel includes two others as among the best makers in Germany: Johann Conrad Heise (Kassel) and G. M. Ulrich (Leipzig).

61. For a photo and description, see Heyde, "Über Rohrblattinstrumente," 382, Abb. 6; Young, *The Look of Music*, 97, no. 101.

62. See Young, *4900 Historical Woodwind Instruments*, 97, 115, the Grenser clarinet dated 1785 is now in Vermillion (US-SD, 7385); the Grundmann clarinet dated 1775 is a clarinet d'amour in G (F-Arnouville-lés-Gonesse). According to Eric Hoeprich, a five-key August Grenser clarinet that he owns has an F♯/C♯ key skillfully added, probably by Grenser; for a photograph see Meloni, 27.

63. Sachs, *Sammlung*, 291–92, nos. 520, 2873. A photograph of the Gehring four-key clarinet is in Kroll, "Vor- und Frühgeschichte," 3. The staff of the Musikinstrumenten-Museum in Berlin verified the loss of these instruments.

64. See Flechsig, "Ostfälische Musikinstrumentenmacher," 55. The author is grateful to Gunther Joppig and Johan van Kalker for information.

65. Flechsig, "Ostfälische Musikinstrumentenmacher," 112–13; Schmidtke, *Musikalisches Niedersachsen*, 90.

66. The author is grateful to Hans Rudolf Stalder for information. For a photograph, see Kjeldsberg, *Musikkinstrumenter*, 62–63.

67. For another photograph, see Bessaraboff, *Ancient European Musical Instruments*, 100, pl. 1.

68. Shackleton made this observation concerning an instrument (GB-Cambridge) similar to Tölcke's by the untraced maker Hespe (Hanover) on a six-key clarinet in a lecture entitled "What Can Be Learned from a Collection of Clarinets" at California Institute of Technology in Pasadena, Calif., in 2001.

69. Johann Friedrich Boie constructed a later seven-key clarinet (1790–1800, D-Darmstadt, Kg 67: 131) of blackwood with ivory ferrules, silver keys, a stock-bell, an A–B trill key with a slightly curved touch piece, and a cross E♭/B♭ key. For a photograph, see *Musik Instrumente*, 52. Boie constructed clarinets with six, seven, and twelve keys. See Young, *4900 Historical Woodwind Instruments*, 33.

70. See Collinson, *Encyclopedias*, 110.

71. "Clarinet, ein Blasinstrument, welches einen mehr molligten Ton von sich giebt, als die Hoboe, und mehr schneidenden, als eine Flöte; das Mittel zwischen Hoboe und Queerflöt. Die raschen Regimentsclarinette, besonders, wenn sie staat hölzernen Scheidel einen von Meßing haben, schreyen mehr als eine Trompete. Hier ist aber die Rede von den sanften Instrumenten, wie sie die neuern Concertisten behandeln. Ein Clarinet scheint wie ein Saite, die vom Ueberspinnen um 5 Töne tiefer wird, auch in einer fünften Verhältniß auf die Welt gekommen zu seyn; weil sie lieber b als h, und leichter aus dem F als C blasen. Ueberhaupt ist kein Instrument, das den Tonsetzern mehr Mühe macht, als das Clarinet. Wenn sie Chalmeau blasen, so geht ein c Clarinet bis ins e und zwey Töne tiefer als die Geige. Ueber das dreygestrichene c oder d darf man sie nicht hinaufsetzen. Ihre Klappen helfen die Semitöne herauszubringen, und ihr Umfang macht in der Mitte die beste Wirkung." Köster, "Clarinet," vol. 5, 685. The author thanks Richard M. Sheirich for help with the translation.

72. Koch, *Musikalisches Lexikon*, 333–34 n. **.

73. Young, *4900 Historical Woodwind Instruments*, 35, nos. Y1–5. The author is grateful to David Ross for information.

74. For photographs, see Stubbins, *The Art of Clarinetistry*, pls. IV and V; Ross, "A Comprehensive Performance Project," 167–68.

75. See Domp, *Studien*, 50.

76. See Bereths, *Die Musikpflege*, 154–55; Davis, "The Orchestra," 99.

77. Examples include a D clarinet by Georg Henrich Scherer (NL-Onnen) about 1750 and an anonymous five-key D clarinet with corps in E♭ (ca. 1835, DK-Copenhagen-H). See Himmer, "Klarinetsamling," 1981.

78. "Eine B Clarinett von schwarz Ebenholz mit 2 Stück 4 Schnabel 3 Birnen und verßilberten Klappen, von Kirst. 7 L'dor." *Journal für Literatur*, cxxiii. Only one clarinet is extant by Kirst; Young, *4900 Historical Woodwind Instruments*, 133. The clarinet in Breslau, no. 117, listed by Young, was destroyed during World War II.

79. "Uebrigens hat dieß Instrument noch das Besondere, daß es nicht in alle Töne einstimmt, sondern bei gewissen Tonarten entweder durch einzusetzende Mittel-stücke dem Tone, aus welchem das Stück geht, angepaßt, oder auch eine ganz andere Clarinette genommen werden muß, daher geibt es B, A, C Clarinetten, u. und es wird die Stimmung derselben jedesmahl mit angegeben." Löbel, *Conversationslexikon*, vol. 1, 270.

80. Ventzke, "Aus Briefen," 631.

81. Backofen, *Anweisung zur Clarinette* (ca. 1803), 8.

82. "Sey man aufmerksam auf die nöthige Gleichheit im Instrumente, dass die Tiefe gehörig und kräftig, und doch die Höhe leicht und angenehm anspreche. Daher sehe man Z.B. bey dem Clarinett darauf, dass der Becher oder Trichter nicht an enge gespannt, sondern von weiterm Unfange, so zu sagen, etwas gewölbt sey." See Fröhlich, *Vollständige Theoretisch-pracktische Musikschule*, 4; trans. Rousseau, "Clarinet Instructional Materials," 165.

83. "Für das auf dem Clarinett dumpfe und nicht reine *Gis* oder *As*, wodurch zugleich das *Cis* oder *Des* verbessert wird, ist bey den neuen Instrumenten noch eine 6*te* Klappe angebracht, welche sich an dem obern Mittelstucke befindet. Auch hat man an manchen Instrumenten, um den *b* Triller zu gewinnen, noch eine besondere Klappe, welche an dem obersten Mittelstücke nächst der *a* Klappe angebracht ist." Fröhlich, *Vollständige Theoretisch-pracktische Musikschule*, 8–9; trans. Rousseau, "Clarinet Instructional Materials," 175.

84. For a photograph, see Borders, *European and American Wind and Percussion Instruments*, 32, no. 615.

85. For the Sellner-system oboe, see Burgess, "Oboe, the Nineteenth Century, Additional Keys," in Sadie, *New Grove,* 2d ed. During the eighteenth and nineteenth centuries, walking sticks incorporated a number of musical instruments such as violins, flute, oboes, clarinets, and trumpets. They are novelty items not seriously used as instruments. Nevertheless, makers occasionally received a commission. A six-key walking stick clarinet (ca. 1820, NL-Den Haag, Ea 138-1950) with a C♯/G♯ key by Johann Georg Braun (Mannheim) consists of wooden keys inserted in slots on the body; a boxwood cover with an ivory cap on the dark wood mouthpiece; and a lower section with a metal tip used to contact the ground. They do not appear to have been very popular, as only a few examples are extant. The German Widmann (Freiburg im Breisgau, ca. 1840, Ch-Luzern, 140) also made them. See Moeck, "Spazierstockinstrumente"; Dike, *Cane Curiosa*; Vannes, *Katalog der städtischen Sammlung*, 27–28. The walking-stick clarinet and a normal clarinet by Widmar were erroneously described by Vannes as having four keys instead of five keys.

86. Michaelis, "Ueber die Klarinette," 387–88, 390. Michaelis states that Kayser made his clarinets. A nine-key clarinet (D-Göttingen) by F. Kayser of Münden is extant according to Waterhouse, *NLI*, 200.

87. This clarinet is a composite instrument with right-hand corps in A and left-hand corps in B♭. See Dibley, *Historic Musical Instruments*, 44.

88. Weber, "Einiges über Clarinett und Bassetthorn," between 40 and 41.

89. In Spohr's German text, there is a typographical error. He should have printed second (*zweiter*) finger, not third (*dritten*) finger. See Kroll, *Die Klarinette*, 48 n. 7.

90. "1. Eine Klappe zum tiefen Es und zu den Trillern D. Es und A. B. für den ersten Finger der rechten Hand, (auch B-Klappe gennant.) 2. Eine Klappe zum mittlern F. und den Trillern E. F. und H. C. für den dritten Finger der linken Hand. 3. Eine Klappe zu den Trillern A. H. und B. C. für der rechten Hand. 4. Eine Klappe zum mittlern As für den ersten Finger der linken Hand, (zur Seite der A-Klappe liegend,) und endlich 5) Eine Klappe zum tiefen B und zu den Trillern A. B. in der Tiefe und E. F. in der Mitte für den dritten Finger der rechten Hand. 6. Zwei nebeneinander stehende Löcher für den dritten Finger der linken Hand, um das tiefe Cis rein zu haben, oder noch besser für den kleinen Finger der linken Hand eine

Klappe zu diesem Behuf. 7. Ein Loch an der untern Seite der Clarinette, welches mit dem Daumen der rechten Hand bedeckt ist, zum tiefen H, und 8. Die beiden langen Klappen so gobogen, dass das mittlere H und Cis schnell aufeinander folgen können." The introduction is transcribed by Stork in "Johann Simon Hermstedt," 797; Kroll, *Die Klarinette*, 48–49; reproduced by Schmatz, "Die Klarinetten." Cf. the descriptions given by Kroll, *The Clarinet*, 25, 72–73.

91. One example (D-Biebrich, K-7) has a cross f/c key instead of a side key; another (D-Markneukirchen, 123) has a side f/c key but a B/F♯ instead of a B♭/F key. For a photograph and description of the Biebrich (Mus. K-7) instrument, see Young, *The Look of Music*, 151, no. 181; for a photograph of the Markneukirchen (123) instrument see Dullat, *Klarinetten*, 265, Abb. 157.

92. Vanderhagen, *Nouvelle méthode* (ca. 1819); Backofen, *Anweisung zur Clarinette* (1824). B. Schott's Söhne published Blatt's twelve-key clarinet tutor about 1828 and also manufactured twelve-key clarinets.

93. There is an extant stock-bell by Hesse (GB-London-W). A five-key Paulus clarinet (D-München-J) includes a stock-bell section; for a photograph see Joppig, "Holzblasinstrumente," 76.

94. Schubart, *Ideen*, 321.

95. Young, *4900 Historical Woodwind Instruments*, 103–4.

96. Halfpenny, "Early English Clarinets," 53.

97. Halfpenny, "The Christ Church Trophies," 82–83.

98. Anderson, *Music in New York*, xv.

99. Kenyon de Pascual, "English Square Pianos," 212.

100. Photographs are found in Rendall, *The Clarinet*, pl. 2a; Montagu, *The World of Baroque and Classical Instruments*, 88, pl. 70.

101. Cf. Halfpenny, "The Earliest English Clarinets," pls. Vd, VIa2.

102. See Young, *4900 Historical Woodwind Instruments*, 165–66; Waterhouse, *NLI*, 265. Instruments not listed by Young include a five-key B♭ Miller clarinet (US-CA-Santa Monica) and a five-key B♭ clarinet in the Smithsonian Institution.

103. Halfpenny, "Early English Clarinet," 45. Both instruments carry the earliest version of Miller's stamp: a sunburst, Miller's name, and a rose on a stem. All subsequent instruments include a unicorn rampant (the entire animal erect), a unicorn's head, or his name and address without a symbol, Young, *4900 Historical Woodwind Instruments*, 165–66.

104. Halfpenny, "Early English Clarinets," 48.

105. For photographs and descriptions, see Halfpenny, "Early English Clarinets," 51–52, pl. V, a–b; Simon, *Handel*, 248, no. 231.

106. Webster, *Johan Zoffany*, 69–70; Hutchins, *Mozart: The Man, the Musician*, 39, ill. 61; Simon, *Handel*, 152, 246–47.

107. See Rendall, *The Clarinet*, 13, 71, 84 n. 9. See Montagu's description in Simon, *Handel*, 248.

108. *The Clarinet Instructor*, "A Scale of Notes for the Clarinet," between 1 and 2; reproduced in Shackleton, "Clarinet," in Sadie, *NGDMI*, vol. 1, 394.

109. At least one clarinet by Thomas Collier illustrates an intermediate step in construction by its offset F♯/C♯ key without a bottom block to guide the key. See Halfpenny, "Early English Clarinet," 50, 52. Early clarinets have a ¼-inch crank.

110. A five-key clarinet marked "SCHUCHART" (J-Tokyo, 99) with six boxwood sections (mouthpiece, barrel, two finger hole joints, stock, and bell) dates to about

1800. Because Charles Schuchart died in 1765, it seems likely that another maker by this name existed or a member of Collier's firm used Schuchart's stamp. Cf. Waterhouse, *NLI*, 364; Young, *4900 Historical Woodwind Instruments*, 216.

111. Waterhouse, *NLI*, 68; Young, *4900 Historical Woodwind Instruments*, 50. A five-key Collier clarinet dated 1774 is in a private collection in America.

112. See Halfpenny, "Early English clarinets," 55, table II. There are two extant Collier B♭ clarinets (1770, GB-Edinburgh, 100, 1154), photographed in Myers, *Historic Musical Instruments*, 90, no. 100, 1154.

113. Ross "A Comprehensive Performance Project," 217; Shackleton,"The Development of the Clarinet," 29.

114. Waterhouse, *NLI*, 157; Young, *4900 Historical Woodwind Instruments*, 121.

115. These makers include Astor, Astor & Horwood, Bilton, Cramer, Cramer & Son, Cramer & Key, Gerock, Gerock & Wolf, Key, Wolf & Co., and Wolf & Figg. See Waterhouse, *NLI*; Dibley, *Historic Musical Instruments*.

116. See Young, *4900 Historical Woodwind Instruments*, 49−50. Only one other London maker, Muræus, used a lion rampant as part of his stamp, Waterhouse, *NLI*, 276.

117. Byrne, "The Church Band at Swalcliffe," 96.

118. Waterhouse, *NLI*, 130.

119. Waterhouse, *NLI*, 381; Hellier, "A Catalogue of Musicall Instruments," 5. For a good overview of Hellier's collection of music, musical instruments, and activities see Young, "The Shaw-Hellier Collection," *Brio*, 65−69.

120. See Young, *4900 Historical Woodwind Instruments*, 85.

121. See Shackleton, "John Hale," 26.

122. Baines, *The Bate Collection of Historical Wind Instruments*, 31, no. 4.

123. For photographs see Melville-Mason, *Exhibition of European Musical Instruments*, VIII(1); Myers, *Historic Musical Instruments*, 91. For a description, see Dibley, *Historic Musical Instruments*, 26−27, 47−48, 73.

124. A unique carved and decorated five-key C clarinet (ca. 1780−90, US-UT, 84150) by the previously unknown maker Wattles was very likely made in England. It consists of six boxwood sections and an additional small barrel below the small long-tenon ivory mouthpiece, evidently added to lower the pitch. Each of the six sections was turned to produce a twelve-sided surface down to a ring in the middle of the bell, at which point sixteen sides were turned, evidently to match the expansion of the bell. For the last 1.2 centimeters, the bell is round. There are ivory diamond-shaped inserts around all the finger holes, and all five keys are ivory. The S, A, and E/B ivory keys are mounted in rings with center marks, and the lower end of the off-set F♯/C♯ key is guided by a thin block. An English attribution of Wattles's instrument is supported by the physical evidence of a long-tenon mouthpiece, the cranked F♯/C♯ key, the shape of the boss for the F/C finger hole, and the mounting of the A♭/E♭ key. This is the only clarinet turned with twelve sides, decorated with ivory inserts around the tone holes, and fitted with ivory keys. Because of the very small bore in the upper joint, it may have been a showpiece rather than a playable instrument. Another clarinet by Wattles is a conventional five-key C instrument (ca. 1785, US-NY-Dewitt). The author is grateful to Phillip Young for information about the twelve-sided clarinet and to Ralph D'Mello for a photo of his Wattles clarinet.

125. See Ross, "A Comprehensive Performance Project," 209; Waterhouse, "RNCM Collection," http://www.mcm.ac.uk/library/hwm1htm.

126. Hopkinson, *A New and Complete Preceptor*, 10. This tutor was previously

known from a second edition printed by Metzler & Co. between 1842 and 1847. See Rendall, *The Clarinet*, 95.

127. Hopkinson, *A New and Complete Preceptor*, 3.

128. See also *Patents for Inventions*, 71.

129. Young, *4900 Historical Woodwind Instruments*, 162.

130. Luke, "The Clarinets of Thomas Key of London," 37.

131. Dibley, *Historic Musical Instruments*, 24–25; Dibley and Myers, *The Historic Clarinet*, 41, no. 39. Other London makers who used a mouthpiece with a socket instead of a tenon include George Wood, Wood & Ivy, Key, D'Almaine & Co., Bilton, and the American makers Camp (Litchfield, Connecticut) and Badger (Buffalo, New York).

132. *Metzler's and Son's Clarinet Preceptor*, 9.

133. Willman, *A Complete Instruction Book for the Clarinet*, 6, 13–16, 26.

134. Wood may have also supplied mouthpieces to Valentine Metzler since a blackwood signed mouthpiece accompanies a ten-key instrument (US-SD, 2849) by Metzler.

135. Rice, "Clarinet Fingering Charts," 28–29, 41 n. 48.

136. Wood, "Clarionet and Other Wind Musical Instruments," 3–4.

137. Ibid., 3. See Lyle, "John Mahon's Clarinet Preceptor," 53. The London flute maker Richard Potter had made flutes with pewter plug keys since the 1780s, and his examples no doubt inspired Wood to apply them to the clarinet.

138. For a detailed photograph, see Myers, *Historic Musical Instruments*, 104, no. 933.

139. Luke, "The Clarinets of Thomas Key of London," 31.

140. Wood, "Certain Improvements," 3.

141. Waterhouse, *NLI*, 435.

142. Burney, "Clarinet."

143. Bainbridge, *Observations on the Cause of Imperfections*, 20.

144. For a photograph, see Ridley, *European Wind Instruments*, 37, no. 326 C/10.

145. Gutteridge, *Introduction to the Art of Playing*, 1.

146. This was one of the earliest attempts to deal with the problem of the double duty for the thumb to play bb (with the A key) and to depress the speaker key. Mazzeo discusses later developments in "The History," 6–9, 33–37.

147. For a photograph, see Ridley, *European Wind Instruments*, 37, no. 248. There is a second Gutteridge clarinet (C-Toronto) identical to this example.

148. See Landon, *Haydn at Eszterháza*, 404 n. 1, 409 n. 2; Maunder, "A Biographical Index," 187.

149. Stradner, *Musikinstrumente*, 167–68, Abb. 12–13.

150. Ibid., 30, Abb. 11. See also Schmatz, "Die Klarinetten," 19.

151. Weston, *More Clarinet Virtuosi*, 165.

152. Hárich, "Documents," 128–29.

153. Meier, "Die Pressburger Hofkapelle," 83–84.

154. Waterhouse, *NLI*, 243–44; Sebasta, "Theodor Lotz," 55–56. Lotz's stamp reads "kk Hof Instrumentmacher," and this designation is also given on the handbill of a concert in Vienna in 1788. See Lawson, "Playing Historical Clarinets," 148.

155. See Hellyer, "Some Documents," 51, 53.

156. See Rendall, *The Clarinet*, 23–24.

157. Ross, "A Comprehensive Performance Project," 245–47, 251–53.

158. Landon, *Haydn at Eszterháza*, 72, 224–25.

159. Weston, *More Clarinet Virtuosi*, 117.

160. Hoeprich, "A Trio of Basset Horns," 229; Waterhouse, *NLI*, 147.

161. Griesbacher's son, Raymund II, succeeded his father in 1818, but instruments were still made with the father's stamp. Waterhouse, *NLI*, 147; Young, *4900 Historical Woodwind Instruments*, 109.

162. Nagy, "Zur Geschichte," 271.

163. Rohrer, *Bemerkungen auf einer Reise* (Vienna, 1804); quoted in Waterhouse, *NLI*, 147.

164. Hellyer, "Some Documents," 54.

165. See Maunder, "A Biographical Index," 183−85. In addition, the author owns a five-key K. Hammig B♭ clarinet (ca. 1820) which includes two additional longer finger hole joints, all of which are marked with a B♭ pitch name but which tune to about A = 445 and 455. The two shorter joints were altered by shortening the tenons, but heavy wear on the finger holes indicates that all these joints were frequently played.

166. Young, *4900 Historical Woodwind Instruments*, 234.

167. See Maunder, "A Biographical Index," 188−89.

168. Ross, "A Comprehensive Performance Project," 252.

169. Hopfner, *Wiener Musikinstrumentenmacher*, 332−33.

170. See Shackleton, "The Development of the Clarinet," 22, fig. 24.

171. For a photograph and description, see Schlosser, *Die Sammlung*, 125, Tafel LIII.

172. Birsak, *The Clarinet*, 105−6.

173. This mechanism was likely modeled on Simiot's nineteen-key clarinet made in 1827 and later by Vinatieri for Ferdinando Busoni's clarinet. See Rendall, *The Clarinet*, 91−92, Hopfner, *Wiener Musikinstrumentenmacher*, 265−66.

174. For a photograph, see Myers, *Historic Musical Instruments*, 93, no. 81. Koch very often used silver-lined saddles on his flutes.

175. Uhlmann was joined in 1833 by his three sons, Jakob, Leopold, and Joseph; Koch was succeeded by his son Johann Baptist, and the firm continued until 1899; see Waterhouse, *NLI*, 407−8, 444; Hopfner, *Wiener Musikinstrumentenmacher*, 519−21.

176. "Vormahls waren die Clarinetten 5klappig, und sie gaben die halben Töne in der Höhe und Tiefe nicht rein an; jetzt sind die beyden Mutationen B und A zusammen (d.i. mit Verwechselung der Zwischenstücke) mit 19 bis 24 Klappen versehen, welches den Vortheil hat, daß sie reiner tönen, und daß man in der Tonleiter bis zum tiefen e geben kann." Keess, *Darstellung*, vol. 3, 163. The author thanks Richard M. Sheirich for help with the translation.

177. An example of a Ziegler twelve-key A clarinet (ca. 1840, A-Salzburg-C, XVIII/25) includes a second metal-lined barrel. For a photograph, see Birsak, *The Clarinet*, 40, pl. 14.

178. *Münchener allgemeine Musik-Zeitung*, 1, no. 17 (January 1828): 26; cited in Masel, "Der Münchener," 74.

179. See Waterhouse, *NLI*, 297. A thorough explanation of Pentenrieder's patent is given in Masel, "Der Münchener," 96−119. A colored drawing of Pentenrieder's "Privilegiums-Gesuch" is reproduced in Birsak, *The Clarinet*, 63, and Dullat, *Klarinetten*, 267, Abb. 166.

180. Fahrbach, *Neueste Wiener Clarinetten-Schule*, 17. See, Birsak, *Die Klarinette* (Buchloe, 1992), 61; trans. in Birsak, *The Clarinet* (Buchloe, 1994), 62.

181. "Klarinet/Pisstiala na spüsob hoboge/wssak o neco tlustssý/o dole ssjrssý.

Clario, onis f. tibia acuti soni, clamosa ribia. Das Klarinet/eine Pfeiffe auf die art einter Hoboy/jedoch um etwas stärcker/und unten breiter. Hlawa. Capitellum. Der Kopf/oder Tüssel. Prostredek. Pars media. Das mittelstuck. Ssiroky Spodek. Pars extrema latoir. Der Becher ohne boden. Obycegne má tri Klapty / nekdy ssest. Ordinariè habet tres valvulas, interdum sex. Hat insgemein drey Klappen/oder Schlüsse/ bisweilen sechse. Péra. Pennæ. Die Federn. Náhubek tlusty. Orificium subscrassulum. Dickes Mundstuck mit Rohr." Rohn, *Nomenclator*, 232–33; trans. Hans Ruyter, Claremont Graduate School.

182. Waterhouse, *NLI*, 22–23.

183. Ibid., 10.

184. Møller, *Fløjte, obo, klarinet og fagot*, 20.

185. Ibid., 19–20.

186. Jensen, "Dulcianen og fagotten," 198.

187. For a photograph, see Møller, *Fløjte, obo, klarinet og fagot*, 18.

188. Ibid., 38–39, 41.

189. Ibid., 92. Other purchases of a C clarinet, B♭ clarinet, and basset horn were imported, probably from Germany.

190. Møller, *Danske instrumentbyggere*, 202–3.

191. Waterhouse, *NLI*, 375.

192. For photographs, see Møller, *Danske instrumentbyggere*, 202, 271.

193. For photographs, see Møller, *Fløjte, obo, klarinet og fagot*, 64, 82.

194. For photographs, see ibid., 57.

195. The patent drawing and Larshoff's explanation of the function of the keys is reproduced in Møller, *Danske instrumentbyggere*, 56. See also Møller, *Fløjte, obo, klarinet og fagot*, 60–61; Ross, "A Comprehensive Performance Project," 238–39.

196. Møller, *Danske instrumentbyggere*, 202–3.

197. Møller, *Fløjte, obo, klarinet og fagot*, 92–93.

198. Møller, *Danske instrumentbyggere*; Himmer, "Den tidlige klarinet," 163–64.

199. "Clarinetti, soldi otto, e denari Quattro—l'uno." *Tariffa delle gabelle*, 70.

200. Toffolo, *Antiche strumenti veneziani*, 213–15; Bernardini, "Woodwind Makers," 53.

201. Young, *4900 Historical Woodwind Instruments*, 79–81. Clarinets were in use at the Pietà in Venice since the early eighteenth century. See Rice, *The Baroque Clarinet*, 99. Abbé Richard reported hearing a concert of wind instruments including the clarinet at the Pietà in 1762 on Pentecost. See Richard, *Description historique et critique de l'Italie*, vol. 2, 333–34.

202. For a photograph, see Bernardini in "Woodwind Makers," 58, fig. 2. Young illustrates Fornari's key head in Young, *4900 Historical Woodwind Instruments*, 80.

203. See Cervelli, *Antichi strumenti*, 60. In Italy, Gervasoni mentions a four-key clarinet in an 1800 treatise, but no extant examples are presently known. See Gervasoni, *La scuola*, 352. A misidentified E♭ clarinet by Pietro Piana actually is part of a five-key clarinet assembled with the top joint of an oboe. Cf. Young, *4900 Historical Woodwind Instruments*, 178. The author thanks Renato Meucci for information.

204. Meucci, "La costruzione di strumenti musicali," 592–93; Young, *4900 Historical Woodwind Instruments*, 21. The author thanks William Maynard and Renato Meucci for information.

205. For a photograph see Guarinoni, *Gli strumenti musicali*, table XX; for a color photograph see Bizzi, *La collezione*, 132.

206. For a photograph, see *Amadeus*, 10–11, no. 4.

207. A five-key example (private collection) includes a strongly curved touch for its Ab/Eb key similar to those on Simiot clarinets; see the exhibition catalog, Lazzari, *Strumenti a fiato in Legno*, 75.

208. This maker was listed by Waterhouse under Tesero as the last name, but this is the location of a maker or dealer. See Waterhouse, *NLI*, 396.

209. Waterhouse, *NLI*, 302.

210. Young, *4900 Historical Woodwind Instruments*, 177–78.

211. Hamilton misinterpreted the text written by the composer Martinez de la Roca (ca. 1720), who referred to "clarines" or trumpets. See Martinez de la Roca, *Suplicatorio*, 14–16, and Hamilton, *Music*, 24, 222–23. In addition, Soriano Fuertes listed musicians in the royal chapel from a list dated 1756. Among the winds are bassoons, oboes, flutes, "dos clarines," and "dos trompas." The two "clarines" refer to trumpets assigned to the highest parts, the players of the "trompas" playing the lower parts. See Soriano Fuertes, *Historia*, vol. 4, 108. The author is grateful to Beryl Kenyon de Pascual for information.

212. See Kenyon de Pascual, "Ventas," 311–15.

213. *Les Instruments de Musique a Bruxelles*, 257–58.

214. See Kenyon de Pascual, "English Square Pianos," 213.

215. Waterhouse, *NLI*, 65, 410.

216. Reynvaan, *Muzijkaal Kunst-Woordenboek*, 410, pl. 30. See Rice, "Clarinet Fingering Charts," 25.

217. Young, *4900 Historical Woodwind Instruments*, 213. In 2001 a clarinet by Schlegel in private ownership was brought to the Gemeentemuseum and shown to a curator.

218. See Küng, " 'Schlegel A Bale,' " 77.

219. Nickel, *Der Holzblasinstrumente*, 123; Küng, " 'Schlegel a Bale,' " 77.

220. "Um 1 Baar von Basel beschriebene Clarinet und 1 Baar Flutravers." See Nösselt, *Ein ältest Orchester*, 95; Waterhouse, *NLI*, 354.

221. Fürstlich Oettingen-Wallerstein'sche Archiv, *Hofhaltungsrechnung 1773*, 84; cited by Piersol in "The Oettingen-Wallerstein Hofkapelle," 53.

222. Küng, " 'Schlegel a Bale,' " 78–79.

223. For a photograph see Zimmermann, *Von Zinken, Flöten, und Schalmeien*, 51, no. 137.

224. Küng, " 'Schlegel a Bale,' " 85; Young, *4900 Historical Woodwind Instruments*, 213, Y no. 1. For photographs, see Dullat, *Klarinetten*, 265, Abb. 156–57.

225. Young, *4900 Historical Woodwind Instruments*, 213, Y no. 3.

226. Waterhouse, *NLI*, 392.

227. Waterhouse, *NLI*, 364.

228. *New York Gazette* (16 November 1761), 12; cited in Gottesman, *The Arts and Crafts in New York*, 368; Corry, Keller, and Keller, *PACN*.

229. A late example of an anonymous, probably American, three-key clarinet (ca. 1820, F-Bayonne) is in a private collection. It is made of stained fruitwood with thin metal ferrules divided in five sections: mouthpiece (a modern replacement), barrel, left-hand joint, right-hand section joined to the stock, and a separate bell. The E/B key is positioned for L4 and its key head is mounted on a block.

230. Cited in Corry, Keller, and Keller, *PACN*.

231. In 1871, an auction of the long-lived Philadelphia music publisher George E. Blake listed forty clarinets with "4 keys." This description was apparently a mistake

for five keys because the speaker key on the back of the instrument was not counted. See *Catalogue of the Large and Valuable Stock*, 50, nos. 2799, 2800, 2804, 2805.

232. *Pennsylvania Gazette-Philadelphia* (5 January 1764), 31; cited in Taricani, "Music in Colonial Philadelphia," 194; Corry, Keller, and Keller, *PACN*.

233. *New York Mercury* (5 October 1772); cited in Corry, Keller, and Keller, *PACN*.

234. *South Carolina & American General Gazette* (6–13 May 1774), 3; cited in Corry, Keller, and Keller, *PACN*.

235. *Royal Gazette-Charleston* (17–20 October 1781), 31; cited in Corry, Keller, and Keller, *PACN*. The ads appeared in 17–20 October, 1781.

236. Frank Kidson and H. G. Farmer, "John Jacob Astor," *NGDAM*, vol. 1, 87. See Waterhouse, *NLI*, 104, and Libin, "The Eisenbrandt Family Pedigree," 338.

237. "Jacob Anthony, Drechsler und Instrumentenmacher . . . macht und verkauft, naeml. allerhand Arten von Queer-Floten, gemeinen Floeten, Hautboys, Clarinetten und Queer-Pfeifen. Er verbessert auch alte Instrumenten, und macht allerhand andere Drechsler-Arbeit." *Der Wochentliche Philadelphische Staatsbote* (29 September 1772), 31. The advertisement appears twice more before 13 October 1772; cited in Corry, Keller, and Keller, *PACN*.

238. Waterhouse, *NLI*, 10.

239. For a photograph, see *Music, Theater, Dance*, 67.

240. Waterhouse, *NLI*, 104. For photographs and a description of a five-key clarinet by Eisenbrandt, see Libin, *American Musical Instruments in the Metropolitan Museum*, 75.

241. For photographs and descriptions of Gütter clarinets, see Carter, "The Gütter Family," 50, 67–69.

242. For a photograph and description of a Whitely clarinet (US-MI-Dearborn) made in the European style, see Eliason, *Graves and Company Musical Instrument Makers*, 7, pl. 5.

243. Waterhouse, *NLI*, 427; Young, *4900 Historical Woodwind Instruments*, 253–54.

244. Eliason, "Graves, Samuel," in Sadie, *New Grove*, 2d ed.; Waterhouse, *NLI*, 144.

245. Young, *4900 Historical Woodwind Instruments*, 93–94. In 1838, Graves offered clarinets in F, E♭, C, or B♭ in boxwood or "cocoa" (cocus) with five, six, eight, nine, eleven, or thirteen keys. For a photograph of a finely made cocus, thirteen-key C clarinet by Graves and Company (US-CT, 3328.67), see Renouf, *A Yankee Lyre*, 22–23. During the 1830s, Graves made clarinets for the dealers John Ashton (Boston), Marsh & Chase (Montpellier, Vermont), and Prentiss (Boston); Eliason, "Letters," 45–46, 50–51.

246. Waterhouse, *NLI*, 206.

247. There is a highly unusual key design on a fourteen-key John Pfaff B♭ clarinet (GB-Cambridge) made in three sections of rosewood. It may have been made for the 1855 Exhibition in Washington, D.C.

248. Simiot, *Tableau explicatif*; reproduced in Jeltsch and Shackleton, "Caractérisation acoustique," 122–24.

249. For a photograph, see Shackleton, "Clarinet," in Sadie, *NGDMI*, vol. 1, 395, ill. 5(a).

250. Shackleton, "Clarinet," Sadie, *NGDMI*, vol. 1, 395.

251. An example of a similar Simiot seven-key clarinet (GB-Cambridge) with this position of the B/F♯ is illustrated and described in Shackleton, "The Development of the Clarinet," 20, fig. 2.2 (c).

252. Moir, "Catalogue du Musée de Nice," 1987.

253. For a photograph see *Musique Bourgeoise*, 37, 23, ill. 12.

254. Moir, "Catalogue du Musée de Nice," 1987.

255. See a letter by Simiot to members of the l'Institut Royal, 26 November 1827; cited in Jeltsch and Shackleton, "Caractérisation acoustique," 111 n. 39.

256. "M. Simiot a aussi exposé une clarinette en *ut* à laquelle il est parvenu à donner les qualities qui jusqu'ici n'avaient appartenu qu'à la clarinette en *si*." Héricart de Thury, *Rapport du jury*, 355–56.

257. Jeltsch and Shackleton, "Caractérisation acoustique," 111–12.

258. See the photographs in Myers, *Historic Musical Instruments*, 92; descriptions in Rendall, *The Clarinet*, 91–92; Dibley, *Historic Musical Instruments*, 71. There is an identical boxwood example of a Simiot nineteen-key clarinet (GB-Cambridge).

259. Institut de France. Académie Royale des beaux-arts (2 October 1827). The author thanks Jean Jeltsch for information. An explanation of Simiot's improvements and the report of the Institut de France is reprinted in Fétis, "Inventions et perfectionnemens d'instruments," 515–17.

260. Fétis, "Nouvelles de Paris," 495.

261. "MM Beer & Mocker tous deux premières clarinettes des Théâtre Royaux des Italiens et de l'Odéon, feront entendre & démonstreront les avantages de ces deux instruments." The author thanks Jean Jeltsch for information.

262. Simiot, "Correspondance," 541–42.

263. Simiot's influence, is clear since B/F♯ provides a usable b in the chalumeau register, a note that normally is badly out of tune on the five-key clarinet. The author thanks Nicholas Shackleton for information.

264. Rendall, *The Clarinet*, 89.

265. Simiot, "Correspondance," 541.

266. Grenser may have begun work on this instrument by March 1808, as suggested by Michaelis in "Ueber die Klarinette," 389–90 n. *. See also "Nachrichten," (1808), 89–91; "Miscellen," 798–99.

267. "Nachrichten," (1809): 653 and n. *. Cf. Rendall, *The Clarinet*, 89.

268. For a report of the concert of 22 October 1809 in Vienna, see "Nachrichten" (1810): 298–99.

269. See L. B. Francoeur, "Rapport fait par M. Francoeur," 42; Estock, "A Biographical Dictionary," 250–54.

270. Cf. Shackleton and Rice, "César Janssen," 187.

271. Müller called his ligature an *anneau* or ring and illustrated a mouthpiece, metal ligature, and reed in his important *Méthode*. See fig. 1.4.

272. Müller, *Méthode*, 5.

273. Shackleton and Rice, "César Janssen," 187.

274. See the photograph and description in Shackleton and Rice, "César Janssen," 188.

275. "Rapport fait par la commission," 593. For a section of the report, see Rendall, *The Clarinet*, 90; Weston, *More Clarinet Virtuosi*, 159–60.

276. Weber, "Das Clarinett," vol. 17, 374. However, a 1997 search in the Paris Conservatory archives by Jeltsch did not locate 1814 documents relating to the Müller clarinet.

277. Héricart de Thury, *Rapport du jury*, 356.

278. Photographs of this instrument are in Weston, *Clarinet Virtuosi*, pl. 4; Dullat, *Klarinetten*, 34, Abb. 15; 266, Abb. 160. Lefèvre dated similar thirteen-key clarinets 1825 and 1827. See Shackleton and Rice, "César Janssen," 187.

279. The author is grateful to Thomas Reil for information about and photographs of this instrument. For a photograph see Meloni, 48.

280. "Letztere nach Iwan Müller's neuester Erfindung." Joppig, "Holzblasinstrumente," 56–57; for a reproduction of the advertisement see Joppig, "Zur Entwicklung," 263, Abb. 135.

281. "Instruments de musique," 16–17.

282. Gardeton, *Annales de la musique*, 65.

283. Advertised in Carl Almenräder, *Abhandlung über die Verbesserung des Fagotts* (Mainz, 1822); reproduced by Joppig in "Holzblasinstrumente," 57.

284. Pierre, *Les facteurs d'instruments*, 301 n. 1. A Müller-system thirteen-key clarinet by Brelet is owned by Jeltsch (F-Le Mans).

285. Backofen, *Anweisung zur Clarinette* (1824), 6.

286. "Anzeige," 28.

287. Héricart de Thury, *Rapport du jury* (1824), 356.

288. Francoeur, "Rapport fait par M. Francoeur," 42.

289. Shackleton and Rice, "César Janssen," 190.

290. For photographs and a description, see Shackleton and Rice, "César Janssen," 190–93. A Lefèvre clarinet (F-Bayonne) dated 1825 is the earliest dated instrument to include rollers. They are medium size and identical to those used on thirteen-key clarinets by Baumann and Gentellet.

291. Paris Conservatoire carton AJ 37 384. The author thanks Jean Jeltsch for information.

292. The instrument was previously owned by the collector Eugène de Bricqueville and photographed in *Musée retrospective*, 83, fig. 50. There were a total of eleven keys mounted in rings, blocks, and saddles for S, A, E♭/B♭, C♯/G♯ (possibly an addition), B/F♯ (possibly an addition), F/C, A♭/E♭ (now missing), F♯/C♯, E/B, D, and C. The author is grateful for information from Keith Puddy, Nicholas Shackleton, and Jean Jeltsch.

293. For reproductions of this program see Poulin, "The Basset Clarinet of Anton Stadler," 72, fig. 3; Jeltsch, "La clarinette de Mozart," 16; Lawson, "Playing Historical Clarinets," 148.

294. *Musikalischer Korrespondenz der teutschen Filarmonischen Gesellschaft für das Jahr 1790* no. 29 (10 November 1790), 146; cited and trans. in Ross, "A Comprehensive Performance Project," 262–63; see also Ness, "Some Remarks Concerning the Basset Clarinet," 11.

295. Gerber, *Historisch-Biographisches Lexikon*, vol. 2, col. 556.

296. Prague (16 October 1791), Berlin (31 January 1792, 23 March 1792), Warsaw (4 May 1792, 11 September 1792), Vilnius (1793, no programs available), Riga (27 February 1794, 5 March 1794, 21 March 1794), St. Petersburg (13 May 1794), Lübeck (16 September 1794, 27 September 1794), Hamburg (29 November 1794, 20 December 1794), and Hanover (12 September 1795). See Poulin, "A Report on New Information," 946–53.

297. *Musikalisches Wochenblatt* (January 1792): 41; cited and trans. in Poulin, "The Basset Clarinet of Anton Stadler," 76.

298. The earliest player to demonstrate that Mozart's concerto can be managed on an historically accurate clarinet is the American Dutch clarinetist Eric Hoeprich. He gave a fine performance on a ten-key basset clarinet of his own design in 1985 with the Orchestra of the Eighteenth Century at the Concertgebouw in Amsterdam.

299. Poulin reproduced all three programs, preserved in the Latvian Fundamental Library, Riga, in "Anton Stadler's Basset Clarinet," 124–25. The author wishes to thank Pamela Poulin for a photograph.

300. During the early 1990s, Hoeprich made an A basset clarinet based on one of the Riga program engravings and successfully performed Mozart's clarinet concerto in 1994. His instrument has six sections of ebony with ivory ferrules; nine keys with a completely chromatic basset range; a blackwood mouthpiece; and a slightly curved, wooden neck. Attached to the lowest section is a "cross-pipe" or small L-shaped section angled at about 90 degrees inserted into a bell that flares outward to a cylindrical section and then inward. The keys are for the S, A, Ab/Eb, F♯/C♯, E/B, Eb, D, Db, and C. For a photograph, see Lawson, *Mozart*, 47, fig. 4.2. In other words, the instrument is a standard five-key clarinet with a four-note extension below e.

301. See also Adelson, "Reading between the (Ledger) Lines," 168 n. 28.

302. *Musikantiquariat Hans Schneider*, 76; Lawson, *Mozart*, 48.

303. *Hannoversiche Anzeige* (7 and 11 September 1795); cited in Fink, "Anton Stadler in Hannover," 20.

304. Sievers, *Hannoversche Musikgeschichte*, 318.

305. See Schönfeld, *Jahrbuch*, 58.

306. See Rice, "The Clarinette d'Amour," 104.

307. "Wiener Kunstnachrichten," 543–44; trans. in Lawson, *Mozart*, 45. This description was paraphrased in Gerber, *Neues Historisch-Biographisches Lexikon*, vol. 4, 248, who corrected the misprint "querrippe" (lateral ridge) to "querpipe" (transverse pipe).

308. *Wiener Zeitung*, 21 August 1799 and 31 May 1800. See Maunder, "A Biographical Index," 187–88.

309. "Anzeige von verbesserten und neu erfundenen Blasinstrumenten," *Wiener Zeitung* (2 April 1803): 1174; cited and trans., along with a reproduction of the original advertisment, in Ross, "A Comprehensive Performance Project," 269–71.

310. Backofen, *Anweisung zur Clarinette* (ca. 1803), 35.

311. Ibid., 8, 37.

312. Ibid., 35. See Ross, "A Comprehensive Performance Project," 272–73. Backofen did not mention extended-range clarinets in the second edition of his tutor, published in 1824.

313. See Riehm, "Zum Problem," 218; Riehm, "Klarinette," in *MGG*, 2d ed., vol. 5 (1996), 187.

314. Waterhouse, *NLI*, 300.

315. See the descriptions in Lawson, *Mozart*, 88–89. The Bischoff basset clarinet includes an E/B key.

316. The author thanks Hans Rudolf Stalder for photographs and information.

317. Haine and Poulin reported a Johann Ziegler basset clarinet (B-Bruxelles, JT 365) at the Brussels museum. In 1990, the curator of the museum collection, Ignace De Keyser, and the author determined that this instrument is an eight-key basset horn made with a straight body in Eb by comparing the finger hole placement of a five-key clarinet d'amour (B-Bruxelles, 932) by Pietro Piana marked with the pitch letter "F." This pitch identification was later confirmed by a playing test. See Haine, *Musica*, 130; Poulin, "A Report on New Information," 951.

318. See Lawson, *Mozart*, 26–27.

CHAPTER 3

1. Corrette, *Le parfait maître*, 20.

2. Garsault, *Notionaire*, 633. For a reproduction of the plate and translation of Garsault's text, see Rice, *The Baroque Clarinet*, 134–36.

3. Roeser, *Essai*, 3–4. The lowest note of the register, e, was placed at the end of the scale, separated from the highest note, f3, by a bar line, perhaps as an indication that the pitch of e could be faulty or questionable on some instruments. Roeser did not explain the numbers 1 and 2 under the notes e and f, but they probably designate these notes as the first and second of the range. His scale omits f♯ and a♭ in the chalumeau register but includes the corresponding twelfths of c♯ and e♭, because the chalumeau notes were considered to be out of tune and unusable.

4. Ibid., 3–4.

5. Roeser, *Gamme de la clarinette*. For a photograph and discussion of this fingering chart, see Rice, "Clarinet Fingering Charts," 23–24, pl. V.

6. Francoeur, *Diapason général*, 18.

7. Ibid., 23–25.

8. See Becker, *Klarinetten-Konzerte des 18. Jahrhunderts*, x, 103–4.

9. Corrette, *Méthode*, 56.

10. Hotteterre, *Méthode*, 24; Castillon, "Clarinette," vol. 2, 450; Vanderhagen, *Méthode nouvelle et raisonnée* (ca. 1785), "Gamme naturelle" and "Gamme Diesée et Bemolisée."

11. Albrechtsberger, *Gründliche Anweisung*, 437.

12. "Es wird . . . hat noch weit mehr Töne im Amfange als die Hoboe, indem es vom E der kleinern Octave bis ins viergestrichene C un D geht." Löbel, *Conversationslexikon*, 269–70.

13. "Vom E der kleinern Octave biß ins dreigestrichene F geht; man will zwar die Höhe bis ins viergestrichene C seßen; allein das Instrument wird dadurch übertrieben." Brockhaus, *Conversations-Lexikon*, vol. 2, 565–66.

14. Lefèvre, *Méthode*, planches 3–4. Lawson reproduces the chromatic fingering chart in "Playing Historical Clarinets," 144.

15. These extremely high pitches never came into general use although fingerings for these notes using the modern clarinet are given by Pace in 1943 and Rehfeldt in 1994. Pace, *Ancie Battenti*, 90; Rehfeldt, *New Directions*, 127.

16. The following section is based on Rice, "Clarinet Fingering Charts," and a separate study of instruction materials.

17. H. Grenser made eleven-key instruments as professional clarinets. However, a fingering chart for an eleven-key clarinet appeared only in an 1842 Italian translation of Lefèvre's *Methode*.

18. "Lorsqu'on a passé le troisième ut, la Gamme n'est plus generale, parce que chacun la fait à son gré." Roeser, *Gamme de la clarinette*; title page reproduced in Rice, "Clarinet Fingering Charts," pl. V.

19. "Da sich wegen des verschiedenen Baues, und der verschiedenen Art des Einblasens der Blas: vorzüglich Rohrinstrumente keine durchaus bestimmte Regeln des Fingersatzes geben lassen, so ist alles, was man hier thuen kann, in einer Scala die gewöhnlichen Griffe anzugeben, und eine Critik über jeden Ton anzuhängen und dabey die verschiedene Art, den nämlichen Ton zugreifen, nebst den Mitteln anzuzeigen, die dumpen Töne heller und klingender zu machen, und die schlechten zu verbessern. Hieraus muss sich nun jeder für sein Instrument seine Scala selbst ausziehen." Fröhlich, *Vollständige Theoretisch-pracktische Musikschule*, 15; trans. in Rousseau, "Clarinet Instructional Materials," 191.

20. Suggested by Baines, *Woodwind Instruments*, 301. In his treatise of 1782, the Norwegian bandmaster L. N. Berg was the first to use a Stutzfinger of R3 in his fingering chart for a three-key clarinet. See Berg, *Den første Prøve*, 50; Rice, *The Baroque Clarinet*, 72–73.

21. Cf. Halfpenny, "The French Hautboy," 51.

22. "Wenn der naturliche *as* Griff wie *B* bey den 1ten X zeichen zu schwer scheinen sollte, so beliebe man der Geschwindigkeit wegen zum *H*: Griff mit der langen Klappe auch die kleine *A* Klappe sammt den linken Zeige Finger zu öffnen und mit Beybehaltung dieses Griffes zum *As* auch den linkcken dritten oder *G* Finger offen zu halten. Zum 2ten X zeichen aber das *E♯* nicht wie *F* mit der Gabel sondern, wie *Fis* oder *F♯* zu grieffen, und dazu den rechten kleinen Finger auf das *C* Loch zu legen." Stadler, *Trois caprices*, 7. Cf. trans. in Carroll, "Anton Stadler's Contributions," 80. The text and part of the music are reproduced in Birsak, *The Clarinet*, 37, pl. 9.

23. Randel, *New Harvard Dictionary of Music*, 284. Du Moutier was probably the earliest to call the clarinet mouthpiece an "embouchure " in his article "Faiseur d'instrument a vent," vol. 1, 439.

24. Identical statements appear in several English and American tutors. See *A New and Complete Preceptor*, 3.

25. Vanderhagen, *Méthode* (ca. 1785), 2–3.

26. Blasius, *Nouvelle méthode*, 48; trans. in Menkin, "Frédéric Blasius," 66.

27. Lefèvre, *Méthode*, 2.

28. Michel, *Méthode*, 3; trans. in Rousseau, "Clarinet Instructional Materials," 125.

29. Hoeprich, "Clarinet Reed Position," 51.

30. Roeser, *Essai*, 12; trans. in Titus, "The Solo Music," 77.

31. Subsequently, three fingering charts for the four-key clarinet published in Paris depicted the reed-above position: Hotteterre, *Méthode*, 24; *Principes de clarinette*, 1–2; and Abraham, *Principes*, 2.

32. Norlind, "Abraham Abrahamsson Hülphers," 56–57; trans. by Mrs. Kirsten Koblik.

33. Vanderhagen (1785, ca. 1799, ca. 1819), Blasius (ca. 1796), Michel (ca. 1801), Lefèvre (1802), Démar (ca. 1808), Bochsa (ca. 1809), Rybicki (ca. 1826), Gambaro (ca. 1830), and Carnaud (1829). See Rice, "Clarinet Fingering Charts."

34. See Hoeprich, "Clarinet Reed Position," 52 and ill. 5.

35. Berg, *Den første Prøve*, 49; cited in Rice, "The Clarinet as Described by Lorents Nicolai Berg," 47; trans. by Mrs. Sonni Marschik.

36. Backofen, *Anweisung zur Clarinette* (ca. 1803), 4; trans. in Hoeprich, "Clarinet Reed Position in the Eighteenth Century," 50.

37. "Soll inzwischen das Instrument die Liebhaber noch mehr reizen. . . . Dahin gehört zuerst, dass mann aufhört, das Blatt oben zu blasen, wie die Franzosen sogar noch in ihrer Anweisung fordern. Man verliert dann freylich jene äussertste Höhe, aber man gewintt dagegen—ich möchte sagen, das ganze Instrument. Selbst die Haltung des Instruments ist nach jener Weise schwieriger, und giebt dem Kopfe eine unangenehme Richtung. Allein wie ist es möglich, einen sauften und zarten Ton zu bilden, wenn man das fibrirende Blatt mit den Zähnen berührt? Hierdurch muss ganz unvermeidlich . . . ein scharfer Ton herauskommen." Michaelis, "Ueber die Klarinette," *AMZ* 10 (1808), 386, trans. Don Halloran.

38. "Es gibt überhaupt zwey Arten das Clarinett zu blasen; eine, wenn man das Blatt ober dem Kopfe, und die andere, wen man es unter demselben hält. Bey dieser letzten hat der Spieler mehr Vortheil mit der Articulation durch den Zungenstoss Z.B. im geschwinderen Vortrage gestossener Passagen, aber den Nachtheil dass er nicht so geschwind mit einer solchen Gleichheit, wie jener, Höhe und Tiefe wechseln kann, wie es jeder leicht beurtheilen kann, der die Natur dieses Instrumentes, und die dazu erforderliche Behandlungsart kennt. Bey der ersten Art lässt sich die Zunge

nicht so genau und sicher anwenden, es entsteht auch durch ihre Anwendung im Blasen ein Pfeifen der Luft, der Ton kann nicht gehörig gebildet werden, und erhält das klangvolle nicht. Unterdessen ist ihre Anwendung auch nicht nothwendig, und diejenigen, welche glauben, dass ohne dem Zugenstosse kein lebendiger, energischer, mannigfaltiger Vortrag Statt finden könne, irren um so mehr, als sie das einzige Ziel aller Instrumentalisten, besonders des Clarinetisten, dem Sänger gleich zu kommen, zu misskennen scheinen." Fröhlich, *Vollständige Theoretisch-practische Musikschule*, 14; trans. in Rousseau, "Clarinet Instructional Materials," 128.

39. Hoeprich, "Clarinet Reed Position," 51.

40. Fétis, "Beer, Joseph," *Biographie Universelle* (Paris, 1860), vol. 1, 297.

41. Gerber, *Neues Historisch-Biographisches Lexikon*, vol. 4, 328; trans. Rendall, *The Clarinet*, 80–81. See also Clinch, "Clarinet Concerto No. 3," 21–22.

42. Vanderhagen's *Nouvelle méthode* (ca. 1819) includes a fingering chart for a twelve-key clarinet identified as the instrument played by Baermann in Paris during 1817 and 1818. For a reproduction of the fingering chart, see Lawson, *The Early Clarinet*, 28–29.

43. "Il y a plusieurs raisons . . . de préférence avec l'anche appuyée sur la lèvre inférieure: 1.o on y gagne, que le pouce de la main droite devient un doigt utile, car on n'en a plus besoin pour soutenir la Clarinette. . . . En second lieu, on a cet avantage, de pouvoir mettre sur les dents de la màchoire inférieure, un petit morceau de carte, et par-là éviter que les dents ne blessent pas la lèvre sur laquelle on met l'anche, ce que les personnes qui mettent l'anche en-dessus ne peuvent guère éviter: et enfin, l'exécutant n'est pas obligé de contracter ses nerfs, et parlà, de défigurer les traits de sa figure, ce qui arrive à ceux qui jouent differemment, parce que la lèvre supérieure est trop petite pour pouvoir naturellement se reployer sur les dents: cette darnière raison n'est pas la moindre, en effet, l'exécutant doit chercher soigneusement à éviter tout ce qui peut inspirer à l'auditeur une sensation désagreable et pénible." Müller, *Méthode*, 23–24; trans. in Rousseau, "Clarinet Instructional Materials," 128, 130.

44. Francoeur, "Rapport fait par M. Francoeur," 44.

45. Backofen, *Anweisung zur Clarinette* (1824), 6.

46. Rybicki (1826), Vaillant (1828), Blatt (1827–28), and Carnaud (1829). See Rice, "Clarinet Fingering Charts."

47. "En France, les hautbois, les flûtes et les bassons ne laissant rien à désirer. La clarinette est moins heureusement cultivée, quoique nous ayons plusieurs artistes recommandables par leur talent. Notre infériorité en ce genre, à l'égard de l'Allemagne, tient au systéme vicieux que nos clarinetistes ont adopté tant par la position de l'anche dans la bouche, que pour la force de ses anches. En Allemagne, où la clarinette est cultivée avec beaucoup de succés, le bec de l'instrument est placé dans la bouche de l'exécutant, de manière que l'anche est pressée par la lèvre inférieure; en France, c'est le contraire, et l'anche est placée en dessus. Les avantages de la manière allemande sont évidens; car la lèvre inférieure a bien plus de moelleux et de velouté que la supérieure, et la langue n'étant point obligée de remonter, comme dans la maniére française." Fétis, "De l'execution musicale," 226.

48. "Les clarinettistes allemands ont une supériorité incontestable sur les Français. Quelques-uns de ceux-ci se sont distingués par un jeu brillant, mais ils n'ont jamais pu acquérir le son doux et velouté de leurs rivaux de l'Allemagne. Divers préjugés les en ont empêchés; par exemple, ils font consister une partie du talent à tirer de leur instrument un son puissant et volumineux, qui est incompatible avec la douceur; de plus, ils s'obstinent à presser l'anche par la lèvre supérieure, au lieu de

l'appuyer sur l'inférieure, qui est à la fois plus ferme et plus moelleuse." Fétis, *La musique*, 292.

49. An early illustration of the reed-below mouthpiece position is found in Wood, "Clarionet and Other Wind Musical Instruments" [English patent specification] (1800).

50. Mahon, *A New and Complete Preceptor*, 1.

51. Hopkinson, *A New and Complete Preceptor*, 2. A unique copy of this tutor (GB-Cambridge) was dated in pen by a previous owner, George Smith, as "24th Sept. 1814." Hopkinson's opinon was quoted by Rendall from a later edition published by Metzler & Co. about 1842. See Rendall, *The Clarinet*, 95.

52. Willman, *A Complete Instruction Book*, 4–6, 8.

53. *Metzler's and Son's Clarinet Preceptor*, 3.

54. The earliest American tutor to illustrate the reed-below position is *A New and Complete Preceptor* (ca. 1825), 3.

55. Vanderhagen, *Méthode* (ca. 1785), 5–9. See Pearson, "Playing Historical Clarinet," 49. For a well-informed discussion concerning ornamentation, see Pearson, "Playing Historical Clarinet," 55–58.

56. Vanderhagen, *Méthode* (ca. 1785), 8.

57. Vanderhagen, *Nouvelle Méthode* (ca. 1799), 36. Michel suggests similar consonants for articulation. For the *coup de langue ordinaire* he recommends the voiced consonant "tû" and for détaché the unvoiced consonant "te," in his *Méthode*, 13.

58. Vanderhagen, *Méthode* (ca. 1785), 9; trans. in Charlton, "Classical Clarinet Technique," 401.

59. *Complete Instuctions* [sic] *for the clarinet*, 7. Mather describes the diaphragm aspiration as "breath stroke" and "slurred staccato" or "pearl stroke." Mather, *Interpretation of French Music*, 47–48.

60. Backofen, *Anweisung zur Clarinette* (ca. 1803), 11–12; trans. in Rousseau, "Clarinet Instructional Materials," 132.

61. Ibid., 12.

62. "Spreche man in das Instrument ein leichtesh (ha) welches nur bey tiefern Tönen härter angesprochen wird, bey deren Vortrage man sich auch etwas Vorschub durch das nachhelfen mit den Lippen verschafft. Jene welche unter sich blasen können sich der Sylbe tü oder tu bedienen." Fröhlich, *Vollständige Theoretisch-pracktische Musikschule*, 14; trans. in Rousseau, "Clarinet Instructional Materials," 188.

63. Fröhlich, *Vollständige Theoretisch-pracktische Musikschule*, 20. See Pearson, "Playing Historical Clarinet," 49.

64. Roeser, *Essai*, 2; Francoeur, *Diapason générale*, 21; and La Borde, *Essai*, vol. 1, 252.

65. Roeser, *Essai*, 5.

66. Ibid., 4–10.

67. Francoeur, *Diapason générale*, 25–30, 32–33. The clefs used are soprano, French violin, mezzo soprano, alto, treble, tenor, and baritone.

68. Roeser, *Essai*, 2, 7–8; Francoeur, *Diapason général*, 21; La Borde, *Essai*, vol. 1, 252.

69. Roeser, *Essai*, 2, 7; Francoeur, *Diapason général*, 25, 27 no. b.

70. Francoeur, *Diapason général*, 27 no. c, 29 no. f.

71. Roeser, *Essai*, 5; Francoeur, *Diapason général*, 21.

72. Norlind, "Abraham Abrahamsson Hülphers," 56–57; cited in Rice, "Clarinet Fingering Charts," 19; trans. by Mrs. Kirsten Koblik.

73. *The Clarinet Instructor*, 7.

74. *Compleat Instuctions* [sic], 8; *New and Complete Instructions* (ca. 1797), 6; *New and Compleat Instructions* (ca. 1798), 6; *The Clarinet Preceptor*, 6; Eley, *New Tutor*, 6.

75. Wesley, "Clarinet Scale," fol. 166.

76. Vanderhagen, *Nouvelle méthode* (ca. 1799), 69–70.

77. Blasius, *Nouvelle méthode*, 45–46; Lefèvre, *Méthode*, 138.

78. Lefèvre, *Méthode*, 138–44.

79. Vanderhagen, *Nouvelle méthode* (ca. 1799), 70.

80. Vanderhagen, *Méthode* (ca. 1785), 19.

81. "Clarinette en Mi Majeur c "est un corps en mi qui se pose sur la Clarinette en ut. . . . Cette Clarinette est un demi ton plus basse que la Clarinette en ut. . . . Il faut en consequence jouer ou écrire un demi ton plus haut que le violon." Vanderhagen, *Nouvelle méthode* (ca. 1799), 70; trans. in Rousseau, "Clarinet Instructional Materials," 114.

82. Gervasoni, *La scuola della musica*, 353.

83. "Si osservi che ciascun pezzo componente il clarinetto, costumasi da'fabbricatori a marcarlo colla lettera iniziale del tuono in cui è costrutto. Quello in cesolfaut porta la lettera C., perchè la posizione del cesolfaut rende realmente il cesolfaut. Quello in befà porta la lettera B., perchè la posizione del C. rende il befà. Il pezzo in alamirè porta la lettera A. . . . Il solo pezzo in bemì è denominato, anzichè dalla posizione C. (che rende il detto bemì) dalla posizione del faut, che rende l'elamì, e da tutt'i fabbricatori si marca in cotal modo = E.♯ =. Non da altra cagione credo si possa ripetere questa distinzione; che dal dubbio, che, marcandosi questo pezzo colla lettera B., arrecar possa confusione col clarinetto in befà, marcato anch'esso colla lettera B. Questo dubbio peraltro sì volesse marcare il clarinetto in befà, non col solo B. (che rigorosamente dice bemì, non befà) ma con un bemolle unito = B.♭ =, ed in allora marcando il pezzo in bemì col solo B." Antolini, *La retta maniera*, 18–19 n. 2; trans. in Rousseau, "Clarinet Instructional Materials," 116.

84. Ross, "A Comprehensive Performance Project," photo 103.

85. Ross, "A Comprehensive Performance Project," 232; Jeltsch, *La clarinette à six clés*, 18–27. The set of clarinets by Roche was offered for sale by the French dealer Jean Michel Renard in 2002.

86. Koch, *Musikalisches Lexikon*, 334.

87. Backofen, *Anweisung zur Clarinette* (ca. 1803), 1.

88. Michaelis, "Ueber die Klarinette," 387.

89. J. P., "On the Clarionet," 57.

90. Catrufo, *Des voix et des instrumens*, 10.

91. See Becker, *Klarinetten-Konzerte des 18. Jahrhunderts*, xi, 105, and Titus, "The Solo Music," 170–73.

92. "Wenn sie Chalmeau blasen, so geht ein c Clarinet bis ins e und zwey Töne tiefer als die Geige." Köster, "Clarinet," vol. 5, 685.

93. Vanderhagen, *Méthode* (ca. 1785), 3. A later writer who called the notes from e to e¹ "chalumeau" is Schneider. See Schneider, *Historisch-technische Beschreibung*, 30. The clarinetist Berr initially provided the commonly accepted names for the parts of the compass in his 1836 *Traité* as e to f¹ (*chalumeau*), g¹ to b♭¹ (*intermédiare*), b¹ to c³ (*clairon*), and d³ to g³ (*aigû*). Berr published a second tutor that provided a chromatic compass of e to f¹, f♯¹ to b♭¹, b¹ to c³, and c♯³ to g³. See Berr, *Traité*, 9–10; *Méthode*, 7.

94. "Wanneer men deezen Term vindt geschreeven, in eene *Clarinetpartije*; geest

het te kennen, dat men die *Passagie*, waarbij dat gevonden wordt, een *Octaaf* Laager moet Speelen. Zijnde dit de Toon der CHALUMEAU, of *Schalmeije*: en wordende dit gedaan; om dat men anderszins den *Bassleutel* zoude moeten bezigen, het welk hier door voorgekoomen wordt." Reynvaan, *Muzijaal Konstwoordenboek*, vol. 1, 117; trans. by Roelof Wijbrandous.

95. Blasius, *Nouvelle méthode*, 51.

96. Vanderhagen provides almost a full page of exercises alternating these two terms in the second issue of his tutor. Vanderhagen, *Méthode* (ca. 1797–98), 8–9. Mahon wrote similar transposition exercises adopting the terms "chalumeau," "clar.," and "clarinet" advocated by Blasius. Mahon, *A New and Complete Preceptor*, 9–10.

97. Backofen, *Anweisung zur clarinette* (ca. 1803), 36.

98. Francoeur, *Diapason général*, 24, 34.

99. Vandenbrœck, *Traité général*, 46–47.

100. Michel, *Méthode*, 2.

101. Ibid., 2.

102. J.P., "On the Clarionet," 57.

103. "Faute de Clarinettes, on pourra les Exécuter avec deux Hautbois Flutes ou Violins." The other composers represented are Wagenseil, Kohaut, and Richter. See Johansson, *French Music Publishers' Catalogues*, fasc. 118; Wolf, *The Symphonies of Johann Stamitz*, pl. 4b; and Hoeprich, "Die Klarinetten Johann Scherers," Abb. 2. A modern edition edited by Riemann printed the third symphony from this collection with the flute listed as an alternate instrument ("flauti o clarinetti"). See Riemann, *Mannheim Symphonists*, 36.

104. Rameau, *Les Boréades*, 1–3.

105. Framery, *L'infante de Zamora*, 248. Guion was unaware that Framery added the clarinet parts to his version of Paisiello's *La frascatana* since Paisiello did not use clarinets in this opera. Guion, "The Instrumentation of Operas," 121, 139–40.

106. Trans. in Spaethling, *Mozart's Letters, Mozart's Life*, letter of 20 Sept. 1786, 179. See also Hamann, "Eine interessante Aufführungsanweisung Mozarts," 139.

107. Roeser, *Essai*, 10; Francoeur, *Diapason général*, 30; Castillon, "Clarinette," vol. 2, 451.

108. Rice, *The Baroque Clarinet*, 119–20.

109. Ibid., 123–26.

110. In one version of a manuscript score of Bach's *Orione*, all the clarinet parts are notated in the treble clef. Bach, *Orione and Zanaida CWB*, vol. 4.

111. Weber, "Einiges über Clarinett und Bassetthorn," 51; Bellini, *Teoriche musicale*, 37–38.

112. In London, selected operas were published in short scores with keyboard accompaniment rather than full scores as was common in Paris. British publishers also offered separate instrumental parts in the more expensive editions. For example, *The Favorite Songs in the Opera Demofoonte* by Vento (Bremner, 1765) is an orchestral score for two violins, viola, and a basso continuo of harpsichord and cello with separate parts for two flutes (doubling oboes in one aria), two clarinets, and two horns.

113. Salieri, *Tarare*, 27–30. Angermüller, editor of the reprint of Salieri's *Tarare*, did not understand clef transposition for the clarinets, and all of the parts are marked for clarinet in C. In Paer's *L'intrigo amoroso* the clarinet part is marked "Clarino in alamirè."

114. Rossini, *Tancredi* (Pesaro, 1984). In the French score of *Tancredi* (ca. 1827) the

overture includes a soprano clef in the margin and a treble clef with a transposed part for A clarinet. A second aria has a tenor clef in the margin and a treble clef with a transposed part for B♭ clarinet. See Rossini, *Tancrède*, 95.

115. Carse, *The History of Orchestration*, 205.

116. Rossini, *Tancredi*, pt. 3, "Commento Critico," 150–51.

117. Kollmann, *An Essay*, 90. Eley stated about 1795, "If a piece of Music is in the key of E[♭] or F, the Clarinet part is printed in f, if the key of B[♭] or C, then in C." *New Tutor*, 6.

118. Backofen, *Anweisung zur Klarinette* (ca. 1803), 34.

119. "La Clarinette en Si bémol se note en clef de Sol, mais le compositeur doit être censé écrire en clef d'Ut quatrième ligne. Pour la Clarinette en La on la note également en clef de Sol; le compositeur est censé écrire en clef d'Ut première ligne." Catrufo, *Des voix et des instrumens*, 11–12.

120. Gianelli, *Grammatica*, 77–79; Weber, "Einiges über Clarinett und Bassetthorn," 50–51 (Weber pointed out that these clefs were used by French composers); Seyfried, *J. G. Albrechtsberger's sämtliche Schriften* (1837), vol. 3, 166–67. Albrechtsberger's earlier treatise of 1790 and Seyfried's first edition of Albrechtsberger's works (1826) did not mention clef notation; cf. Birsak, *The Clarinet*, 49. As late as 1856, Andries mentions that composers also use the C clef on the fourth line (i.e., the tenor clef) in order to indicate B♭ clarinet, but he appears to be quoting outdated information including a mention of the clarinet in B♮. See Andries, *Aperçu théorique*, 4, 24. In Italy during the twentieth century, clarinet training included the identical use of tenor and soprano clefs for transposing as confirmed in a 1951 article by Napoleon Cerminara, formerly clarinetist with the New York Philharmonic-Symphony. See Cerminara, "To B or Not to B," 12–22.

121. See also Prout, *The Orchestra*, 154.

122. In correspondence with the author.

123. Salieri, *La cifra*. The author thanks John Rice for information.

124. Colin Lawson suggests this transposition as one possibility of Pasiello's use of the tenor clef in correspondence with the author.

125. Paisiello, *La Passione di Gesù Cristo*, 54–55.

126. Ibid., 132. Saint-Arroman states that the use of the tenor clef in eighteenth-century French music means that the parts were to be played an octave lower but did not clearly identify his source of information. In fact, there seems to be no evidence to support this claim. Every use of the tenor clef should be examined individually to determine whether transposition fits into the texture and whether it is possible to play the part an octave lower. See Saint-Arroman, *L'interprétation de la musique française*, 109.

127. *The Symphony in Poland*, TS, ed. J. Pronak, ser. F, vol. 7 (New York: Garland, 1982), 11.

128. The *Concertone* by Gherardeschi is in the library of the Basilica di Santo Zeno, Archivio Capitolare in Pistoia. See Pineschi, "Gherardeschi, Giuseppe," in Sadie, *New Grove*, 2d ed. The *Concertone* by Sarti is in the Conservatorio Statale di Musica Luigi Cherubini in Florence. See Pace, *Ancie Battenti*, 129. The author thanks Luigi Magistrelli for photocopies of these works.

129. Palese, *Tre duetti*, Ricordi pl. no. 1616. See Heck, "Ricordi Plate Numbers in the Earlier Nineteenth Century," 117–24. See also Rau, "Die Kammermusik für Klarinette," 349–50. The author thanks Luigi Magistrelli for a photocopy of the works by Palese and Bottesini.

130. La Borde, *Annette et Lubin*, 1–7, 54–58.

131. Ibid., 68–70, 107–13.

132. La Borde, *Annette et Lubin*, parts in the Bibliothèque Nationale de France, Vm⁵ bis 76.

133. Floquet, *L'union de l'amour et des arts*, 26–29, 38–39, 40–41, 57–60, 61–84, 85–88, 89–90, 91–96, 114–19, 134–37, 143–47, 166–86.

134. Gossec, *Messe des Morts*, 1–5, 9–25, 51–66, 127–35, 163–70. See Macdonald, "François-Joseph Gossec," vol. 1, 448–49 nn. 210, 511. The overture is illustrated in Rice, "The Clarinette d'Amour," 100.

135. Charlton, "Orchestration and Orchestral Practice," 283–84.

136. Sacchini, *L'Olympiade*, 177–95; Sacchini, *Dardanus*, 89–93.

137. Cherubini, *Lodoïska*, 32–50, 200–207, 224–46, 249–60.

138. D'Herbain, *Célime*, 1–14, 29, 72–79. Cucuel, *Études*, 18.

139. D'Herbain, *Célime*, 29, 80–82, Bibliothèque Nationale, Vm² 93. Ibid., 18.

140. These include the seven Paris operas published in Gluck, *Sämtliche Werke*, and the second version of *Cythère assiégée* (Paris, 1775).

141. Czerny, *School of Practical Composition*, vol. 3, 6.

142. Heyde, "Blasinstrumenten," 63. Page, "To Soften the Sound," 66.

143. Page, "To Soften the Sound," 66.

144. "Bei Stücken von sehr trauriger und sanfter Empfindung." F. D. Weber, *Allgemeine theoretisch-praktische Vorschule der Musik*, 113.

145. Page, "To Soften the Sound," 71.

146. J. Rice, *Antonio Salieri*, 570.

147. Spontini, *Milton*, 156–91.

148. See the photograph of this section in Libby, "Spontini, Gaspare," in *New Grove*, 18, 20, ill. 3. The second version of *Fernand Cortez* (1817) includes this march as a "Trio, choeur et danse" in act 3, no. 4. See Spontini, *Fernand Cortez*, 423.

149. "En renferment le bas de l'instrument dans une bourse de peau." Spontini, *Fernand Cortez*, 394.

150. "Il faut envelopper l'instrument dans un sac de toile ou de peau." Berlioz, *Lélio, ou Le retour à la vie* (Paris, 1855) cited in Berlioz, *Choral Works*, XVI; Berlioz, *Grand traité*, 144 and n. 1.

151. Page, "To Soften the Sound," 75; Haynes, *The Eloquent Oboe*, 194.

152. F. D. Weber, *Allgemeine theoretisch-praktische Vorschule der Musik*, 113. Paper or a damp sponge was used for muting oboes during the early eighteenth century; the lip of the oboe's bell held the mute in the bell. This material was not an option for the clarinet since clarinet bells do not have lips. Haynes, *The Eloquent Oboe*, 78 n. 37.

153. For a photograph and description, see Ridley, *European Wind Instruments*, 23.

154. Montagu, *The Bate Collection*, 18.

155. "Nog voor acht clarinetten met vier A Stuckken, twee D stukken, twee sour, 105 gulden." Van Aerde, *Les Tuerlinckx*, 163.

156. Van Aerde, *Les Tuerlinckx*, 164.

157. Ibid., 167.

158. "Wie rührend ist ubrigens nicht der Ton dieses Instruments, wenn seine Stärke durch den angebrachten Becher (das ist, durch den ihm eigenthümlichen zugehörigen Dämpfer) moderirt wird?" "Berichtigungen," vol. 6, 41–42.

CHAPTER 4

1. *Compleat Instuctions*, 1.

2. Marsh, *Hints to Young Composers*, 64.

3. Vanderhagen, *Méthode* (ca. 1785), 4; trans. in Birsak, *The Clarinet*, 15.

4. Schubart, *Ideen*, 320; trans. in Kroll, *The Clarinet*, 54.

5. "Die Clarinette ist . . . der Menschenstimme aber am gleichsten." Albrechtsberger, *Gründliche Anweisung*, 424.

6. Koch, *Musikalische Lexikon*, 332; trans. in Birsak, *The Clarinet*, 15.

7. Grétry, *Mémoires*, 279. In Grétry's opera *Anacréon* (1797), two people dance in a slow (lento) duet to the accompaniment of two B♭ clarinets.

8. Löhlein, *Anweisung zum Violinspielen*, 3d ed., ed. J. F. Reichardt (Leipzig, 1797), 97. In this edition, Reichardt prefers the tone of the clarinet above the oboe. The first edition (1774) describes Stradivari violins as having a strong, penetrating, oboelike tone. See Walls, "Mozart and the Violin," 9, 26.

9. Kratochvíl, "Koncertantní klarinet," 313. Rochlitz, "Nachrichten," *AMZ* (1816): 321–23; "Nachrichten," *AMZ* (1818): 555–57. See also Sacchini, "The Concerted Music for the Clarinet," 274; cf. Weston, "Players and Composers," 96.

10. Additional operas are investigated in chapter 3 concerning playing techniques.

11. See Rice, *The Baroque Clarinet*, 114–28, 134–36.

12. A one-act ballet entitled *Célime* (1756) by d'Herbain includes clarinet parts written in a clarino style in the Ouverture, "Fanfares pour les chasseurs et Chasseresses," and Ariette. The fanfare and aria were meant to be transposed on D and B♭ clarinets, and the instruments used were probably two- or three-key clarinets, but four-key clarinets may have been available. See d'Herbain, *Célime*, 1–11, 29, 72–79; Rice, *The Baroque Clarinet*, 134.

13. During the late eighteenth century only four full scores were published in London: J. C. Bach's *La clemenza di Scipione* (1778), Sacchini's *L'amore soldato* (1778), William Jackson's *Lord of the Manor*, and Steven Storace's *No Song, No Supper* (1790). See Price, Milhous, and Hume, *Italian Opera in Late Eighteenth-Century London*, vol. 1, 195; Fiske, *English Theatre Music*, 587–88.

14. See Fiske, *English Theatre Music*, 294–96; and Fiske, "Opera, §V, 1: England," in Sadie, *New Grove*.

15. Unverricht, "Glaser, Johann Wendelin," vol. 1, 60.

16. Treiber, "Kantor Johann Wendelin Glaser," 64–68, 70.

17. Ibid., 50, 66, and ex. 17, between 48 and 49.

18. See Cucuel, "Notes sur la Comédie Italienne," 164; and Charlton, *Grétry and the Growth of Opéra-Comique*, 333 n. 9.

19. La Borde, *Gilles, garçon peintre*, 1–12, 113–17, 122–31.

20. Cucuel, "Notes sur la Comédie Italienne," 164–65; Rice, *The Baroque Clarinet*, 153–54. About the same time that La Borde began to write for clarinets in his operas, B♭ clarinets appear in the motet "Benedicam dominum" (1757), with a text based on Psalm 33, by the Parisian church music composer Esprit Joseph Antoine Blanchard. In one choral section in E-flat major, the orchestra has two violins, oboe, clarinet, and basso continuo. The parts are marked "ob. et clar.," suggesting that both instruments could be played together or either used as an alternative. Transposed for a B♭ clarinet, the compass is limited to at most a twelfth, f^1 to a^2 and b♭ to f^2. Blanchard, "Benedicam dominum," 550–58. See also Cucuel, *Études*, 21 and his transcription of four measures of Blanchard's motet.

21. La Borde, *Annette et Lubin*, 1–7, 54–58, 64–67, 68–70, 107–13. There are also transposed clarinet parts among a set of orchestral parts published by Moria (Paris) in 1762, preserved in the Bibliothèque Nationale (F-Pn, Vm⁵bis 76).

22. By the early nineteenth century, E♭ and F clarinets had replaced the E clarinet.

23. Fend, "La Borde, Jean Benjamin-François de," in Sadie, *NGDO*.

24. La Borde, *Ismène et Isménias*, 1–9, 44; act 2, 23–29, 32, 40–47; act 3, 3–5, 11–13, 14–35.

25. La Borde, *Amphion*, 65, 67–68, 68–70, 96–97, 98, 125–33.

26. Blanchard, "Benedicam dominum," 550; Cucuel, *Études*, 21.

27. Arne, *Thomas and Sally*, 6–7. The beginning of this work is illustrated in Baines, *Woodwind Instruments*, 298.

28. *Thomas and Sally* arrived in America only a year after publication. Rivington and Brown (New York) advertised its availability in 1762 in the *New York Gazette & Weekly Post Boy*. This popular opera had fifteen performances in Philadelphia; New York; Annapolis, Maryland; Williamsburg, Virginia; Charleston, South Carolina; and Baltimore, Maryland, up to 1783. Corry, Keller, and Keller, *PACN*.

29. Arne, *Artaxerxes*, 86–89.

30. Ibid., 134–37.

31. Performances of *Artaxerxes* continued in London until the end of the century, and in 1839, Covent Garden produced a revival. Robert Wells's 1766 advertisement of the score of *Artaxerxes* was the first in America, but subsequent advertisements in various cities mention only selected arias because of the florid and difficult music written for the Italian singers Tenducci and Peretti. See Fiske, *English Theatre Music*, 306; Fiske, "Opera," in Sadie, *New Grove*; and Corry, Keller, and Keller, *PACN*.

32. Arne, *The Fairy Prince*, 32–34.

33. Gossec, *Eight Symphonic Works*, TS, ser. D, vol. 3, xii.

34. Gossec, *Messe des Morts*, 1–5, 9–25, 51–66, 127–35, 163–70. See also Macdonald, "François-Joseph Gossec," vol. 1, 302; Fend, "François-Joseph, Gossec," in Sadie, *New Grove*.

35. Gossec did not use the clarinet in his three most successful operas of the 1760s: *Le tonnelier* (1765), *Les pêcheurs* (1766), and *Toinon et Toinette* (1767). The author thanks Ingrid Pearson for information.

36. Warburton, "Bach, Johann Christian," in Sadie, *NGDO*.

37. Bach, *Orione*, parts; Bach, *Orione and Zanaida*, CWB, vol. 4, 2–40, 99–113, 200–14, 118–20; vol. 12, 385–94.

38. Burney, *A General History*, vol. 2, 865. Apparently, Burney was unaware of Arne's earlier use of the clarinet in *Thomas and Sally* (1760).

39. Bach, *Orione*; *Orione and Zanaida*, CWB, vol. 4, 2–61. There are also additional handwritten parts for oboes transposed from the taillies parts in the music library of the University of California at Berkeley.

40. See CWB, vols. 4–17, 25; Bach, *Amadis des Gaules*; and Maunder, "J. C. Bach and the Basset-Horn," 42–47.

41. Cf. Weimer, *Opera Seria*, 103.

42. See Bach, *Edimione*, CWB, vol. 14, 320–26; Bach, *Cefalo e Procri*, CWB, vol. 13, 330–43. Bach included D clarinets in the English ode "Happy morn, auspicious rise" (1768–69) and B♭ clarinets in two arias written to Italian texts (1779 and 1770s); Bach, *Works with English texts*, CWB, vol. 25; "Ah, che gl'istessi numi" and "Cara, ti lascio," in Bach, *Miscellaneous Works to Italian Texts*, CWB, vol. 16.

43. Bach, *Amor vincitore*, CWB, vol. 15, 94–100. James Harris, the queen's secre-

tary, reports the performance with these soloists in a manuscript. See Bach, *Part One, Thematic Catalogue, CWB*, vol. 31, 327–29.

44. Petty, "Vento, Matia," in Sadie, *NGDO*; Bach, *Adriano in Siria, CWB*, vol. 5, no. 22, 489–512.

45. Vento, *The Favorite Songs in the Opera Demofoonte*, 6–9, 14–22. In the unpaginated full score autograph of *Sonfonisba* the transposed clarinet parts were marked "clarinet B♭," "clarinet in E♭," "and "clarinetti in Befa."

46. Vento, *The Favourite Songs in the Opera Sonfonisba*, 14–22. At least one more use of the clarinet in England is recorded during the 1760s. Dibdin included four measures of cues for C clarinet in the short score of his 1768 pastiche *Lionel and Clarissa*, 25.

47. Vento, *The Favourite Songs in the Opera La vestale*. This pitch indication was not a mistake but written by Italian composers to indicate B♭ clarinets in E-flat major. For example, Paer uses this term for the B♭ clarinet in *L'intrigo amoroso* ("clarinetto in Elafá,"1795), *Sargino* ("clarinetto in E," 1803), and *L'agnese* (1809). The author is grateful to Ingrid Pearson for information.

48. Charlton, "Grétry," in Sadie, *NGDO*.

49. "Si l'on n'a point de Clarinettes, les hautbois peuvent jouer leurs parties en-jouant un ton plus haut." Grétry, *Le Huron*, scene 4, 42–47, and scene 12. Charlton found that in one copy of the score the aria was removed; see *Grétry*, 333 n. 9.

50. Grétry, *Zemire et Azor*, 147–50.

51. O'Connor, "Floquet, Etienne Joseph," in Sadie, *NGDO*.

52. Floquet, *L'union de l'amour et des arts*, ouverture, 19–22, 26–29, 38–39, 40–41, 47–51, 53–55, 57–60, 61–84, 86–88, 89–90, 114–19, 134–37, 143–47, 166–86.

53. Floquet, *Le siegneur bienfaisant*, 67–81, 131–46, 166, 237, 239–42, 243–60, 469–73.

54. Grétry, *Céphale et Procris*, 1–19, 94–97, 111–16, 147–59, 160–64, 175–80, 181–83, 183–88, 190–212, 213–14, 225–27, 241–52.

55. Grétry, *Guillaume Tell*, 1–2, 14–17, 18–21, 42–47, 51–52, 53, 55–62, 69–94, 148–43, 144–47. The opening measures of the overture are quoted in Charlton, *Grétry*, 313, ex. 35.5. A more famous version of the "ranz des vaches" by Rossini in *Guillaume Tell* (1829) utilizes an English horn solo.

56. Excerpts of *Amor e Psiche* survive at the Deutche Staatsbibliothek in Berlin. See Helm and Berg, "Agricola, Johann Friedrich," in Sadie, *New Grove*, 2n ed.

57. "Als eine Seltenheit merken wir die Clarinetten an, die in dem Chore auf dem Theater mit zum Vorscheine kommen. Ein verständiger Componist weis zu seiner Zeit von allem Gebrauch zu machen, und es ist kein Zweifel, daß dieses durchdringende und kräfftige Instrument einen ansehnlichen Rang unter den Blaßinstrumenten behaupten könnten, wenn es von geschikten Leuten mit Ernst getrieben würde; bisher hat es freilich nur gedient, den Klang der Queerpfeife martialischer, und den Larm der Trommel erträglicher zu machen." Hiller, "Fortsetzung über die Oper," 87. The translation is based on Robin Chatwin's unpublished translation of part of Hiller's comment in Kroll, "Vor- und Frühgeschichte der Klarinette," 6.

58. Cannabich, *Le rendes-vous, ballet de chasse, RRMCE*, vol. 45, pt. 1, 7–10; 22–23; 30–36; 37; 38–40; Vogler, *Le rendez-vous de chasse, RRMCE*, vol. 45, pt. 1, 85–86; 103–8.

59. Cannabich, *Médée et Jason, RRMCE*, vol. 47, pt. 2, 76–79; 180; 181; 185–98. The incorrect key signature is used for A clarinets in no. 21 and the C parts in the D major section, no. 20, were probably played on A clarinets because of the awkward finger-

ing required. Clarinets in A were also required in Carl Stamitz's viola concerto in D, op. 1, published by Heina of Paris about 1773 and by Haveisen in Frankfurt shortly afterward. They are used with two horns in supporting and sustaining roles with the widest compass of f¹ to c³. See Cooper, *Concerto IV*.

60. Reichardt, *Der Geisterinsel*.

61. See Gluck, *Sämtliche Werke* and *Cythère assiégée*.

62. See Francoeur, *Diapason général*, 26–34.

63. *Orphée et Eurydice, SWG*, pt. 1, vol. 6, 324–25.

64. Clarinets were used in only three sections of *Iphigénie en Tauride* (1779) and in one section of *Iphigenie auf Tauris* (1781) *SWG*, pt. 1, vols. 9 and 11.

65. The author thanks Ingrid Pearson for information.

66. Giordani, *A Collection of Favourite Songs*, 10–16, 22.

67. In another Vauxhall song for Mrs. Weichsel, "Behold the Heav'ns how beauteous and serene," in *The Favourite Cantatas*, B♭ clarinets are given a range of f¹ to d³ and c¹ to c³. The author thanks Ingrid Pearson for information.

68. Giordani, *The Favourite Songs in the Opera Antigono*, 1–5.

69. Giordani, *The Favorite Songs as Sung by Sigra. Sestini*, 5–7.

70. Ibid., 15–19. According to Parke, Thomas Linley was praised for his use of clarinets and horns in the song "O ponder well," which he added to a performance of *The Beggar's Opera* given in 1777 at the Drury Lane Theatre. See Parke, *Musical Memoirs*, vol. 1, 11–12. Unfortunately, the score of Linley's additions has not survived.

71. Giordani, *The Favorite Songs and Rondeaus*, 6–11. In a contemporary review of *Il bacio* (1782), Giordani's hunting call theme with a clarinet-horn quartet was described as exhilarating. See Petty, *Italian opera*, 190.

72. See Robinson and Hofmann, *Giovanni Paisiello*, 105. Paisiello did not include the clarinet in *La frascatana* (1774), as stated in Guion, "The Instrumentation of Operas," 121. However, C clarinets are included in one aria (marked "Clarino ou Flautto") of the French version of this opera first performed in Strasbourg in 1779, entitled *L'infante de Zamora*, 248–57.

73. Robinson and Hofmann, *Giovanni Paisiello*, 216, 220, 222.

74. Ibid., 219–22, 245–53.

75. Ibid., 254, 256–58, 261, 263, 269–72, 280, 284, 291, 293, 295–99. The French version of *Il matrimonio inaspetto*, entitled *Le marquis Tulipano*, also included B♭ clarinets in the finale of act 3.

76. Ibid., 825.

77. Batta, *Opera*, 370.

78. Paisiello, "Il barbier di Siviglia," vol. 1, fols. 103r–113v; vol. 2, act 4, 26v–68r.

79. Ibid., vol. 2, fols. 25r–45r. To ensure that this aria would be performed, a note in the Paris score states that if a clarinetist was not available the part could be played on an oboe or a flute. Paisiello, *Le barbier de Seville*, 139.

80. Paisiello, "Il barbier di Siviglia," vol. 2, fols. 46v–47r. In the printed Paris edition of this opera, the cadenza was omitted.

81. See *Le roi Théodore à Venise*; performances of the Italian version include five sections for B♭ clarinet and two sections for A clarinet. See Robinson and Hofmann, *Giovanni Paisiello*, 332–35.

82. Paisiello, *Serenata in Do Maggiore per otto strumenti*.

83. Ward, "Mozart and the Clarinet," 152–53: *Idomeneo* (1781), *Die Entführung aus dem Serail* (1782), *Der Schauspieldirector* (1786), *Le nozze di Figaro* (1786), *Don Giovanni* (1787), *Così fan tutte* (1790), *Die Zauberflöte* (1791), and *La clemenza di Tito* (1791).

84. Mozart, *Thomas Attwood Theorie- und Kompositionsstudien*, NMA, ser. 10, wg. 30, pt. 1, 124.

85. Ibid., 157.

86. Lawson, "The Authentic Clarinet: Tone and Tonality," 357. Mozart wrote the Kyrie in Munich from 1780 to 1781 or possibly in Vienna during the late 1780s. See Mozart, Kyrie, *MW*, ser. 3, vol. 1, 31–46. In 1808, Rochlitz wrote of the different tone colors between clarinets and advised that clarinetists play the C, B♭, and A clarinets as intended by Mozart in *Don Giovanni*. Rochlitz, "Etwas über die Aufführung von Lieb und Treue," 23 n. **.

87. *Les petits riens*, NMA, ser. 2, wg. 6, vol. 2.

88. Two arias in E major, no. 15 and no. 19 require B♮ clarinets. Mozart, *Idomeneo*, NMA, ser. 2, wg. 5, vol. 11, 283–94, 352–62.

89. Mozart, *Die Entführung aus dem Serail*, NMA, ser. 2, wg. 5, vol. 12, 279.

90. Ibid., 348, mm. 83–86.

91. Mozart, *Der Schauspieldirector*, NMA, ser. 2, wg. 5, vol. 15, 53.

92. Mozart, *Le nozze di Figaro*, NMA, ser. 2, wg. 5, vol. 16, 94–102.

93. Ibid., 161–66.

94. Ibid., 175–82. See Kozma, "Heroes of Wood and Brass," 27–28.

95. Mozart, *Don Giovanni*, NMA, ser. 2, wg. 5, vol. 17, 201–2. Cf. Lawson, *Mozart*, 23.

96. Mozart, *Così fan tutte*, NMA, ser. 2. wg. 5, vol. 18, 391, mm. 78–79. In no. 25, the E major rondo "Per pieta ben mio," B♭ clarinets are in F major, 400–414.

97. Mozart, *Die Zauberflöte*, NMA, ser. 2, wg. 5, vol. 19, 191–92.

98. Mozart, *La clemenza di Tito*, NMA, ser. 2, wg. 5, vol. 20, 102–16.

99. Ibid., 265–81.

100. Mozart includes clarinets in his arrangements of five Handel oratorios for performances in Vienna: *Acis and Galatea* (1788), *Messiah* (1789), *Alexander's Feast* (1790), and *Ode to St. Cecilia* (1790). The orchestras include flutes, oboes, bassoons, horns, strings, and basso continuo. Mozart avoids scoring flutes, oboes, and clarinets together, and the clarinets' compass is limited to two octaves and a fourth at most, from a to d³. C and B♭ clarinets in ten sections of *Acis and Galatea* have a few short solos but usually double the flutes or oboes. In *Messiah*, C, B♭, and A clarinets play in fourteen sections, occasionally as the only winds, but usually to double voice parts, oboes, or flutes. NMA, ser. 28, wg. 1, vols. 1–2.

101. Shield, *Rosina*, MB, vol. 72, 1–10, 43–46, 47–55. Although the key signature for the B♭ clarinets in the overture is in D major, they begin playing after a modulation to E-flat major in m. 58, placing them in the key of F major.

102. Shield, *Robin Hood*, 62.

103. Fiske, *English Theatre Music*, 465. Although Arnold used the clarinet in his operas *Children of the Wood* (1794) and *Obi, or Three-finger'd Jack* (1800), he decided not to use them in his "historical" editions of Handel's oratorios during the late 1780s and 1790s. See Arnold, *The Works of Handel*. Others in England sometimes included clarinet parts in Handel's works to replace a missing oboe or flute. For example, Fisher Littleton (also known as John Smith), active in the Aberdeen Musical Society from the mid-1780s, wrote clarinet parts for at least one of Handel's oratorios, *Samson*, in the Staffordshire County Public Office. However, the parts were probably not used for a performance. The author thanks Graydon Beeks for information.

104. Cf. Fiske's observation in Storace, *No Song, No Supper*, MB, vol. 16, 28–32, 112.

105. Ibid., 53–68, 82–89.

106. Anton Stadler may have adapted this aria for his basset clarinet. See Pohl, *Denkschrift*, 67; Weston, "Players and Composers," 93; Lawson, *Mozart*, 26.

107. Haydn, *Die Schöpfung/The Creation*, 67–75, 210–18.

108. Brown, *Performing Haydn's "The Creation*," 2–7; Haydn, *Die Schöpfung/The Creation*, vi; MacIntyre, *Haydn: The Creation*, 232–35.

109. Haydn, *Messen, HW*, ser. 23, vol. 2, 237–39, 240–42; Lawson, "Haydn and the Clarinet," 7, 9–10.

110. Lawson, "Haydn and the Clarinet," 9–10.

111. See Briquet and Charlton, "Isouard, Nicolas," in Sadie, *NGDO*. On the title pages of his printed operas, he often uses the name Niccolò.

112. See also Fueter, "Die Notierung der Klarinetten," 169.

113. Weber, *Der Freischütz*, 8, 11–12, 18–19.

114. Titus provides a checklist of all concerto composers and those listed in publishers' catalogues in Appendix B of "The Solo Music," 575–81. See also Pound, "A Study of Clarinet Solo Concerto Literature"; Kratochvíl, "Koncertantní klarinet v českém klasicismu," 285–372; Balássa, "Az első bécsi klasszikus iskola klarinétversenyei," 49–74, 134–83; Newhill, "The Contribution," 90–122; Sacchini, "The Concerted Music for the Clarinet"; and Jacob, *Die Klarinettenkonzerte*.

115. Titus, "The Solo Music," 43. J. M. Molter was the only composer to write for the D clarinet in his six concertos.

116. This estimate was given by Spicknall, "The Solo Works of Bernhard Henrik Crusell," 151 n. 159, based on the works investigated by Titus in "The Solo Music."

117. Examples of concertos for A clarinet, before Mozart's concerto, were written by Baron Theodor von Schacht and Michel Yost. Schacht wrote three concertos, one of the manuscripts of which is dated 1781 (MS. Rtt Schacht 33); the other two manuscripts (MS. Rtt Schacht 41 and 43) were probably written during the 1780s. See Titus, "The Solo Music," 284–94; Färber, "Der Fürstlichen Thurn und Taxissche Hofkomponist Theodor von Schacht," 11–192. Yost wrote two concertos for A clarinet in A and E major, nos. 4 and 6; see Titus, "The Solo Music," 257. Whistling and Hofmeister list them in the *Handbuch der musikalischen Litteratur*, 196.

118. See Stoltie, "A Symphonie Concertante Type"; Brook and Gribenski, "Symphonie concertante," in Sadie, *New Grove*, 2d ed. The Free Library of Philadelphia owns two manuscript scores of solos for clarinet and string orchestra, one attributed to Nicolò Jommelli, the other to Baldassare Galuppi. There is absolutely no evidence to establish that either work is authentic, and the scores appear on modern ruled paper, perhaps as a composition assignment. Cf. Pound, "Two Eighteenth Century Clarinet Arias," 8–9.

119. The Carl Stamitz concerto for clarinet and bassoon was an arrangement of a concerto for oboe or flute and bassoon published in 1778. See Kaiser and Wolf, "Carl Stamitz, Worklist," in Sadie, *New Grove*, 2d ed. The Concerto in B-flat Major for violin, oboe, clarinet, and orchestra by Karl Friedrich Abel, recorded by Dieter Klöcker (BASF, 21191, 1973), was very likely an arrangement of a concerto for violin, oboe, and cello published in 1781. See Knape, Charters, and McVeigh, "Carl Friedrich Abel, Worklist," in Sadie, *New Grove*, 2d ed.

120. See the manuscript salary list (Besoldungslite) reproduced in Münster, "Johann Anton Fils," 39–40, 41 nn. 5, 6. Michael Quallenberg and Johannes Hampel are listed as clarinetists from 1758. See Würtz, *Verzeichnis*, 30, 43, 49.

121. Gradenwitz, "The Beginnings of Clarinet Literature," 145–50. Lebermann, the

editor of the published score, added two horn parts since they were missing from the manuscript parts; see J. Stamitz, *Konzert für Klarinette*. Gradenwitz published a piano and clarinet arrangement of this concerto with an overly edited clarinet part in J. Stamitz, *Concerto*. Lebermann also edited a piano and clarinet arrangement; J. Stamitz, *Konzert*, Klavierauszug.

122. Gradenwitz, "The Beginnings of Clarinet Literature," 145–50. See also the discussion by Titus, "The Solo Music," 149–64.

123. Kratochvíl, "Koncertantní klarinet v českém klasicismu," 317–18; Newhill, "The Contribution," 111; Wolf, *The Symphonies of Johann Stamitz*, 343 n. 16; and Wolf, "Johann Stamitz," in Sadie, *New Grove*, 2d ed.

124. Newhill, "The Contribution," 111. The concerto was likely performed in 1772 by one of Regensburg's court clarinetists, since this performance date is found on the manuscript. See Gradenwitz, "The Beginnings of Clarinet Literature," 146–47.

125. The following performers have recorded the Johann Stamitz concerto playing five-key clarinets: Hans Rudolf Stalder, Henry Kusder, London, ca. 1780 (Ex Libris EL 16804, 1979) and Alan Hacker, George Miller, London, ca. 1780 (L'Oiseau-Lyre DSLO 505, 1975). Gerber credited a clarinet concerto to Anton Filtz, a Czech composer active at Mannheim. Unfortunately, this concerto has not been found; see Newhill, "The Contribution," 100, and Komma, "Filtz, Anton," in *MGG*.

126. See Birsak, "Salzburg, Mozart, and the Clarinet," 28. Sherman and Thomas give ten separate movement incipits, but Kalmár combined the short Menuetto (movement 7) and Trio (movement 8) into one movement, as found in the autograph. See Sherman and Thomas, *Johann Michael Haydn*, 25, and M. Haydn, *Divertimento in D*.

127. Birsak, "Salzburg, Mozart, and the Clarinet," 28. Haydn's obbligato C clarinet part to "Kommt her, ihr Menschen," ST 180, for soprano and strings (1772) is confined to the clarino register from g^1 to c^3 and is technically considerably simpler than the earlier divertimento of 1764. For an excerpt, see Birsak, *The Clarinet*, 28–29. The author thanks Stewart Carter and Howard Weiner for identifying the type of trombone played in the divertimento.

128. Münster, "Mannheim and Vienna (1760–1800)." Three concertos (one solo and two for two clarinets) attributed to Joseph Haydn and recorded by Dieter Klöcker are not considered authentic, Feder, "Franz Joseph Haydn, Work-List," in Sadie, *New Grove*, 2d ed. See also Ellsworth, "Haydn Clarinet Concertos."

129. See Becker, *Klarinetten-Konzerte*, 53–91, 105; Angerer, "Franz Xaver Pokorny," in Sadie, *New Grove*, 2d ed.

130. Francoeur, *Diapason général*, 22–25.

131. See the edition for clarinet in B♭ and piano of C. Stamitz, *Konzert F-dur*. Boese, *Die Klarinette*, 23–52, 123–25; Newhill, "The Contribution," 103–11; and Jacob, *Die Klarinettenkonzerte*, 43–48.

132. Held on 24 December 1771, 2 February 1772, and 28 May 1772.

133. Pierre, *Histoire du Concert Spirituel*, 299–300, 303–7, 310–12. The only other contemporary German composer reported as writing a clarinet concerto is Konrad Starck [Stark] whose lost concerto in B-flat major appears in supplement VII (1772) of *BTC*, 470. About 1765 Stark was a composer at the court of Trier and, about 1781, Kapellmeister at Koblenz; both cities employed clarinetists. See Eitner, *Biographisch-Bibliographisches Quellen-Lexikon*, vol. 9, 256.

134. Johansson, *French Music Publishers' Catalogues*, vol. 2, fascs. 108–11. Cf. Jacob, *Die Klarinettenkonzerte*, 14; Devriés and Lesure, *Dictionnaire*, vol. 1, no. 86 (1777); no.

88 (1783). The Concerto for Two Clarinets or Clarinet and Violin was written about 1777; see Kaiser and Wolf, "Carl Stamitz, Work-List," in Sadie, *New Grove*, 2d ed.

135. Gerber, *Historisch-Biographisches Lexikon*, vol. 2, 559; Wojciechowski, preface to C. Stamitz, *Klarinetten-Konzert Nr. 3*; Titus, "The Solo Music," 185, 200.

136. The concerto was advertised in the *Berlinische musikalische Zeitung* (1793): 156, according to Boese, *Die Klarinette*, 33. See Newhill, "The Contribution," 107–8; Jacob, *Die Klarinettenkonzerte*, 99; Kratochvíl, "Koncertantní klarinet v českém klasicismu," 293; C. Stamitz, *Concerto in E♭*.

137. Friedrich Carl Kaiser, "Carl Stamitz (1745–1801)" (Ph.D. diss., Marburg, 1962), 86–91; cited in Jacob, *Die Klarinettenkonzerte*, 12.

138. Ernest Eichner, a bassoonist and composer active in Paris from 1771, wrote Concerto no. 2, listed as an oboe concerto in the supplement to Breitkopf & Härtel's 1781 catalog. Newhill, "The Contribution," 98–99; *BTC*, supplement XIV (1781), 730.

139. Boese, *Die Klarinette*, 125; C. Stamitz, *Konzert Es-dur*.

140. Diderot, *Recueil*, vol. 2, pl. 4, "Chasse, Venerie, Chasse du Sanglier." This plate includes four printed horn calls. Jacob found the hunting call "Das große Halali" in mm. 213–35 of this movement; see *Die Klarinettenkonzerte*, 78–79.

141. See Weston, *Clarinet Virtuosi of the Past*, 251; Thomas, "John Mahon Concerto No. 2," 5; *LS*, pts. IV and V; Weston, *Yesterday's Clarinettists*, 110.

142. Boydell, *Rotunda Music*, 137, 141, 219–20; Weston, *Clarinet Virtuosi of the Past*, 252; *BD*, vol. 10, 56–57; Johnston, "Concerts," 280; "Summary of Concerts"; Weston, *Yesterday's Clarinettists*, 110.

143. *LS*, pt. IV (1747–76), 1869; Weston, *Clarinet Virtuosi of the Past*, 251. The popular ballad for soprano "The Wanton God" appears in act 3 of Arne's 1738 opera *Comus*, the theme of which begins the Rondo finale, third movement of Mahon's Second Concerto. See Arne, *Comus*, *MB*, vol. 3, 107–9.

144. Johnston, "Concerts," 552, ill. 22.

145. *A Catalogue of Vocal and Instrumental Music*. The author thanks Ingrid Pearson for information.

146. Thomas, "John Mahon," 8–9. Copies of the Second Concerto are in the Henry Watson Music Library, Manchester, and the Austrian National Library, Vienna. Thomas, the editor of the published edition, wisely chose to supply cadenzas taken from Mahon's examples published in his *Preceptor*. See Mahon, *Clarinet Concerto No. 2*.

147. In 1797, Ignace Pleyel published at least one concerto for C clarinet with an optional solo part for flute or violoncello; see Benton, *Ignace Pleyel*, 6; Pleyel, *Clarinet Concerto*.

148. *Rivington's New York Gazette* advertised Mahon's concertos from 20 October 1779 through 5 February 1780. A performance of a clarinet concerto by "Mahoy" is in *Rivington's New York Gazette* on 27 April 1782; see Corry, Keller, and Keller, *PACN*.

149. Titus, "The Solo Music," 404.

150. Titus and Pound observed that the work is better suited to the oboe, flute, or violin due to its limited range and lack of rests. Titus, "The Solo Music," 405; Pound, "A Study of Clarinet Solo Concerto Literature," 155 n. 2. Vanhal's Concerto for C Clarinet, composed after 1775 was transcribed from a flute concerto and has an even more limited range of g^1 to c^3. See Bryan, "Johann Baptist Vanhal," in Sadie, *New Grove*, 2d ed., and the score of Vanhal, *Concerto*.

151. "How oft Louisa" is also printed as duet no. 3, entitled "Scot's Air," in Mahon's *A New and Complete Preceptor*, 26. Lawson identified the song in the second movement as "The birks of Endermay" in his recording of Mahon's *Second Concerto* on a five-key clarinet on Hyperion CD A66896 (1997).

152. Cramer, *Magazin der Musik*, 757–58; Dlabacž, "Versuch eines Verzeichnisses," vol. 7, 137–38; Dlabacž, *Allgemeines historisches Künstler-Lexikon*, 65–66. See also Weston, *Clarinet Virtuosi of the Past*, 29–38.

153. *LS*, part IV (1747–76), 1785.

154. Fétis, "Beer, Josef," in *Biographie Universelle* (1837), vol. 2, 99.

155. Pierre, *Histoire du Concert Spirituel*, 305–7, 310–12.

156. Fétis, "Beer, Joseph," in *Biographie universelle* (1873–80); English trans. in Rees-Davies, *Fétis on Clarinettists*, 8–9.

157. Mooser, *Annales de la musique*, vol. 2, 246, 308, 364–66; Weston, *Clarinet Virtuosi of the Past*, 36–38; Morrow, *Concert Life in Haydn's Vienna*, 346.

158. *BTC*, 860. The C. F. Peters firm also published this concerto sometime after 1814, when it acquired the Kühnel firm; see Pound, "A Study of Clarinet Solo Concerto Literature," 103.

159. Weston reproduced two pages of Beer's Concerto, op. 1, published by Peters, in *Clarinet Virtuosi of the Past*, 32–33.

160. A piano and clarinet arrangement was transcribed by Pound in "A Study of Clarinet Solo Concerto Literature," vol. 2, 1–45. This concerto has been recorded by Joost Hekel playing a five-key clarinet on Erasmus Muziek Producties, 1997, CD, WVH199.

161. Pohl, *Denkschrift*, 57–58; cited in Morrow, *Concert Life in Haydn's Vienna*, 242, 244; Weston, *Clarinet Virtuosi of the Past*, 47.

162. Poulin, "The Basset Clarinet of Anton Stadler," 69; Link, *The National Court Theatre*, 202.

163. 8 February 1782. See Link, *The National Court Theatre*, 209 n. 15. See also Weston, *More Clarinet Virtuosi*, 246–47; Pisarowitz, "'Müaßt ma nix in übel aufnehma," 30.

164. 24 April 1782; see Link, *The National Court Theatre*, 209 n. 15.

165. 20 February 1788; Link, *The National Court Theatre*, 121. The handbill is reproduced in Poulin, "The Basset Clarinet of Anton Stadler," 72; Lawson, "The Basset Clarinet Revived," 487; and Lawson, "Playing Historical Clarinets, 148.

166. Kratochvíl initially proposed the name "basset clarinet" in"Koncertantní klarinet v českém klasicismu," 262.

167. Österreichische Nationalbibliothek, Vienna, MS 5856. The author attributed this concerto to Leopold Kozeluch in a letter to the editor of *Clarinet* 2, no. 4 (Aug. 1975): 4. This attribution was repeated by Weston in *More Clarinet Virtuosi of the Past*, 217. Incipits of the movements of the concerto are under the name Michl in Supplement 15 (1782–84) of the Breitkopf catalog. See *BTC*, 799; Ross, "A Comprehensive Performance Project," 259; Lawson, *Early Clarinet*, 104.

168. The Breitkopf & Härtel edition was advertised in the "Intelligenz-Blatt" of the *AMZ* in March 1801; *AMZ* 3 (1 April 1801): between 468 and 469. The later editions are dated by their plate numbers: Pleyel (no. 399), André (no. 1595 and nos. 1595 and 1613 on orchestral parts), and Sieber (no. 1552). See Devriès and Lesure, *Dictionnaire*; Deutsch, *Musikverlags Nummern*; and cf. Ness, "Some Remarks," 35–43, and Lawson, *Mozart*, 38.

169. This draft is in Mozart, *Konzerte*, NMA, ser. 5, wg. 14, vol. 4, 165–76. The editor Giegling notes the darker ink and sharper point of the notes in A major on IX, and Ness suggests that Mozart wrote this later part in order to orient himself to the different key for the basset clarinet in A. See Ness, "Some Remarks," 31. Alan Tyson dated the basset horn draft to about 1791 based on the watermark on pp. 1–6 of the

draft, and on the stylistic similarities to the basset clarinet concerto. See Lawson, *Mozart*, 34.

170. Lawson, *Mozart*, 35. In order to perform the basset horn draft, the maker/performer Gilles Thomé made a reproduction of an eight-key basset clarinet in G, completed the scoring of the 199 measures of the concerto and performed it in 1994 in Le Mans, France. See Thomé, "Anton Stadler: le miracle Bohémien," 14–24. Thomé later recorded the concerto draft with orchestra in 1999 on a CD, "Une soirée chez les Jacquin," with Ensemble 415 on Zig Zag Territoires ZZT 99 07 01.

171. Rochlitz, "Recension," 408–14; trans. in Kroll, *The Clarinet*, 63. A complete English translation of the entire review by McColl is in Lawson, *Mozart*, 79–83.

172. Dazeley, "The Original Text of Mozart's Clarinet Concerto," 166–72; Kratochvíl, "Betrachtungen über die Urfassung des Konzerts für Klarinette," 263–68; Hess, "Die Ursprüngliche Gestalt," 13–30; Hacker, "Mozart and the Basset Clarinet," 361; Sheveloff, "When Sources Seem to Fail," 386, 393–99. See also Lawson's discussion in *Mozart*, 52–59.

173. Mozart, *Concerto for Clarinet or Basset Clarinet*.

174. Mozart, *Concerto K 622: Edition for Basset Clarinet in A and Clarinet in A*.

175. *Verzeichniss der von dem verstorbenen Herrn Musikdirecktor C. F. G. Schwencke* (Hamburg, 1824), no. 424; cited in Ness, "Some Remarks," 44, and Weston, "Schwencke's Mozart Concerto," 65.

176. See also the discussion of Schwencke's edition and reconstructions of the text in Adelson, "Reading between the (Ledger) Lines," 158–65.

177. Lawson describes this dialogue as occurring between the soprano and baritone registers in *Mozart*, 64. Adelson makes the same observation and cites a similar phrase in the act 1 quintet and the act 2 trio in Mozart's *Die Zauberflöte*. See Adelson, "Reading between the (Ledger) Lines," 185–91.

178. The passage was illustrated in Hacker, "Mozart and the Basset Clarinet," 360, and the autograph is reproduced in Lawson, "The Basset Clarinet Revived," 494–96.

179. Poulin, "An Updated Report," 24, and "Anton Stadler's Basset Clarinet," 123, fig. 7.

180. A detailed review of Tausch's life is given in Weston, *Clarinet Virtuosi of the Past*, 40–44.

181. Most young musicians in the court orchestra were appointed to a student position (Akzessisten) in which they would learn the craft and art of performing. Usually students were promoted to a higher position by the death or departure of the older musicians. See Würtz, *Verzeichnis*, 27–28, 55.

182. Nösselt, *Ein ältest Orchester*, 235. According to Weston, Jacob retired from playing in 1786 or 1787; *Clarinet Virtuosi of the Past*, 42.

183. Franz's brother Joseph was an assistant in 1779 and promoted to Franz's position as first clarinet in 1788. Joseph remained with the court orchestra until some time before 1824. See Nösselt, *Ein ältest Orchester*, 235.

184. Tausch, *Concerto no. 3 in E Flat*, score; *Concerto for Clarinet and Orchestra*; *Konzert Es-dur*. Clinch's designation "Concerto no. 3" actually referred to the numbering in a collection of concertos by different composers. See Newhill, "The Contribution," 113.

185. All of these concerts were reviewed in the *AMZ* according to Boese, *Die Klarinette*, 63.

186. Gerber, *Neues*, vol. 2, 326–28; Fétis, *Biographie Universelle*, vol. 8, 191–92. See Clinch, "Clarinet Concerto no. 3," 21, 23–24; and Lawson, *Mozart*, 11.

187. Newhill, "The Contribution," 115.

188. Michaelis, "Ueber die Klarinette," 386.

189. Newhill, "The Contribution," 114.

190. Tausch, *Concerto pour la clarinette*, 2, 4.

191. Clinch believed that Tausch continued to play on a five-key clarinet until his death but does not provide evidence to support this contention. See Clinch, "Clarinet Concerto no. 3," 18, 22, 30.

192. Dahlström, "Bernhard Henrik Crusell," in Sadie, *New Grove*, 2d ed. For Crusell's career, see Weston, *Clarinet Virtuosi of the Past*, 67–76; Weston, *More Clarinet Virtuosi of the Past*, 74–77; Spicknall, "The Solo Works of Bernhard Henrik Crusell," 13–35; and Weston, "An Assessment of Crusell The Man," 30–33.

193. Most of the reviews were published in the *AMZ*. See Spicknall, "The Solo Works of Bernhard Henrik Crusell," 51–52 n. 87.

194. It is possible that in 1797 Crusell owned a five-key clarinet made by the Stockholm maker Johan Carlström. Crusell recorded the purchase of a mouthpiece by Amlingue on 2 June and a C clarinet by Baumann on 14 September 1803 in his diary; Dahlström, *Bernhard Henrik Crusell*, 74–75, 278; Weston, *Yesterday's Clarinettists*, 58.

195. Dahlström, *Bernhard Henrik Crusell*, 79–80.

196. See Young, *4900 Historical Woodwind Instruments*, 103, Y9. A photograph of the entire instrument (S-Stockholm, 43554), missing its upper ferrule (on the barrel) and mouthpiece, and of both upper joints is in Dahlström, *Bernhard Henrik Crusell*, 313, 315. The photograph in Weston, *Clarinet Virtuosi of the Past*, pl. 6, shows the clarinet with its B♭ upper joint but the G♯ key is not visible. Dahlström suggests that Crusell purchased his Grenser clarinet about 1810, and may have purchased the A joint during his visit to Dresden in 1811. See Dahlström, "Bernhard Henrik Crusell," in Sadie, *New Grove*, 2d ed.

197. Dahlström, *Bernhard Henrik Crusell*, 80–81. Spicknall described and illustrated a B♭ clarinet with ebony corps in A with ivory ferrules that appears to have ten keys, although he states the instrument has eleven and describes nine keys. Spicknall, "The Solo Works of Bernhard Henrik Crusell," 47–48, 50. The Stockholm Museum owns five clarinets by Grenser & Wiesner, dating from 1822 or later. Four of the instruments have eleven keys, another has ten keys. See Young, *4900 Historical Woodwind Instruments*, 108, Y4–5, Y7–9; Weston, *Yesterday's Clarinettists*, 58–59.

198. Dahlström suggests composition dates for op. 1 (ca. 1808), op. 11 (ca. 1807), op. 3 (1808), and op. 5 (1815); see "Bernhard Henrik Crusell," in Sadie, *New Grove*, 2d ed.

199. See Spicknall, "The Solo Works of Bernhard Henrik Crusell," 151; Titus, "The Solo Music."

200. Spicknall, "The Solo Works of Bernhard Henrik Crusell," 181–82.

201. Ibid., 194–95; Dahlström, "Bernhard Henrik Crusell," in Sadie, *New Grove*, 2d ed. In a communication to Ingrid Pearson in August 2000, Dahlström quoted Henrik Reinholm in *Finlands minnesvärde män* (Helsingors: J. C. Frenckel, 1853), who describes Crusell as playing with the reed-above embouchure because his teeth were uneven.

202. Spohr wrote three concert pieces for Hermstedt: on a theme from his opera *Alruna* (1809), on themes written by Peter von Winter (1811), and on a theme by Franz Danzi (1814). The first two included an orchestral accompaniment, the third, a string quartet accompaniment. Subsequently, all three were published with piano accompaniment.

203. Brown, *Louis Spohr*, 50; Kroll, *The Clarinet*, 72, 127; Johnston, "The Clarinet

Concertos of Louis Spohr," 72, 126; Brown, "Louis Spohr, Worklist," in Sadie, *New Grove*, 2d ed.

204. Spohr, *Lebenserinnerungen*, vol. 1, 121–22; trans. and cited in Johnston, "The Clarinet Concertos of Louis Spohr," 52–53, 132.

205. See the translation in Johnston, "The Clarinet Concertos of Louis Spohr," 53–54. The introduction is transcribed in Stork, "Johann Simon Hermstedt," 797; Göthel, *Thematisch-bibliographisches Verzeichnis*; and reproduced in Schmatz, "Die Klarinetten."

206. Brown, *Louis Spohr*, 50. For a detailed description of Hermstedt's life and career, see Weston, *Clarinet Virtuosi of the Past*, 77–99.

207. Three contemporary concertos for B♭ clarinet are Krommer's Concerto in E-flat Major, op. 36 (1803); Riotte's Concerto in B-flat Major (ca. 1809); and Hook's Concerto in E-flat Major (1812). They all include technically brilliant solos. However, the runs and arpeggios of the clarinet parts stay within the confines of F and C major that are more idiomatic than is the solo part of Spohr's Concerto no. 1, and there is less chromatism in the solo and orchestral parts. The Riotte concerto, published by Breitkopf & Härtel, carries a plate number of 1308. See Pound, "A Study of Clarinet Solo Concerto Literature," vol. 1, 177; Deutsch, *Musikverlags Nummern*, 9.

208. For an analysis of Spohr's use of chromatic harmony in his concertos see Johnston, "The Clarinet Concertos of Louis Spohr," 98–101.

209. The *ossia* passages were supplied by Spohr, Hermstedt (in the first movement of Concerto no. 3, mm. 162–63), and possibly the publishers of printed editions. See Johnston, "The Clarinet Concertos of Louis Spohr," 106–7, 109.

210. Spohr, *Concerto no. 3*, 2, mm. 56–58; 73–75.

211. Spohr, *Concerto no. 2*, second movement, mm. 1–8.

212. Ibid., third movement, mm. 242–45.

213. Johnston, "The Clarinet Concertos of Louis Spohr," 38; Weston, *Clarinet Virtuosi of the Past*, 83–99.

214. "Hermstädt übertrifft in Ueberwindung der Schwierigkeiten und durch seinen höchst ausdrucksvollen Vortrag alle Uebrigen." Backofen, *Anweisung zur Klarinette* (1824), 3.

215. This account of Baermann's life and career is based on Weston, *Clarinet Virtuosi of the Past*, 38, 116–20.

216. See Carl Baermann, *Vollständige Clarinett Schule*, vol. 1, 1. The maker's name was mispelled in Baermann's tutor as Kriesling und Schlott.

217. Weston, foreword to Weber, *Concerto for Clarinet no 1*.

218. Weston, *Clarinet Virtuosi of the Past*, 78.

219. Weber, *Diary*, 27 September 1812; quoted in Weber, *Writings on Music*, 375. The translation here is in Weston, *Clarinet Virtuosi of the Past*, 78.

220. Warrack, *Carl Maria von Weber*, 126.

221. At m. 143, Baermann composed sixteen additional bars followed by a short cadenza in a performance copy of the manuscript. The violinist Täglichsbeck provides the orchestration of these measures, and they first appeared in print in Schlesinger's or Peters's edition about 1870. These additions appear in almost every subsequent edition. Baermann's additional measures and cadenza are printed along with Jähn's alteration to mm. 141–43 and Baermann's alteration to mm. 117–21. See Sandner, *Die Klarinette bei Weber*, 63–64, and Weston, introduction to Weber, *Concerto for Clarinet no. 1*.

222. Warrack, *Carl Maria von Weber*, 127–28.

223. Coincidently, the clarinet solo of Hook's clarinet concerto (1812) begins with a similar arpeggio "rocket" passage on f ending on f³, but with longer note values. See Hook, *Concerto for Clarinet and Orchestra*.

224. Cudworth, quoting Marsh in "John Marsh," 133.

225. Wolf, *The Symphonies of Johann Stamitz*, 343 n. 15. One of these works was the Stamitz symphony "avec clarinets et cor de chasse," performed on 26–27 March 1755 at a Concert Spirituel; see Pierre, *Histoire du Concert Spirituel*, 269, nos. 537–38.

226. *VI Sinfonie, a piu istrumenti intitolate La Melodia Germanica composte da vari autori . . . Opera XI*. The title page is illustrated in Wolf, *The Symphonies of Johann Stamitz*, pl. 4b, and Hoeprich, "Die Klarinetten Johann Scherers," Abb. 2.

227. "Faute de Clarinettes, on poura les Exécuter avec deux Hautbois, Flutes ou Violons." The other composers in this collection are Franz Richter (no. 2), Georg Wagenseil (no. 4), and Karl Kohaut (no. 6).

228. See Riemann, *Symphonien der pfaelzbayerischen Schule*; Riemann, *Mannheim Symphonists*, vol. 1, 14–35, 36–63. Riemann did not republish Symphony no. 5.

229. Brook, *La symphonie française*, vol. 2, 314–15; Macdonald, "Gossec, François-Joseph," vol. 1, 299, 303–4.

230. Gossec, *Eight Symphonic Works*, TS, ser. D, vol. 3, xv, xxxi. Brook transcribed the beginning of the Adagio (second movement) of op. 8, no. 1, with clarinets in B♭ in *La symphonie française*, vol. 1, 158–59. Other composers who included optional clarinets parts were Schencker, op. 1, no. 3 (1761); Beck, op. 3 (1762) and op. 4 (1767); Toeschi and Holzbauer, op. 3 (ca. 1765); Leemans, op. 1 (ca. 1765) and op. 2 (ca. 1766); Dittersdorf, op. 17 (1775); Vanhal, op. 17 (1775); and Roeser, op. 12 (1776). See Cucuel, "La question," 281–82; and Cucuel, *Études*, 19, 55; Leemans, *One Symphony*, TS, ser. D, vol. 2, xxi; xxxv, nos. 1–3, 7; xxxvi, no. 8; *Almanach Musical*, 83, nos. 199, 200; and Roeser, *One Symphony*, TS, ser. D, vol. 2, xli.

231. Edited in Gossec, *Eight Symphonic Works*, TS, ser. D, vol. 3, 151–67.

232. Gossec, *Eight Symphonic Works*, TS, ser. D, vol. 3, xxxiii–xxxiv.

233. Weston, *Clarinet Virtuosi of the Past*, 251; BD, vol. 10, 58.

234. See Cannabich, *The Symphony at Mannheim*, TS, ser. C, vol. 3, lix, and Riemann, *Symphonien der pfaelzbayerischen Schule*. Cannabich's *Sinfonia a 12* includes B♭ clarinets with a restricted range of g¹ to d³ and e♭¹ to a2. A C major *Ouverture a 15* includes clarinets in B♭ in D major, but the use of awkward accidentals suggests the original parts were in C. See Riemann, *Mannheim Symphonists*, vol. 2, 103–41, 142–60.

235. Fränzl, *Three Symphonies*, TS, ser. C, vol. 11.

236. 15 January 1752. The author is grateful to Pamela Weston for a transcription of this benefit concert from the British Library.

237. LS, 534; BD, vol. 1, 280; and Weston, *More Clarinet Virtuosi of the Past*, 39.

238. LS, 774.

239. Herschel, *Three Symphonies*, TS, ser. E, vol. 2, xxi–xxiii, xxxv. Carl Friedrich Abel is sometimes credited with using the clarinet in one of his symphonies. Mozart copied Abel's Symphony in E-flat Major, op. 7, no. 6 (1763–64); it had previously been attributed to Mozart himself (the former K. 18). Mozart substituted B♭ clarinets for oboes in the original symphony published by Bremner (London) in 1767. There is no other evidence to suggest that Abel included clarinets in any of his symphonies. Knape and Charters, "Abel, Carl Friedrich," in Sadie, *New Grove*, 2d ed.; Mozart, *Symphonie no. 3*, MG, ser. 8, no. 3; Knape, *Bibliographisch-thematisches Verzeichnis*, 30–31.

240. See Erskine, *Periodical Overture, no. 28, TS,* ser. E, vol. 1, xli–ii, xlvi, no. 8. Erskine's works, now lost, includes a "Concerto with Clarinitts" (performed 15 November 1771); "Overture with Clarinett solos" (performed 13 December 1771); and a "Concerto with Clarinets" (performed 7 April 1780). Johnson, *Music and Society,* 82–83.

241. Barthélemon, *The Symphony, TS,* ser. E, vol. 1, lxxxvii–viii; xci, no. 6; xciii, no. 18. Vanhal's Sinfonia no. 42, a symphony in C published in 1774 in London, includes a part for two "Clarinetti." However, these parts were intended for clarini (trumpets), since they include many repeated notes and the compass is restricted to notes in the overtone series. See Floyd, "The Clarinet Music of Johann Baptist Vanhal," 67–68.

242. Bach, *Symphonies II; Symphonies III; Simphonies Concertantes II, CWB,* vols. 27, 28, 31. See also Bach, *The Concerted Symphonies.*

243. Bach, *Symphonies Concertantes II, CWB,* vol. 31, ix.

244. Pokorny, *Seven Symphonies, TS,* ser. C, vol. 7, xviii.

245. Scharnagl, "Pokorny, Franz Xaver," in Sadie, *New Grove;* Pokorny, *Seven Symphonies,* xxxiv–xli, xlvi; symphonies D60, D61, D63, E♭3, E♭9, B♭3, B♭4.

246. Scharnagl, "Schacht, Theodor," in Sadie, *New Grove;* Schacht, *Two Symphonies, TS,* ser. C, vol. 7, xlviii, xlix, l.

247. Poštolka, "Pichl, Václav," in Sadie, *New Grove.* Pichl, *Three Symphonies, TS,* ser. B, vol. 7, lix. The 1775 Breitkopf catalog supplement lists this symphony with clarinets as no. 6 of their publication. See *BTC,* 564.

248. Pierre, *Histoire du Concert Spirituel,* 309, no. 983. See the discussion in Zaslaw, *Mozart's Symphonies,* 330–31.

249. See Spaethling, *Mozart's Letters, Mozart's Life,* letter of 4 Jan. 1783, 337–39; Zaslaw, *Mozart's Symphonies,* 377–79.

250. Zaslaw, *Mozart's Symphonies,* 434.

251. Haydn, *Londoner Sinfonien, HW,* ser. 1, vols. 17–18. Lawson, "Haydn and the Clarinet," 8–9. The earliest American use of the clarinet appears in the first published orchestral score, Hans Gram's setting of "The Death Song of an Indian Chief" for soprano and an orchestra of two B♭ clarinets (untransposed), two E♭ horns (transposed), violins, violas, and cellos. The clarinet parts double the first and second violins in most passages. The first page of the score in *Massachusetts Magazine* 3, no. 3 (March 1791): between 186–187 is reproduced by Howard in *Our American Music,* between 60–61, although the indications for clarinets are missing in his reproduction. See also Koegel, "The Indian Chief," 479, 487.

252. Lawson, "The Development of Wind Instruments," 81.

253. Schindler mentions that Friedlowsky taught Beethoven about the clarinet. See Schindler, *Beethoven as I Knew Him,* 58. However, it is uncertain when Friedlowsky moved from Prague to Vienna. See Lawson, "The Development of Wind Instruments," 82; Weston, *Clarinet Virtuosi of the Past,* 169.

254. Weber, "Einiges über Clarinett und Bassetthorn," 39. However, Weber's fingering charts for nine- and eleven-key clarinets ascend to c4.

255. Other examples of Beethoven's use of color to determine his choice of clarinet are the C clarinets in the B-flat march in *Fidelio* and the C clarinets in the D major Gloria of the *Missa solemnis.* Lawson, "The Development of Wind Instruments," 82.

256. Ibid., 73.

257. See the detailed discussion of salon concerts by Viano in "By Invitation Only," 131–62.

258. In the Bibliothèque Nationale, Paris, Vm⁷ 6942.

259. Fétis, *Biographie universelle,* 2d ed., vol. 1, 12; Mendel, *Musikalisches Conversations-Lexicon,* vol. 1, 9.

260. Whistling and Hofmeister, *Handbuch der musikalischen Litteratur.* The majority of works in the first edition of this trade listing were published between 1790 and 1816. See the introduction by Ratliff, viii, ix, xii and Rees-Davies, *Whistling and Hofmeister.*

261. "On ne trouvera dans ces Recueils que des Morceaux don't l'execution sera très practicable sur l'Instrument, attendu qu'ils seront tous executes avant que de les y mettre."

262. Abraham, *Nouveaux recueils,* 20.

263. In the Bibliothèque Nationale, Paris, Vm⁷. 640.

264. Cf. the list of these works in Lawson, *Mozart,* 91.

265. Whistling and Hofmeister, *Handbuch der musikalischen Litteratur,* 212–15.

266. Randall, "A Comprehensive Performance Project;" Randall, "The Clarinet Duet," 9–11.

267. Jones, "Bates, William," in Sadie, *New Grove,* 2d ed. Bates's *Eighteen Duettino's for Two Guitars, Two French Horns, or Two Clarinets* was advertised in Longman & Co.'s 1769 *Catalogue of Vocal and Instrumental Music.*

268. The author thanks Ingrid Pearson for information.

269. See Randall, "A Comprehensive Performance Project," 21–22 and Randall, "The Clarinet Duet," 10. The anonymous duets are discussed and no. 3 is reproduced in Rice, *The Baroque Clarinet,* 81.

270. Randall reproduced a two-line duet headed "Adagio" from a later anonymous printing of Roeser's *Gamme de la clarinette* in "The Clarinet Duet," 10, preserved in the Bibliothèque Nationale, Paris, Ch. 90.

271. See Corrette, *Méthode,* with duets "pour la Flute, Haut-bois et Clarinette" (56–66); *Principes de clarinette*; and Abraham, *Principes.*

272. The letters were transcribed by Théophile Dufour in *Correspondence générale de J. J. Rousseau* (Paris, 1924–35), vol. 19, 346; cited in Randall, "A Comprehensive Performance Project," 22–23.

273. A modern edition of these duos appears in Becker, *Klarinetten-Duette,* 7–10.

274. Autograph in the Brussels Conservatory Library; see Becker, *Klarinetten-Duette,* 11–13.

275. Advertised in *Avant-coureur* and *Mercure de France*; see Cucuel, *Études,* 60. Gaspard's fourth collection of twenty-five airs for two clarinets is listed along with *Six duos pour la clarinette* (Berault) by Johann Kuchler in the *Almanach Musical* (1775), 68, nos. 125–26.

276. Gaspard, *VIIIe recueil.* A copy is in the Bibliothèque Nationale, Paris, Cons. A. 34.026. This work was also advertised by the Parisian publisher Tarade in his 1777 catalog; see Devriès and Lesure, *Dictionnaire,* vol. 1, no. 203 (1777). Numbers 7, 18, 21, and 34 were edited and republished by Cucuel in *Études,* 53–54. See also Cucuel, *Études,* 60 n. 5.

277. Procksch also wrote a duo for clarinet and cello, now lost, dedicated to the clarinetist Count Michael Ogínsky in 1773 entitled *Sei sonate a clarinetteo e accompagnameto di violoncello, dedicate à S. E. il signore Conte Oginsky. . . composte dal signor Gasparo Procksch.* Advertised in *Avant-coureur* according to Cucuel in *Études,* 60 n. 3.

278. Roeser, *Premier recueil de duo tirés des opera-comiques, avec accompagnement*

de clavecin ou de forte-piano, See *Journal de musique* 63, no. 1. A later edition of the *Premier recueil* (ca. 1781) survives in two separate parts of seven pages with eighteen airs from operas by Dezède, Grétry, Louis-Emmanuel Jadin, Martini, Monsigny, Sacchini, and Pierre Vachon.

279. Abraham published his *Premier recueil d'ariettes* about 1778, since it is listed in *Almanach Musical* (1778), 92, no. 174. At least six more publications of duets by Abraham, published in 1788–89, are in the Bibliothèque Nationale, Paris. In the Bibliothèque Municipal of Dijon, Abraham's one-page fingering chart entitled *Principes de clarinette* was bound with all thirty-two collections of Abraham's *Recueil d'ariettes*.

280. Vanderhagen's *Duo de clarinettes* (Chevardiere) is listed in the *Almanach Musical* for 1776, 77, no. 118, 144–45, along with the presumably lost *Sonate de M. Baer, pour la clarinette et le basson* (Le Marchand) and *Duo per clarinetto e fagotto dall Sig. Moriggi* (Berault). The oboist Giuseppe Ferlendis wrote twelve divertimenti for two clarinets in 1799; see Ferlendis, *12 Divertimenti*.

281. Crusell, *Trois duos pour deux clarinettes d'une difficulté progressive* (Leipzig, 1821). For an analysis and discussion, see Dahlström, *Bernhard Henrik Crusell*, 185–98.

282. Lefèvre published nine sets of six duos in Paris from 1786 to 1805, preserved in the Bibliothèque Nationale. See Randall, "A Comprehensive Performance Project," 114.

283. Stadler, *Six Duettinos*.

284. Yost wrote eight books of six duets for two clarinets consisting of ops. 1–7, and op. 10 published during the 1780s. Additional duets were published as *Six Favorite Duets*, op. 12, and *Sett of Three Original Duets* (London, ca. 1800); *Six petits duos* (Paris, 1801); *Duos non difficiles* (Paris, 1803, 1805); two books of six duets for clarinet and violin as ops. 8 and 9; and twelve arias for clarinet and viola. Six duets for two clarinets are in manuscript at the library of the Conservatory of Music in Genoa. In addition, Devienne, Garnier, and Vanderhagen transcribed many duets by Michel during the early nineteenth century. See Bacci, "Michel Yost," 60–63; Randall, "A Comprehensive Performance Project," 125–26.

285. Twelve duets by Devienne were published in two sets for clarinet and bassoon (ca. 1788 to ca. 1803). See Montgomery, "François Devienne," in Sadie, *New Grove*, 2d ed.

286. Garnier's three duos, op. 4, were very likely for oboe with an alternate part for clarinet and bassoon. See Cotte, "Garnier, François-Joseph," in Sadie, *New Grove*, 2d ed.

287. Charlton and Audéon, "Gebauer, François René," in Sadie, *New Grove*, 2d ed.

288. Goepfert, *Trois duos concertantes op. 22* (ca. 1821). André, in Offenbach, published earlier duos by Goepfert for clarinet and bassoon in 1813. See Weston, *Clarinet Virtuosi of the Past*, 114–15.

289. Johnson and Burnham, "Beethoven, Ludwig, van; Worklist, Works of Doubtful Authenticity, Probably Spurious," in Sadie, *New Grove*, 2d ed.

290. Two eighteenth-century sonatas advertised in catalogs have not been found. They include one by Schirmor listed by Tarade in the 1778 catalog and one by D. Chiapperelli listed by Boyer in the 1785 catalog. See Devriès and Lesure, *Dictionnaire*, vol. 1, no. 13 and Johansson, *French Music Publishers' Catalogues*, vol. 2, fasc. 91. Newman credited Narcisco Casanova and Antonio Soler with clarinet sonatas, but this statement appears to be an error. Cf. Newman, *The Sonata in the Classical Era*, 296; Voxman and Mead, "Some Notes," 28.

291. "Pour faciliter le Professeur qui n'est pas tenu de savoir bien jouer du violon-celle ou de l'alto ces Sonates devant être executées avec la clarinette en Si♭, on bais-sera le violoncelle ou l'alto d'un ton et on jouera comme c'est écrit." Buteux, *Meth-ode*, 98. Trans. in Voxman and Mead, "Some Notes," 29. Earlier, Backofen included a duo for clarinet in B♭ and cello in his tutor about 1803. See Backofen, *Anweisung zur Klarinette* (ca. 1803), 18–20.

292. Jackman, "Sciroli, Gregorio," in Sadie, *New Grove*, 2d ed.

293. Delius "Wiederentdeckte italienische Klarinettenmusik," 41–42; Jackman, "Sciroli, Gregorio," in Sadie, *New Grove*, 2d ed.

294. Sciroli, Sonata for Clarinet and Basso Continuo. This work is recorded by Luigi Magistrelli playing a nine-key clarinet by Kohlert (Graslitz) on Bayer Records, CD, BR 100 223, 1996.

295. Voxman expressed doubts that this work was originally written for clarinet in Voxman and Mead, "Some Notes," 28.

296. See Lefèvre, *Trois grandes sonates*. Previous accounts and editions of Lefèvre's sonatas relied on an erroneous dating of 1804–5 in Hopkinson, *A Dictionary*. Janet's address in 1793 and 1794 was rue St. Jacques no. 31, where these sonatas were pub-lished. See Devriès and Lesure, *Dictionnaire*, vol. 1, 234. Voxman suggests a date of about 1788 for Devienne's sonatas for clarinet and bass, but Porthaux published three of his sonatas for clarinet and bass in 1802 (pl. 104); and Sieber published three other sonatas from 1803 to 1805 (pl. 1245). In addition, Frères Gaveaux published three sonatas for clarinet and bass by Duvernoy as opp. 1 and 5 between 1797 and 1812. See Voxman, "Some Notes," 29; Kennedy, "The Clarinet Sonata in France," 48, 123–24; Cotte, "Duvernoy," in *MGG*, vol. 15, 1893–94; Devriès and Lesure, *Dictionnaire*, vol. 2, 74, 135, 146–47, 234.

297. Blasius (ca. 1803) and Baissiere, *fils* (ca. 1808), wrote sonatas for clarinet and unrealized bass. See Merriman, "Early Clarinet Sonatas," 28. In England and Amer-ica, song sheets or sheet music for keyboard and voice sometimes includes an easier, transposed version of the melody placed at the end of the song written for amateur players of the violin, recorder (marked as flute), transverse flute, English guitar (marked as guitar), or clarinet. American arrangements for clarinet appear from the 1790s through the early nineteenth century and usually include a melody transposed to F or C major. See Rice, "Some Performance Practice Aspects," 229–47; Girdham, *En-glish Opera*, 84, 105–9.

298. The first sonata was written for keyboard and violin, the second for keyboard and clarinet or violin obligato. Eberl's sonatas were also published in 1802 in Vienna by the Bureau d'arts et d'industrie, pl. 2. See Balássa, "Az elsó bécsi klasszikus iskola zongora-klarinét szonárái," 39; Deutsch, *Musikverlags Nummern*, 10.

299. Voxman and Mead, "Some Notes," 30.

300. Balássa, "Az elsó bécsi klasszikus iskola zongora-klarinét szonárái," 15–18; Voxman and Mead, "Some Notes," 30–32.

301. Weber was not happy that Hermstedt, Baermann's rival, requested a concerto, stating "this was small satisfaction to me." Weber wrote in his diary during 1812 and 1815 that he had composed or was composing a "Savoysche Lied und am Clarinette-Concert" for Hermstedt. Neither a Savoyard song nor a clarinet concerto has been found. See Weber, *Writings on Music*, 375; Weston, *Clarinet Virtuosi of the Past*, 88–89; and Warrack, *Carl Maria von Weber*, 165.

302. Warrack, *Carl Maria von Weber*, 374.

303. Warrack, *Carl Maria von Weber*, 167. An early performance of the entire work

was by the clarinetist Johann Gottlieb Kotte and the pianist Julius Benedikt on 23 December 1823 at Dresden as a "new concerto for clarinet" by Weber. See Weston, *Clarinet virtuosi of the past*, 89.

304. "Das Werk bestehet aus einem feurigen, in Einem Gusse fortströmenden Allegro aus Es, einem ungemein zarten, aber keineswegs weichlichen Andante aus C moll; und einem heitern, zum Theil sehr pikanten Rondo aus Es, in welchem sich ganz besonders männliche Fröhlichkeit mit tiefem Ernst und sogar wehmüthigen Anklängen, gar wunderbar und effectreich mischt." Rochlitz, "Anzeigen," 443.

305. Cf. Warrack's description in *Carl Maria von Weber*, 178.

306. Struck, *Grand duo pour le piano-forte et clarinette ou violon* (Bonn, 1804); see Balássa, "Az elsó bécsi klasszikus iskola zongora-klarinét szonárái," 22–25, 39–40.

307. Franz Anton Hoffmeister, *Six duos pour le piano forte et clarinette* (Vienna, ca. 1812). Balássa gave incipits of all six duos, but nos. 2–4 match the three sonatas by Vanhal. See Balássa, "Az elsó bécsi klasszikus iskola zongora-klarinét szonárái," 25–33, 40–41.

308. See the detailed analysis by Balássa, "Az elsó bécsi klasszikus iskola zongora-klarinét szonárái," 33–36, and Harlow, "The Chamber Music," 51–53.

309. Originally for C clarinet and orchestra, Rossini wrote a more ornate and musically interesting solo for B♭ clarinet and piano published by Breitkopf & Härtel, 1823–24. Rossini wrote a third, simpler solo for B♭ clarinet and piano published by Ricordi in 1829. See Sacchini, "The Concerted Music," 141.

310. The Mendelssohn sonata is included in *Masterworks*. Additional sonatas by K. Arnold (1816) for clarinet in A and R. N. C. Bochsa (ca. 1812) are listed in Merriman, "Early Clarinet Sonatas," 28.

311. Vanhal limits the compass of the clarinet parts from c to d³, and there are many charming moments throughout his sonatas. The Heine sonata is a more virtuosic work with a wider range. Rossini wrote an early student work that consists of a simple melody followed by five variations. Hoffmeister's sonata is one of the earliest works for A clarinet and piano and, along with Ries's sonata, is an effective concert piece. The Danzi sonata is technically more challenging than the earlier works, probably written for an eleven-key clarinet. Archduke Rudolph's sonata is even more demanding technically for the clarinetist and especially for the pianist. Mendelssohn's sonata is a musically weak student work.

312. Lefèvre is sometimes mistakenly credited with writing the earliest reed trio for oboe, clarinet, and bassoon. This was based on an erroneous interpretation of Fétis's list of Lefèvre's published music. Fétis's second work for Lefèvre was "Deux symphonies concertantes pour clarinette et basson," followed by "Une concertante pour hautbois, clarinette et basson." The latter is now correctly identified as the Symphonie concertante for oboe, clarinet, bassoon, and orchestra, published in Paris by Janet & Cotelle, ca. 1819. See *Einzeldrucke vor 1800*, vol. 12, 408; cf. Gillespie, *The Reed Trio*, 10; Fétis, *Biographie universelle*, vol. 5, 283.

313. See Gassmann, *Trio D-dur*.

314. See Charlton and Audéon, "René François Gebauer," in Sadie, *New Grove*, 2d ed.

315. See Montgomery, "François Devienne," in Sadie, *New Grove*, 2d ed.

316. Manuscripts of Crusell's "Pot-pourri pour clarinette, cor & bassoon" and a "Concert-Trio för Clarinet, Waldhorn & Fagott" are in the library of the Kungliga Musikaliska Akademiens in Stockholm. See Dahlström, *Bernhard Henrik Crusell*, 198.

317. Scholz-Michelitsch, *Georg Christoph Wagenseil*, 46–47, 85–90.

318. See Wagenseil, *Sonata*.

319. Bryan, "Vanhal, Johann Baptist," in Sadie, *New Grove*, 2d ed.

320. *Almanach Musical*, 71, no. 144. A manuscript from the Rheda collection in Münster of a "Trio B♭ Clarinetto Solo violino con Basso" includes attributions in different hands to "Signor Stamitz" and Haydn. According to Eugene K. Wolf in a 1991 letter to the author, the conflicting attributions and the fact that the Rheda collection is unreliable argue against an attribution to Johann Stamitz or Haydn. Furthermore, the form and style of the piece suggest a later composer other than Johann Stamitz, possibly Carl Stamitz.

321. Vanhal, *Sei trios*. Subsequently, the English publisher Bland published two trios, no. 2 for C clarinet and no. 3.

322. Another work by Vanhal advertised but not found is the *Six trios pour une clarinette, un bassoon et basse, ou deux clarinettes et basse, oeuvre 18*, published by Berault, in the *Almanach Musical*, 72, no. 147.

323. Helm "Bach, Carl Philipp Emanuel," in Sadie, *New Grove*.

324. C. P. E. Bach, *Six Sonatas*.

325. Mozart, *Trio per il clavicembalo o forte piano, con l'accompagnemento d'un violino e viola . . . La parte del violino si può eseguire anche con un clarinetto* (Vienna, ca. 1788; second printing, ca. 1802; third printing, Johann Cappi. ca. 1804). Twelve other editions list the alternate instrumentation: Le Duc (Paris, ca. 1788), Götz (Mannheim, Munich and Dusseldorf, ca. 1789), Longman & Broderip (London, ca. 1790), Hummel (Berlin, Amsterdam, ca. 1792), André (Offenbach, ca. 1793), Sieber (Paris, 1790s), Magazin de Musique (Braunschweig, ca. 1799), Böhme (Hamburg, after 1800), Breitkopf & Härtel (Leipzig, ca. 1802), Simrock (Bonn, ca. 1803), Chemische Druckerey (Vienna, ca. 1811), and Steiner (Vienna, ca. 1822). See *Einzeldrucke*, vol. 6, 190 and Köchel, *Chronologisch-thematisches Verzeichnis*, 555.

326. Mozart, *Trio pour clavecin*, pl. 581. See Deutsch, *Musikverlags Nummern*, 6.

327. Roger Hellyer, "Wind instruments," 288.

328. *Grand trio pour le piano-forte avec un clarinette ou violon, et violoncelle* (Vienna, 1798). See Kinsky, *Das Werk Beethovens*, 25–27.

329. See Kinsky, *Das Werk Beethovens*, 25.

330. Lawson, "The Development of Wind Instruments," 77.

331. Harlow, "The Chamber Music with Clarinet," 51.

332. Tuthill, "The Quartets and Quintets for Clarinet and Strings," 11–15; Rau, "Die Kammermusik." See also Sundet, "A Study."

333. Whistling and Hofmeister, *Handbuch*; see also Rees-Davies, *Whistling and Hofmeister*.

334. "Le partie de Clarinette peut se jouer par un Hautbois ou Violon et la partie de l'Alto peut se jouer avec un Cor de chasse." Stamitz, *Six quatuors*. Other quartets published with alternate oboe or violin parts include those by Struck, Carl Stamitz, and Cannabich. See Sundet, "A Study," 149, 298; Cannabich, *Deux quatuors* and *Quartett*.

335. Cannabich, *Deux quatuors* and *Quartett*; Kichler, *Six quatuors*; Stamitz, *Six quatuor*.

336. See Rau, "Die Kammermusik," 111–12; Bacci, "Michel Yost," 58–59.

337. Rau, "Die Kammermusik," 179; Poštolka, "Pichl, Václav," in Sadie, *New Grove*, 2d ed.

338. Bochsa, *Trois quatuors*; see Devriès and Lesure, *Dictionnaire*, vol. 1, 85; Rau, "Die Kammermusik," 122–23.

339. Arranged by André in Offenbach about 1799, see the informative article by Newhill, "The Mozart Clarinet Quartets," 26–28.

340. See Rau, "Die Kammermusik," 185–93.

341. Goepfert, *Quatuor*, pl. 386. See Sundet, "A Study," 129–32; and for dating the work, Deutsch, *Musikverlags Nummern*, 6, 26.

342. See Rau, "Die Kammermusik," 143.

343. Müller, *Premier quatuor*, pl. 3788. Whistling and Hofmeister, *Handbuch*, (1818), 16, cf. Rau, "Die Kammermusik," 166 and Deutsch, *Musikverlags Nummern*, 6.

344. Tuthill, "The Quartets and Quintets," 3–11.

345. Other publications were Artaria (Vienna, ca. 1802); Mollo & Co. (Vienna, ca. 1802); and Sieber (Paris, ca. 1802). See *Einzeldrucke*, vol. 6, 170; vol. 13 (1998), 137. In 1808, Artaria published an arrangement of the quintet for piano with clarinet or violin. In the ninth measure of the second trio of the clarinet part, the triplet d2–a–f is replaced by two eighth notes notated in the bass clef as d–f. See Mozart, *Grande sonate*, 3. This is evidence that some players owned and perfomed this work on a basset clarinet during the early nineteenth century. This is the only passage in the entire work that uses a note below e.

346. Hellyer, "Wind Instruments," 288.

347. Newhill, "The Adagio," 170. The increased technical demands by composers reflect both the romantic nature of the music, the rise in players' techniques, and the increasing sophistication of the clarinets' mechanism.

348. Krachtovíl, "Betrachtungen," 268–70; Mozart, *Quintette mit Bläsern, NMA*, ser. 8, wg. 15, pt. 2; Krachtovìl, "Otázhka původního znění Mozartova Koncertu," 63–67; Croll and Birsak, "Anton Stadlers Bassettklarinette," 8–10; and Sheveloff, "When Sources Seem to Fail," 387–401.

349. Backofen, "Quintetto, oeuv. 15" advertised in the "Intelligenz-Blatt" 11, col. 49, in *AMZ* 6 (1804). See Rau, "Die Kammermusik," 255.

350. Rudolf Argermüller, "Neukomm, Sigismund Ritter von," *New Grove*, 2d ed., and Rau, "Die Kammermusik," 283. The work. entitled Introduction, Thema und Variationen, published in Berlin in 1962, and attributed to Carl Maria Weber, is actually Küffner's Quintet in B-flat Major, op. 32. See Rau, "Von Wagner, von Weber?" 172–75; Newhill, "Küffner's Works," 34; Weston, *More Clarinet Virtuosi*, 149.

351. Weber had been working on a quintet for clarinet and string quartet for Baermann since 1811, finishing it in 1815. It was published in Berlin by Schlesinger about 1820, and in Paris by Richault (pl. 2105) about 1827. See Warrack, *Carl Maria von Weber*, 167; Devriès and Lesure, *Dictionnaire*, vol. 2, 369.

352. Romberg, *Quintetto*, pl. 1459; see Deutsch, *Musikverlags Nummern*, 14.

353. Krommer, *Quintuor*.

354. Rau, "Die Kammermusik," 300. The Adagio for clarinet and string quartet by Richard Wagner, published by Breitkopf & Härtel in 1926, is actually the second movement of Baermann's Quintet, op. 23. See Newhill, "The Adagio," 167–71; and Rau, "Von Wagner, von Weber?" 170–72.

355. Warrack, *Carl Maria von Weber*, 167.

356. Morrow, *Concert Life in Haydn's Vienna*, 256. First edition, *Quintuor concertant pour piano forte, hautboy, clarinette, cor & basson* (Augsburg: Gombert, 1799); see Köchel, *Chronologisch-thematisches Verzeichnis*, 487. Later editions were published by Artaria (1803), Sieber (1803), Cappi (1804), Simrock (ca. 1807), and André (ca. 1813). See Köchel, *Chronologisch-thematisches Verzeichnis*, 488 and *Einzeldrucke vor 1800, Wolfgang Amadeus Mozart*, 152.

357. Spaethling, *Mozart's Letters, Mozart's Life*, letter of 10 April 1784, 366–67.

358. Smallman, *The Piano Quartet and Quintet*, 21.

359. First edition, *Grand Quintetto* (Vienna: Mollo, 1801). See Kinsky, *Das Werk Beethovens*, 37. In Mollo's transcription for piano, violin, viola, and cello, the piano part remains unchanged but the string parts include octave transpositions, new parts, and the addition of ornamentation. Writers suggest that this arrangement was more satisfactory than the one with winds and cite the popularity of the piano quartet in Vienna at the time. See Smallman, *The Piano Quartet and Quintet*, 21–22; Warrack, "Chamber Works with Wind Instruments," 300.

360. Smallman, *The Piano Quartet and Quintet*, 21. An illuminating analysis and comparison of the Mozart and Beethoven *Quintets* is given by Tovey, *Essays in musical analysis*, 109–20.

361. Morrow, *Concert Life in Haydn's Vienna*, 294; Weston, *Clarinet Virtuosi*, 40.

362. Suppan, "Wind Quintet," in Sadie, *New Grove*, 2d ed.

363. The work was listed in the *BTC*, Supplement 15 for 1782, 40. See Kaul, *Thematische Verzeichnis*, 13; Sirker, *Die Entwicklung*, 21, 24.

364. Fétis reports that the Schmitt quintet, now lost, was published by Pleyel; Cambini's three *Quintetti Concertants* were published by Sieber in 1802, pl. 1571. See Devriès and Lesure, *Dictionnaire des éditeurs*, vol. 2.

365. See K. Moeck, "The Beginnings of the Woodwind Quintet," 22, 31–33; Suppan, "Wind Quintet," in Sadie, *New Grove*, 2d ed.; Stone, "Reicha, Antoine," in Sadie, *New Grove*, 2d ed.

366. Important works for larger ensembles include Beethoven's Septet, op. 20 (1799–1800); Spohr's Nonet, op. 32 (1813), Octet, op. 41 (1814), and Schubert's Octet (1824).

CHAPTER 5

1. Carse, *The Orchestra*, 130. Solinus and Leander were horn players but the clarinetists are not mentioned in this advertisement. See *BD*, vol. 9, 182; vol. 14, 195.

2. *LS*, vol. 4, 942.

3. Croft-Murray and McVeigh, "London," in Sadie, *New Grove,* 2d ed.; Hogwood, "The London Pleasure Gardens," general intro. to J. C. Bach, *Favourite Songs*, ix–x; William Weber, "London: A City of Unrivalled Riches," in *The Classical Era*, ed. N. Zaslaw (1989); cited in Haynes, *The Eloquent Oboe*, 442.

4. Cucuel, "La question de clarinettes," 281; Rice, *The Baroque Clarinet*, 154.

5. Capon and Yve-Plessis, *Paris gallant*, 133; see also Hellyer, "'Harmoniemusik': Music for Small Wind Band," 82.

6. See Green, *The Hurdy-Gurdy*, 22–23.

7. Whitwell, *The Wind Band*, 4–5. A thorough discussion of Harmoniemusik in Moravian communities is given by Hellyer, "The Harmoniemusik of the Moravian Communities," 95–108.

8. For a detailed description of the autograph, see Feder, "Das Autograph," 156–58. Haydn, *Divertiment in C* for *Bläserdivertimenti und "Scherzandi," HW*, ser. 8, vol. 2.

9. Landon, *Haydn: The Early Years*, 522; Haydn, *Divertimento in C.*

10. *Divertisement pour deux clarinettes, deux hautbois, deux cors et deux Bassons.* See Hellyer, "'Harmoniemusik': Music for Small Wind Band," 105; Croft-Murray, "The Wind-Band," 144.

11. Jensen, "Dulcianen," 198.

12. Meier, "Die Pressburger Hofkapelle," 83–84; see also Sehnal, "Das Musikinventar," 294 n. 48.

13. Mozart, *Orchesterwerke, NMA*, ser. IV, wg. 12, vol. 2, vii, and Blazin, "The Two Versions," 32.

14. This dating is based on an analysis of Mozart's handwriting and paper types used in the separate wind score. See Blazin, "The Two Versions," 33.

15. Mozart, *Orchesterwerke, NMA*, ser. IV, wg. 12, vol. 2, 12–28.

16. Blazin, "The Two Versions," 43–44.

17. Ibid., 32–33, 47.

18. Mozart, *Ensemblemusik, NMA*, ser. VII, wg. 17, vol. 1, XVI. See Blazin, "The Two Versions," 33–34; however, K. 186 may have been written in Milan in March 1773, see Eisen and Sadie, "Mozart, Wolfgang Amadeus: Works," in Sadie, *New Grove*, 2d ed.

19. Mozart, *Ensemblemusik, NMA*, ser. VII, wg. 17, vol. 1, , 3–38. Hellyer, "Harmoniemusik and Other Works," 283.

20. See Spaethling, *Mozart's Letters, Mozart's Life*, letter of 3 November 1781, 291–93. See Mozart, *Ensemblemusik, NMA*, ser. VII, wg. 17, vol. 2, 3–40.

21. Hellyer, "Harmoniemusik and Other Works," 284. For a discussion of the extant transcriptions for Harmonie of *Die Entführung aus dem Serial*, see Hellyer, "The Transcriptions for *Harmonie*," 53–66.

22. Mozart, *Ensemblemusik, NMA*, ser. VII, wg. 17, vol. 2, 41–96. The clarinet parts are almost identical to those in the earlier sextet version.

23. Ibid., vol. 2, 97–140.

24. Hellyer, "Harmoniemusik and Other Works," 284.

25. See Link, *The National Court Theatre*, 209 and n. 15, 406–7, 410. In 1783, Cramer mentioned the personnel of the Kaiserlich-Königlichen Harmonie in *Magazin der Musik*, 1401 n. 190.

26. Hellyer, "Harmoniemusik and Other Works," 284, 286.

27. Ibid., 284.

28. Mozart, *Ensemblemusik, NMA*, ser. VII, wg. 17, vol. 2, 141–222.

29. Morrow, *Concert Life*, 256. A detailed discussion of the Serenade in B♭ is given in Leeson and Whitwell, "Concerning Mozart's Serenade," 97–130.

30. Schink, *Litterarische Fragmente*, 286. The performance of the serenade that Schink heard was apparently shortened to four movements. See the trans. by Lawson, "Playing Historical Clarinets," 143, and Weston, *Clarinet Virtuosi*, 48–49.

31. A good overview of the history and literature of Harmonie bands is found in Hellyer, "'Harmoniemusik': Music for Small Wind Band," and Whitwell, *The Wind Band*.

32. See Haynes, *The Eloquent Oboe*, 161–62; Camus, "Military Music of Colonial Boston," 81.

33. The band is reproduced in *A View of [the] Royal Building for his Majesty's Horse & Foot Guards, St. James's Park, London*, in Croft-Murray, "The Wind Band," 152, pl. 110. A hand-colored engraving (1753) of the band is reproduced in Camus, "Military Music of Colonial Boston," 82, fig. 72.

34. According to James A. Browne in *England's Artillerymen* (1865), this document was found among the papers of the 1st Battalion Royal Artillery. See Farmer, *History*, 9–10.

35. Farmer, *The Rise*, 58.

36. Richard Hinde, *The Discipline of the Light Horse* (London, 1778), 206–7; quoted in Hellyer, "'Harmoniemusik': Music for Small Wind Band," 56. Two clarinetists may be on horseback in the anonymous engraving "Mounted Band in the

Procession accompanying the State Entry of the Venetian Ambassadors, Querini and Morosini, into London, April 18th, 1763," in Croft-Murray, "The Wind Band," 152, pl. 111.

37. William Gardiner, *Music and Friends* (London, 1853), vol. 3, 7; quoted in Hind, "The British Wind Band," 185.

38. Parke, *Musical Memoirs*, vol. 2, 239.

39. Farmer, *The Rise*, 69–70.

40. Wroth, *The London Pleasure Gardens*, 311. Hellyer suggests that it was more likely that two bands were employed at Vauxhall, a clarinet-horn band and a fife-drum band; Hellyer, "'Harmoniemusik': Music for Small Wind Band," 32.

41. Croft-Murray and McVeigh, "London," in Sadie, *New Grove*, 2d ed. In 1793, Lord George Macartney brought five German musicians among his official representatives to China with two violins, a viola, cello, oboe, bassoon, clarinet, flute, fife, and two basset horns. Chinese painters traced the outline and details of several instruments onto sheets of large paper. See Cranmer-Byng, *An Embassy to China*, 104, 364 n. 22.

42. Croft-Murray, "The Wind-Band," 143.

43. Weston, *Clarinet Virtuosi*, pl. 14, provides the entire illustration. Kramer was a member of the Prince of Wales and the Prince Regent's Band at Brighton before becoming Master of the King's Music in 1817. See Weston, *Clarinet Virtuosi*, 136–37.

44. *Pennsylvania Gazette*, 26 June 1755; see Camus, *Military Music*, 42.

45. *New York Gazette & Weekly Post Boy*, in Corry, Keller, and Keller, *PACN*.

46. Camus, *Military Music*, 179–82.

47. Ibid., 48.

48. Ibid., 50, 179.

49. *Pennsylvania Journal*, 13 August 1777; *Rivington's New York Gazette*, 18 July 1778, 14 April 1779. See Corry, Keller, and Keller, *PACN*.

50. Hardy, *Rudolf Kreutzer*, 10–11. He quotes the *État militaire de France* for 1 June 1763, p. 175, and gives 1762 as the date in the body of the text. According to Biber, the 1763 "Ordonnance du Roi concernant le régiment des Gardes Suisses" also specifies a "Bande turque" but does not provide evidence for this statement. See Biber, "Aus der Geschichte," 133.

51. "La musique de cors, de clarinettes & de bassons admise dans les régimens d'Infanterie, par une ordonnace du 19 Avril 1766. . . . Il y a seize Musiciens attachés au régiment des Gardes-Françoises, indépendamment des Tambours & des Fifres par compagnie." Turpin de Crissé, *Commentaire*, vol. 2, 8–9. Cotte quotes part of this ordinance but misdates it as 19 April 1756; cf. Cotte, "Blasinstrumente," 316; Haynes, *The Eloquent Oboe*, 287.

52. Robert, "Militaire (musique)," 466.

53. See Pierre, *Le Conservatoire*, 99; and Whitwell, *The Wind Band*, 170–71, 180–81.

54. Whitwell, *The Wind Band*, 150 n. 439.

55. Vanderhagen, *La naissance*.

56. Kastner, *Manuel général*, 170 and note 1.

57. *Dispositions sur la composition des musique militaries* (13 Oct. 1823); cited by Pierre in *Le Conservatoire*, 404.

58. *Casselisch Polizey- und Commercien-Zeitung* (1763), 407, cited and trans. by Whitwell, *The Wind Band*, 97.

59. Hiller, "Fortsetzung über die Oper," 87.

60. Reschke, *Studie*, 26, 38, these marches were destroyed during World War II. Many sources, including Page, "Band," in Sadie, *New Grove*, 2d ed., state that Frederick the Great stipulated that Prussian army bands consist of a Harmonie octet of pairs of oboes, clarinets, horns, and bassoons in 1762. Documentation of the date of this instrumentation is lacking. See Hellyer, "'Harmoniemusik': Music for Small Wind Band," 47–48; Whitwell, *The Wind Band*, 95–96.

61. Habla, *Besetzung*, 229, 231.

62. Burney, *The Present State of Music in Germany*, vol. 1, 17–18.

63. Compare the description in Croft-Murray, "The Wind Band," 153–54. An arrangement of the Allegretto movement of Haydn's Symphony no. 99 (1793) comprises a Turkish band of flute and two oboes, two C clarinets, two bassoons, two horns, clarino, serpent, and percussion instruments indicated only by a waving line for a bass drum. Other percussion in Symphony no. 99 probably used in this arrangement are timpani, triangle, and cymbals. See Haydn, *Londoner Sinfonien, HW*, ser. 1, vol. 17, 227–33.

64. The manuscript score of two quartets, "Grenadiers Marche" and "Mousquetiers Marche," are marked "kayserlich-königlichen Exercitium de anno 1765" with two parts for "Pfeifer" and two marked "Clarinetten in B." Reproduced in Brixel, Martin, and Pils, *Das ist Oesterreichs Militär Musik*, 46–47.

65. See Rameis, *Die Österreichische Militärmusik*, 19.

66. See Birsak and König, *Das grosse Salzburger Blasmusik Buch*, 63, Abb. 56, 64, 66. Birsak describes the pitch of the two- and three-key Walch clarinets in the Salzburg Museum as "almost exactly a whole tone lower than our modern concert A." "Salzburg, Mozart, and the Clarinet," 26.

67. Ibid., 68.

68. Ibid., 69. An eight-bar illustration of "Turkish" music played in Salzburg in 1812 was written for fife in D, clarinet in D, trumpet in D, and side drum. See Birsak, *The Clarinet*, 119.

69. Ibid., 69.

70. Christoph Friedrich Nicolai, *Beschreibung einer Reise durch Deutschland und in die Schweiz im Jahre 1781* (Berlin: Stetin, 1784), vol. 4, 558, cited by Michael Pirker, "Pictorial Documents," 8–9.

71. Hoftheater-Rechnungsbücher 13./14. Halbjahr-Rechnung 1782/83, pp. 52–56, Staatsarchiv Wien, cited by Michael Pirker, "Pictorial Documents," 9.

72. Stekl, "Harmoniemusik," 167.

73. Schönfeld, *Jahrbuch*, 98; see Page, "Band," in Sadie, *New Grove*, 2d ed.

74. See Beethoven, *Militair-Marsch*.

75. Suppan and Suppan, "Band," table 2, in Sadie, *New Grove*, 2d ed.

76. Farhbach suggested a band of fifty-five in 1846 that included one A♭ clarinet, one E♭ clarinet, and about thirteen B♭ clarinets. See Joseph Fahrbach, *Organizzazione della musica militaire* (Milan, 1846) cited in Suppan and Suppan, "Band," table 2, in Sadie, *New Grove*, 2d ed.

77. The first page is reproduced in Kenyon de Pascual, "Carlos III," 34.

78. Iriarte mentions the martial clarinets (*clarinetes marciales*) in *La música*, 82. In 1780, the clarinet is also listed as a military instrument in *Diccionario de la Lengua Castellana*, s.v. "Clarinete."

79. Hülphers, *Historisk*, 103 n. 23; cf. the translation by Harker in *Historical Disquisition*, 48 n. 23.

80. Norlind, "Abraham Abrahamsson Hülphers," 56 n. 2. Helistö states, without

documentation, that Count Fersen supplied the Life Guard band with a clarinet in 1756. See Helistö, *Klaneetti*, 20–21.

81. See Norlind, "Abraham Abrahamsson Hülphers," 44; trans. Kirsten Koblik.

82. Ibid., 44; trans. Kirsten Koblik.

83. Ibid., 56; trans. Kirsten Koblik.

84. Hernes, *Impuls,* 297.

85. See Berg, *Den første prøve*, 51; see Rice, "The Clarinet as Described," 48–49, 53.

86. Helistö, *Klaneetti*, 29; the original letter is reproduced on p. 30; trans. Marketta Kivimäki.

87. Ibid., 31.

88. See Henry Lichtenstein, *Travels in Southern Africa in the Years 1803, 1804, 1805, and 1806* (London, 1812); cited in Jooste, "The History," 36.

89. Kroeger, "The Church-Gallery Orchestra," 25.

90. Weir, *Village and Town Bands*, 13.

91. Kroeger, "The Church-Gallery Orchestra," 29.

92. Weir, *Village and Town Bands*, 13. Thomas Webster's painting "The Village Choir" (1847) clearly illustrates a three-member band including a musician playing a six-key English clarinet, along with a bassoon, and cello or bass viol with choir members in the west gallery of Bow Brickhill church in Buckinghamshire. Weir, *Village and Town Bands*, cover, 12; also reproduced in *EM* 8, no. 3 (July 1980): 395; *EM* 12, no. 1 (Feb. 1984): 19, fig. 8.

93. Niemöller, *Kirchenmusik*, 65–66, 68, 237, 257.

94. Charlton, "Orchestra and Chorus," 96.

95. See Weston, *Clarinet Virtuosi of the Past;* Viano, "By Invitation Only."

96. Wolf, "On the Composition of the Mannheim Orchestra," 118, 125.

97. Kaul, *Geschichte der Würzburger Hofmusik*, 100.

98. Gruhn, "Zweibrücken," vol. 1, 180–81.

99. Bereths, *Die Musikpflege am kurtrierischen Hofe*, 46, 48, 51, 68, 88, 147.

100. Schweickert, *Die Musipflege*, 49.

101. François-Sappey, "Le personnel," 155.

102. Zaslaw, "Towards the Revival," 171–72, 174.

103. Beusker, *Die Münsterische*, 140, 142, 159.

104. Spitzer and Zaslaw, "Orchestra, §5: Eighteenth Century," table 1, in Sadie, *New Grove*, 2d ed.; Friis, *Det Kongelige Kapel*, 72.

105. Link, *The National Court Theatre*, 209 n. 15.

106. Schmidt, *Die Musik am Hofe*, 84.

107. Spitzer and Zaslaw, "Orchestra, §5: Eighteenth Century," table 1, in Sadie, *New Grove*, 2d ed.

108. McVeigh, *Concert Life*, 207, table 10.

109. Landmann, "Die Entwicklung," 181. Cf. Zaslaw, "Towards the Revival," 171, 175–77; Weston, *More Clarinet Virtuosi*.

110. Whitwell, *The Wind Band*, 169.

111. Ibid., 170–71.

112. Pierre, *Le Conservatoire*, 124–25.

113. Peter Cahn, "Conservatories, 1790–1945," in Sadie, *New Grove,* 2d ed.; E. Douglas Bromberger, "The Conservatory and the Piano," in *Piano Roles*, 154; Weston, *Clarinet Virtuosi*, 38, 117; Becker, *History*, 25; see also Sowa, *Anfänge institutioneller Musikerziehung in Deutschland*.

BIBLIOGRAPHY

MUSIC SOURCES

Abraham. *Recueil d'ariettes choisies des meilleurs autéurs et de divers operas comiques arrangées pour deux clarinettes.* 32 vols. Paris: Frère, [ca. 1777–85].

———. *Nouveaux recueils pour une clarinette seule d'ouvertures, morceaux de chant, airs de danse, et autres airs agréables.* Vol. 2. Paris: Bignon, [ca. 1789].

Arne, Thomas Augustine. *Artaxerxes: An English Opera.* London: John Johnson, 1762.

———. *The Fairy Prince: A Masque.* London: Welcker, 1771.

———. *Thomas and Sally, or the Sailor's Return.* London: The author, 1761.

Arnold, Samuel. *British Opera in America: Children of the Wood.* New York: Garland, 1994.

———. *Obi, or, Three-Finger'd Jack.* London: Stainer & Bell, 1996.

———. *The Works of Handel,* 45 vols. London: The author, 1786–97.

Bach, Carl Philipp Emanuel. "Duet für 2 Clarinetten." Autograph MS., Brussels: Bibliothèque du Conservatoire Royale de Musique de Bruxelles.

———. *6 Sonatas for Clarinet, Bassoon, and Piano.* Edited by G. Piccioli. New York: International, 1955.

Bach, Johann Christian. *Amadis des Gaules.* Paris: Sieber, [ca. 1780]; reprint, Farnborough, 1972.

———. *The Collected Works of Johann Christian Bach, 1735–1782.* Edited by Ernest Warburton. 48 vols. New York: Garland, 1984–99.

———. *The Concerted Symphonies: Three Symphonies in Score.* Edited by Joseph A. White Jr. Tallahasee: Florida State University, 1963.

———. *Favourite Songs Sung at Vauxhall Gardens,* introduced by Christopher Hogwood. Tunbridge Wells: R. Macnutt, 1985.

———. *Orione.* London: I. Walsh, 1763.

———. *Orione and Zanaida. CWB,* vol. 4, edited by E. Warburton. New York: Garland, 1989.

Backofen, Johann Heinrich Georg. *Quintetto pour clarinette, violon, deux altos et violoncelle,* op. 15. Leipsic: Breitkopf & Härtel, [1803].

Bates, William. *Eighteen Duettino's for Two Guittars, Two French Horns, or Two Clarinets.* London: J. Longman, [ca. 1769].

Becker, Heinz, ed. *Klarinetten-Duette aus der Frühzeit des Instrumentes.* Wiesbaden: Breitkopf & Härtel, 1954.

————. *Klarinetten-Konzerte des 18. Jahrhunderts*. Das Erbe Deutscher Musik, 41. Wiesbaden: Breitkopf & Härtel, 1957.

Beer, Joseph. *Concerto No. 1 for Clarinet and Orchestra*. Edited by J. Madden. London: Musica Rara, 1978.

Beethoven, Ludwig van. *Militair-Marsch: Vollständige kritisch durchgesehene überall berachtigte Ausgabe*. Leipzig: Breitkopf & Härtel, 1862–88; reprint, Ann Arbor: Edwards, 1949, part 287, serie 2, no. 15.

Berlioz, Hector. *Choral Works with Orchestra*. Part 1. Edited by J. Rushton. Vol. 12a of *New Edition of the Complete Works*. Kassel: Bärenreiter, 1991.

Bianchi, Francesco. *La villanella rapita ou La villageoise enlevée*. Paris: Sieber, 1789.

Blanchard, Esprit Joseph Antoine. "Benedicam dominum: Psalm XXXIII employé a grand choeur avec simphonie pour la chapelle du roi en l'annèe 1757," edited by M. F. Beche, MS. (Versailles, 1788), Vm¹. 1323, Bibliothèque Nationale.

Blasius, Frédéric. "Three Quartetti for Clarinet, Violin, Viola, and Cello." MSS. (ca. 1810). Vienna: Österreichsche Nationalbibliothek, SM 22113.

Bochsa, Charles. *Trois quatuors concertans pour clarinette, violon, alto, et basse*. Paris: Imbault, [ca. 1795].

Boieldieu, François-Adrien. *Sonata*. Transcribed for clarinet by G. Gambaro, edited by G. Balássa. Budapest: Editio Musica, 1981.

Bottesini, Pietro. *Divertimento per clarinetto con accompagnamento di due violini, viola e violoncello*. Milan: G. A. Carulli, [ca. 1827].

Cannabich, Christian. *Deux quatuors pour un hautbois ou clarinette, violon, alto, violoncelle ou basson*. Paris: Berault, 1774.

————. *Quartett für Oboe (Klarinette), Violine, Viola, und Violoncello (Fagott)*. Edited by H. Steinbeck. Munich: Doblinger, 1969.

Catel, Charles-Simon. *Quartet in D minor*, op. 2, no. 3. Edited by H. Voxman. Monteux: Musica Rara, 1984.

Cherubini, Maria Luigi. *Démophoon*. Paris: Le Duc, 1788; facsimile ed., New York: Garland, 1978.

————. *Lodoïska*. Paris: Naderman, 1791; facsimile ed., New York: Garland, 1978.

Cimarosa, Domenico. *Il matrimonio secreto*. Paris: O. Lecouix, [ca. 1820].

————. *Gli orazi e i curiazi*. Paris, 1796; Paris: Imbault, 1802; facsimile ed., Milan: Edizioni Suvini Zerboni, 1986.

Cooper, Kenneth, ed. *Concerto IV. Classical Strings and Winds (c. 1770–1828): Classical Solo Concerti*. New York: Garland, 1990.

Corri, Domenico. *A Select Collection of the Most Admired Songs, Duetts, &c. from Operas in the Highest Esteem, and from Other Works, in Italian, English, French, Scotch, Irish &c*. Edinburgh: J. Corri, 1779; reprint, New York: Garland, 1993.

Crusell, Bernhard Henrik. *Concerto for Clarinet and Orchestra*, op. 11. Edited by P. Weston. Vienna: Universal Edition, 1988.

————. *Konzert f-moll für Klarinette und Orchester*, op. 5. Edited by J. Michaels. Hamburg: H. Sikorski, 1962.

————. *Quatuor op. 2, no. 1 mi bémol major, pour clarinette, violon, alto et violoncelle*. Basel: Kneusslin, 1960.

————. *Quatuor pour clarinette, violon, alto et violoncelle*, ouevre 4. Paris: Richault, ca. 1827.

————. *Quatuor pour clarinette, violon, alto et violoncelle*, ouevre 7. Paris: Richault, ca. 1827.

D'Herbain, Chevalier. *Célime, ballet en un acte: représenté par l'Accademie Royale de*

Musique le 28ᵉ jour de Septembre 1756. Paris: Aux addresses ordinaires, 1756.

Danzi, Franz. *Sonate B-dur Klarinette und Klavier*. Edited by J. Wojciechowski. Hamburg: N. Simrock, 1960.

Dibdin, Charles. *Lionel and Clarissa: A Comic Opera, as Performed by Several Eminent Masters*. London: J. Johnson, 1768.

Donizetti, Gaetano. *Maria Stuarda*, 1834; facsimile ed., Milan: Ricordi, 1991.

Ferlendis, Giuseppe. *12 Divertimenti in stile classico*. Edited by L. Magistrelli. Pian Camuno: Eufonia, 1998.

Floquet, Etienne Joseph. *Le siegneur bienfaisant*. Paris: L'auteur, 1780.

———. *L'union des l'amour et des arts*. Paris: L'auteur, [ca. 1773].

Framery, Nicolas Etienne. *L'infante de Zamora*. Paris: Leduc, [ca. 1781].

Fuchs, Johann Nepomuk. *Trio in D-dur für Klarinette, Viola und Violoncello*. Winterthur: Amadeus Verlag, 1979.

Gassmann, Florian Leopold. *Trio D-dur für Klarinette in A, Horn in D und Fagott*. Edited by K. Janetzky. Adliswil: Edition Kunzelmann, 1982.

Gherardeschi, Giuseppe. "Concertone a violini, viola, clarinette obbligato, corni, violoncello et contrabasso." MS., 1784, Pistoia, Basilica di S. Zeno, Archivio Capitolaro.

Giordani, Tommaso. *A Collection of Favourite Songs Sung by Mrs. Weichsell at Vauxhall*. London: W. Napier, 1772.

———. *The Favourite Cantatas and Songs Sung at Vaux Hall by Mrs. Weichsell*. London: Welcker, 1773.

———. *Three Songs and a Cantata Sung by Mrs. Weichsel at Vaux Hall*. London: Johnston, 1772.

———. *The Favorite Songs and Rondeaus as Sung by Sigra. Toddi and Sigra. Prudom in the Comic Opera of La due contesse*. London: Welcker, 1777.

———. *The Favorite Songs as Sung by Sigra. Sestini in the Comic Opera La marchesa giardiniera*. London: Welcker, 1775.

———. *The Favourite Songs in the Opera Antigono*. London: Welcker, 1774.

———. *The Favorite Songs Sung by Sigra. Pozzi and Sigr. Jermoli in the Comic Opera La vera costanza*. London: Longman & Broderip, 1778.

Glaser, Johann Wendelin. "Ihr müsset gehasset werden von Jedermann," MS., ca. 1760–80, Frankfurt am Main, Stadt und Universität-Bibliothek, Ms. FF.Mus. 221.

Gluck, Christoph Willibald. *Cythère assiégée*. Paris: Des Lauriers, 1789.

———. *Sämtliche Werke*, edited im Auftrage des Staatlichen Instituts für Musikforschung, Berlin, mit Unterstützung der Stadt Hannover. 26 vols. Kassel: Bärenreiter, 1951–97.

Goepfert, Karl Andreas. *Quatuor pour la clarinette, violon, alto et violoncelle*. Bonn: Simrock, ca. 1803.

———. *Trois quatuors pour clarinette, violon, alto et violoncelle*, ouevre 36. Offenbach: André, ca. 1818.

Gossec, François-Joseph. *Messe des morts*. Paris: M. Henry, 1780.

Grétry, André-Ernest-Modeste. *L'amitié à l'épreuve*. Paris: Aux addresses ordinaires de musique, 1772.

———. *Anacréon*. Paris: Frey, 1799.

———. *La caravane du Caire*. Lyon: Castaud, 1784.

———. *Céphale et Procris*. Lyon: Castaud, 1775.

———. *Colinette à la cour*. Paris: Houbaut, 1782.

———. *Collections complètes*. 49 vols. Leipzig: Breitkopf & Härtel, 1884–1936.

————. *Les deux avares*. Paris: P. R. C. Ballard, 1771.

————. *Elisca*. Paris: L'auteur, 1812.

————. *L'embarras des richesses*. Paris: Huguet, 1783.

————. *Guillaume Tell*. Paris: L'auteur, 1794.

————. *Le Huron*. Paris: Beraux, Haubaut, 1768.

————. *Les mariages samnites*. Paris: Houbaut, 1776.

————. *Panurge dan l'île des lanternes*. Lyon: Castaud, 1785.

————. *Zémire et Azor*. Paris: Houbaut, 1772.

Haydn, Franz Joseph. *"Bläserdivertimenti" und "Scherzandi."* Ed. S. Gerlach, H. Walter, and M. Ohmiya. Joseph Haydn Werke, Reihe 8, band 2. Munich: G. Henle, 1991.

————. *Divertimento in C für 2 Klarinetten, 2 Hörner*. Ed. H. C. Robbins Landon. Vienna: Doblinger, 1959.

————. *Die Schöpfung/The Creation*. Edited by A. Peter Brown. Oxford: Oxford University Press, 1995.

————. *Werke*. 79 vols. Munich: G. Henle, 1958–.

Haydn, Michael. "Divertimento." MS., 4 August 1764. Budapest: Országos Széchényi Könyvtár, Mus. ms. II.84.

————. *Divertimento in D*. Edited by L. Kalmár. Budapest: Zenemúkiadó Vállalat, 1965.

Heine, S. Frederic. *Sonata*. Edited by L. Merriman. San Antonio: Southern, 1969.

Hoffmeister, Johann Anton. *Zwei Quartette Klarinette, Violine, Viola & Violoncello*. Edited by W. Höckner. Hamburg: N. Simrock, 1964.

————. *Sonata for Clarinet and Piano*. London: Musica Rara, 1970.

Hook, James. *Concerto for Clarinet and Orchestra*. Edited by J. Brymer. London: Josef Weinberger, 1983.

Hummel, Johann Nepomuk. *Quartet for Clarinet and Strings*. Edited by K. Janetsky. London: Musica Rara, 1958.

Isouard, Nicolas. *Les Confidences*. Paris: Cherubini, Méhul, Kreutzer, Rode, N. Isouard, et Boieldieu, 1803.

————. *Joconde*. Paris: Bochsa, 1814.

————. *Lulli et Quinault*. Paris: Bochsa, 1812.

————. *Les rendez-vous bourgeois*. Paris: Cherubini, Méhul, Kreutzer, Rode, N. Isouard, et Boieldieu, 1807.

Jackson, William. *The Lord of the Manor*. London: J. Preston, 1781.

Kichler [Kuchler], Johann. *Six quatuors concertantes pour une clarinette, violin, alto, fagotto ou violoncello*. Paris: Aux addresses ordinaires de musique, 1774.

Krommer, Franz. *Quintuor pour clarinette, violin, deux altos et violoncelle, oeuvre 95*. Offenbach: Jean André, [ca. 1819].

La Borde, Jean-Benjamin de. *Amphion: ballet en un acte*. Paris: Aux addresses ordinaires de musique, 1767.

————. *Annette et Lubin*. Paris: Le Marchand, 1762.

————. *Annette et Lubin* [orchestral parts]. Paris: Moria, 1762.

————. *Gilles, garçon peintre, z'amoureux-t-et rival*. Paris: Sieber, 1765.

————. *Ismène et Isménias*. Paris: Le Marchand, 1771.

Lefèvre, Jean-Xavier. *Trois grandes sonates pour clarinette et basse, 1793*, facsimile ed. edited by J. Jeltsch. Courlay: J. M. Fuzeau, 1998.

Mahon, John. *Clarinet Concerto no. 2*. Edited by E. Thomas. London: Novello, 1989.

————. *Second Concerto for the Clarinett*. London: J. Bland, [ca. 1790]. Vienna: Österreichische Nationalbibliothek, Mus. M.S. 16781.

Michl, Josef. "Concerto." MS., Österreichische Nationalbibliothek, Vienna, Mus. 5856.

Mozart, Wolfgang Amadeus. *Concerto for Clarinet or Basset Clarinet in A.* Edited by A. Hacker. London: Schott, 1974.

————. *Concerto K 622: Edition for Basset Clarinet in A and Clarinet in A.* Edited by P. Weston. Vienna: Universal Edition, 1997.

————. *Grande sonate pour le piano-forte avec accompage d'un clarinette ou violon oblige.* Vienna: Artaria, 1808.

————. *Neue Ausgabe sämtlicher Werke,* 78 vols. Kassel: Bärenreiter, 1978–.

————. *Trio pour clavecin, ou forte-piano, avec accompagnement de clarinette ou violon, et viola composé par Mr Mozart, oeuvre 14me.* Offenbach: J. Andre, 1793.

————. *Wolfgang Amadeus Mozart's kritisch durchgesehene Gesamtausgabe* (Leipzig: Breitkopf & Härtel, 1877–).

Müller, Iwan. *Premier quatuor pour clarinette, violon, alto et violoncelle.* Offenbach: André, [ca. 1818].

Paer, Ferdinando. "L'agnese." MS., 1808, New York Public Library, Mus. Res. Paër *MSI.

————. "L'intrigo amoroso." MS., 1795, New York Public Library, Mus. Res. * MSI.

————. "Sargino." MS., 1803, New York Public Library, Paër *MSI.

Paisiello, Giovanni. *Le barbier de Seville.* Paris: Baillon, 1784.

————. "Il barbier di Siviglia: opera buffa in quatro atti." MS., 2 vols., 1782, Claremont, Honnold Library, Seymour Fol M1500.P3 B37x.

————. "Elfrida." MS., 1792, New York, New York Public Library, Mus. Res. *MSI.

————. *L'infante de Zamora.* Paris: Leduc, 1781.

————. *Le marquis Tulipano.* Paris: Imbault, [1789?].

————. "La serva padrona." MS., 1781, New York, New York Public Library, Mus. Res. *MSI.

————. "Nina, la pazza per amore." MS., 1789, New York, New York Public Library, Mus. Res. *MSI.

————. *La Passione di Gesù Cristo.* Paris, 1783; facsimile ed., New York: Garland, 1987.

————. *Le roi Théodore à Venise.* Paris: Hughet, 1787.

————. *Serenata in do maggiore per otto strumenti* [adapted from "Elvira," 1794]. Edited by G. C. Ballola. Milan: Edizioni Suvini Zerboni, 1985.

————. "I zingari in Fiera." MS. (Rome: Gaetano Rosati), 1789, Claremont, Honnold Library, Seymour Fol M1500.P3 B.

Palese, Pascotino. *Tre duetti per flauto e clarinetto.* Milan: Ricordi, [ca. 1823].

Piccinni, Niccolò. *Roland.* Paris: L'auteur, 1778.

Pichl, Wenzel. *Three Quartetto's for a Clarinet, Violin, Tenor and Violoncello.* London: Longman and Broderip, [ca. 1795].

Pleyel, Ignace. *Clarinet Concerto.* Edited by G. Dobrée. London: Musica Rara, 1968.

Pokorny, Franz Xaver. *Konzert B-dur für Klarinette.* Wiesbaden: Breitkopf & Härtel, 1958.

————. *Konzert Es-dur für Klarinette.* Wiesbaden: Breitkopf & Härtel, 1958.

[Procksch], Gaspard. *VIIIe. recueil contenant 38 airs en duo pour deux clarinettes ou deux cors de chasse.* Paris: Bignon, [ca. 1776].

Rameau, Jean-Phillipe. *Les Boréades (1764): tragédie lyrique,* facsimile ed. Paris: Stil, 1982.

Recent Researches in the Music of the Classica Era. Middleton, Wisc.: A-R Editions, 1975–.

Reicha, Antoine. *Quintet in B♭ for Clarinet and String Quartet*. Edited by K. Janetzky. London: Musica Rara, 1962.

Reichardt, Johann Friedrich. *Der Geisterinsel*. New York: Garland, 1986.

Riemann, Hugo, ed. *Mannheim Symphonists: A Collection of Twenty-Four Orchestral Works*. 2 vols. New York: Broude Brothers, 1956.

———. *Symphonien der pfaelzbayerischen Schule (Mannheimer Symphoniker)*. Jahrgang III, no. 1, vol. 4 of *Denkmäler der Tonkunst in Bayern*. Braunschweig: H. Litolff's Verlag, 1902.

Ries, Ferdinand. *Sonata for Clarinet or Violin and Piano*. Edited by W. Lebermann. Mainz: Schott, 1967.

———. *Trio, op. 28, for Clarinet, Cello, and Piano*. London, 1969.

Roeser, Valentin. *Premier recueil d'airs d'opera comique aranges pour deux clarinettes*. Paris: Aux addresses ordinaires de musique, [ca. 1781].

Romberg, Andreas. *Quintetto per il clarinetto, violino, due viole et violoncello op. 57*. Leipzig: C. F. Peters, [ca. 1818].

Rossini, Gioacchino. *Tancrède*. Paris: Troupenas, [ca. 1827].

———. *Tancredi*. Edited by Philip Gossett. Vol. 10 of *Edizione critica delle opere di Gioacchino Rossini*. Pesaro: Fondazione Rossini, 1984.

———. *Variations for Clarinet and Piano*. Edited by M. Lurie. Los Angeles: Artransa Music, 1967.

Rudolph, Archduke. *Sonata for clarinet and piano*. Edited by H. Voxman. London: Musica Rara, 1973.

Sacchini, Antonio. *Dardanus*. Paris: L'auteur, 1784.

———. *L'Olympiade*. Paris: Mr. D'Enouville, [1777].

Salieri, Antonio. *La cifra*. MS., 1789, autograph.

———. *Tarare: Opera en cinq actes avec un prologue*. Edited by R. Angermüller. 2 vols. Paris: Imbault, 1787; Munich: G. Henle Verlag, 1978.

Sarti, Giuseppe. "Concertone à per più strumenti obbligati." MS., Conservatorio Statale di Musica Luigi Cherubini, Florence.

———. *Les noces de Dorine*. Paris: Sieber, [ca. 1789].

Sciroli, Gregorio. *Sonata for Clarinet (Flute, Oboe) and Basso Continuo, B♭ major*. Edited by N. Delius. Mainz, 1990.

Sebastiani, Ferdinando. "Canto religioso per clarinetto e piano forte." MS., 1845.

Shield, William. *Robin Hood, or Sherwood Forest*. London: G. Goulding, [ca. 1800].

———. *Rosina*. Edited by J. Drummond. Musica Britannica, vol. 72. London: Stainer & Bell, 1998.

Simon, Eric, ed. *Masterworks for Clarinet and Piano*. New York: G. Schirmer, 1951.

Spohr, Louis. *Concerto no. 1, opus 26*. Boston: Cundy-Bettoney, n.d.

———. *Concerto no. 2, opus 57*. Edited by F. Demnitz. Leipzig, 1882.

———. *Concerto no. 3 in F Minor for Clarinet and Piano*. Edited by S. Drucker. New York: International, 1965.

Spontini, Gasparo. *Fernand Cortez*. Paris, 1817, 2d version; New York: Garland, 1980.

———. *Milton*. Paris: Erard, [ca. 1804].

Stadler, Anton. *Trois caprices pour la clarinette seule*. Vienna: Au magasin de l'imprimerie chimique, [ca. 1808].

———. *Trois fantaisies ou potpourris pour clarinette seule*. Vienna: Jean Traeg, [ca. 1809].

———. *Six duettinos progressives pour deux clarinettes*. Vienna: Magasin de l'imprimerie chimique, [ca. 1808].

————. *Variations sur differents themas favorites pour la clarinette seule.* Vienna: J. Cappi, [ca. 1810].

Stamitz, Carl. *Concerto no. 3.* Edited by S. Drucker. New York: International, 1969.

————. *Concerto in E♭ for Clarinet and Piano.* Edited by A. H. Christmann. New York: G. Schirmer, 1968.

————. *Klarinetten-Konzert Nr. 3.* Edited by J. Wojciechowski. New York: C. F. Peters, 1957.

————. *Konzert Es-dur für Klarinette und Orchester.* Edited by J. Wojciechowski. Hamburg: H. Sikorski, 1953.

————. *Konzert F-dur für Klarinette und Orchester.* Edited by G. Balássa and O. Nagy. Budapest: Editio Musica, 1970.

————. *Konzert für Klarinette in B und Orchester (Es-Dur) (Darmstädter Konzert).* Edited by H. Boese. Leipzig: VEB Friedrich Hofmeister, 1956.

————. *Six quatuor a une clarinette violon alto et basse.* Paris: Sieber, 1773.

Stamitz, Johann. *Concerto in B-flat Major for Clarinet and Strings.* Edited by J. Gradenwitz. New York: MCA Music, 1953.

————. *Konzert für Klarinette.* Edited by W. Lebermann. Partitur and Klavierauszug. Mainz: B. Schott's Söhne, 1967.

Storace, Stephen. *La cameriera astuta.* London, [ca. 1793].

————. *No Song, No Supper.* Edited by R. Fiske. Musica Brittanica, vol. 16. London: Stainer & Bell, 1959.

Struck, Paul. *Quatuor pour clarinette, violon (ou deux violins), alto et violoncelle.* Offenbach: André, [ca. 1795].

The Symphony, 1720–1840: A Comprehensive Collection of Full Scores in Sixty Volumes. Edited by Barry S. Brook and Barbara B. Heyman. New York: Garland, 1979–85.

Tausch, Franz. *Concerto no. 3 in E Flat.* Edited by P. Clinch. Nedlands, 1974.

————. *Concerto for Clarinet and Orchestra: No. 3 in E flat.* Edited by P. Clinch. London, 1979.

————. *Concerto pour la clarinette* [ca. 1815]. Berlin, Staatsbibliothek, MS., Mus. ms. 30077.

————. *Konzert Es-dur für Klarinette und Orchester.* Edited by G. Balássa. Budapest, 1978.

Vanderhagen, Amand. *Air de danse de Chimène, opera de Sacchini, varié pour la clarinette.* Paris: Imbault, 1807–11.

————. *La naissance du roi de Rome: symphonie militaire à grand orchestre.* Paris: Imbault, 1811–12.

Vanhal [Wanhal], Johann Baptist. *Concerto in C Major for Clarinet and Orchestra.* Edited by G. Balássa and M. Berlász. London: Boosey & Hawkes, 1972.

————. *Deux trios a clarinetto, violino et violoncello.* London: Bland, [ca. 1785].

————. *Sei trios per violino clarinetto e basso, op. 20.* Paris: Le Duc, [ca. 1781].

————. *Sonata for Clarinet (Violin, Flute, or Oboe) and Piano.* Edited by B. Tuthill. New York, 1948.

————. *Sonata No. 2 for Clarinet and Piano.* Edited by L. Merriman. San Antonio: Southern, 1968.

————. *Sonate Es-Dur für Klarinette in B und Klavier.* Edited by D. Stofer. Mainz: B. Schott's Söhne, 1971.

Vento, Mattia. *The Favorite Songs in the Opera Demofoonte.* London: R. Bremner, [ca. 1765].

————. *The Favourite Songs in the Opera Sofonisba.* London: R. Bremner, [ca. 1766].

————. *The Favourite Songs in the Opera La vestale*. London: R. Bremner, 1776.

————. "Sofonisba." Autograph MS., 1766, Library of Congress, M1500 V46285.

Wagenseil, Georg Christoph. *Sonata per Clarinetto, Violino e Basso Continuo*. Edited by R. Scholz. Vienna: Doblinger, 1977.

Weber, Carl Maria von. *Concertino*. Edited by G. Haußwald. Wiesbaden: Breitkopf & Härtel, 1974.

————. *Concerto No. 1 in F Minor*. Edited by P. Weston. Corby, Northants: Fentone Music, 1987.

————. *Concerto No. 2 in E-flat, opus 74*. Edited by R. Kell. New York: International, 1958.

————. *Der Freischütz*. New York: Dover, 1977.

————. *Variations, op. 33 for Clarinet and Piano*. Edited by S. Drucker. New York: International, 1960.

Winter, Peter von. *Concertino Es-dur für Klarinette, Violoncello und Orchester*. Edited by J. Michaels. Hamburg: H. Sikorski, 1966.

[Yost], Michel, and [Johann Christoph] Vogel. *Six quatuors concertants pour clarinette, violon, alto et basse, 5me livre de quatuor*. Paris: Sieber, [ca. 1789].

PRIMARY AND SECONDARY SOURCES

Abraham. *Principes de clarinette suivis de pas redoubles et de marches les plus a la mode*. Paris: Frère, [ca. 1782].

Adelson, Robert. "Reading between the (Ledger) Lines: Performing Mozart's Music for the Basset Clarinet." *Performance Practice Review* 10, no. 2 (fall 1997): 137–91.

Adlung, Jacob. *Anleitung zu der Musikalischen Gelahrtheit*. 2 vols. Erfurt: J. D. Jungicol, 1758; facsimile ed., Kassel: Bärenreiter, 1953.

Albrechtsberger, Johann Georg. *Gründliche Anweisung der Composition . . . und mit einem Anhange: Von der Beschaffenheit und Anwendung aller jetzt üblichen Musikalischen Instrumente*. Leipzig: J. G. I. Breitkopf, 1790.

Almanach Musical. Paris, 1775–83; reprint, Geneva: Minkoff.

Amadeus, His Music, and the Instruments of Eighteenth-Century Vienna: An Exhibition Presented by the Shrine to Music Museum (Vermillion, S.D.: Shrine to Music Museum, 1990).

Anderson, Gillian B. *Music in New York during the American Revolution: An Inventory of Musical References in Rivington's New York Gazette*. Boston: Music Library Association, 1987.

Andries, Jean Jacques. *Aperçu théorique de tous les instruments de musique, actuellement en usage*. Gand: Gevaert, 1856.

Antolini, Francesco. *La retta maniera di scrivere per il clarinetto ed altri istromenti da fiato*. Milan: C. Buccinelli, 1813.

"Anzeige." In "Intelligenz-Blatt." *AMZ* 27 (June 1825): 28.

"BSO Collection Reinstalled." *Newsletter of the American Musical Instrument Society* 20 (1991): 1, 6–7.

Bacci, Alessio. "Michel Yost, il creatore della scuola clarinettistica francese." *Tetraktýs* 1 (1997): 49–63.

Backofen, Johann Georg Heinrich. *Anweisung zur Clarinette mit besonderer Hinsicht auf die in neuern Zeiten diesem Instrument beigefügten Klappen nebst einer kurzen Abhandlung über das Basset-Horn*. Leipzig: Breitkopf & Härtel, 1824.

————. *Anweisung zur Clarinette nebst einer kurzen Abhandlung über das Basset-Horn*. Leipzig: Breitkopf & Härtel, [ca. 1803]; reprint, Celle: Moeck, 1986.

Baermann, Carl. *Vollständige Clarinett Schule von dem ersten Anfange bis zur höchsten Ausbildung des Virtuosen*. 2 vols. Offenbach: André, 1864–75.

Bainbridge, William. *Observations on the Cause of Imperfections in Wind Instruments.* London: The author, 1823.

Baines, Anthony. *The Bate Collection of Historical Wind Instruments: Catalogue of the Instruments.* Oxford: University of Oxford, 1976.

———. *European and American Musical Instruments.* 3d ed. New York: Viking Press, 1966.

———. *Woodwind Instruments and Their History.* London: Faber, 1967.

Balássa, György. "Az elsó bécsi klasszikus iskola klarinétversenyei (1770–1810)." *Magyar Zene* 18 (1977): 48–74, 134–83.

——— . "Az elsó bécsi klasszikus iskola zongora-klarinét szonárái." *Magyar Zene* 17 (1976): 12–41.

Bartenstein, Hans. "Die frühen Instrumentationslehren bis zu Berlioz." *Archive für Musikwissenschaft* 28, no. 2 (1971): 97–118.

Batta, András. *Opera: Composers, Works, Performers.* Cologne: Könermann, 2000.

Becker, Heinz. *History of Instrumentation.* Cologne: A. Volk, 1964.

———, ed. *Klarinetten-Duette aus der Frühzeit des Instrumentes.* Wiesbaden: Breitkopf & Härtel, 1954.

———, ed. *Klarinetten-Konzerte des 18. Jahrhunderts.* Vol. 41 of *Das Erbe Deutscher Musik.* Wiesbaden: Breitkopf & Härtel, 1957.

Bellini, Fermo. *Teoriche musicale su gli istromenti e sull'istrumentazione.* Milan: G. Ricordi, 1844.

Benton, Rita. *Ignace Pleyel: A Thematic Catalogue of His Compositions.* Stuyvesant, N.Y.: Pendragon Press, 1977.

Bereths, Gustav. *Die Musikpflege am kurtrierischen Hofe zu Koblenz-Ehrenbreitstein.* Mainz: B. Schott's Söhne, 1964.

Berg, Lorents Nicolai. *Den første Prøve for Begyndere udi Instrumental-Kunsten.* Kristiansand: A. Swane, 1782.

"Berichtigungen und Zusätze zum den Musikalischen Almanachen auf die Jahre 1782, 1783, 1784." *Musikalische Korrespondenz der teutschen Filarmonischen Gesellschaft für Jahr 1791,* vol. 6 (1791), 41–2.

Berlioz, Hector. *Grand traité d'instrumentation et d'orchestration moderne.* Paris: Schonenberger, 1843; reprint, Paris: H. Lemoine, 1952.

Bernardini, Alfredo. "Woodwind Makers in Venice, 1790–1900." *JAMIS* 15 (1989): 52–73.

Berr, Frédéric. *Méthode complète de clarinette,* Paris: J. Meissonnier, [ca. 1836].

———. *Traité complet de la clarinette à quatorze clefs.* Paris: E. Duverger, 1836.

Bessaraboff, Nicholas. *Ancient European Musical Instruments: An Organological Study of the Musical Instruments in the Leslie Lindsey Mason Collection at the Museum of Fine Arts, Boston.* New York: October House, 1941.

Beusker, Gerd. *Die Münsterische Dom-, Hof- und Musikkapelle, 1650–1802.* Kassel: Bärenreiter, 1978.

Biber, Walter. "Aus der Geschichte der Blasmusik in der Schweiz." In *Bericht über die Erste Internationale Fachtagung zur Erforschung der Blasmusik Graz, 1974,* edited by W. Suppan and E. Brixel, 127–43. Tutzing: H. Schneider, 1974.

Birsak, Kurt. *Die Holzblasinstrumente im Salzburger Museum Carolino Augusteum: Verzeichnis und Entwicklungsgeschichten Unterschungen.* Salzburg: Salzburger Museum Carolino Augusteum, 1973.

———. *Die Klarinette: Eine Kulturgeschichte.* Buchloe: Obermayer, 1992. Translated by G. Schamberger under the title *The Clarinet: A Cultural History.* Buchloe: Obermayer, 1994.

————. "Salzburg, Mozart und die Klarinette." *Mitteilungen der Internationalen Stiftung Mozarteum* 33 (1985): 40–47. Translated by G. Schamberg under the title "Salzburg, Mozart, and the Clarinet." *Clarinet* 13 (1985): 26–31.

Birsak, Kurt, and Manfred König. *Das grosse Salzburger Blasmusik Buch.* Vienna: Brandstätter, 1983.

Bizzi, Guido. *La collezione di strumenti musicali del Museo Teatrale alla Scala: studio, restauro e restituzione.* Milan: Silvano Editoriale, 1991.

Blasius, Mathieu-Frédéric. *Nouvelle méthode de clarinette.* Paris: Porthaux, [ca. 1796]; reprint, Geneva: Minkoff, 1972.

Blatt, Franz Thaddäus. *Méthode complette de clarinette.* Mainz: Les fils de B. Schott, [ca. 1827–28].

Blazin, Dwight. "The Two Versions of Mozart's Divertimento K. 113." *Music and Letters* 73 (1992): 32–47.

Bochsa, Charles. *Méthode instructive pour la clarinette.* Paris: Imbault, [ca. 1808].

Boese, Helmut. *Die Klarinette als Solo Instrument in der Mannheimer Schule.* Dresden: Dittert, 1940. Translated by Kenneth Kawashima under the title "The Clarinet as a Solo-Instrument in the Music of the Mannheim School." D.M.A. diss., Peabody Conservatory of Music, 1965.

Bonanni [Buonani], Filippo. *Descrizione degl'Istromenti Armonico.* Rome: V. Monaldini, 1776.

Borders, James M. *European and American Wind and Percussion Instruments: Catalogue of the Stearns Collection of Musical Instruments, University of Michigan.* Ann Arbor: University of Michigan Press, 1988.

Boydell, Brian. *Rotunda Music in Eighteenth-Century Dublin.* Dublin: Irish Academic Press, 1992.

Bragard, Roger, and Ferdinand J. De Hen. *Musical Instruments in Art and History,* translated by B. Hopkins. New York: Viking Press, 1968.

Brixel, Eugen, Günther Martin, and Gottfried Pils. *Das ist Oesterreichs Militär Musik: Von "Turkischen Musik" zu den Philharmonischen in Uniform.* Graz: Kaleidoskop, 1982.

Brockhaus, F. A., ed. *Conversations-Lexikon; oder, Encyclopädisches Handwörterbuch für gebildete Stände.* 3d ed. 10 vols. Leipzig: F. A. Brockhaus, 1814–19.

Bromberger, E. Douglas. "The Conservatory and the Piano." In *Piano Roles: Three Hundred Years of Life with the Piano,* edited by J. Parakilas, 152–55. New Haven: Yale University Press, 1999.

Brook, Barry S. *La symphonie française dans la seconde moitié XVIIIe siècle.* 3 vols. Paris: Publications de L'Institut de Musicologie de l'Université de Paris, 1962.

————, ed. *The Breitkopf Thematic Catalogue: The Six Parts and Sixteen Supplements, 1762–1787.* New York: Dover, 1966.

Brown, A. Peter. *Performing Haydn's "The Creation": Reconstructing the Earliest Renditions.* Bloomington: Indiana University Press, 1986.

Brown, Clive. *Louis Spohr: A Critical Biography.* Cambridge: Cambridge University Press, 1984.

Burney, Charles. *The Present State of Music in Germany, The Netherlands, and United Provinces.* 2d ed. 2 vols. London, 1775; reprint, New York: Broude Brothers, 1969.

————. *A General History of Music from the Earliest Ages to the Present Period.* 2 vols. London, 1789; reprint, New York: Dover, 1957.

————. "Clarinet." In *The Cyclopedia: or Universal Dictionary of Arts, Sciences, and Literature,* edited by A. Rees, vol. 8. London, 1819.

Buteux, Claude François. *Méthode de clarinette d'apres celle composée par Xavier Le Fèvre adoptée par le Conservatoire de Musique augmentée du mécanisme de l'instrument perfectionné par Ivan Muller.* Paris: F. Troupenas, [1836].

Byrne, Maurice. "The Church Band at Swalcliffe." *GSJ* 17 (1964): 89–98.

———. "Cramer, John." *NGDMI*, vol. 1, 512.

Camus, Raoul F. *Military Music of the American Revolution.* Chapel Hill: University of North Carolina Press, 1976.

———. "Military Music of Colonial Boston." In *Music in Colonial Massachusetts 1630–1820 I: Music in Public Places*, 75–103. Boston: Colonial Society of Massachusetts, 1980.

Capon, Gaston, and Robert Yve-Plessis. *Paris gallant au dix-huitième siècle; vie privée du prince de Conty, Louis-François de Bourbon (1717–1776).* Paris: J. Schmit, 1907.

Carnaud. *Nouvelle méthode de la clarinette moderne à six et à treize clefs.* Paris: Collinet., 1829.

Carroll, Elizabeth A. "Anton Stadler's Contributions to the Clarinet, Clarinet Playing, and Late Eighteenth-Century Music Pedagogy." Master's thesis, Bowling Green State University, 1986.

Carse, Adam. *The History of Orchestration.* London: Kegan Paul, Trench, Trubner and Co., 1925; reprint, New York: Dover, 1964.

———. *Musical Wind Instruments.* London, 1939; reprint, New York: Da Capo Press, 1965.

———. *The Orchestra in the XVIIIth Century.* Cambridge: W. Heffner & Sons, 1940; reprint, New York: Broude Brothers, 1969.

Carter, Stewart. "The Gütter Family: Wind Instrument Makers and Dealers to the Moravian Brethren in America." *JAMIS* 37 (2001): 48–83.

Castillon, Frédéric Adolphe Maximilian Gustav de. "Clarinette." In *Supplément à l'Encyclopédie, ou Dictionnaire Raisonné des Sciences, des Arts et des Métiers par un Société de Gens de Lettres*, edited by J. B. Robinet, vol. 2, 450–51. 5 vols. Amsterdam: M. M. Rey, 1776–80; facsimile ed., Paris: Au Cercle du livre précieux, 1977.

Catalogue of the Crosby Brown Collection of Musical Instruments of All Nations. 5 vols. New York: Metropolitan Museum of Art, 1901–14.

Catalogue of the Large and Valuable Stock of Music Plates, Sheet Music, Musical Instruments, Material, &c. Being the Entire Stock of the Late George E. Blake. [Philadelphia]: M. Thomas & Sons, 1871.

A Catalogue of Vocal and Instrumental Music, Engraved, Printed and Sold Wholesale and Retail by John Welcker. London: J. Welcker, 1774.

Catalogue of Vocal and Instrumental Music, Printed and Sold by Longman, Lukey and Co. London: Longman, Lukey and Co., 1772.

Catrufo, Gioseffo. *Des voix et des instrumens à cordes à vent et à percussion.* Paris, 1832.

Cerminara, Napoleon. "To B or Not to B." *Clarinet* 1, no. 7 (fall 1951): 19–22.

Cervelli, Luisa. *Antichi strumenti musicali in un moderno museum: Museo Nazionale Strumenti Musicali, Roma.* 2d ed. Rome: Gela Editrice, 1986.

Charlton, David. "Classical Clarinet Technique: Documentary Approaches." *EM* 16 (1988): 396–406.

———. *Grétry and the Growth of Opéra-Comique.* Cambridge: Cambridge University Press, 1986.

———. "Orchestra and Chorus at the Comédie-Italienne (Opéra-Comique),

1755–99." In *Slavonic and Western Music: Essays for Gerald Abraham*, 87–108. Ann Arbor: UMI Research Press, 1985.

———. "Orchestration and Orchestral Practice in Paris, 1789 to 1810." Ph.D. diss., University of Cambridge, 1973.

Chouquet, Gustave. *Le Musée du Conservatoire National de Musique catalog raisonné des instruments de cette collection.* 4 vols. Paris, 1875–1903.

The Clarinet Instructor by Which Playing on That Instrument Is Rendered Easy. London: Longman & Broderip, [ca. 1780].

The Clarinet Preceptor. London: C. Wheatstone, [ca. 1801].

Clinch, Peter. "Clarinet Concerto No. 3 by Franz Tausch (1762–1817)." *Studies in Music* 8 (1974): 17–31.

Collinson, Robert. *Encyclopedias: Their History throughout the Ages.* New York: Hefner, 1966.

Complete Instuctions [sic] for the Clarinet. London: S. A. & P. Thompson, [ca. 1781].

Corrette, Michel. *Méthode pour apprendre aisément à joüer de la flutte traversiere . . . Nouvelle édition, revûe, corigée et augmentée de la Gamme du Haut-bois et de la Clarinette.* Paris: Addresses ordinaires de musique, [ca. 1773]; reprint, Geneva: Minkoff, 1977.

———. *Le parfait maître à chanter: Méthode pour apprendre facilement la musique vocale et instrumentale.* Paris: L'auteur, 1758 ; reprint, Geneva: Minkoff, 1999.

Corry, M. J., K. Van Winkle Keller, and R. M. Keller, eds. *The Performing Arts in Colonial Newspapers, 1690–1783: Text Database and Index.* New York: University Music Editions, 1997 [CD-ROM].

Cotte, Roger. "Blasinstrumente bei freimaurerischen Riten." *Tibia* 2 (1979): 315–17.

Cramer, Carl Friedrich. *Magazin der Musik.* Hamburg, 1783; reprint, Hildesheim: G. Olms, 1971.

Cranmer-Byng, J. L., ed. *An Embassy to China: Being the journal kept by Lord Macartney during his embassy to the Emperor Ch'ien-lung, 1793–1794.* Hamden: Archon, 1963.

Croft-Murray, Edward. "The Wind-Band in England, 1540–1840." In *Music and Civilisation*, 135–63. London: British Museum Publications, 1980.

Croll, Gerhard, and Kurt Birsak. "Anton Stadlers 'Bassettklarinette' und das 'Stadler-Quintett' KV 581." *Oesterreichische Musikzeitschrift* 24, no. 1 (January 1969): 3–11.

Cucuel, Georges. *Études sur un orchestre au XVIIIᵐᵉ siècle.* Paris: Fischbacher, 1913.

———. "Notes sur la Comédie Italienne de 1717 à 1789." *Sammelbände der Internationalen Musikgesellschaft* 15 (1913–14): 154–66.

———. "La question des clarinettes dans l'instrumentation du XVIIIe siècle." *Zeitschrift der Internationallen Musikgesellschaft* 12 (1911): 280–84.

Cudworth, Charles. "John Marsh on the Subscription Concert." *GSJ* 19 (1966): 132–34.

Czerny, Carl. *Practical School of Composition; or, Complete Treatise on the Composition of All Kinds of Music, Both Instrumental and Vocal.* Vol. 3. London: R. Cocks, 1839; reprint, New York: Da Capo Press, 1979.

Dahlström, Fabian. *Bernhard Henrik Crusell: Klarinettisten och hans store instrumentalverk.* Helsingfors: Svenska Litteratursällskapet I Finland, 1976.

Davis, Shelley. "The Orchestra under Clemens Wenzeslaus: Music at a Late Eighteenth-Century Court." *JAMIS* 1 (1975): 86–112.

Dazeley, George. "The Original Text of Mozart's Clarinet Concerto." *Music Review* 9 (1948): 166–72.

Delius, Nikolaus. "Wiederentdeckte italienische Klarinettenmusik." *Tibia* 15, no. 1 (1990): 41–42.

Démar, [Sébastian]. *Nouvelle méthode pour la clarinette.* Orléans: L'Auteur, [ca. 1808].

Deutsch, Otto Erich. *Musikverlags Nummern: Eine Auswahl von 40 datierten Listen 1710–1900.* 2d ed. Berlin: Merseburger, 1961.

Devriès, Anik, and François Lesure. *Dictionnaire des éditeurs de musique français.* 2 vols. Geneva: éditions Minkoff, 1979, 1988.

Dibley, Tom. *Historic Musical Instruments in the Edinburgh University Collection.* Vol. 2, part f, fascicle i: Clarinets. Edinburgh: Edinburgh University Collection of Historic Instruments, 1995.

Dibley, Tom, and Arnold Myers. *The Historic Clarinet: Edinburgh International Festival Exhibition Handbook.* Edinburgh: Edinburgh University Collection of Historic Musical Instruments, 1986.

Diccionario de la lengua Castellana compuesto por la Real Academia Española. Madrid: Joaquin Ibarra, 1780.

Diderot, Denis. "Clarinette." In *Encyclopédie, ou Dictionnaire raisonné des sciences, des arts et des métiers par un société de gens de lettres,* edited by Denis Diderot and Jean Le Rond D'Alembert, vol. 3, 505. 17 vols. Paris: Briassoon, David, Le Breton, 1751–65; facsimile ed., Paris: Au Cercle du livre précieux, 1977.

Diderot, Denis, and Jean Le Rond D'Alembert, eds. *Recueil de planches sur les sciences, les arts libéraux et les arts méchaniques, avec leur explication.* 11 vols. Paris: Braisson, David, Le Breton, 1762–72.

Diemand, Anton. "Anwesenheit des Kaisers Franz I . . . zu Wallerstein I. J. 1764." *Unterhaltungsblatt der Augsburg Postzeitung,* no. 100 (1899), as cited in Diemand, "Josef Haydn und der Wallerstein Hof," *Zeitschrift des historischen Vereins für Schwaben und Neuburg* 44 (1921): 2 n. 3.

Dike, Catherine. *Cane Curiosa: From Gun to Gadget.* Geneva: Les editions de l'amateur, 1983.

Dlabacž, Gottfried Johann. *Allgemeines historisches Künstler-Lexikon für Böhmen und zum Theil auch für Mähren und Schlesien.* Prague: G. Haase, 1815; reprint, Hildesheim: Olms, 1973.

———. "Versuch eines Verzeichnisses der vorzüglichen Tonkünstler in oder aus Böhmen." In *Materialien zur alten und neun Statistik von Böhmen,* edited by J. A. S. von Riegger, vol. 7, 135–61; vol. 12, 227–99. Leipzig: Widtmann, 1787–93.

Domp, Joachim. *Studien zur Geschichte der Musik an Westfällischen Adelshöfen im XVIII. Jahrhundert.* Düsseldorf: H. Krumbiegel, 1934.

Dullat, Günther. *Klarinetten: Grundzüge ihrer Entwicklung.* Frankfurt: E. Bochinsky, 2001.

Du Moutier. "Faiseur d'instrument a vent." In *Dictionnaire portatif des arts et metiers,* edited by P. Macquer, vol. 1, 439–40. 2 vols. Paris: Lacombe, 1766.

Eberhardt, Hans. "Johann Simon Hermstedt, 1778–1846: Seine Bedeutung als Klarinettenvirtuose." *Mitteilungen des Vereins für deutsche Geschichte und altertumskunde in Sondershausen* 10 (1940): 95–143.

Einzeldrucke vor 1800. 14 vols. Kassel: Bärenreiter, 1971–99.

Einzeldrucke vor 1800: Wolfgang Amadeus Mozart Verzeichnis von Erst- und Frühdrucken bis etwa 1800. Kassel: Bärenreiter, 1978.

[Eisel, Johann Phillip]. *Musicus Autodidaktos, oder Der sich selbst Informirende Musicus*. Erfurt: J. M. Funcken, 1738.

Eitner, Robert. *Biographisch-Bibliographisches Quellen-Lexikon der Musiker und Musikgelehrten der christlichen Zeitrechnung bis zur mitte des neunzehnten Jahrhunderts*. 10 vols. Leipzig, 1900–1904; reprint, New York: Musurgia, 1947.

Eley, Christoph Friedrich. *A New Tutor for the Clarinet*. London: Lewis, Houston & Hyde, [ca. 1795].

Eliason, Robert E. *Graves and Company Musical Instrument Makers*. Dearborn, Mich.: Edison Institute, 1975.

———. "Letters to Marsh and Chase from Graves and Company, Musical Instrument Makers." *JAMIS* 4 (1978): 43–53.

Ellsworth, Jane. "Haydn Clarinet Concertos: A Case of Wishful Thinking." *Clarinet* 29, no. 3 (June 2002): 50–53.

Ersch, J. S. and J. G. Gruber, eds. *Allgemeine Encyclopädie der Wissenschaften und Künste*. 167 vols. Leipzig: J. F. Gleditsch, 1818–89.

Estock, Joseph James. "A Biographical Dictionary of Clarinetists Born before 1800." Ph.D. diss., University of Iowa, 1972.

Fahrbach, Joseph. *Neueste Wiener Clarinetten-Schule*. Vienna: A. Diabelli, [ca. 1841].

Fallon, John P. *Marks of London Goldsmiths and Silversmiths, Georgian Period (ca. 1697–1837): A Guide*. New York: Arco, 1972.

Färber, Sigfrid. "Der Fürstlichen Thurn und Taxissche Hofkomponist Theodor von Schacht und seine Opernwerke." In *Studien zur Musikgeschichte der Stadt Regensburg*, vol. 1, edited by H. Beck. Regensburg: G. Bosse, 1979.

Farmer, Henry George. *History of the Royal Artillery Band, 1762–1953*. London: Royal Artillery Institution, 1954.

———. *The Rise and Development of Military Music*. London: W. Reeves, 1913.

Feder, Georg. "Das Autograph von Haydns Divertimento in C-Dur für 2 Klarinetten und 2 Fagotte." *Haydn-Studien* 6, part 2 (November 1988): 156–58.

Fétis, François Joseph. *Biographie universelle des musiciens et bibliographie génerale de la musique*, 8 vols. Brussels: Meline, Cans et Compagnie, 1837. 2d ed., 8 vols., Paris: Firmin Didot Frères, fils et cie., 1860–65.

———. "Correspondance." *Revue musicale* 6, no. 23 (January 1830): 541–42.

———. "De l'execution musicale." *Revue musicale* 5 (1829): 224–28.

———. "Inventions et perfectionnemens d'instrumens: Clarinette de M. Simiot." *Revue musicale* 5, no. 21 (18 December 1829): 515–17.

———. *La musique mise à la portée de tout le mode*. Paris: A. Mesnier, 1830.

———. "Nouvelles de Paris." *Revue musicale* 2, no. 45 (December 1827): 494–95.

Fink, Heinrich. "Anton Stadler in Hannover." *Tibia* 11 (1986): 20, 22–24.

Fiske, Roger. *English Theatre Music in the Eighteenth Century*. 2d ed. London: Oxford University Press, 1980.

Flechsig, Werner. "Ostfälische Musikinstrumentenmacher des 18. und frühen 19. Jahrhunderts." *Braunschweigische Heimat* 48 (1962): 46–9, 89–96, 110–15; 49 (1963), 9–16, 42–48, 83–89, 109–13; 50 (1964), 9–14, 53–59.

Floyd, Samuel Russell. "The Clarinet Music of Johann Baptist Vanhal." Ph.D. diss., Michigan State University, 1988.

Follan, James E. "The Historic Clarinet: The Edinburgh University Collection." *Clarinet* 14 (1987): 20–25.

Forkel, Johann Nicolaus. *Musikalischer Almanach für Deutschland auf das Jahr 1782*. Leipzig, 1781; reprint, Hildesheim: G. Olms, 1974.

Francoeur, Louis-Benjamin. "Rapport fait par M. Francoeur, au nom du Comité des arts mécaniques, sur une nouvelle clarinette présentée à la Société par M. Janssen, rue l'Évêque, no. 14, butte des Moulines, à Paris." *Bulletin de la Société d'encouragement pour l'industrie nationale* 212 (1822): 40–45.

Francoeur, Louis-Joseph. *Diapason général de tous les instrumens à vent.* Paris: Le Marchand, 1772; reprint, Geneva: Minkoff, 1972.

François-Sappey, Brigitte. "Le personnel de la Musique Royale de l'avènement de Louis XVI à la chute de la monarchie (1774–1792)." *Recherches* 26 (1988–90): 133–72.

Friis, Niels. *Det Kongelige Kapel fem Aarhundreder ved Hoffet, paa Teatret og i Koncertsalen.* Copenhagen: P. Haase & Søns, 1948.

Fröhlich, Joseph. *Vollständige Theoretisch-pracktische Musikschule für alle beym Orchester gebräuliche wichtigen Instrumente.* Bonn: Simrock, 1810–11.

Fueter, Eduard. "Die Notierung der Klarinetten in der älteren französischen Oper." *Schweizerische Musikzeitung und Sängerblatt* 65, no. 13 (1925): 169–70.

Gambaro, [Jean-Baptiste]. *Méthode facile de clarinette à six clefs.* Paris: Gambaro, [1820].

Gandini, Alessandro. *Cronistoria dei Teatri di Modena dal 1539 al 1871.* Modena: Tipografia Sociale, 1873; reprint, Bologna: Forni Editori, 1969.

Gardeton, César. *Annales de la musique ou almanach musical de Paris.* Paris, 1820; reprint, Geneva: Minkoff, 1978.

Garsault, François Alexandre Pierre de. *Notionaire, ou Mémorial raisonné.* Paris: G. Desprez, 1761.

Gérard, Bernadette. "Inventaire alphabétique des documents répertoriés relatifs aux musiciens parisiens conservès aux archives de Paris." *Recherches* 13 (1973): 181–212.

Gerber, Ernst Ludwig. *Historisch-Biographisches Lexikon der Tonkünstler.* Leipzig: J. G. I. Breitkopf, 1790–92; reprint, Graz: Akademische Druck- u. Verlagsanstalt, 1977.

———. *Neues Historisch-Biographisches Lexikon der Tonkünstler.* Leipzig: A. Kühnel, 1812–14; reprint, Graz: Akademische Druck- u. Verlagsanstalt, 1966.

Gervasoni, Carlo. *La scuola della musica.* Piacenza: N. Orcesi, 1800; reprint, Bologna: Forni, 1969.

Gétreau, Florence. *Aux origines du Musée de la Musique: Les collections instrumentales du Conservatoire de Paris, 1793–1993.* Paris: Editions Klincksieck, 1996.

Gianelli, Pietro. *Grammatica ragionata della musica.* 2d ed. Milan: A. Santini, 1820.

Giannini, Tula. "A French Dynasty of Master Woodwind Makers Revealed: Bizey, Prudent and Porthaux, Their Workshop in Paris, Rue Dauphine, St. André des arts, ca. 1745–1812, New Archival Documents." *NAMIS* 27, no. 1 (1998): 7–10.

———. *Great Flute Makers of France: The Lot and Godfroy Families, 1650–1900.* London: Tony Bingham, 1993.

Gillespie, James E., Jr. *The Reed Trio: An Annotated Bibliography of Original Published Works.* Detroit: Information Coordinators, 1971.

Girdham, Jane. *English Opera in Late Eighteenth-Century London: Stephen Storace at Drury Lane.* Oxford: Oxford University Press, 1997.

Gossec, François-Joseph. "Notice sur l'introduction des cors, des clarinettes et des trombones dans les orchestres français; extraite des manuscripts autographes de Gossec." *Revue musicale* 5, no. 10 (13 April 1829): 217–23.

Göthel, Folker. *Thematisch-bibliographisches Verzeichnis der Werken von Louis Spohr.* Tutzing: H. Schneider, 1981.

Gottesman, Rita S. *The Arts and Crafts in New York, 1726–1776*. New York: New-York Historical Society, 1936; reprint, New York: Da Capo Press, 1970.

Gradenwitz, Peter. "The Beginnings of Clarinet Literature." *Music and Letters* 17 (1936): 145–50.

Green, Robert A. *The Hurdy-Gurdy in Eighteenth-Century France*. Bloomington: Indiana University Press, 1995.

Grenser, Heinrich. "Erklärung an Tromlitz über die Flöten." *AMZ* 2 (1799), between 454 and 455 ; "Intelligenz-Blatt" 11 (March 1800).

Grétry, André-Ernest-Modeste. *Mémoires, ou Essai sur la musique*. Paris: L'auteur, 1789; reprint, New York: Da Capo Press, 1971.

Gruhn, Wilfried, "Zweibrücken." In Hubert Unverricht, *Musik und Musiker am Mittelrhein: Ein biographisches, orts- und landesgeschichtliches Nachschlagewerk*, vol. 1, 171–83. Mainz: B. Schott's Söhne, 1974.

Guarinoni, Eugenio De'. *Gli strumenti musicali nel museo del Conservatorio di Milano*. Milano: U. Hoepli, 1908.

Guion, David. "The Instrumentation of Operas Published in France in the Eighteenth Century." *Journal of Musicological Research* 4 (1982): 115–41.

Gutteridge, William. "Clarionets," British Patent, No. 4398, 18 March 1824; reprint, London: G. E. Eyre and W. Spottiswoode, 1857.

———. *Introduction to the Art of Playing on Gutteridge's New Patent Clarinet*. London: Clementi, 1824.

Habla, Bernhard. *Besetzung und Instrumentation des Blasorchesters seit der Erfindung der Ventile für Blechblasinstrumente bis zum zweiten Weltkrieg in Österreich und Deutschland*. Tutzing: Hans Schneider, 1990.

Hacker, Alan. "Mozart and the Basset Clarinet." *Musical Times* 110 (1969): 359–62.

Haine, Malou. *Musica: Musical Instruments in Belgian Collections*. Liège: Mardaga, 1989.

Haine, Malou, and Nicolas Meeùs, eds. *Instruments du musique anciens à Bruxelles et en Wallonie*. Brussels: Centre culturel de la Communauté française Wallonie-Bruxelles, 1985.

Halfpenny, Eric. "Castilon on the Clarinet." *Music and Letters* 35 (1954): 332–38.

———. "The Christ Church Trophies." *GSJ* 28 (1975): 81–85.

———. "Clarinet Mouthpieces." MS, n.d., GB-London-Waterhouse Collection.

———. "Early English Clarinets." *GSJ* 18 (1965): 42–56.

———. "The French Hautboy: A Technical Survey, Part II." *GSJ* 8 (1956): 50–59.

Halle, Johann Samuel. *Werkstätte der heutigen Künste, oder die neue Kunsthistorie*. 6 vols. Brandenburg and Leipzig: J. W. Halle and J. S. Halle, 1761–79.

Hamann, Heinz-Wolfgang. "Eine interessante Aufführungsanweisung Mozarts." *DMf* 10, no. 1 (1957): 139–40.

Hamilton, Mary Neal. *Music in Eighteenth Century Spain*. Urbana, 1937; reprint, New York: Da Capo Press, 1971.

Hardesty, Kathleen. *The Supplément to the Encylopédie*. The Hague: M. Nijhoff, 1977.

Hardy, Joseph. *Rudolf Kreutzer: Sa jeunesse à Versailles, 1766–1789*. Paris: Fischbacher, 1910.

Hárich, János II. "Documents from the Esterházy Archives in Eisenstadt and Forchtenstein." *Haydn Yearbook* 19 (1994): 1–359.

Harlow, Martin. "The Chamber Music with Clarinet of Ferdinand Ries." *Clarinet* 27, no. 3 (June 2000): 50–54.

Haynes, Bruce. *The Eloquent Oboe: A History of the Hautboy, 1640–1760*. Oxford: Oxford University Press, 2001.

————. "Pitch Standards in the Baroque and Classical Periods." Ph.D. diss., Université de Montréal, 1995.

Heck, Thomas F. "Ricordi Plate Numbers in the Earlier Nineteenth Century: A Chronological Survey." *Current Musicology* 10 (1970): 117–24.

Heckel, Wilhelm. "Holz und Metall als Baustoff für Musikinstrumente." *Zeitschrift für Instrumentenbau* 53, no. 18 (15 June 1933), 289.

Helistö, Paavo. *Klaneetti: Suomalaisen kansanklarinetin vaiheita.* Kaustinen: Kansanmusiikki-instituutti, 1988.

Hellier, Samuel. "A Catalogue of Musicall Instruments," edited by Eric Halfpenny. *GSJ* 18 (1965): 5–6.

Hellyer, Roger. "'Fidelio' für neunstimmige Harmonie." *Music and Letters* 53, no. 3 (July 1972): 242–53.

————. "Harmoniemusik and Other Works for Multiple Wind Instruments." In *The Mozart Compendium*, edited by H. C. Robbins Landon, 283–87. New York: Schirmer Books, 1990.

————. "The Harmoniemusik of the Moravian Communities in America." *Fontes Artis Musicae* 17, no. 2 (April–June 1980): 95–108.

————. "'Harmoniemusik': Music for Small Wind Band in the Late Eighteenth and Early Nineteenth Centuries." Ph.D. diss., Oxford University, 1973.

————. "Some Documents Relating to Viennese Wind-Instrument Purchases." *GSJ* 28 (1975): 50–59.

————. "The Transcriptions for *Harmonie* of *Die Entführung aus dem Serail.*" *Proceedings of the Royal Musical Association* 102 (1975–76): 53–66.

————. "The Wind Ensembles of the Esterházy Princes, 1761–1813." *Haydn Yearbook* 15 (1984): 5–92.

————. "Wind Instruments with Strings and Piano." In *The Mozart Compendium*, edited by H. C. Robbins Landon, 287–89. New York: Schirmer Books, 1990.

Héricart de Thury, Louis-Etienne-François. *Rapport du jury d'admission des produits de l'industrie française.* [Paris]: Pélicier, 1824.

Hernes, Asbjørn. *Impuls og tradisjon i norsk musikk, 1500–1800.* Oslo: J. Dybwad, 1952.

Hess, Ernst. "Die Ursprüngliche Gestalt des Klarinettenkonzertes KV 622." *Mozart Jahrbuch* 15 (1967): 13–30.

Heyde, Herbert. "Blasinstrumente und Bläser der Dresdner Hofkapelle in der Zeit des Fux-Schülers Johann Dismas Zelenka (1710–1745)." In *Johann Joseph Fux und die Barocke Bläsertradition Kongreßbericht Graz 1985*, 39–65. Tutzing, 1987.

————. "Über Rohrblattinstrumente des Musikinstrumentenmuseums der Karl-Marx-Universität Leipzig." *Tibia* 4 (1979): 378–83.

Highfill, Philip H., Kalman A. Burnim, and Edward A. Langhans, eds. *A Biographical Dictionary of Actors, Actresses, Musicians, Dancers, Managers, and Other Stage Personnel in London, 1600–1800.* 16 vols. Carbondale: Southern Illinois University Press, 1973–1993.

Hiller, Johan Adam, "Fortsetzung über die Oper: l'Amore di Psiche vom Herrn Agricola." *Wöchentliche Nachrichten und Anmerkungen die Musik betreffend* 3, Anhang (11 September 1769; reprint, Hildesheim: G. Olms, 1970): 81–88.

Himmer, Otto. "Klarinetsamling." MS., 1981.

————. "Den tidlige klarinet i Danmark." In *Musa-Årbog*, edited by N. Bindex and M. Friis, 159–81. Århus: Musa-Print, 1992.

Hind, Harold C. "The British Wind Band," *Hinrichsen's Musical Year Book* 7 (1952): 183–94.

Hitchcock, H. Wiley, and Stanley Sadie, eds. *The New Grove Dictionary of American Music.* 4 vols. London: Macmillan, 1986.

Hoeprich, T. Eric. "Clarinet Reed Position in the Eighteenth Century." *EM* 12 (1984): 49–55.

———. "Die Klarinetten Johann Scherers." *Tibia* 10 (1985): 435–38.

———. "A Trio of Basset Horns by Theodor Lotz." *GSJ* 50 (1997): 228–36.

Hopfner, Rudolf. *Wiener Musikinstrumentenmacher, 1766–1900: Adressenverzeichnis und Bibliographie.* Tutzing: H. Schneider, 1999.

Hopkinson, Cecil. *A Dictionary of Parisian Music Publishers, 1700–1950.* London: The author, 1954.

Hopkinson, John. *A New and Complete Preceptor for the Clarinet.* London: Wm. Milhouse, [ca. 1814].

Hotteterre, Jacques, le Romain. *Méthode pour apprendre a jouer en très peu de tem de la Flute traversiere, de la Flute à bec et du Haut-bois . . . Augmentée des Principes de la musique et des Tablatures de la Clarinette et du Basson.* Paris: Bailleux, [ca. 1775].

Howard, John Tasker. *Our American Music.* New York: Crowell, 1931.

Huber, Renate. *Verzeichnis sämtlicher Musikinstrumente im Germanischen Nationalmuseum Nürnberg.* Wilhelmshaven: F. Noetzel, 1989.

Hülphers, Abraham Abrahamsson. *Historisk Afhandling om Music och Instrumenter.* Westerås: J. L. Horrn, 1773; reprint, Stockholm: Svenskt musikhistoriskt arkiv, 1969. Translated by J. W. Harker under the title *Historical Disquisition on Music and Instruments.* Omaha: J. W. Harker, 1992.

Hutchins, A, ed. *Mozart: The Man, the Musician.* New York: Schirmer, 1976.

"Instrumens de musique, confectionnés par B. Schott fils à Mayence," in "Intelligenzblatt no. 9." *Cäcilia: Eine Zeitschrift für die musikalische Welt* 11 (1825): 16–17.

Instruments de Musiques, 1750–1800. Echevinage-Saintes: Musée des Beaux-Arts, 1982.

Iriarte, Tomas de. *La Música, Poema.* Madrid: En La Imprenta Real de la Gazeta, 1779.

Jacob, Michael. *Die Klarinettenkonzerte von Carl Stamitz.* Wiesbaden: Breitkopf & Härtel, 1991.

Jeltsch, Jean. *La clarinette à six clés: Un jeu de clarinettes du facteur parisien Jean-Jacques Baumann.* Courlay: J. M. Fuzeau, 1997.

———. "La clarinette de Mozart." *Crescendo* 34 (July–Aug. 1990): 12–24.

———. "'Prudent à Paris': vie et carrière d'un maître faiseur d'instruments à vents." *Musique, images, instruments* 3 (1997) : 129–52.

Jeltsch, Jean, and Nicholas J. Shackleton. "Caractérisation acoustique de trois clarinettes de facteurs lyonnais: Alexis Bernard et Jacques François Simiot." In *Colloque acoustique et instruments anciens factures, musiques et science,* 103–24. Paris: Musée de la Musique, 1998.

Jeltsch, Jean, and Denis Watel. "Maîtrises et jurandes dans la communauté des faiseurs instruments à Paris." *Musique, images, instruments* 4 (1998): 9–31.

Jenkins, Jean L. *Musical Instruments: Horniman Museum London.* London: Inner London Education Authority, 1970.

Jensen, Verner. "Dulcianen og fagotten I Danmark I 1600- og 1700-tallet." In *Musa-Årbog,* edited by N. Bindex and M. Friis, 182–209. Århus: Musa-Print, 1992.

Johansson, Cari. *French Music Publishers' Catalogues of the Second Half of the Eighteenth Century.* 2 vols. Stockholm: Almquist & Wiksells, 1955.

Johnson, David. *Music and Society in Lowland Scotland in the Eighteenth Century.* London: Oxford University Press, 1972.

Johnston, Roy. "Concerts in the Musical Life of Belfast to 1874." Ph.D. diss., Queen's University of Belfast, 1996.

Johnston, Stephen Keith. "The Clarinet Concertos of Louis Spohr." D.M.A. diss., University of Maryland, 1972.

Jooste, Fanie. "The History of Wind Bands in South Africa, Part I." *Journal of Band Research* 22, no. 2 (spring 1987): 34–43.

Joppig, Gunther. "Holzblasinstrumente." In *Fünf Jahrhunderte Deutscher Musikinstrumentenbau,* edited by H. Moeck, 39–90. Celle: Moeck, 1987.

———. "Zur Entwicklung des Deutschen Fagotts." In *Studia Organologica: Festschrift für John Henry van der Meer zu seinem fünfundsechzigsten Geburstag,* 253–76. Tutzing: H. Schneider, 1987.

———. "Zur Geschichte der Klarinette anhand von Erstausgaben früherer Klarinettenschulen." *Die Klarinette* 2 (1987): 62–68.

Journal de musique, theorique, pratique, dramatique et instrumentale. Paris: Rualt, 1774; reprint, Geneva: Minkoff, 1972.

Journal für Literatur, Kunst, Luxus und Mode. Weimar, 1793.

Kastner, Jean-Georges. *Manuel Général de Musique Militaire à l'usage des Armée Françaises.* Paris: Didot Frères, 1848.

Kaul, Oskar. *Geschichte der Würzburger Hofmusik im 18. Jahrhundert.* Würzburg: C. J. Becker, 1924.

———. *Thematische Verzeichnis der Instrumentalwerke von Anton Rosetti.* Wiesbaden: Breitkopf & Härtel, 1968.

Keess, Stephen Edler von. *Darstellung des Fabricks- und Gewerbswesen in Seinem Gegenwärten Zustande, Vorzüglich in Technischer, Mercantilischer und Statistischer Beziehung.* 2d ed. 3 vols. Vienna: Morschner und Jaspar, 1829.

Kennedy, Dale Edwin. "The Clarinet Sonata in France before 1800 with a Modern Performance Edition of Two Works." Ph.D. diss., University of Oklahoma, 1979.

Kenyon de Pascual, Beryl. "Carlos III: un rey protector de la música." *Reales sitias* 97 (1988): 33–38.

———. "English Square Pianos in Eighteenth-Century Madrid." *Music and Letters* 64 (1983): 212–17.

———. "Ventas de instrumentos musicales en Madrid durante la segunda mitad del siglo XVIII." *Revista de musicologia* 5 (1982): 309–23.

Kinsky, Georg. *Das Werk Beethovens: Thematisch-Bibliographisches Verzeichnis seiner Sämtlichen Vollendeten Kompositionen.* Munich, 1955.

Kjeldsberg, Peter Andreas. *Musikkinstrumenter ved Ringve Museum: The Collection of Musical Instruments.* Trondheim: Ringve Museums Skifter, 1976.

Knape, Walter. *Bibliographisch-thematisches Verzeichnis der Kompositionen von Karl Friedrich Abel.* Cuxhaven: The author, 1971.

Koch, Heinrich Christoph. *Musikalisches Lexikon.* Frankfurt: H. dem Jüngern, 1802; reprint, Hildesheim: Olms, 1964.

Köchel, Ludwig Ritter von. *Chronologisch-thematisches Verzeichnis sämtlicher Tonwerke Wolfgang Amadé Mozarts.* 6th ed. Wiesbaden: Breitkopf & Härtel, 1964.

Koegel, John. "'The Indian Chief' and 'Morality': An Eighteenth-Century British Popular Song Transformed into a Nineteenth-Century American Shape-Note Hymn." In *Music in Performance and Society: Essays in Honor of Roland Jackson,* edited by M. Cole and J. Koegel, 437–508. Warren, Mich.: Harmonie Park Press, 1997.

Kohler, Susan Carol. "J. G. H. Backofen's *Anweisung zur Klarinette nebst einer kurzen Abhandlung über das Basset-Horn*: Translation and Commentary." D.M.A. diss., University of Washington, 1997.

Kollmann, Augustus Frederic Christopher. *An Essay on Practical Musical Composition*. London: The author, 1799; reprint, New York: Da Capo Press, 1973.

Köster, H. M. G. "Clarinet." In *Deutsche Encyclopädie oder Allgemeines Real-Wörterbuch aller Künste und Wissenschaft*, edited by H. M. G. Köster. Vol. 5, 685. Frankfurt: Varrentrapp Sohn und Wenner, 1781.

Kozma, Tibor. "Heroes of Wood and Brass: The Clarinet in *Figaro*." *Opera News* 16, no. 17 (25 February 1952): 26–28.

Kratochvíl, Jiří. "Betrachtungen über die Urfassung des Konzerts für Klarinette und des Quintetts für Klarinette und Streicher von W. A. Mozart." In *Internationale Konferenz über das Leben und Werk W. A. Mozarts, Praha, 27.–31. Mai 1956*, 262–71. Prague, [ca. 1958].

———. "Koncertantní klarinet v českém klasicismu." *Ziva Hudbá* 9 (1968): 285–371.

———. "Otázka původního znění Mozartova Koncertu pro klarinet a Kvintetu pro klarinet a smyčce." *Hudebni Veda* 1 (1967): 44–70.

Kreitzer, Amy. "Serial Numbers and Hallmarks on Flutes from the Workshop of Monzani and Hill." *GSJ* 48 (1995): 168–80.

Kroeger, Karl. "The Church-Gallery Orchestra in New England." *American Music Research Center Journal* 4 (1994): 23–30.

Kroll, Oskar. *Die Klarinette: Ihre Geschichte, ihre Literatur, ihre Grossen Meister*. Edited by D. Riehm. Kassel: Bärenreiter, 1965. Translated by H. Morris under the title *The Clarinet*, revised and with a repertory by D. Riehm, translation edited by A. Baines. New York: Taplinger, 1968.

———. "Vor- und Frühgeschichte der Klarinette." *Musik im Krull Zeitbesusstein* 2, no. 15 (14 April 14 1934): 3–7.

Küng, Andreas. "'Schlegel A Bale': Die erhaltenen Instrumente und ihre Erbauer." *Basler Jahrbuch für Historiches Musikpraxis* 11 (1987): 63–88.

La Borde, Jean-Benjamin de. *Essai sur la musique ancienne et moderne*. 4 vols. Paris: P. D. Pierres, 1780.

Landmann, Ortrun. "Die Entwicklung der Dresdener Kofkapelle zum 'Klassischen' Orchester." *Basler Jahrbuch für Historische Musikpraxis* 17 (1993): 175–90.

Landon, H. C. Robbins. *Haydn at Eszterháza, 1766–1790*. Bloomington: Indiana University Press, 1978.

———. *Haydn: The Early Years, 1732–1765*. Bloomington: Indiana University Press, 1980.

Lawson, Colin. "The Authentic Clarinet: Tone and Tonality." *Musical Times* 124 (1983): 357–58.

———. "The Basset Clarinet Revived." *EM* 15, no. 4 (November 1987): 487–501.

———. "The Development of Wind Instruments." In *Performing Beethoven*, edited by R. Stowell, 70–84. Cambridge: Cambridge University Press, 1994.

———. *The Early Clarinet: A Practical Guide*. Cambridge: Cambridge University Press, 2000.

———. "Haydn and the Clarinet." *Haydn Society Journal of Great Britain* 17 (1997): 2–10.

———. *Mozart: Clarinet Concerto*. Cambridge Music Handbooks. Cambridge: Cambridge University Press, 1996.

———. "Playing Historical Clarinets." In *The Cambridge Companion to the Clarinet*, 134–49. Cambridge: Cambridge University Press, 1995.

Lawson, Colin, ed. *The Cambridge Companion to the Clarinet*. Cambridge: Cambridge University Press, 1995.

Lazzari, Gianni, ed. *Strumenti a fiato in Legno dalle collezioni private italiana*. Ferrara: Casa Editrice, 2001.

Leeson, Daniel N., and Robert D. Levin. "Mozart's Deliberate Use of Incorrect Key Signatures for clarinets." *Mozart Jahrbuch* (1998): 139–52.

Leeson, Daniel N., and David Whitwell. "Concerning Mozart's Serenade in B♭ for Thirteen Instruments, K. 361 (370a)." *Mozart Jahrbuch* (1976–77): 97–130.

Lefèvre, Jean-Xavier. *Méthode de clarinette*. Paris, 1802; reprint, Geneva: Minkoff, 1974.

Lescat, P., and J. Saint-Arroman, eds. *Clarinette: Méthodes et traités-dictionnaires*. Courlay: Editions J. M. Fuzeau, 2000.

Les instruments de musique a Bruxelles et en Wallonie: Inventaire descriptif. Liège: Mardaga, 1992.

Libby, Dennis. "Spontini, Gaspare." *New Grove*, vol. 8, 16–25.

Libin, Laurence. *American Musical Instruments in the Metropolitan Museum of Art*. New York: W. W. Norton, 1985.

———. *Clarinets from the Collection of William J. Maynard*. New York: Metropolitan Museum of Art, 1994.

———. "The Eisenbrandt Family Pedigree." In *Studia Organologica: Festschrift für John Henry van der Meer zu seinem fünfundsechzigsten Geburtstag*, 335–42. Tutzing: H. Schneider, 1987.

———. *Musical Instruments in the Metropolitan Museum*. New York: Metropolitan Museum of Art, 1978.

Link, Dorothea. *The National Court Theatre in Mozart's Vienna: Sources and Documents, 1783–1792*. Oxford: Clarendon Press, 1998.

Löbel, R. G., ed. *Conversationslexikon mit vorzüglicher Rücksicht auf die gegenwärtigen Zeiten*. Leipzig: F. A. Leupold, 1796.

Luke, James N. "The Clarinets of Thomas Key of London." D.M.A. diss., University of Missouri, 1969.

Lyle, Andrew. "John Mahon's Clarinet Preceptor." *GSJ* 30 (1977): 52–55.

Macdonald, Robert James. "François-Joseph Gossec and French Instrumental Music of the Second Half of the Eighteenth Century." 3 vols. Ph.D. diss., University of Michigan, 1968.

MacIntyre, Bruce C. *Haydn: The Creation*. New York: Schirmer Books, 1998.

Made for Music: An Exhibition to Mark the Fortieth Anniversary of the Galpin Society for the Study of Musical Instruments. London: Galpin Society, 1986.

Mahillon, Victor-Charles. *Catalogue descriptif et analytique du musée instrumental du Conservatoire royale de musique de Bruxelles*. 2d ed. 5 vols. Ghent: Libraire générale de A. Hoste, 1893–1922.

Mahon, John. *A New and Complete Preceptor for Clarinet*. London: Goulding, Phipps & D'Almaine, [ca. 1803].

Malot, Joseph-François. *L'art de bien faire une anche de clarinette*. Avallon: Oddoul, 1820.

Marcuse, Sibyl. "The Instruments of the King's Library at Versailles." *GSJ* 14 (1961): 34–36.

Marsh, John. *Hints to Young Composers of Instrumental Music*. London: Clementi, Banger, Hyde, Collard & Davis, [ca. 1806]; reprinted and edited by C. Cudworth in John Marsh, "Hints to Young Composers of Instrumental Music." *GSJ* 18 (1965): 57–71.

Martinez De La Roca, Joaquin. *Suplicatorio sobre del memorial dirigido a V.S.I. por D. Pedro Paris y Rojo, músico en la real capilla de S.M. cuyo assumpto es quexarse del estillo en que se pratica hoy la música figurada, o canto de organo.* Madrid, [ca. 1720]. Barcelona, Biblioteca de Catalunya, MS., 910744 M.369.

Masel, Andreas. "Der Münchener Holzblasinstrumentenmacher Benedikt Pentenrieder (1809–1849)." Master's thesis, Ludwig-Maximilians-Universität, 1986.

The Massachusetts Magazine, or Monthly Museum of Knowledge and Rational Entertainment 3, no. 3 (March 1791).

Mather, Betty Bang. *Interpretation of French Music from 1675 to 1775 for Woodwind and Other Performers.* New York: McGinnis & Marx, 1973.

Maunder, Richard. "A Biographical Index of Viennese Wind-Instrument Purchases, 1700–1800." *GSJ* 51 (1998): 170–91.

———. "J. C. Bach and the Basset-Horn." *GSJ* 37 (1984): 42–47.

Mazzeo, Rosario. "The History of the Clarinet's B♭ Mechanisms." *Clarinet* 27, no. 2 (1980): 6–9, 33–37.

McVeigh, Simon. *Concert Life in London from Mozart to Haydn.* Cambridge: Cambridge University Press, 1993.

Meier, Adolf. "Die Pressburger Hofkapelle des Fürstprimas von Ungarn, Fürst Joseph von Batthyany, in den Jahren 1776–1784." *Das Haydn Jahrbuch* 10 (1978): 81–89.

Meloni, Fabrizio. *Il clarinetto.* Varese: Zecchini Editore, 2000.

Melville-Mason, Graham. *Exhibition of European Musical Instruments: The Galpin Society, Twenty-First Anniversary Exhibition.* Edinburgh: Reid School of Music, 1968.

Mendel, Hermann. *Musikalisches Conversations-Lexicon.* 11 vols. Berlin: R. Oppenheim, 1870–76.

Menkin, William. "Frédéric Blasius: Nouvelle Méthode de Clarinette et Raisonnement des Instruments: A Complete Translation and Analysis with an Historical and Biographical Background of the Composer and his Compositions for Clarinet." D.M.A. diss., Stanford University, 1980.

Merriman, Lyle. "Early Clarinet Sonatas." *Instrumentalist* 21, no. 9 (April 1967): 28.

Metzler's and Son's Clarinet Preceptor. London: Metzler & Son, [ca. 1825].

Meucci, Renato. "La costruzione di strumenti musicali a Roma tra XVII e XIX secolo, con notizie inedite sulla famiglia Biglioni." In *La musica a Roma attraverso le fonti d'archivio*, edited by B. M. Antolini, A. Morelli, and V. V. Spagnuolo, 581–93. Lucca: Libreria Musicale Italiana, 1994.

[Michaelis, Christian Friedrich]. "Ueber die Klarinette." *AMZ* 10 (1808): 369–75, 385–91.

Michel, V. *Méthode de clarinette.* Paris: Cochet, [ca. 1801].

"Miscellen." *AMZ* 11 (1809): cols. 798–800.

Moeck, Hermann. "Spazierstockinstrumente: Eine kurze Vorstudie zu folgendem Aufsatz." *Studia Instrumentorum Musicae Popularis* 3 (1974): 149–51.

Moeck, Hermann, ed. *Fünf Jahrhunderte Deutscher Musikinstrumentenbau.* Celle: Moeck Verlag, 1987.

Moeck, Karen. "The Beginnings of the Woodwind Quintet." *NACWPI Journal* 26, no. 2 (winter 1977–78): 22, 31–33.

Moir, Joseph. "Catalogue du Musée de Nice." MS., 1987.

Møller, Dorthe Falcon. *Danske instrumentbyggere, 1770–1850: En erhvervshistorisk og biografisk frenstiling.* Copenhagen: G. E. C. Gad, 1983.

————. *Fløjte, obo, klarinet og fagot: Træblæsertraditionen i dansk instrumentbygning.* Copenhagen: Falcon, 1987.

Montagu, Jeremy. *The Bate Collection of Historical Instruments: Checklist of the Collection.* Oxford: Bate Collection, 1988.

————. *The World of Baroque and Classical Instruments.* New York: Overlook Press, 1979.

Monzani, Tebaldo. "Clarionets and Flutes." British Patent no. 3586, 9 September 1812. Reprint, London: G. E. Eyre and W. Spottiswoode, 1856.

Mooser, R. Aloys. *Annales de la musique et des musiciens en Russie au XVIIIme siècle.* 3 vols. Geneva: Mont-Blanc, 1951.

Morrow, Mary Sue. *Concert Life in Haydn's Vienna: Aspects of a Developing Musical and Social Institution.* New York: Pendragon Press, 1989.

Müller, Iwan. *Gamme pour la nouvelle clarinette inventée p: Iwan Müller.* Bonn: N. Simrock, [ca. 1812].

————. *Méthode pour la nouvelle clarinette & clarinette-alto.* Paris: Gambaro, [ca. 1821]; Italian ed., Milan: G. Ricordi, [ca. 1826]; German ed., Leipzig: F. Hofmeister, [1825].

Münster, Robert. "Johann Anton Fils und das Mannheimer Orchester in den Jahren 1754 bis 1760." In *Johann Anton Fils (1733–1760): Ein Eichstätter Komponist der Mannheimer Klassik*, ed. H. Holzbauer, 33–46. Tutzing: H. Schneider, 1983.

————. "Mannheim and Vienna (1760–1800)." Liner notes. Deutsche Grammophon Gesellschaft Archiv 198415, [ca. 1967] [recording of Michael Haydn, Trumpet Concerto].

Musée retrospective de la Classe 17: Instruments de Musique Matériel, Procédés et Produits a l'Exposition Universelle Internationale de 1900, A Paris. Paris, 1900.

Music, Theater, Dance: An Illustrated Guide. Washington, D.C.: Library of Congress, 1993.

Musica Britannica. General ed., A. Lewis. 78 vols. London: Stainer & Bell, 1951–.

Musik Instrumente aus dem Hessischen Landesmuseum 16–19. Jahrhundert. Darmstadt: Hessisches Landesmuseum, 1980.

Musikantiquariat Hans Schneider, Katalog: Musikerautographen, no. 308. Tutzing: Hans Schneider, [ca. 1988].

Musique bourgeoise au dix-nouvième siècle: Collection d'instruments de musique anciens des musées de Nice. Nice: Musée des Beaux-Arts, 1995.

Myers, Arnold, ed. *The Glen Account Book, 1838–1853.* Edinburgh: Edinburgh University Collection of Historic Musical Instruments, 1985.

————. *Historic Musical Instruments in the Edinburgh University Collection.* Vol. 1, *The Illustrations.* Edinburgh: Edinburgh University Collection of Historic Musical Instruments, 1990.

"Nachrichten." *AMZ* 11 (1808): cols. 89–91.

"Nachrichten." *AMZ* 11 (1809): cols. 649–55.

"Nachrichten." *AMZ* 12 (1810): col. 298–99.

"Nachrichten." *AMZ* 34 (1832): cols. 870–71.

Nagy, Michael. "Zur Geschichte und Entwicklung der Wiener Holzbläserschule." In *Klang und Komponist: Ein Symposon der Wiener Philharmoniker*, edited by O. Biba and W. Schuster, 263–82. Tutzing: H. Schneider, 1992.

Nectoux, Jean-Michel. "Trois orchestras Parisiens en 1830: l'Académie Royale de Musique, le Théâtre-Italien et la Société des Concerts du Conservatoire." In *Music in Paris in the Eighteen-Thirties*, edited by P. Bloom, vol. 4, 471–505. 4 vols. Stuyvesant, N.Y.: Pendragon Press, 1987.

Ness, Arthur J. "Some Remarks Concerning the Basset Clarinet and Mozart's Concerto in A Major (KV 622)." Master's thesis, Harvard University, 1961.

Neue Mozart-Ausgabe. 130 vols. Ed. International Stiftung Mozarteum, Salzburg. Kassel: Bärenreiter, 1978–.

New and Compleat Instructions for the Clarionet. London: A. Bland & Weller, [ca. 1798].

New and Complete Instructions for the Clarionet. London: Preston & Son, [ca. 1797].

A New and Complete Preceptor for the Clarinet. Boston: John Ashton, [ca. 1825].

Newhill, John. "The Adagio for Clarinet and Strings by Wagner/Baermann." *Music and Letters* 55, no. 2 (April 1974): 167–71.

———. "The Contribution of the Mannheim School to Clarinet Literature." *Music Review* 40 (1979): 90–122.

———. "Küffner's Works for Clarinet." *Clarinet* 13, no. 4 (Summer 1986): 34–37.

———. "The Mozart Clarinet Quartets." *Clarinet* 17, no. 1 (Nov.–Dec. 1989): 26–28.

Newman, William S. *The Sonata in the Classical Era.* 3d ed. New York: Norton, 1983.

Nickel, Ekkehart. *Der Holzblasinstrumente in der freien Reichsstadt Nürnberg.* Munich: E. Katzbichler, 1971.

Niemöller, Klaus Wolfgang. *Kirchenmusik und reichsstädtische Musikpflege im Köln des 18. Jahrhundert.* Cologne: A. Volk, 1960.

Nösselt, Hans-Joachim. *Ein ältest Orchester 1530–1980: 450 Jahre Bayerisches Hof- und Staatsorchester.* Munich: Bruckmann, 1980.

Norlind, Tobias. "Abraham Abrahamsson Hülphers och frihetstidens musikliv." *Svensk Tidskrift för Musikforskning* 19 (1937): 16–64.

P., J. "On the Clarionet." *The Harmonicon* 8 (1830): 57–58.

Pace, Temistocle. *Ancie Battenti: Storia-fisica-letterature.* Florence: Carlo Cya, 1943.

Page, Janet K. "'To Soften the Sound of the Hoboy': The Muted Oboe in the Eighteenth and Early Nineteenth Centuries." *EM* 21 (1993): 65–80.

Parke, William T. *Musical Memoirs.* 2 vols. London: H. Colburn and R. Bentley, 1830; reprint, New York: Da Capo Press, 1970.

Patents for Inventions: Abridgements of Specifications relating to Music and Musical Instruments, A.D. *1694–1866.* London: G. E. Eyre and W. Spottiswoode, 1871; reprint, Longon: T. Bingham, 1984.

Pearson, Ingrid. "Playing Historical Clarinets." In *The Early Clarinet: A Practical Guide,* edited by Colin Lawson, 41–62. Cambridge: Cambridge University Press, 2000.

Petty, Frederick. *Italian Opera in London, 1760–1800.* Ann Arbor: UMI Research Press, 1980.

Pierre, Constant. *Le Conservatoire National de Musique et de Déclamation: Documents historiques et administratifs recueillis ou reconstitués.* Paris: Imprimerie Nationale, 1900.

———. *Les facteurs d'instruments de musique.* Paris: E. Sagot, 1893.

———. *Histoire du Concert Spirituel, 1725–1790.* Paris: Heugel, 1975.

Piersol, Jon R. "The Oettingen-Wallerstein Hofkapelle and Its Wind Music." Ph.D. diss., University of Iowa, 1972.

Pillaut, Léon. *Le Musée du Conservatoire National de Musique: 3e supplément au catalogue de 1884.* Paris: Librairie Fischbacher, 1903.

Pirker, Michael. "Pictorial Documents of the Music Bands of the Janyssaries (Mehter) and the Austrian Military Music." *Ridlm Newsletter* 15, no. 2 (Fall 1990): 2–12.

Pisarowitz, Karl Maria. "'Müaßt ma nix in übel aufnehma . . .' : Beitragsversuche zu einer Gebrüder-Stadler-Biographie." *Mittleilungen der Internationalen Stiftung Mozarteum* 19, no. 1–2 (February 1971): 29–33.

Pohl, Carl Ferdinand. *Denkschrift aus Anlass des hunderjährigen Bestehens der Tonkünstler-Societät in Wien.* Vienna: Im Selbstverlage des Vereines, 1871.

Pontécoulant, Louis Adam de. *Organographie: Essai sur la facture instrumentale.* 2 vols. Paris: Castel, 1861; reprint, Amsterdam: F. Knuf, 1972.

Poole, H. Edmund. "A Catalogue of Musical Instruments Offered for Sale in 1839 by D'Almaine & Co., 20 Soho Square." *GSJ* 35 (1982): 3–36.

Poulin, Pamela. "Anton Stadler's Basset Clarinet: Recent Discoveries in Riga." *JAMIS* 22 (1996): 110–27.

———. "The Basset Clarinet of Anton Stadler." *College Music Symposium* 22, no. 2 (fall 1982): 67–82.

———. "A Report on New Information Regarding Stadler's Concert Tour of Europe and Two Early Examples of the Basset Clarinet." In *Bericht über den Internationalen Mozart-Kongreß Salzburg 1991,* edited by R. Angermüller et al., 946–53. Kassel: Bärenreiter, 1992.

———. "An Updated Report on New Information Regarding Stadler's Concert Tour of Europe and Two Early Examples of the Basset Clarinet." *Clarinet* 22, no. 2 (February–March 1995): 24–28.

Pound, Gomer J. "A Study of Clarinet Solo Concerto Literature Composed before 1850: With Selected Items Edited and Arranged for Contemporary Use." Ph.D. diss., Florida State University, 1965.

———. "Two Eighteenth Century Clarinet Arias." *Woodwind World* 4, no. 9 (February 1963): 8–9.

Powell, Ardal, ed. *The Keyed Flute by Johann George Tromlitz.* Oxford: Clarendon Press, 1996.

Price, Curtis, Judith Milhous, and Robert D. Hume. *Italian Opera in Late Eighteenth-Century London.* 2 vols. Oxford: Clarendon Press, 1995, 2001.

Principes de clarinette avec la tablature des meilleurs mtres. pour cet instrument et plusieur duo pour cet instrument. [Paris: Girard, ca. 1775].

Prout, Ebenezer. *The Orchestra.* London: Augener, 1897.

Quantz, Johann Joachim. *Versuch einer Anweisung die Flöte Traversiere zu Spielen.* Berlin: J. F. Voss, 1752; reprint, Leipzig: C. F. Kahnt, 1906. Translated by E. R. Reilly under the title *On Playing the Flute.* New York: Schirmer, 1966.

Rameis, Emil. *Die Österreichische Militärmusik: Von Anfängen bis zum Jahre 1918.* Tutzing: H. Schneider, 1976.

Randall, David M. "The Clarinet Duet from 1715 to 1780." *Clarinet* 2, no. 2 (February 1975): 9–11.

———. "A Comprehensive Performance Project in Clarinet Literature with an Essay on the Clarinet Duet from ca. 1715 to ca. 1825." D.M.A. diss., University of Iowa, 1970.

Randel, Don M., ed. *New Harvard Dictionary of Music.* Cambridge: Belknap Press of Harvard University Press, 1986.

"Rapport fait par la commission chargée d'examiner la nouvelle clarinette proposée par M. Muller, et la clarinette alto perfectionnée par la même artiste." *Gazette Nationale, ou Le Moniteur Universel* 152 (1812): 593–94.

Rau, Ulrich. "Die Kammermusik für Klarinette und Streichinstrumente im Zeitalter der Wiener Klassik." Ph.D., diss., Universität des Saarlandes, 1977.

———. "Von Wagner, von Weber? Zwei Kammermusikwerke für Klarinette und

Streichinstrumente unter falscher Autorschaft." *DMf* 29, no. 2 (April–June 1976): 170–75.

"Recension," *AMZ*, 3, no. 6 (5 November 1800): 95–96.

Rees-Davies, Jo. *Fétis on Clarinettists and Clarinet Repertoire.* Brighton: The author, 1988.

———. *Whistling and Hofmeister, 1817–1827: The Clarinet Repertoire.* Brighton, [ca. 1988].

Rehfeldt, Phillip. *New Directions for the Clarinet.* Rev. ed. Los Angeles: University of California Press, 1994.

Rendall, F. Geoffrey. *The Clarinet: Some Notes upon Its History and Construction.* 3d ed. revised and with some additional materials by P. Bate. New York: W. W. Norton, 1971.

Renouf, Nicholas. *A Yankee Lyre: Musical Instruments by American Makers.* New Haven: Yale University Collection of Musical Instruments, 1985.

Reschke, Johannes. "Studie zur Geschichte der brandenburgisch-prußischen Heeresmusik." Ph.D. diss., Friedrich-Wilhelms-Universität zu Berlin, 1936.

Reynvaan, Joos Verschuere. *Muzijkaal Konstwoordenboek.* 2 vols. Middelburg: W. A. Keel and J. de Jongh, 1789–90.

———. *Muzijkaal Kunst-Woordenboek.* Amsterdam: W. Brave, 1795.

Rice, Albert R. *The Baroque Clarinet.* Early Music Series 13. Oxford: Clarendon Press, 1992.

———. "Berr's Clarinet Tutors and the 'Boehm' Clarinet." *GSJ* 41 (1988): 11–15.

———. "The Clarinet as Described by Lorents Nicolai Berg." *JAMIS* 5–6 (1979–80): 43–53.

———. "The Clarinette d'Amour and Basset-Horn." *GSJ* 39 (1986): 97–111.

———. "Clarinet Fingering Charts, 1732–1816." *GSJ* 37 (1984): 16–41.

———. "An Eighteenth Century Description of the Five-Key Clarinet." *Clarinet* 4 (1977): 29–30.

———. "Garsault on the Clarinet." *GSJ* 32 (1979): 99–103.

———. "Some Performance Practice Aspects of American Sheet Music, 1793–1830." In *Music in Performance and Society: Essays in Honor of Roland Jackson*, 229–47. Warren: Harmonie Park Press, 1997.

Rice, John A. *Antonio Salieri and Viennese Opera.* Chicago: University of Chicago Press, 1998.

Richard, Jérôme. *Description historique et critique de l'Italie, ou, Nouveaux mémoires sur l'etat actuel de son gouvernement, des sciences, des arts, du commerce, de la population et de l'histoire naturelle.* 6 vols. Dijon: François Des Ventes, 1766.

Ridley, E. A. K. *European Wind Instruments.* London: Royal College of Music, 1982.

Riehm, Diethard. "Zum Problem der tiefen Klarinetten in Johann Christian Bachs Opern." In *Festschrift Klaus Hortschansky zum 60. Geburtstag*, edited by A. Beer and L. Lütteken, 211–20. Tutzing: Schneider, 1995.

Robert, Fréderick. "Militaire (musique)." In *Dictionnaire de la musique en France aux XVIIᵉ et XVIIIᵉ siècles*, edited by Marcelle Benoit. Paris: Fayard, 1992.

Robinet, J. B., ed. *Suite du recueil de planches.* Paris: Panckoucke, Stoupe, Brunet, 1777.

———. *Supplément à l'encyclopédie, ou dictionnaire raisonné des sciences, des arts et des métiers par un société de gens de lettres.* 5 vols. Amsterdam: M. M. Rey, 1776–1780.

Robinson, Michael F., and Ulrike Hofmann. *Giovanni Paisiello: A Thematic Catalogue of his Works.* Thematic Catalogues Series 15. Stuyvesant, N.Y.: Pendragon Press, 1991.

[Rochlitz, Johann Friedrich]. "Anzeigen." *AMZ* 20, no. 24 (17 June 1818): 443.

———. "Etwas über die Aufführung von Lieb und Treue: Intelligenz-Blatt 6." *AMZ* 10 (February 1808): 21–25 between 350–53.

———. "Nachrichten." *AMZ* 18, no. 29 (8 May 1816): 321–23.

———. "Nachrichten." *AMZ* 20, no. 31 (August 1818): 555–57.

———. "Recension." *AMZ* 4 (1802): cols. 412–13.

Roeser, Valentin. *Essai d'instruction à l'usage de ceux qui composent pour la clarinette et le cor.* Paris: Le Menu, 1764; reprint, Geneva: Minkoff, 1972.

———. *Gamme de la clarinette avec six duos pour cet instrument.* Paris: Le Menu, 1769.

Rohn, Jan Karel. *Nomenclator artifex mechanicus. To Gest: Gmenowatel W trogi Řžeči.* Prague: J. Prussowý, 1768.

Ross, David. "A Comprehensive Performance Project in Clarinet Literature with an Organological Study of the Development of the Clarinet in the Eighteenth Century." D.M.A. diss., University of Iowa, 1985.

Rousseau, Eugene E. "Clarinet Instructional Materials from 1732 to ca. 1825." Ph.D. diss., State University of Iowa, 1962.

Rousselet, William. "La foire aux 'bouts' de clarinettes." *Larigot* 29 (July 2002): 28.

Rybicki, François. *Méthode pour la clarinette.* Paris: Arnaud, [ca. 1826].

Sacchini, Louis Vincent. "The Concerted Music for the Clarinet in the Nineteenth Century." Ph.D. diss., University of Iowa, 1980.

Sachs, Curt. *Sammlung alter Musikinstrumente bei der Staatlichen Hochschule für Musik zu Berlin: Beschreibender Katalog.* Berlin: J. Bard, 1922.

Sadie, Stanley. "The Wind Music of J. C. Bach." *Music and Letters* 37, no. 2 (April 1956): 107–17.

Sadie, Stanley, ed. *The New Grove Dictionary of American Music.* 3 vols. London: Macmillan, 1986.

———. *The New Grove Dictionary of Music and Musicians.* 20 vols. London: Macmillan, 1980.

———. *The New Grove Dictionary of Music and Musicians.* 29 vols. London: Macmillan Reference, 2001.

———. *The New Grove Dictionary of Musical Instruments.* 3 vols. London: Macmillan, 1984.

———. *The New Grove Dictionary of Opera.* 4 vols. London: Macmillan, 1988.

Saint-Arroman, Jean. *L'interprétation de la musique française, 1661–1789.* Paris: Honoré Champion, 1983.

Sandner, Wolfgang. *Die Klarinette bei Weber.* 2d ed. Wiesbaden, 1974.

Schindler, Felix. *Beethoven as I Knew Him.* Edited by D. W. MacArdle. Chapel Hill: University of North Carolina Press, 1966.

Schink, Johann Friedrich. *Litterarische Fragmente.* Graz: Widmanstättenschen Schriften, 1785.

Schlosser, Julius. *Die Sammlung Alter Musikinstrumente: Beschreibendes Verzeichnis.* Vienna: A. Schroll, 1920.

Schmatz, Gerald. "Die Klarinetten in der Musikinstrumentensammlung des Grazer Joanneums." Master's thesis, Hochschule für Musik und Darstellende Kunst in Graz, 1985.

Schmidt, Günther. *Die Musik am Hofe der Markgrafen von Brandenburg-Ansbach.* Kassel: Bärenreiter, 1956.

Schmidtke, Gotthard. *Musikalisches Niedersachsen, Künstler aus Braunschweig und der Heide: Eine Porträtreihe.* Brunswick: Waisenhaus-Buchdruckerei, 1969.

Schneider, Wilhelm. *Historisch-technische Beschreibung der Musicalischen Instrumente.* Neisse and Leipzig: T. Hennings, 1834.

Scholz-Michelitsch, Helga. *Georg Christoph Wagenseil: Hofkomponist und Hofklaviermeister der Kaiserin Maria Theresia.* Vienna: W. Braumüller, 1980.

Schönfeld, Johann Ferdinand von, ed. *Jahrbuch der Tonkunst von Wien und Prag.* Vienna, 1796; reprint, Munich: E. Katzbichler, 1976.

Schröder, Hans. *Verzeichnis der Sammlung alter Musikinstrumente.* Hamburg: Alster, 1930.

Schubart, Christian Friedrich Daniel. *Ideen zu einer Ästhetik der Tonkunst* [dictated 1783–85]. Vienna: J. V. Degen, 1806; reprint, Hildesheim: G. Olms, 1969.

Schultze, Bernhard. *Querflöten der Renaissance und des Barock: Eine historisierende literarische Anthologie.* Munich: The author, 1984.

Schweickert, Karl. *Die Musipflege am Hofe der Kurfürsten von Mainz im 17. und 18. Jahrhundert.* Mainz: I. Wilckens, 1937.

Sebasta, Robert. "Theodor Lotz: Musician, Instrument Maker, and Composer." Booklet. *Une soirée chez les Jacquin.* Zig-Zag Territoires, 990701, 1999.

Sehnal, Jiří. "Die Musikkapelle des Olmützer Bischofs Maxmilian Hamilton." *DMf* 21 (1971): 411–17.

———. "Das Musikinventar des Olmützer Bischofs Leopold Egk aus dem Jahre 1760 als Quelle vorklassischer Instrumentalmusik." *Archiv für Musikwissenschaft* 29 (1972): 285–317.

Seifers, Heinrich. *Die Blasinstrumente im Deutschen Museum: Beschreibender Katalog.* Munich: R. Oldenbourgh, 1976.

Seyfried, Ignaz Ritter von. *J. G. Albrechtsberger's sämtliche Schriften über Generalbaß, Harmonie-Lehre, und Tonseßkunst zum Selbstunterrichte.* Vienna: A. Strauss, 1826.

———. *J. G. Albrechtsberger's sämtliche Schriften über Generalbaß, Harmonie-Lehre, und Tonseßkunst zum Selbstunterrichte.* 2d rev. ed. Vienna: T. Haslinger, 1837.

Shackleton, Nicholas. "Clarinet." *NGDMI*, vol. 1, 389–403.

———. "Clarinet." *New Grove*, 2d ed., vol. 21, 895–910.

———. "The Development of the Clarinet." In *The Cambridge Companion to the Clarinet*, edited by Colin Lawson, 16–32. Cambridge: Cambridge University Press, 1995.

———. "John Hale." *FoMRHIQ* 48 (1987): 26.

Shackleton, Nicholas, and Albert Rice. "César Janssen and the Transmission of Müller's Thirteen-Keyed Clarinet in France." *GSJ* 52 (1999): 183–94.

Sherman, Charles H., and T. Donley Thomas. *Johann Michael Haydn (1737–1806): A Chronological Thematic Catalogue of His Works.* Stuyvesant, N.Y.: Pendragon Press, 1993.

Sheveloff, Joel. "When Sources Seem to Fail: The Clarinet Parts in Mozart's K. 581 and K. 622." In *Critica Musica: Essays in Honor of Paul Brainard*, edited by John Knowles, 379–401. London, 1996.

Sievers, Heinrich. *Hannoversche Musikgeschichte: Dokumente, Kritiken, und Meinungen.* Tutzing: H. Schneider, 1979.

Simiot, Jacques-François. "Correspondance." *Revue musicale* 6 (1830): 541–42.

————. *Tableau explicatif des innovations et changements faits à la clarinette*. Lyons: The author, 1808.

Simon, J., ed. *Handel: A Celebration of Life and Times, 1685–1759*. London: National Portrait Gallery, 1986.

Sirker, Udo. *Die Entwicklung des Bläserquintetts in der ersten Hälften des 19. Jahrhunderts*. Regensburg: G. Bosse, 1968.

Smallman, Basil. *The Piano Quartet and Quintet*. Oxford: Clarendon Press, 1994.

Smith, David Hogan. *Reed Design for Early Woodwinds*. Bloomington: Indiana University Press, 1992.

Soriano Fuertes, Mariano. *Historia de la música española*. 4 vols. Madrid: D. Bernabé Carrafa, 1855–59.

Sowa, Georg. *Anfänge institutioneller Musikerziehung in Deutschland (1800–1843)*. Regensburg: E. Bosse, 1972.

Spaethling, Robert, ed. and trans. *Mozart's Letters, Mozart's Life*. New York: W.W. Norton, 2000.

Spicknall, John Payne. "The Solo Works of Bernhard Henrik Crusell (1775–1838)." D.M.A. diss., University of Maryland, 1974.

Spohr, Louis. *Lebenserinnerungen*. Edited by F. Göthel. 2 vols. Tutzing: H. Schneider, 1968.

Spohr, Peter. *Kunsthandwerk im Dienste der Musik*. [Exhibition catalog, Historisches Museum, Frankfurt.] Frankfurt am Main: K. Reichmann, 1991.

Stekl, Hannes. "Harmoniemusik und 'türkische Banda' des Fürstenhauses Liechtenstein." *Haydn Yearbook* 10 (1978): 164–75.

Stoltie, James Merle. "A Symphonie Concertante Type: The Concerto for Mixed Woodwind Ensemble in the Classic Period; Illustrated with a Score of François Devienne's *IIᵉ simphonie concertante pour hautbois ou clarinette et bassoon principal*." Ph.D. diss., State University of Iowa, 1962.

Stork, Karl. "Johann Simon Hermstedt: Zum Gedächtnis des berühmten Klarinettenvirtuosen und ersten Kappellmeisters des ehemaligen Hofkapelle, jetzt staatliches Loh-Orchester, zu Sondershausen." *Deutsche Musiker Zeitung* 60 (1929): 796–98.

Stradner, Gerhard, *Musikinstrumente in Grazer Sammlungen*. Vienna: Verlag das Österreichischen Alademie der Wissenschaften, 1986.

————. "Zur Stimmtonhöhe der Blasinstrumente zur Zeit Joseph Haydns." In *Joseph Haydn: Bericht über den Internationalen Joseph Haydn Kongress*, edited by Eva Badura-Skoda, 81–86. Munich: G. Henle, 1986.

————. "Stimmtonhöhe, Tonarten-und Klangcharaker." In *Strumenti per Mozart*, edited by Marco Tiella and Romano Vettori, 284–90. Bologna: Longo, 1991.

Streitwolf, Johann Heinrich Gottlieb. "Verkauf: Intelligenz-Blatt 6." *AMZ* 30 (1828): 24, between 284–85.

————. "Verzeichniss von Flöten, Clarinetten, Oboën, Fagotten, Basshörnern, Flageoletten, etc." Unpublished ms., ca. 1830–35.

Stubbins, William. *The Art of Clarinetistry*, 2d ed. Ann Arbor: Ann Arbor Publishers, 1965.

Sundet, Jerrold A. "A Study of Manuscript, Out-of-Print, and Currently Published Compositions for Single Oboe or Single Clarinet with Small String Group (c1750–1820)." D.Ed. diss., Colorado State College, 1964.

Taricani, Jo Ann. "Music in Colonial Philadelphia: Some New Documents." *Musical Quarterly* 65 (1979): 185–99.

Tariffa delle gabelle per Firenze. Florence: Cambiagi, 1781.

Thomas, Elaine. "John Mahon Concerto No. 2 for Clarinet and String Orchestra." Master's thesis, City University [London], 1987.

Thomé, Gilles. "Anton Stadler: le miracle Bohémien." *Clarinette magazine* 27 (January 1995): 14–24.

Titus, Robert Austin. "The Solo Music for the Clarinet in the Eighteenth Century." Ph.D. diss., State University of Iowa, 1962.

Toffolo, Stefano. *Antiche strumenti veneziani, 1500–1800: Quattro secoli di liuteria e cembalaria.* Venice: Arsenale editrice, 1987.

Tovey, Donald Francis. *Essays in Musical Analysis: Chamber Music.* London: Oxford University Press, 1944.

Treiber, Richard. "Kantor Johann Wendelin Glaser (1713–1783) und die Wertheimer Kirchenmusik im 18. Jahrhundert." *Jahrbuch des Historischen Vereins "Alt-Wertheim"* (1936): 39–57; (1937): 37–76.

Turpin De Crissé, Lancelot. *Commentaire sur les institutions militaires de Végèce.* 2d ed. Vol. 2. Paris: Nyon l'aîné, 1783.

Tuthill, Burnet C. "The Quartets and Quintets for Clarinet and Strings." *NACWPI Journal* 23 (summer 1974): 3–15.

Unverricht, Hubert, ed. *Musik und Musiker am Mittelrhein: Ein biographisches, orts- und landesgeschichtliches Nachschlagewerk,* 2 vols. Mainz: B. Schott's Söhne, 1974.

———. "Glaser, Johann Wendelin." In Hubert Unverricht, *Musik und Musiker am Mittelrhein: Ein biographisches, orts- und landesgeschichtliches Nachschlagewerk,* vol. 1, 60–68. Mainz: B. Schott's Söhne, 1974.

Vaillant, [Pierre]. *Nouvelle méthode de clarinette à cinq et à treize clefs.* Paris: L'Auteur, [ca. 1826].

Van Acht, Rob, Wot Bosma, and Carole Hoekman. *List of Technical Drawings of Musical Instruments.* 2d ed. The Hague: Haags Gemeentemuseum, 1992.

Van Aerde, Raymond. *Les Tuerlinckx, luthier à Malines.* Mechlin: L. & A. Godenne, 1914.

Vandenbrœck, Othon. *Traité général de tous les instrumens à vent.* Paris: Boyer, 1794; reprint, Geneva: Minkoff, 1974.

Vanderhagen, Amand. *Méthode nouvelle et raisonnée pour la clarinette.* Paris: Boyer and Le Menu, [ca. 1785]; reprint, Geneva: Minkoff, 1972.

———. *Méthode nouvelle et raisonnée pour la clarinette.* Paris: Nadermann, [ca. 1797–98].

———. *Nouvelle méthode de clarinette divisée en deux parties.* Paris: Pleyel, [ca. 1799].

———. *Nouvelle méthode pour la clarinette moderne à douze clés.* Paris: Pleyel & Fils Aîné, [ca. 1819].

van Kalker, Johan. *Die Geschichte der Klarinetten: Eine Dokumentation.* Oberems: Verlag Textilwerkstatt, 1997.

van Lennep, W., et al., eds. *The London Stage, 1660–1800.* 5 parts. Carbondale: Southern Illinois University Press, 1960–68.

Vannes, René. *Katalog der städtischen Sammlung alter Musikinstrumente im Richard-Wagner-Museum Tribschen, Luzern.* Luzern: Richard-Wagner-Museum, 1956.

Ventzke, Karl. "Aus Briefen des Flötenbauers Wilhelm Liebel in Dresden an den Flötisten Robert Frisch in Dublin von 1847." *Tibia* 16, no. 4 (1991): 629–31.

Vermeersch, Valentin. *Musiques et sons (Bruges Musées communaux Museumpromenade).* Brugge: Les Amis des Musées communaux, 1990.

Viano, Richard J. "By Invitation Only: Private Concerts in France during the Second Half of the Eighteenth Century." *Recherches* 27 (1991–92): 131–62.

Voxman, Himie, and Maurita Murphy Mead. "Some Notes on the Early Clarinet Sonatas and Anton Eberl's Sonata in B♭, Op. 10, No. 2." *Clarinet* 22, no. 4 (July–August 1995): 28–32.

Wachmann, Eric. "Clarinet Woodworking: The Tools Used in the Construction of the Clarinet between 1775 and 1843." D.M.A. diss., University of North Carolina at Greensboro, 1996.

Walker, Aidan, ed. *The Encyclopedia of Wood: A Tree-by-Tree Guide to the World's Most Versatile Resource.* New York: Facts on File, 1989.

Walls, Peter. "Mozart and the Violin." *EM* 20 (1992): 7–29.

Ward, Martha Kingdon. "Mozart and the Clarinet." *Music and Letters* 28 (1947): 126–53.

Warrack, John. *Carl Maria von Weber*, 2d ed. Cambridge: Cambridge University Press, 1976.

———. "Chamber Works with Wind Instruments (from 1700)." In *Chamber Music*, edited by A. Robertson. Harmondsworth: Penguin Books, 1957.

Watel, Denis. "Michel et François Amlingue, facteurs d'instruments à Paris de 1780 à 1830." *Larigot* 15 (1994): 16–21.

Waterhouse, William. *The New Langwill Index: A Dictionary of Musical Wind-Instrument Makers and Inventors.* London: Tony Bingham, 1993.

———. "RNCM Collection of Historic Musical Instruments Catalogue." Available online at http://www.mcm.ac.uk/library/hwm1.htm.

Weber, Carl Maria von. *Writings on Music.* Edited by John Warrack, translated by Martin Cooper. Cambridge: Cambridge University Press, 1981.

Weber, Friedrich Dionysious. *Allgemeine theoretisch-praktische Vorschule der Musik.* Prague, 1828.

Weber, Gottfried. "Das Clarinett." In *Allgemeine Encyclopädie der Wissenschaften und Künste*, edited by J. S. Ersch and J. G. Gruber, vol. 17, 374. Leipzig: J. F. Gleditsch, 1818–89.

———. "Einiges über Clarinett und Bassetthorn." *Cäcilia: Eine Zeitschrift für die musikalische Welt* 11 (1829): 35–57.

Weber, Rainer. "Eine symmetrisches Klarinettenpaar im Städischen Museum Ingolstadt." *Oboe, Klarinette, Fagott* 4, no. 2 (June 1989): 72–75. Translated by Allan Ware under the title "A Symmetrical Pair of Clarinets in the City Museum of Ingolstadt, GDR." *Clarinet* 17, no. 2 (February–March 1990): 31–33.

Webster, Mary. *Johan Zoffany, 1733–1810.* London: National Portrait Gallery, 1976.

Weimer, Eric. *Opera Seria and the Evolution of Classical Style, 1755–1772.* Ann Arbor: UMI Research Pess, 1984.

Weir, Christopher. *Village and Town Bands.* Aylesbury: Shire Publications, 1981.

Wesley, Samuel. "Clarinet Scale in the Hand of Samuel Wesley" [ca. 1789]. British Library, MS., Add. 35011, fol. 166.

Weston, Pamela. "An Assessment of Crusell the Man." *Clarinet* 22, no. 1 (November–December 1994): 30–33.

———. *Clarinet Virtuosi of the Past.* London: R. Hale, 1971.

———. *More Clarinet Virtuosi of the Past.* London: The author, 1977.

———. "Players and Composers." In *The Cambridge Companion to the Clarinet*, edited by Colin Lawson, 92–106. London: Cambridge University Press, 1995.

———. "Schwencke's Mozart Concerto: A Hypothesis." *Clarinet* 24, no. 1 (November–December 1996): 64–66.

———. *Yesterday's Clarinettists: A Sequel.* York: Emerson, 2002.

Whistling, Carl Friedrich, and Friedrich Hofmeister. *Handbuch der musikalischen Litteratur.* Leipzig: A. Meysel, 1817; reprint, New York: Garland, 1975.

Whitwell, David. *The Wind Band.* Northridge, Calif.: Winds, 1984.

"Wiener Kunstnachrichten." *Journal des Luxus und der Moden* 16 (1801): 538–45.

Willman, Thomas L. *A Complete Instruction Book for the Clarinet.* London: Goulding, D'Almaine, 1826.

Wolf, Eugene K. "On the Composition of the Mannheim Orchestra, ca. 1748–1778." *Basler Jahrbuch für Historische Musikpraxis* 17 (1993): 113–38.

———. *The Symphonies of Johann Stamitz.* The Hague: M. Nijhoff, 1981.

Wolf, Georg Friedrich. *Kurzgefaßtes musikalisches Lexikon.* Halle, 1792.

Wood, James. "Certain Improvements on the German Flute, Applicable also to the Clarionet and Bassoon," British Patent No. 3797, 10 May 1814. London: G. E. Eyre and W. Spottiswoode, 1856.

———. "Clarionet and Other Wind Musical Instruments." British Patent No. 2381, 19 March 1800. London: G. E. Eyre and W. Spottiswoode, 1856.

———. "An Improvement in the Formation and Position of the Long Keys b Natural and C Sharp, used upon the Musical Instrument commonly called the Clarionet, for the more easily Fingering of the Same." British Patent No. 4423, 14 February 1820. London: G. E. Eyre and W. Spottiswoode, 1856.

Wroth, Warwick. *The London Pleasure Gardens of the Eighteenth Century.* London: Macmillan, 1896.

Würtz, Roland. *Verzeichnis und Ikonographie der kurpfälzischen Hofmusiker zu Mannheim nebst darstellendem Theaterpersonal 1723–1803.* Quellenkataloge zur Musikgeschichte 8. Wilhelmshaven: Heinrichshofen's Verlag, 1975.

Young, Percy. "The Shaw-Hellier Collection." *Brio* 23 (winter 1986): 65–69.

———. "The Shaw-Hellier Collection." In *Handel Collections and their History*, edited by T. Best, 158–70. Oxford: Clarendon Press, 1993.

Young, Phillip T. *4900 Historical Woodwind Instruments: An Inventory of 200 Makers in International Collections.* London: Tony Bingham, 1993.

———. *The Look of Music: Rare Musical Instruments, 1500–1900.* Vancouver: Vancouver Musueums and Planetarium Association, 1980.

Zaslaw, Neal. *Mozart's Symphonies: Context, Performance Practice, Reception.* Oxford: Clarendon Press, 1989.

———. "Towards the Revival of the Classical Orchestra." *Proceedings of the Royal Musical Association* 103 (1976–77): 158–87.

Zimmermann, Josef. *Von Zinken, Flöten, und Schalmeien: Katalog einer Sammlung historischer Holzblasinstrumente.* Düren, 1967.

INSTRUMENT MAKERS, MOUTHPIECE MAKERS, AND INSTRUMENT DEALERS INDEX

GENERAL INDEX

Abel, Karl Friedrich: Concerto for violin, oboe, and clarinet, 250 n. 119; Symphony in E-flat, 257 n. 239

Abraham, 29; duets, 186, 260 n. 279; *Nouveaux recueils*, 182–83; *Principes de clarinette*, 260 n. 279

Agricola, Johann, 128–29; *Amor e Psiche*, 128, 247 n. 56

Albrechtsberger, Johann Georg, 80, 111

Alto clarinet, 35, 66, 68–69, 211, 220 n. 54

Andries, Jean Jacques, 243 n. 120

Angermüller, Rudolph, 242 n. 113

Antolini, Francesco, 21, 93–94

Arne, Thomas, 117–21; *Artaxerxes*, 119–20, 198; *Comus*, 252 n. 143; *Fairy Prince*, 119, 121; *Thomas and Sally*, 117–19, 145

Arnold, Samuel: *Children of the Wood*, 249 n. 103; *Obi, or Three-finger'd Jack*, 249 n. 103

Articulation, 83–85, 87–90; chest, 84, 88; diaphragm or lips, 89–90; legato, 88; throat, 89–90; tongue, 88–90

Attwood, Thomas, 134

Bach, Carl Philipp Emanuel: Duet, 185, 193, Six Little Sonatas for clarinet, bassoon, and basso continuo, 190, 193

Bach, Johann Christian, 121–26, 129; *Adriano in Siria*, 124, 126; "Ah, che gl'istessi numi," 246 n. 42; *Amadis et Gaules*, 124; *Amor vincitore*, 124–26; "Cara, te lascio," 246 n. 42; *Carattaco*, 124; *Cefalo e Procri*, 124; "Cruel Strephon will you leave me," 102; *Endimione*, 124; "Happy

morn, auspicious rise," 246 n. 42; *La clemenza di Scipione*, 124, 245 n. 13; *Lucio Silla*, 124; *Menalcas*, 124; *Orione*, 99–100, 122–24; symphonies, 178; *Temistocle*, 124

Backofen, Johann Georg Heinrich, 13, 20, 39, 41, 74–75, 81, 84, 86, 89, 95, 97, 102, 171–72, 217 n. 9, 227 n. 92; Duo for clarinet and cello, 261 n. 291; Concertante for two A clarinets, 150; Quintet for clarinet, violin, two violas, and cello, 195

Baermann, Heinrich, 86, 165, 172–73, 196–97, 264 n. 351; comparison with Hermstedt, 172–73

Bähr, Josef, 197

Bainbridge, William, 50

Balássa, György, 189

Barbandt, Charles, 177–78; Great Concerto, 178

Barrel, 11, 15–17, 30, 37; convex, 37, 45–46; metal-lined, 19, 48, 54, 230 n. 177; sockets, 16

Barthélemon, François-Hippolyte, 178

Basset clarinet, 56, 71–76, 138, 145, 183, 195, 264 n. 345; L-shaped section, 72–74

Basset horn, 56–7, 71–72, 74, 124, 138, 144–45, 156, 160, 204, 211; in G, 162

Bass-Klarinett, 72

Bates, William, 183–85; *Eighteen Duettino's*, 184–85

Batthyány, Cardinal Prince Joseph von, 199

Bazin, Pierre, 84